D1714511

Historians and sociologists of Israeli society agree on the crucial role played by the Eastern European agricultural workers of the Second *Aliya* which, despite resistance from the Ottoman government, reached Palestine between 1904 and 1914 and gave important shape to the emerging Israeli society. However, they disagree over what the immigrants actually did, partly because of a more general disagreement over what exactly is involved in the formation of a nation state. Furthermore, they tend to see these processes as separate from Israeli–Palestinian relations, failing to assert that the shaping of the Israeli state and nation and the social origins of the Israeli–Palestinian conflict are bound and inexorably shaped by each other.

In this highly researched book, which demystifies much of the Zionist wisdom on the subject, Professor Shafir argues that in Palestine, as in other European 'pure settlement' colonies, the policies implemented in the creation of the nation were based upon attempts to gain control of the land and labor markets. Indeed, it was not the ideologies imported by the Jewish settlers nor the intra-Jewish political conflicts, but the particular conditions of the conflict in the land and labor markets between the Jewish settlers and the Palestinian Arab population which gave rise to the most typical characteristics of Israeli society, such as the collective forms of life and organisation, the close association of soldier and settler, the subordinate position of non-European Jews, the hegemony of the labor movement and, lastly, in the context of the Israeli–Palestinian conflict, the militant stance for separatism tempered by willingness to concede territorial partition.

The nature of the land and labor markets in late Ottoman Palestine undeniably facilitated the entry of Jewish settlers, but they also in several ways limited Palestine's attractiveness to the potential settler. The author highlights the fact that this situation introduced two contradictions into the growing state which today still characterize Israeli institutions. The first is that between the market-oriented approach to Israeli–Palestinian relations and the internal collectivism of Israeli society and economy; the second, now more dominant than the first, is that between Jewish exclusivity and the real potential for separate Israeli and Palestinian Arab developments.

Land, labor and the origins of the
Israeli–Palestinian conflict 1882–1914

CAMBRIDGE MIDDLE EAST LIBRARY

Series list continues on page 288

Land, labor and the origins of the Israeli–Palestinian Conflict 1882–1914

GERSHON SHAFIR

LECTURER IN SOCIOLOGY AND ANTHROPOLOGY,
TEL AVIV UNIVERSITY, AND
ASSISTANT PROFESSOR OF SOCIOLOGY,
UNIVERSITY OF CALIFORNIA, SAN DIEGO

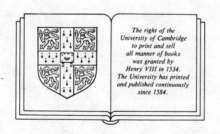

The right of the
University of Cambridge
to print and sell
all manner of books
was granted by
Henry VIII in 1534.
The University has printed
and published continuously
since 1584.

CAMBRIDGE UNIVERSITY PRESS

CAMBRIDGE
NEW YORK   PORT CHESTER
MELBOURNE   SYDNEY

Published by the Press Syndicate of the University of Cambridge
The Pitt Building, Trumpington Street, Cambridge CB2 1RP
40 West 20th Street, New York, NY 10011, USA
10 Stamford Road, Oakleigh, Melbourne 3166, Australia

First published 1989

Printed in Great Britain at the University Press, Cambridge

British Library cataloguing in publication data

Shafir, Gershon
Land, labor and the origins of the Israeli–Palestinian conflict 1882–1914.–
(Cambridge Middle East Library).
1. Palestine. Social conditions, 1640–1948
1 Title
956.94′03

Library of Congress cataloguing in publication data

Shafir, Gershon.
Land, labor and the origins of the Israeli–Palestinian conflict 1882–1914
– (Cambridge Middle East Library).
Bibliography.
Includes index.
1. Jewish–Arab relations – To 1917.   2. Jews – Colonization – Palestine.
3. Labor Zionism – Palestine.   4. Land settlement – Palestine. 1. Title.
II. Series.
DS119.7.S3818   1989   956′.02   88-25681

ISBN 0 521 35300 9

To all those Israelis and Palestinians
who are struggling for peace,
and to Daphie, Gil, and Jamie Neiree,
who will benefit from it

Contents

Contents

Preface

This study was engendered by the dislocating experience of growing into maturity as part of the Israeli generation of 1967. For me, the aftermath of the Six Day War revealed the gap between the evidence of Israeli society's gradual but definite transformation through its manifold relationships with the Palestinian Arabs who came under Israeli occupation, and the Palestinians' invisibility in historical and sociological accounts of the early formation of Israeli society. Although throwing off mental habits is always a slow process, I came eventually to the conclusion that, during most of its history, Israeli society is best understood not through the existing, inward-looking, interpretations but rather in terms of the broader context of Israeli–Palestinian relations. Nor was Israel completely different from some of the other European overseas societies that were also shaped in the process of settlement and conflict with already existing societies. To comprehend the complex character of the Israeli state and nation, I decided, after further reflection, to approach their formation from this comparative perspective.

In an analogous, and in part autonomous, fashion, my methodological approach underwent a similar transformation. Initially, being awed by the positivist distinction between history and theory, I viewed my project as essentially one of the reinterpretation of existing historical sources. As the research progressed and I became more acquainted with the historical material, and especially with the archival sources, it dawned on me that I would have to rewrite portions of the history of early Zionist settlement. The reason was that I could no longer accept the simple attribution of some of the important social experiments of the period to the organized Eastern European agricultural workers of the Second *Aliya*. Retrospectively, the predominance of this form of tunnel vision might be understandable, since the impact of the labor movement was enormous and decisive, but, in fact, the labor movement was also the inheritor, and subsequent shaper and interpreter, of the agendas of the World Zionist Organization and some segments of the First *Aliya* – and of various European models of colonization. At the conclusion of this

xi

work I view historical sociology not as interdisciplinary cooperation but rather as an integrated enterprise of historically grounded theory formation, i.e. the generation of theoretical propositions and concepts by means of the analytic ordering of the past in its relation to the structures of present-day society.

By engaging in a historical–sociological analysis from this vantage, I felt well positioned to point to the formative impact of the Palestinian–Israeli conflict on Israeli state and nation formation. Its influence gave shape precisely to those aspects of their society which Israelis pride themselves on being most typically Israeli: the protracted hegemony of the labor movement, the close association of soldier and farmer, the cooperative forms of social and economic organization – but also the secondary status of Middle Eastern and North African Jews. Simultaneously, I was able to accent the two major interconnected dilemmas that accompanied Israel's formation, and still characterize Israeli state and society. The first is the disjunction between the market-oriented cast of Israeli–Palestinian relations and the internal collectivism of the Israeli economy and society. The second is the growing tension between two competing visions of building an excusively Jewish nation in Palestine: maximalist territorial exclusivism, the logical conclusion of which is the removal of the Palestinian Arabs; and the territorial partition of Eretz Israel /Palestine, leading to separate Israeli and Palestinian national development.

This brings me to another somewhat less tangible but nonetheless important facet of this study, which concerns the inferences that may be drawn from the analysis of the past for the shaping of the future. Since these inferences are rarely self-evident, I might at least try and prevent the misinterpretation of my own.

In this century, the potentially tragic consequences of the severance of Jews from a territory of their own was only too clearly revealed, justifying a desire for political normalcy by standards of the modern world order. Hence, reviewing the history of Israel's creation, the first stage of which is examined in this study, does not present us, even with the wisdom of hindsight, with a realistic alternative course to the pursuit of nationhood and sovereignty. Nor does there seem to have been much leeway for carrying out this project differently, given the inauspicious conditions under which, and narrow time frame within which, Jewish immigrant-settlers labored. Nonetheless, I argue in this study that we should also recognize that the epic of Zionism, in addition to the necessary and the heroic, was not devoid of a tragic dimension: the creation of Israel through encroachment on and, subsequently, displacement of the majority of the Arab residents of Palestine.

Most Israelis are accustomed to view early Zionist history, as indeed most people view the dawn of their national histories, as a saga. Seldom is the many-sidedness of such epochs acknowledged, and even more rarely is their complexity assimilated more than temporarily. Sometimes, the reappropriation process of the multifaceted character of history is sped up. The desire to produce a complex picture emerges usually when a society is thrust into that murky domain we are wont to call a "crisis," i.e., a historical interval calling for a portentous decision. But where should we start the reassessment?

Those who do not learn the lessons of history, Santayana has already taught us, are bound to repeat its mistakes. I take one of the potential meanings of his maxim to be that a major fallacy in studying the past is to assume that history is bound to repeat itself. It is this repetition – as if going through it all again were part of natural history – that engenders a mistake by betraying our most human ability – the gift of learning. Not only of individuals, but also of historical periods it may be said that *si duo faciunt idem, non est idem.*

The post-1967 mistake would be the view that the process of Israeli territorial accumulation did not end in 1948 but should continue through the *de facto* or *de jure* annexation of the occupied territories and their population to Israel, thus eliminating the possibility of a Palestine side by side with Israel. Today, there are many, in Israel and elsewhere, who in that case foresee an Israel resembling South Africa (whose so-called apartheid is in reality a white supremacist regime), and equally suffering from unending cycles of violence generated by exclusivist practices. But Israeli history did not start in 1967 and the unexpected conquests of the Six Day War were but one phase in a protracted conflict. If there is a potential for similarity in present-day Israel to South Africa, its roots must be found in the inability of these, and similar, societies to come to terms with the legacy of their histories of colonization.

There is, however, one difference between these, and other related, cases. While starting out with the maximalist aim of Jewish territorial supremacy in Palestine, under the unauspicious circumstances for colonization in both land and labor markets in this part of the Ottoman Empire, the aims of the Zionist mainstream were transformed. Failing to attract the masses of the Jewish people and remaining dependent on massive outside financial subsidy, the Israeli labor movement perforce limited its ambition and condoned a course that potentially diverted it from the South African path: it sought a bifurcated model of economic development leading to territorial partition. This strategy, though it originated not in the appreciation of Palestinian national aspirations but in the inescapable facts of Palestinian demography, was expected by the labor movement to go a long way toward the resolution of the Israeli–Palestianian conflict, and subsequently became the legacy of its, and simultaneously the WZO's, mainstream. Consequently, the gradual abandonment of partition plans, with their accompanying vision of an Israeli and an Arab state side by side in Eretz Israel/Palestine, in favor of returning to earlier dreams of Israeli territorial maximalism, with all its deplorable results, would signal the final superseding and/or the transformation of the labor movement. Concomitantly this would entail the repudiation of the painfully learned historical lesson that in Eretz Israel/Palestine there is no realistic alternative to sovereignty expressed through and limited by territorial partition.

Still the question remains: how do we learn from history? Baruch Kimmerling observed that whereas Israelis tend to focus on the non-colonialist reasons and motivations for their immigration to Palestine, Arabs direct their attention to its results. Until the former learn about results and the latter about intentions, neither is likely to gain access to new knowledge. My study, looking at the actions of Jews in the process of the formation of the Israeli state and nation, necessarily focuses mostly on results, but it also examines at several points the intentions of Jewish immigrants. Indeed, the two cannot be sealed off hermetically, since motivations produce actual results while unexpected realities generate new motivations.

Combining the scrutiny of intents and results in one perspective is not a self-evident intellectual and moral route. Lecturing in 1918, Max Weber recognized an "ethic of conviction," i.e. acting rightly and leaving the results to the discretion of impersonal forces, to be an honorable course for those who professed intimacy with the aims of history. Weber, while empathizing with this ethical choice, distinguished it from an equally potent "ethic of responsibility," which focused on the foreseeable results of our actions and thus was, in his view, more appropriate for politics. Weber admitted that in desperate circumstances an "ethic of conviction," with its attitude of "all or nothing," might be an unavoidable last resort, but he argued equally forcefully that to resort to it too easily would signify an abdication of moral responsibility. For us, on the other side of the savage tide of history in the twentieth century, only a more modest, but in its admission of the conflict of values more profound, "ethic of responsibility" is left. Zionism, having been nourished and legitimated by idealistic intentions, now has to pay attention to their consequences. Israelis cannot be excused from ignoring the "other," their imprint on it, and the way they themselves were formed while shaping it. We need to keep the whole picture in sight, even if only to help us prevent the mistake of repetition.

Three-fifths of the manuscript were written while I was at Tel Aviv University, the balance during a year at the University of California at Berkeley, and the work of revision was completed at the University of California in San Diego. During the years of research and writing I was fortunate to have received support and encouragement of colleagues, friends and family members, to whom I am grateful in more ways than I know how to say on paper. Roger Owen, Yoav Peled, Michael Shalev, Yonathan Shapiro, and John H. Zammito saw the point of the manuscript when it was still in a rough and preliminary stage. Roger Owen and John Zammito patiently and dependably accompanied it to completion, and by providing me with innumerable helpful comments and concrete signs of support all along made a vast difference. Michal Innerfield Shafir sustained, encouraged, and sometimes endured me during the intensive years of working out and putting these ideas on paper. Avishai Ehrlich, Roger Friedland, David Matza, Jane Rubin, Lyn Spilman, Kim Voss, Carlos Waisman, Jeff Weintraub, and Leon Zamosc read some of the many versions of the introduction; Dani Diner, Huri Islamoğlu-Inan, Ruth Kark and Ilan Pappe chapter 2; Ephi Yaar and Ian Lustick chapter 3; Meir Amor, Bat-Zion Eraqi-Klorman, and Shlomo Swirski chapter 4; Uri Ben-Eliezer chapter 6. I take special pleasure in thanking Jonathan Frankel, without whose suggestions chapter 7 would have been much weaker. Meir Amor, Nitza Berkovitch, Ronit Etstein, Sibylle Heilbrunn, and Franziska Spronz helped me with the collection of the sources. Robert N. Bellah, Noah Lewin-Epstein, George Fredrickson, Shula Gubkin, Shulamit Laskov, Tim McDaniel and others shared on occasion their keen insight and knowledge with me. Yoram Mayorek of the Central Zionist Archives advised me in regard to archival sources. Emanuel Kochavi of Hadera put at my disposal and patiently explained his copies of the Protocols of the Hadera Board and General Assembly between 1891 and 1913. This research was supported by grants from the Alice and Beno Gitter Research Foundation, the Ford Foundation (received through the Israel Foundations Trustees), and the Fund for Basic Research of the Israeli Academy of Sciences and Humanities.

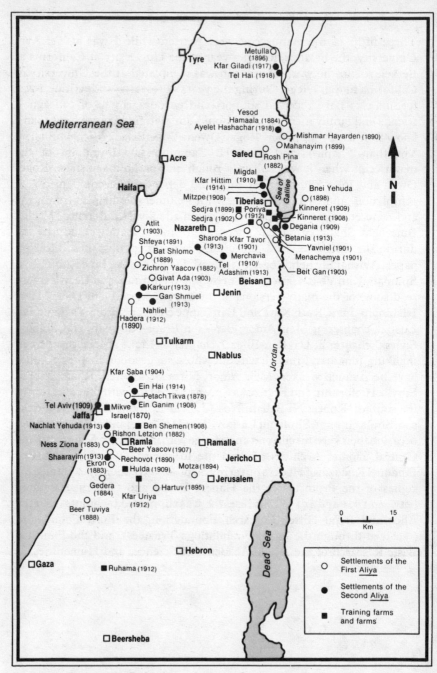

Mediterranean Sea

Tyre

Metulla (1896)
Kfar Giladi (1917)
Tel Hai (1918)

Yesod Hamaala (1884)
Ayelet Hashachar (1918)
Mishmar Hayarden (1890)
Mahanayim (1899)

Acre

Safed
Rosh Pina (1882)

Haifa

Migdal (1910)
Kfar Hittim (1914)
Mitzpe (1908)
Sedjra (1899)
Sedjra (1902)
Poriya (1912)
Tiberias
Sea of Galilee
Bnei Yehuda (1898)
Kinneret (1909)
Kinneret (1908)
Degania (1909)
Betania (1913)
Yavniel (1901)
Menachemya (1901)
Beit Gan (1903)

Atlit (1903)
Shfeya (1891)
Bat Shlomo (1889)
Zichron Yaacov (1882)
Givat Ada (1903)
Karkur (1913)
Gan Shmuel (1913)
Nahliel
Hadera (1912)
(1890)

Nazareth
Sharona (1913)
Kfar Tavor (1901)
Merchavia (1910)
Tel Adashim (1913)

Beisan

Jenin

Tulkarm

Nablus

Kfar Saba (1904)
Ein Hai (1914)
Petach Tikva (1878)
Tel Aviv (1909)
Mikve Israel (1870)
Ein Ganim (1908)
Jaffa
Nachlat Yehuda (1913)
Ben Shemen (1908)
Rishon Letzion (1882)
Ness Ziona (1883)
Ramla
Beer Yaacov (1907)
Shaarayim (1913)
Rechovot (1890)
Ekron (1883)
Hulda (1909)
Gedera (1884)
Kfar Uriya (1912)
Hartuv (1895)
Beer Tuviya (1888)

Ramalla

Jericho

Motza (1894)
Jerusalem

Jordan

Dead Sea

0   15
Km

Hebron

Gaza
Ruhama (1912)

○ Settlements of the First Aliya

● Settlements of the Second Aliya

■ Training farms and farms

Beersheba

N

Jewish settlements in Palestine, 1878–1918

xvi

Chapter one

Introduction

The substance of nationalism as such is always morally, politically, humanly ambiguous. This is why moralizing perspectives on the phenomenon always fail, whether they praise or berate it.

Tom Nairn, "The Modern Janus," in his *The Break-Up of Britain,* 1977

Historical research . . . can . . . extract from the vast storehouse of the past . . . sets of intelligent questions that may be addressed to current materials. The importance of this contribution should not be exaggerated. But it should not be underrated either. For the quality of our understanding of current problems depends largely on the broadness of our frame of reference . . . The answers themselves, however, are a different matter. No past experience, however rich, and no historical research, however thorough, can save the living generation the creative task of finding their own answers and shaping their own future.

Alexander Gerschenkron, *Economic Backwardness in Historical Perspective,* 1962

The sociology of Israeli society

A small stratum of organized Eastern European Jewish agricultural workers who reached Palestine in the Second *Aliya* (wave of immigration) between 1904 and 1914 shouldered the major burden of Israel's creation. Their leaders, David Ben-Gurion, Itzhak Ben-Zvi, Joseph Shprintzak, Berl Katznelson, Itzhak Tabenkin, etc., and their political heirs from the Third *Aliya* of 1918–23, Golda Meir, and others, gave determinate shape to emerging Israeli society and simultaneously fashioned its labor movement into the dominant political force until 1977. While Israeli sociologists and historians agree that this stratum played a pivotal historical role, they disagree over what its members actually did and, more generally, over what the tasks of state and nation formation involved. In this study I will seek to provide answers to these two questions. In turn, these answers will allow me to address a third, and integrally related, question: what were the social origins of the Israeli–Palestinian conflict?

1

So far, two major sociological perspectives have predominated in interpreting the shaping of the Israeli state and nation: functionalism and elitism. S. N. Eisenstadt, and his disciples Dan Horowitz and Moshe Lissak, looking through the prism of the value-consensus approach, derived from the more general functionalist perspective, have claimed that "the history of the *Yishuv*'s [the modern Jewish community, literally "settlement," in Palestine] development shows that the Second *Aliya* ... was that period in which social, political, and organizational activities were most dominated by the creation and interpretation of values." These core values of asceticism, emphasis on manual and especially agricultural work, self-defense and self-reliance, Hebrew culture, and future orientation – in short, the pioneering ethos formed in the process of modernization – served as the basis of voluntary solidarity between successive Jewish immigrants and alone made possible a consistent institution-building effort.[1]

Yonathan Shapiro, from the vantage point of Michels' and Mosca's elite theories, has asserted that "the priority given by the founding fathers ... to the conscious action of political organization, enabled them to turn the Jewish community into a stable and modern political state." Shapiro demonstrated that the functionalists had refused to recognize the existence, among the groups constituting emerging Israeli society, of grave internal conflicts, in which the labor movement won out because of its superior organizational skills. He concluded that only the agricultural workers' party apparatus provided an instrument for the cooptation and manipulation of other interest groups and the laying of a foundation for unified action. This political leadership and bureaucracy already served, in his analysis, as a substitute state with a modicum of coercive power, and, aided by the formative generational experience of its leaders and cadre, actually concentrated the resources and man- and womanpower required for the workings of a central authority.[2]

My aim in this study is to pose an *alternative theoretical perspective* to both functionalism and the elitist approach, though I hardly hold them in equal esteem. This study rejects *in toto* the extreme voluntarism of the functionalist perspective, while it complements the elitist approach, with which it shares certain basic assumptions about the importance of power and organization and their uses. While the elite approach is superior in many ways to functionalism, the two theories do share three limitations.

(1) According to Eisenstadt, the experiments undertaken by the agricultural workers of the Second *Aliya* "to find organizational solutions to practical problems were made in conjunction with their ideological orientations, and not as a consequence of the daily, concrete problems of

adaptation to the existing environment." An ideological attitude supposedly shaped even the most menial of tasks, and the practical activities
of this early era were but "symbolic expressions" of solutions to the
problems of future society.[3] When examining political or organizational
processes Eisenstadt inquires whether "ideology was . . . equipped to
handle" them, thus reducing politics to a problem of legitimacy.[4] And his
analysis of economic development is restricted to the gradual and partial
displacement of the Second *Aliya*'s ideological intents by market forces
after independence. This approach never views the agricultural workers
of the Second *Aliya*, therefore, as having had to labor under economic
constraints or in pursuit of economic interests of their own.

In fact, hardly has another period in Zionist history seen such a hiatus
between "ideology" and "reality," the contrary poles of interpretation
employed by Israel Kolatt and Yosef Gorny, the two major historians of
the Second *Aliya*.[5] Kolatt and Gorny recognize only too well that
"reality" – the character of which they fail to explicate clearly and which
it will be my task to explore in these pages – unmade the "ideologies"
imported from the Pale of Settlement (a segregated area of the Russian
Empire, to which Jews were restricted) and imposed a veritable cultural
crisis on the Second *Aliya*. Nevertheless, they, like Eisenstadt, Lissak,
and Horowitz, are reluctant to accept the obvious conclusion – namely
that to survive, let alone to thrive, the immigrants of the Second *Aliya*
had to become eminently practical-minded – and wish instead to uphold
their uninterruptedly ideological character. In fact, when Second *Aliya*
members and leaders had to make choices, adopt or reject models, and
change strategies of action, they constructed these not so much from the
grand cloth of general ideologies as from the simpler materials of concrete
methods of settlement.

Shapiro's elite perspective is more multi-dimensional. His account of
the ascendance of the leadership of the workers' parties emphasizes its
determination to "fight for jobs and decent salaries" for the new
immigrants. Thus he presents the party as an instrument for the
domination of the economy in the undeveloped conditions of Palestine.[6]
Nevertheless, elite theory inherently entails a perspective on politics
which gives precedence to the interests of leaders and the organizations
they control to amass power, over a view of the party as a tool for the
articulation of the followers' economic interests. Furthermore, its
approach to politics as the struggle for control of scarce resources
frequently embraces a narrow notion of economics as a mechanism of
distribution.

Jonathan Frankel, in the most trenchant and thorough history of the
Second *Aliya*, also observes the uniqueness of the Second *Aliya*'s hard

3

core in their "exceptional degree . . . [of] political energy" derived, in his view, in equal measure from the Russian revolutionary experience and Jewish messianism.[7] But in his focus on politics Frankel views it essentially in terms of voluntary factors such as individual motivation, ideology, and party ethos, while the economic side in the life of the Second *Aliya* immigrants is relegated to the background.

Thus both perspectives neglect the impact of economic interests and the structure of production as phenomena in their own right. They see the participants in the process of state and nation formation as possessing greater freedom in the pursuit of their intrinsic designs than the study of the economic conditions under which they operated would lead us to believe.

(2) Both schools take as the beginning of Israeli society's formative period the British Mandate following the First World War. Shapiro's study focuses on the first decade, 1919–30, in the life of the Achdut Haavoda Party of the workers; Lissak and Horowitz examine the entire Mandate period until 1948; and Eisenstadt analyzes both the Mandate and independent Israel till the mid 1960s. Lissak and Horowitz pay only passing attention to the pre-Mandate period, while Shapiro and Eisenstadt preface their analyses with short historical summaries in which the First and Second *Aliyot* comprise only a few pages. Only Eisenstadt keeps referring back to the ideological influences emanating from the era of the Second *Aliya*, but even he has not studied it directly.

This point of departure stems from a teleological reading of Israeli history which considers the Second *Aliya* only in terms of its impact on later waves of immigrants. Before exerting authority over later *aliyot*, and opposing their contending strategies, the agricultural workers of the Second *Aliya*, however, had to crystallize their own method of state and nation formation. Had they not found solutions to their own problems, there would have been no reason for later immigrants to follow in their footsteps, nor would the Second *Aliya* have had the wherewithal to extract such compliance from them.

These solutions responded to economic constraints, though significantly they were not market solutions. Indeed, the methodical bypassing of the market, which started during the last years of the Second *Aliya*, required an ever-expanding political and cultural mobilization, which culminated in the labor movement's *hegemony*. In one of the Gramscian senses of the word, hegemony refers to the political and cultural leadership of a rising social group,[8] but the latter's role is not as idealistic as Eisenstadt's nor as voluntaristic as Shapiro's theories imply. The labor movement's hegemonic position in the *Yishuv* derived not from values or

organizational capacity alone but from the effective combination of its
ideal of state building with an ability to address the interests –
particularly in obtaining employment – of those "building the state."
Indeed, the labor movement's hegemony was grounded in and preceded
by the growth of a sectoral economy and, in the 1920s, as Shapiro so
persuasively demonstrates, by the construction of a paid apparatus, which
augmented its political control. Dan Giladi's observation that the labor
movement's preeminence in the *Yishuv* was consolidated only in the
period between 1936 and Israel's establishment confirms the late arrival
of its hegemonic stage.[9]

(3) Functionalist and elite perspectives view the evolution of the Israeli
state and nation as resulting from interaction among Jewish groups
exclusively and thus render invisible the impact of the Israeli–Palestinian
conflict on the formation of Israel. Eisenstadt, who surveys eighty years
of the *Yishuv*, only analyzes Palestinian Arab society in a concerted way
at the end of his book under the chapter heading: "Non-Jewish Minority
Groups in Israel." But the Arab population of Palestine did not
constitute a minority at the beginning of Zionist settlement, and even
today Arabs living in Israel constitute only part of the Palestinian people
which plays an active role, or on whose behalf other Arabs play a role, in
shaping Israeli society. Lissak, Horowitz, and Shapiro also pay only
passing attention to Arabs in relation to Jews in their respective studies.
Finally, the pervasive but never clearly delineated "reality," that so
seriously constrained "ideology" in Kolatt's and Gorny's historical
studies of the Second *Aliya*, is nothing but this Palestinian presence, i.e.,
a euphemism for the Israeli–Palestinian conflict.

It was essentially in the context of this national conflict that both the
Jewish and Arab sides assumed their modern identities. It transformed
the Jewish immigrants into Israelis, and the inchoate Zionism of Eastern
Europe into the concrete practices of Israeli state and nation formation.
The Arab residents of Palestine developed their own distinct nationalism
and became Palestinians in the same context.

It would not be fair to single out Eisenstadt, Lissak, Horowitz, and
Shapiro for an omission that is shared by virtually all Israeli sociologists.
In introducing a recent anthology of Israeli political sociology, Karl
Deutsch pointed to the paucity of research on Arabs and by Arabs as the
blind spot of Israeli sociology.[10] Not only is the study of Arabs in Israeli
society limited, but, as Avishai Ehrlich indicates in an essay remarkable
for its acuity:

even fewer are researches which deal with consequences of the [Israeli–Arab]
conflict on Israeli structure from a macro-societal point of view using a

historical–comparative method or trying to establish connections between the dynamics of the conflict and processes of social change in Israel. There does not exist yet in Israeli sociology, and not due to its underdevelopment, a trend or school which takes the conflict and its multiple aspects as a starting point for the specificity of Israeli society.[11]

As Ehrlich cogently observes, the reason for this hiatus is that "the mental conception of separatism [between Jews and Arabs in Israeli society] was also carried into research . . . In this context research itself was divided."[12] The one notable exception to this fundamental perspective is found in the work of Baruch Kimmerling, who has probably done more than anybody else to fill the gap described by Ehrlich. Kimmerling lists many spheres in which the conflict had an impact on Israeli society, but has done so in a sparing and piecemeal fashion and has not presented a credible theoretical alternative to either functionalism or elite theory.[13]

In this study, I will seek to convince the reader that, if Palestine at the end of the nineteenth century had been an expanse of land empty of population, the shape assumed by Israeli society would have been much different. In fact, I will argue that what is unique about Israeli society emerged precisely in response to the conflict between the Jewish immigrant-settlers and the Palestinian Arab inhabitants of the land. Among these features I list the precocious political organization of the labor movement, the tight bond between settler and soldier, the evolution of cooperative forms of life, the amalgamation of the organized expressions of these phenomena – the political party, the paramilitary organization, the kibbutz (and later the moshav) – under the aegis of the General Federation of Hebrew Workers in Eretz Israel (the Histadrut), the latter's disproportionate influence in comparison with unions elsewhere, and, finally, the ever-widening division of Israeli society into Jewish and Arab sectors.

Of course, the character of the conflict changed as it evolved from an intra-state conflict between two national movements before the establishment of Israel in 1948, to an inter-state conflict between Israel and its Arab neighbors that were backed by foreign allies and, after 1967, into a fully internationalized conflict. But in Ehrlich's words: "the extension of the conflict and the change of phases did not [lead to] the disappearance of features characteristic of previous phases."[14] Consequently many of the features shaped by the earliest phase remain at the core of the conflict and are easily recognized in the social structure of Israel. The Ottoman period, stretching from the beginning of Zionist immigration in 1882 until the British military conquest during the First World War, is therefore the chronological focus of this study.

The most important methods of Israeli state and nation formation had already evolved by 1914. Fundamentally, I will contend, they were connected with alternative views as to how conditions in the land and labor markets might best be exploited to enable Jewish immigration and settlement and the development of a Jewish economic infrastructure. Concretely, I wish to explain how the agricultural workers of the Second *Aliya*, under the guidance and with the financial assistance of the World Zionist Organization, selected the method of state and nation formation which became dominant after the First World War, and to this end I will examine the social experiments they undertook.

Though the method chosen during the Second *Aliya* was unique, the elements from which it was assembled were not, nor was the experience of the Second *Aliya* unique. To understand not only what its members actually did, but, more generally, what the tasks of state and nation formation involved under the conditions they faced, we must invoke an appropriate comparative perspective.

Settlement and nationalism

Hugh Seton-Watson characterized Jews in the diaspora, anachronistically I believe, as a community "already united by ancient religious culture and a profound solidarity for which the modern phrase 'national consciousness' is perhaps appropriate."[15] He failed to note that nations, unlike ethnic groups, require a territory, and ethnic communities can "become nations only through the movement toward political independence." Nationalism serves then, in Katherine O'Sullivan See's terms, a "dual purpose" for an ethnic group: the transformation of ethnicity into national identity through the development of a territorial community, i.e., *nation formation*, and the setting up of an autonomous political community, i.e., *state formation*.[16]

In the last two decades of the nineteenth century, the undermining of the traditional Jewish middleman role in the manorial economy of the Pale of Settlement and Central Europe called into question Jewish ethnic and cultural distinctiveness. In a remarkable outburst of creativity Jews experimented with a variety of potential identities in the modern era: in the few areas of Central Europe where the benefits of modernity were extended to Jews, large numbers chose assimilation;[17] in the Pale of Settlement, many elected universal or Jewish socialism, "cultural nationalism,"[18] or orthodoxy, which was in part also a novel response; while multitudes emigrated to the New World. The step toward Zionism was neither self-evident nor widespread.[19] Before 1933, only a small minority chose Zionism – the Jewish national movement aiming at the acquisition of territorial rights and political sovereignty in parts of Palestine. Territorial nationalism – so different from and alien to the ethnic Jewish way of life[20] – was, as it were, imposed on Jews as a last resort, in response to Nazi persecutions and genocide, and forced migration from Eastern Europe, North Africa, and the Middle East.

Zionism was founded, like other types of nationalism, on a "theory of political legitimacy, which requires that ethnic boundaries should not cross political ones."[21] The conditions under which nation-states come into existence do, however, call for strikingly different methods of mobilization, which accordingly generate distinct societies. To which of these configurations does Zionism belong?

Obviously, Zionism cannot be classed with the English or French cases. Western European state formation did not require a nationalist movement since it was carried out from above, by emerging Absolutism. Its method called for the *integration* of outlying areas into its core region, and the homogenization of the population through bureaucratic measures.[22] Faced with the multi-ethnic Habsburg, Romanov, and Ottoman Empires, which impeded modern state formation, the Eastern European method[23] did require nationalist ideological mobilization for *secession*. This model is applicable to Israeli state and nation formation, but only in part. At the outset, Zionism was a variety of Eastern European nationalism, that is, an ethnic movement in search of a state. But at the other end of the journey it may be seen more fruitfully as a late instance of European overseas expansion, which had been taking place from the sixteenth through the early twentieth centuries. How can these two methods be linked? To understand that we have to look briefly at the forms of European expansion.

D.K. Fieldhouse and, following him, George Fredrickson offer a four-way typology: the *occupation* and *mixed* models worked out by Spain, the *plantation* model of Portugal, and the *pure settlement* of England.[24] The occupation colony – the typical colonial state – aimed at military and administrative control of a potentially strategic region, and consequently its European administrators attempted to exploit and intensify the existing economic order rather than seeking direct control of local land or labor. The other three models were based on settlement by Europeans. Plantation colonies, due to the presence of a dense agricultural population as well as geographic obstacles, attracted only few settlers. In the plantation (and the mining) colony, in want of "a docile indigenous labor force," the settlers acquired land directly and imported an unfree or indentured labor force to work their monocultural plantations. By contrast, mixed and pure settlement colonies were based on substantial European settlement involving direct control of land. The former required labor coercively elicited from the native population, though the distance between the two groups was cushioned through miscegenation. The latter had "an economy based on white labor," which together with the forcible removal or the destruction of the native population allowed the settlers "to regain the sense of cultural or ethnic homogeneity identified with a European concept of nationality."[25]

The opening up of mixed and pure overseas settlement colonies was justified by the "surplus" populations created by the capitalist transformation of the metropolitan societies. England, which invented the pure settlement colony (later to be imitated by France), experienced two such periods. In Elizabethan and early Stuart times, with the spread of capitalist relations of production, Sir Francis Bacon, one of the principal architects of the Ulster plantation, argued for the colonization of Ireland as a way of relieving England of overpopulation. Others pointed to the social dangers of vagabondage to support emigration to the American colonies. Starting in the nineteenth century, under the full impact of capitalized agriculture, the Malthusian theory of population, and Wakefield's detailed colonization plans, Australia and New Zealand came to be viewed as safety valves to alleviate poverty among rural English workers and allay the agitation of the Chartists.[26] This stage also saw British settlers in such places as Rhodesia, and French and Italian settlers in Algeria, steering these occupation colonies toward a fifth, hybrid, form that I will call an *ethnic plantation settlement*. The new type was based, like both the mixed and the plantation colony, on European control of land. Unlike the plantation colony, it employed local rather than imported labor; but, in distinction to the miscegenation prevalent in the mixed colony, it possessed a full-blown European national identity and opposed ethnic mixture. Finally, inconsistently and ultimately unsuccessfully, the ethnic plantation colony, in spite of its preference for local labor, toyed with the idea of massive European immigration and settlement.

At the same time, the successful settlement of the target territory, the *frontier* where the "interpenetration between [the] two previously distinct societies" took place,[27] was contingent on the low density of its population. "The victims of despoliation were a potential threat," hence only in sparsely inhabited regions was the security risk posed by the native population containable. Furthermore, dense populations usually exhibited more advanced levels of economic life and posed the danger of economic competition to the settlers with low-status occupations.[28]

The transfer not only of capital but also of members of all strata of the population and ultimately of financial decision-making centers, in de Silva's and Arghiri Emmanuel's view, generated the rapid development of pure settlement colonies. As their economies were internally oriented, their profits became reinvested, agriculture intensified, technological innovation encouraged, and secondary industries developed. Conversely, plantation colonies (and mixed colonies in lesser degree) suffered either from the extraterritoriality of investors who repatriated profits or from having being fitted into an imperial division of labor that demanded mostly primary products and, in consequence, they were rendered a complementary and dependent sector of the metropolitan economy. Plantation colonies, in short, were colonized by exploitative colonial investment, while pure settlement colonies were colonized by nation-forming investment with ethic plantation colonies being somewhere in the middle of the continuum. Hence, pure settlements have reproduced, in varying degrees, the complex economies and social structures of the metropolitan societies, competing and often clashing sharply with them, and ultimately breaking away to claim their independence and leave behind their colonial phase, though not necessarily its legacy.[29]

The *pure settlement* of European overseas expansion in a frontier region, based on relatively homogeneous population and on separate markets, is different from both the Western European method of integration or the Eastern European method of secession, but may be seen as *a third method of state and nation formation.* The distinctiveness of this method is obvious from the failure of attempts to expand England and France, states originally created by Western European methods, into Ireland and Algeria respectively, through the settlement method.[30]

The appropriateness of the model of European colonization for the Israeli case is due in part to some structural similarities which I shall introduce in the next two sections of this chapter, but also to attempts, undertaken at various levels of self-consciousness, to emulate its distinctive versions by different groups of Jewish settlers or settlement bodies. We find four alternative models, which will be discussed in later chapters. At this point it is sufficient to list them. Between 1882 and 1900, Baron Edmund de Rothschild followed the model of French agricultural colonization in Algeria and Tunisia, which was based on the development of privately owned monocultural agriculture. When this French model floundered, three others were suggested in its place in the first decade of our century. First, Aharon Eisenberg of the First *Aliya*, who directed Agudat Netaim (The Planters' Society), the largest capitalist company in Palestine before the First World War, recommended a Californian design for enabling urban people to move to the countryside. Secondly, members of Hashomer (The Guard) organization of the Second *Aliya* longed to emulate the Cossacks' military colonization of parts of south-eastern Russia. Other members of the Second *Aliya* also suggested methods tried in other mixed or pure European settlements though, in general, without evolving these into a complete model. Thirdly, Otto Warburg and Arthur Ruppin, the heads of the World Zionist Organization's Palestine Land Development Company, highly consciously tried to reproduce the "internal colonization" model developed by the Prussian government to create a German majority in some of its eastern, ethnically Polish territories, as well as to utilize the Polish measures developed to counter this policy. Eisenberg's and Hashomer's methods, which were perhaps too whimsical, never got off the ground, but the Rothschild and PLDC plans were serious and sincere, and each had its part in shaping the social character of the First and Second *Aliyot*, though only after adaptation to local conditions.

In fact, fitting together the concepts of the Fieldhouse–Fredrickson typology and the Rothschild, PLDC and the First and Second *Aliya*'s efforts, I will try to demonstrate that the most sensible way of analyzing the major intra-Jewish conflict during the Ottoman period of Jewish settlement in Palestine is as one taking place between the pure settlement strategy of the First *Aliya*, which was diverted *malgré lui* into an ethnic plantation type, and the pure settlement form of the Second *Aliya* which, after a similar period of crisis, gained vitality but, in the longer run, in a limited area of Palestine. The different outcomes of the two waves' efforts largely related to the alternative models of colonization chosen by Rothschild and the WZO.

The emulation of the French and German methods of colonization by Rothschild and the PLDC should alert us to the mistaken attribution of the origins of Zionism, by virtually every historian, exclusively to ideological influences emanating from the Pale of Settlement, whence the settlers came. The formative influences that issued from the West, whence the finances of the Zionist project derived, were just as crucial, and it seems to me necessary, therefore, to round out our understanding of early Zionism by exploring this source of material and cultural influence. Such "imported" ideas and methods were important and consequential in shaping Israeli state and nation formation when they were offered by those who could provide the financial backing required for their realization.

Though I start out by placing Israel within the general phenomenon of settlement societies, and therefore the comparative examples I offer will be from appropriate phases in the histories of Virginia and California, Australia, South Africa, Algeria, Tunisia, Prussia, etc., my methodological approach is based on the recognition that differences between instances even of the same category frequently loom very large and, therefore, that comparisons can best be used to "suggest new problems of interpretation and point to discrete patterns of causation."[31]

Frontier and land

Even pure settlement societies are not made of one cloth, though there are obvious analogies between them. I wish to locate some of the "crucial variables" that account for these parallels and the conditions under which they exert their influence. George M. Fredrickson presents three major factors in his masterful historical comparison of the first two "white settler" societies: the US, a combined society of plantation and pure settlement; and South Africa, blending mixed and pure settlement. These are: the "demographic ratio" between the settler and the indigenous populations; the "physical or geographic environment and the possibilities that it offered for economic development" (indirectly also affecting the demographic situation); and the measure of the settler population's semi-autonomous government.[32] The relative weight of these factors, in each case, can be evaluated in terms of the influence they exerted on the struggle for territorial supremacy, and the choice of a labor system (as well as other processes, such as the wars of independence fought against Great Britain, industrialization, etc., whose parallels in our case fall beyond the chronological framework of this study).[33]

The first factor that distinguishes settlement societies from either the Western or the Eastern European configurations of state formation is rooted in their typical desire to expropriate the land resources of the new domain and gain territorial supremacy. The centrality of this interest may be observed through an analysis of the methods of *land allocation*.

In the United-States-to-be, settlement was carried out by joint stock companies that received generous land grants from the Crown. These lands, in turn, were granted by the governors of Virginia and Maryland to individuals, or in the Puritan colonies by a general court, to new townships, which were free to give it away or sell it. In the southern Tidewater colonies a "head-right" of fifty acres was also given to anyone transporting a servant to America.[34] In southern Africa, the early approach developed by the Dutch East India Company permitted settlers to use, for a small annual fee, a circular area measured by half an hour's horse ride from a center point, but squatting was also tolerated on the remote frontier.[35] The first Australian system of land allocation, which lasted from 1787 to 1831, evolved out of grants to settlers and free "tickets of occupation" for pastoralists.[36]

The control of land by its new inhabitants was tied up with effective demographic presence, giving rise to what I will call in this study a *demographic interest*. The demographic interest of a settler population (or, in the case of multi-ethnic societies in general, of any of the respective social groups) emerges from interrelationships of two factors: land and population, and it is best expressed in terms of the ratio between the two, i.e., ranging from moderate to high levels of population density per square unit of land measurement. We may speak, therefore, of the demographic interests of different groups on the frontier, each of which, for example on the basis of its priority of arrival and preferred type of settlement, might seek different population sizes corresponding to the land mass it feels able to command. Initial land allocation methods, none the less, were always designed to encourage, through the incentive of virtually "free land," vigorous settlement and the creation of a critical mass of settlers. "Free land" – the foundation of Frederick Jackson Turner's frontier thesis of American exceptionalism[37] – was the myth that emerged from the realization of the demographic interest at the first stage of settlement, since afterwards the metropolitan or the local government proved quite willing to replace land grants with the land market, even if subsequently they also favored colonization through homesteads.

The demographic differences and the pursuit of the demographic interest found organizational and legal expression in the state structure of settlement societies. The establishment of settler colonies, according to Kenneth Good, "implied the existence of a particularly active and interventionist state." Frequently, this signalled the imposition of an extramarket mechanism on land allocation.[38] In examining the "white economies" of Kenya and Southern Rhodesia, Paul Mosley concluded that they exhibited "a distinctive pattern of extramarket operations," of which land allocation was the most prominent example.[39] Even in the US, and especially on the West Coast, the role of the state was "positive" and "significant" not "passive or minimal."[40] Even after adopting the mechanism of the land market, wrote Turner in regard to the US, "the public domain has been a force of profound importance in the nationaliz-ation and development of the government," generating some of its "highest and most vitalizing activities."[41] The "positive government intervention" of some of the Australian colonies was viewed by con-temporaries as "colonial socialism,"[42] while "the standard interpretation of the entire history of the Canadian economy assigns the state a major role in guiding and stimulating development."[43]

But we should not exaggerate the strength of the state in the settlement colony. The significant question, from the viewpoint of the two interpenetrating societies, is: when did the establishment of the settler

13

society become irreversible? Where the settlers' demographic superiority was established at a relatively early stage, a less powerful state sufficed as far as land disposal was concerned. Where demography favored the native peoples, private settlement companies, colonial government, and autonomous settler states or proto-states effectively extended their powers through the institution and maintenance of state control of land, subsidies for settlers, and restricted access for native people. In this sphere and, as we shall see, also in the labor sphere, the state did not rely on the working of the market. The state not only intervened in the distribution of resources but actually attempted to structure the market itself: hence, its approach is best described as *structural intervention*.

Frontier and labor

In Palestine, as in other settlement societies, the nature of the relations between the settler and local societies was not exhausted by questions of presence on, ownership of, and sovereignty over land.[44] Settler populations on agricultural frontiers invariably needed large unskilled laboring masses to make use of their newly gained land. All settlement societies, therefore, had to decide which of three potential labor forces, or combinations thereof, they would employ. Mixed colonies incorporated the native peoples, plantation colonies "imported" slaves or indentured workers, while pure settlement societies preferred poor white settlers.

The ultimate composition of the labor force in most colonies was not accidental, but the result of careful deliberation by the dominant classes and various commercial and colonizing bodies. In South Africa and Australia these deliberations are well documented. The Council of Seventeen, which ruled the Dutch East India Company from Amsterdam, had regrets about the early introduction of slave labor in southern Africa and sought, in 1716, the advice of the Governor of the Cape of Good Hope Colony and his Council of Policy "whether European farm hands and agriculturalists would be less expensive than slaves." With the dissent of one member, the Council of Policy concluded that "white laborers . . . would be less controllable, as well as more expensive, and they could not be expected to do 'slaves' work.'" Their debate, as pointed out by Fredrickson, gave birth to "a conscious and explicit decision in favor of a labor force composed of non-white slaves rather than free and semi-free whites."[45] When, in 1841, the Immigration Committee of the Australian colony held a similarly broad discussion, it reached the opposite conclusion. Indentured coolie laborers – alien, servile, and introduced "with the expressed expectation that their labor would be cheap" – were presumed to have a detrimental effect on immigration.

Upon taking employment after their term expired, coolies would compete with European laborers, lower their wages, and "dislike of such competition would check British immigration." Pastoralist schemes for coolie labor were consequently rejected.[46] When Chinese and Kanaka immigrants and laborers did, nevertheless, enter the labor market of New South Wales, and later Queensland, they were driven out at the beginning of this century through the mobilization of various groups, above all European workers, for a "White Australia."[47]

The choice ultimately made between alternative labor forces had far-reaching consequences for the social order of settlement societies, and accounts in large part for the differences between them. South Africa made its decision in favor of a mixed type society, while Australia resolved to have a white working class in order to promote the ethnic homogeneity of its future population in accordance with European nationalist aims. Such ambition introduced the added dimension of working-class nationalism to settler state and nation formation.

These and similar phenomena have aroused the interest of a number of sociologists, and as a central tool for analyzing this dynamic I will make use of Frank Parkin's neo-Weberian attempt to build a comprehensive theory of stratification around the concept of "closure" and Edna Bonacich's neo-Marxist "split labor market" approach, two theories which evince surprising similarity. The major mechanism of social stratification, in Parkin's view, is not free competition or class struggle, but social closure, which maximizes rewards by "restricting access to resources and opportunities to a limited circle of eligibles."[48] The advantage of Parkin's approach is in bringing under one umbrella class conflict and intra-class conflict based on ethnic, religious, linguistic, and sexual divisions.[49] Its comprehensiveness leaves us, however, without an explanation of the reasons leading to the espousal of exclusionary strategies. Where Parkin is too broad, Bonacich is just sufficiently specialized.[50]

Split labor market theory locates one important type of ethnic or national antagonism in social processes that hurl together, through settlement or importation, distinct labor forces that originate from unevenly developed regions of the world economy. Such groups possess different *resources*, such as standard of living attained prior to entry into this market, extent of information and trade-union experience; and they evince different *motivations* for seeking employment, for example as permanent or temporary, or as a source of regular or supplementary income. As wages reflect historical standards (that are partially based on past bargaining power), the price of workers from groups with higher resources, such as from the capitalist or proto-capitalist European countries who possess knowledge of a market's workings and a sense of their strength in it, would be more expensive than that of workers from a pre-capitalist economy. If the latter are temporary migrants from rural areas who seek supplementary income, the difference between the two groups' wages would be even larger. In consequence, in multi-ethnic societies, e.g. mixed or plantation colonies or even in some phases of pure settlement colonies, different prices are or would be paid for the same work when performed by members of different groups.

As capital naturally gravitates toward the employment of cheaper labor, it threatens the higher-paid workers with *displacement*, thus initiating a triangular conflict. In order to protect themselves, higher-paid workers are more than likely to launch a struggle not against the capitalists, who usually appear too formidable an opponent, but against the lower-paid workers. Though the fundamental social difference is that between higher-paid and lower-paid workers, the higher-paid workers will attempt to couch it in ethnic or national terms. The two major manifestations of ethnic conflict in the labor market appear antithetical: *exclusion movements* and *caste systems*. In the former, members of one ethnic group are prevented from entering the labor market, or are forced out of it; in the latter, they are confined to the lower rungs of the occupational structure. Both strategies, however, signal the success of higher-paid workers. A third strategy is conceivable: *equalization of pay* may do away with both the threat of displacement and ethnic conflict. This solution, however, is rarely attempted by the higher-paid workers since it may demand sacrifices that contradict their short-term interests. It is even more rarely carried to a successful conclusion, since the world capitalist system functions like a gigantic multi-layered split labor market, and the equalization of pay in one place may result in the flight of capital elsewhere.

Bonacich's theory is still narrowly economistic and ignores the prospect that the mobilization of the higher-priced workers will usually take place on both an ideological and a political level.[51] It is again Parkin who points to the interaction between various forms of closure practices as an important area of analysis. Closure, as we saw in Bonacich's analysis of the labor market, might be a response to exploitation and displacement, but the likelihood of undertaking and legitimating it, in Parkin's opinion, is to be found in prior closure practices. In his view, proletarian exclusion occurs only in the wake of similar policy conducted by the state and the employers, which already deprive the group singled out for exclusion from equal access to rights and resources.[52] The formation of an exclusionary or caste-based labor market, then, is basically *secondary closure* – a demand for the extension of the state-initiated principle of closure. And as we remember from our analysis of land allocation methods, states most likely to impose restrictive closure are found above all in pure settlement colonies.

Wherever working-class nationalism emerges on top of nationalism based on demographic interest and control of land resources it demands the further extension of the state. The reason is that the workers cannot prevail upon the capitalist planters or industrialists to favor them over the lower-paid native or imported workers and shoulder expenses above the market rate alone. Even if the capitalists did so, they would not be able to compete in the international market with other suppliers of the same product who use cheaper labor. Only the state can redistribute the costs of subsidizing the higher-priced white workers among all sectors of society and in this fashion hide the responsibility of the employers who, through practices and threats of displacement, initially pitted the two groups of workers against one another. To enlist the state on their side, workers resort to nationalist claims that resonate well with the aim and structure of the pure settlement colony.

Settlement and Palestine

What was the role played by natural resources, demographic ratio *vis-à-vis* native population, and political self-government – i.e. the three conditions that Fredrickson views as determining the struggle for territorial supremacy and the choice of the labor force – in the colonization of Palestine? How did they inform the two strategies, one associated with the First *Aliya* (1882–1903), an inhibited pure settlement drive that reconciled itself to a plantation type colony, the other, connected with the new pure settlement drive of the agricultural workers of the Second *Aliya* (1903–14), which, initially, was also threatened with disaster? At this point I can only touch upon the major outlines of the argument. The balance of this study will present a thorough analysis.

The conditions of Palestine were not favorable to the creation of a plantation or extractive colony. The virtual absence of major natural resources and comparative advantages for agricultural production discouraged large private investment. In fact, capitalism was not introduced into Palestine by the Jewish settlers, but by the Ottoman government, under heavy European prodding, as part of a policy for all its domains. Furthermore, Jews could not claim the land, as Britain and France did in North America, Australia, North and East Africa etc., by "right of discovery," "right of conquest," and "right of protectorate,"[53] and had neither military might nor governmental backing to expropriate and transfer to them land in support of their ancient historical claim. Hence

Jewish immigrant-settlers and their philanthropists had to purchase land on the market, though frequently from absentee landowners and not from the actual cultivators. Not surprisingly, the average size of the Jewish-owned vineyards and orange groves proved immeasurably smaller than the plantations of Algeria, Kenya, and other colonies of the period. Finally, Jewish planters were not able to emulate the new plantation pattern of employing indentured workers from regions under other forms of imperial control, or of imposing draconian master–servant and vagrancy codes as was the case in South Africa. Instead, they employed a seasonal and unskilled Palestinian Arab wage labor force.

Palestine was even less favorably equipped, with the exception of one condition, to become a pure settlement colony. In Fredrickson's summary: "what seemed required for the emergence of this pattern was a population surplus at home and a relatively sparse indigenous population that is politically and economically at a 'primitive' (normally a hunting–gathering) stage of development."[54] Though the "surplus" population of Jews certainly was there, other conditions differed substantially. Palestine did not possess a tribal society but had a sedentary agrarian population and was part of the Ottoman Empire. Though its agriculture was largely of a subsistence type, the share of the cash crops it exported to European markets showed a continuous rising trend. But while the Palestinian Arab population was hardly sparse, its settlement pattern made it vulnerable to outside penetration. It was concentrated in the hilly regions of the country, and had begun expanding and settling in the coastal zone and inland valleys only a generation or two before the outset of Jewish immigration. Hence these regions were sufficiently unoccupied to become exposed, though not without opposition, to Jewish settlement.

Zionism's main source of strength was outside Palestine, and it was rooted in part in the WZO. The Zionist movement was poor and weak, as its initial refusal to consider active colonization in Palestine, and indeed its uncertainty whether it should aim for Palestine at all, amply reveal. But the WZO was an autonomous body, set in motion by an authentic crisis in Jewish life, and as such was able to elicit continuous support for experimenting and initiating various settlement methods. The need to purchase land and support settlers engendered the organization of a vast and formidable network of fundraising, generally in the form of small contributions, thus enhancing the popular and national character of the movement. Of equal importance was the intervention of the European great powers to protect Jewish immigrants – strictly as part of their aim to ensure a free hand for all foreign nationals against Ottoman restrictions –

and their indirect influence as initiators of capitalist market relations, especially in regard to land-ownership and sale.

To turn Palestine into a settlement colony, and especially of a pure type, Jewish settlement bodies could not rely on the workings of the market. They had to capitalize on minimal initial opportunities and create appropriate conditions in a deliberate way; to set up, as it were, greenhouse conditions. It was this idiosyncratic character of Zionist colonization, its superficially voluntary and political character, that has misled functionalists and elitists, respectively, into assuming that this is all there was to Israeli state and nation formation. But the voluntary political organizations were generated with the express purpose of allowing the formation of a pure or national settlement society, aimed at the reshaping of the land and labor markets along the economic and political lines outlined in the previous two sections, and they remained restricted and dominated by the unfavorable circumstances of Palestine. Continuous economic dependence on outside subsidies and militarization confirm that Israel has not yet escaped these conditions.

This predicament introduced two fundamental tensions that accompanied Israeli state and nation formation: the first between the alternatives of Jewish territorial maximalism and the potential of separate Jewish and Palestinian development, the other between the capitalist character of Jewish–Palestinian economic relations and the internal collectivism of the Jewish economy. During the later years of the Second *Aliya*, pure, i.e. Jewish, settlement came to be seen as feasible only through the *bifurcation* of the economy. This prognosis called for the formation in addition to the First *Aliya*'s ethnic plantation, of a new Jewish-owned and -operated economic and social structure. But while the exclusive Jewish economy was to exist side by side with the Palestinian economy it was also integrally linked with the latter in several respects, such as its continuous objective to purchase land. (Given this continued dependency relationship I prefer to use the term bifurcation over separatism in the economic sphere, while I will reserve the latter term for denoting the method of settlement strategy and the type of nationalism.) And while Jewish settlement became conceivable only through the penetration of European capitalism and Ottoman reforms, above all through the creation of a land market, the accepted formula for the success of the Jewish economy derived from its cooperative and subsequently collectivist practices. These tensions came to reside above all in the new Jewish sector of the economy in which exclusive Jewish employment and collectivism went hand in hand.

The *separatist method of pure settlement* stood on two legs: the WZO's

Jewish National Fund and the agricultural workers' Histadrut, operating to circumvent the land and labor markets respectively. It was around them that the practices of Israeli nationalism evolved. The alliance between the initiators of these two bodies and the forces they represented – Jewish nationalists in Western and Eastern Europe, and the Eretz Israeli labor movement – initiated in the years before the First World War and cemented in the years after the war, provided the bedrock of Israeli state formation. (Since the geographical area under study was unified as a single administrative unit and officially named Palestine only during the British Mandate, that is subsequent to the period under study, I will refer to it as Eretz Israel or Palestine depending on the context.) The process of forging this alliance, and the transformative impact it had on both bodies, making the WZO into a truly popular movement, and the agricultural workers into agricultural settlers, is the culmination of the story told and analyzed in this study.

In Chapter Two, I will examine the land market created by the Ottomans, as the backdrop to Jewish settlement. Most of the rest of the presentation will be focused on the labor market, the major arena of state and nation formation. Chapter Three will review the attempt of the agricultural workers to integrate themselves into the plantation structure in three successive steps – by downward wage equalization with Palestinian workers, through the latter's exclusion, and via caste formation – and explain the virtual failure of all three. Chapters Four to Seven will examine the fate of two alternative methods for increasing the Jewish population of Palestine. Chapter Four will examine the practice of *Israeli nation formation* by focusing on an attempt to "square the circle:" to ensure the planters' economic success while accomplishing pure settlement aims through the employment of lower-paid Jewish workers from Yemen in the Jewish-owned plantations of Palestine. This method proved another and even more tragic failure for the immigrants involved. Chapters Five, Six and Seven will point to the route finally taken in *the formation of the Israeli state*: bypassing the plantation's labor market via three organizational innovations: the political organization of the agricultural workers, their assumption of guard work, and their cooperative settlement. These three innovations made it possible to bifurcate the economy in Palestine and set up an exclusive Jewish employment sector – the infrastructure of a separate Israeli state and nation.

In the Conclusion, I will examine the implications of the labor movement's dominant method of state formation for the entwined national destinies of Israelis and Palestinians, and will argue that the basic forms and arguments of the Israeli–Palestinian conflict were developed before the First World War. The formative period, studied in these pages, laid down inescapable structural constraints, and by closing off certain paths opened up others. The particular shape given to the exclusivist aim of an all-Jewish labor force by the predominance of the labor movement's strategy of economic bifurcation encouraged *separatism* as the predominant form of nationalism. It is the irony of history that the separatism practiced by the Jewish labor movement reduced its initial hostility to Palestinian national interests and made possible the acquiesence of parts of the labor movement, since the late 1930s, in solutions involving territorial partition of Palestine between Jews and Palestinians; but its exclusionary strategy in the labor market also opened the door to more extreme Israeli nationalisms. The present debate in Israeli society, ushered in with the Six Day War, is whether the alternative of territorially separate Israeli and Palestinian development be pursued further and given for the first time a real prospect or be replaced by the more extreme exclusivist alternative – Israeli territorial maximalism.

Chapter two

The framework of dependent development in the Ottoman Empire

Frontiers, by definition, are a meeting area between two societies at different levels of material and political development.[1] On all mixed or pure settlement frontiers, whether on the American, African, or the Australian continents, the invaded society had never reached the stage of development usually associated with state formation, and suffered from vast military inferiority *vis-à-vis* the invading society. The Ottoman Empire, however, was a political entity of four centuries of duration and in possession of territories on three continents. Though a tottering Empire by the late nineteenth century, as the telling expression "the sick man of Europe" indicates, it was weak only in comparison with the nation states of Western Europe and certainly not in contrast with the movement of Jewish settlers, who had thin support even among the Jews of Eastern and Western Europe. When it came to Zionism, the Ottomans were well informed and determined. Even before the first settler of the *Bilu* society of the First *Aliya* set foot in Jaffa on July 6, 1882, the Ottomans, alerted by their consul in Odessa, forbade Jewish immigration and land purchase in Palestine, and tried to uphold these bans in practice during their reign.[2] Nevertheless, they posed a serious obstacle to Jewish colonization only during the First World War. The question, then, is what circumstances enabled Jewish settler-immigrants, in spite of the resolute opposition of the Ottoman government, to keep coming, staying, and sinking roots, tenuous as these were at the time, and turning Palestine into a frontier of settlement?

The integration of the Middle East, including the Ottoman Empire, into the world economic system in a peripheral status seems to hold the answer to this query. We must place Zionism in this broader context of the intervention and penetration of outside forces into the Ottoman Empire as part of its dependent modernization. Jewish colonization was part of this process – otherwise, indeed, it could have hardly taken place, though obviously Zionism had its distinct agenda and qualities as well. In this sense, the "late Ottoman period," which saw initial Jewish settlement, may be called, with equal justification, the "pre-Mandate era," to

22

be followed by the continuation and further expansion of Jewish colonization during the British Mandate proper.

If European penetration provided a large part of the context of Jewish settlement in Palestine, the creative response of the Ottoman government intent on arresting outside intervention, but in the process begetting further weaknesses, supplied an equally portentous element. By the time Jewish settler-immigrants arrived, the Ottoman Empire was not merely a state of past grandeur held together by inertia. The Tanzimat, a grand movement of top-down internal reforms between 1839 and 1878, reformed taxation, land tenure, public administration, and many other facets of life and concomitantly transformed the social hierarchy in the Empire and, within it, in Palestine. By so doing the Tanzimat created the specific legal and economic preconditions that served as the backdrop to Jewish colonization.

Palestine's vulnerability that rendered it susceptible to Jewish settlement in the second half of the nineteenth century may be observed in regard to the two elements of potential colonists' "demographic interest": land and people.

On most settlement frontiers colonial *land appropriation* generally involved outright expropriation of the land resources of the native populations. In Australia, the British Crown took over from the Aboriginal inhabitants the ownership of public domain – defined to include the entire continent – by "right of discovery," and recognized no rights of Aborigines to conclude treaties in this respect.[3] North America was claimed by England as a result of Cabot's discovery,[4] but throughout the expansion of the frontier native American title was expected to be extinguished by treaty and purchase, which, nevertheless, frequently amounted to no more than intimidation and paltry presents.[5] The Cape area of southern Africa came, in 1657, under the control of the Dutch East India Company, which behaved, for all practical purposes, as a sovereign government of the area.[6] In the later example of Kenya, the British government replaced the Imperial British East Africa Company in 1895, and subsequently took claim of all land by the "right of protectorate."[7] On almost all frontiers, at one point or another, tribal reserves were set aside for the native populations, thus making room for additional European settlement.[8] Behind all these cases stood the superior military might of the colonial power, which was ready to enforce respect for its claims.

Jewish colonists in Palestine had neither military nor political power to conclude the one-sided treaties which the British mastered so well. Nor did they partake in the first stage of *land allocation*: the free or virtually free grants from the colonial power, such as "head-rights," "tickets of

23

occupation," squatting, etc., discussed in the Introduction. Paradoxically, Jewish colonization of Palestine, hardly a case of what Donald Denoon calls "settler capitalism,"[9] was, more than any of the other settlement colonies, dependent on the purchase of privately owned land on the open market.[10] The need to buy land in order to create a settlement colony proved a decisive historical anomaly structuring Jewish settlement in Palestine and was one of the factors contributing to its limited territorial expansion. Even so, without the double creations of the Tanzimat – a land market and a new, in part absentee, landowning class, willing to sell land recently acquired – Zionist colonization would have remained inconceivable.

Side by side with nineteenth-century Ottoman dynamism, local patterns of adaptation to the undisputedly "fitful" character of Ottoman control over greater Syria from the sixteenth century on,[11] created another essential precondition for Zionist colonization. Lack of protection by the central authority was responsible in part for Palestine's Achilles heel – the sparseness of population in the coastal zone and the inland valleys. In consequence, Zionism saw a remarkable territorial shift of the Jewish homeland: while in antiquity Jews inhabited mostly the hilly regions of the West Bank, modern Jewish settlers did not penetrate into this area until some years after 1967. Jewish immigrant-settlers lived until 1948 mostly in the coastal region, certain portions of which, in biblical times, were the home of the Philistines, and in the inland valleys. The reason was not lack of interest. In fact, Jewish settlers during the period under study were all territorial maximalists, even seeking to buy land and settle in such remote parts as the Houran Mountains in southern Syria or in Transjordan. The reason for the "relocation" of the Jewish homeland was that the hills of Judea, Samaria, and the Galilee were densely settled by the Palestinian population even in the nineteenth century.

Though without European intervention and Ottoman reform Jewish colonization could not have come about, this dynamism also produced inhibiting circumstances for the Jewish settlers. The modernizing processes contributed to demographic growth of the Palestinian population and attracted various strata to the settlement and expanded cultivation of the self-same coastal regions and valleys. This process contributed a cardinal factor to the emergence of the conflict between the Palestinian Arabs and Eastern European Jewish settlers.

The Jewish settlers' ability to establish a foothold in Palestine derived, in sum, in about equal measure from the historical weakening of the central authority in the Ottoman Empire and from nineteenth-century European penetration, from the government-initiated internal reforms aimed at the modernization of the Empire, and the social forces opposed not to reforms but to the strengthening of state power. The intersection of this complex congeries of interrelated, historical and contemporary, causes generated the preconditions which alone made feasible the turning of Palestine into a settlement frontier, but also boded ill for the immigrant-settlers. In this chapter European penetration and the Ottoman reform movement will be presented in the first section and subsequently their consequences will be surveyed in three central domains. The second section will examine their impact on the characteristics of Palestinian pre-industrial agriculture in the nineteenth century, and the extent and character of changes it underwent. The focus of the third section is reforms of taxation and land tenure and their impact on the social hierarchy of the Middle East, especially in Palestine and Syria. In the next section I will review changes in demography and settlement patterns bearing on the question of "sparsely populated and empty land" in Palestine. Finally, I will examine the nature of these accumulated changes, particularly with a view to their significance for the facilitation and obstruction of Jewish immigration, settlement, and land purchase.

World economy: dependency and reform

The nineteenth century was the period of unrivalled European hegemony, during which, and decisively after the Crimean War, the Middle East was incorporated, as a peripheral region, into the European-dominated world economic system.[12] Trade, and the steamship which made it possible, were followed by the investment of European finance capital, subsequently by political and religious intervention, and finally by military conquest. European influence was especially marked in Palestine, where the religious motive gave further stimulus to economic processes, and Christian religious orders were feverishly busy erecting new churches and monasteries, hospitals and schools, mostly in Jerusalem, but in other loci of religious geography as well.[13]

In theoretical terms, Roger Owen views "the result of the whole process [as] the creation of a pattern of dependence."[14] The perspective of "dependency theory" is based on the abandonment of the view of modernization as a universal process which takes in its train one country after another. The modern world economic system, which came into existence in the sixteenth century, is seen instead as reproducing the duality inherent in the traditional structure of an empire with a *core* and *peripheral* regions which subsidize the core by means of their tribute. There were, however, a number of novel features, with far-reaching

25

implications, in the new world system. First, the political centralization typical of the Empire, and so wasteful of its resources, was replaced by the decentralized order of a large number of autonomous nation states, which, however, were reintegrated by means of an international market. Secondly, between these states a division of labor emerged. Some countries were able to turn a slight edge over other countries, at the beginning of the process, into a greater disparity and even into a monumental difference later, and entrenched themselves as the core of the world economy. As such they successfully industrialized, while peripheral regions supplied them with raw materials and less demanding labor forces. Dependent peripheral countries, then, were not un-developed on the way to development, but "underdeveloped" countries following a course of their own. Thirdly, the development of the social classes in the two regions diverged: instead of an industrial bourgeoisie, intent on national independence, a *comprador* bourgeoisie grew up in the periphery, animated, except in periods of international crisis, by its ties with the world economy.[15]

Traditional Ottoman economic policy, which, in Issawi's view, was similar to the medieval European "policy of provision" in aiming to supply the urban population and the fiscal needs of the government adequately, taxed exports at a higher rate than imports, and hence played into the hands of European economic penetration.[16] For the pre-industrial economy of the Middle East, integration into the world economy – based, among other things, on the abolition of governmental monopolies and the transformation of the Middle East into "one of the lowest duty areas in the world" – meant the debilitation of its limited manufacturing potential. At the same time, it encouraged the boosting of agricultural production to satisfy the rapid expansion of the European market. The Middle East, in sum, became "a producer of primary products and market for manufactured goods and colonial products,"[17] while European finance capital came to control all but one of the big banks, as well as shipping, imports and exports, railways, ports, power and water supply, and mining in the region.[18]

One facet of European ascendancy over the Ottoman Empire was the transformation of the "capitulation" type agreements between them. Originally, capitulations served the sultan as a method for the granting of temporary rights, in the form of a status of conditional extraterritoriality, to foreign citizens. With changing power and economic relations between the parties the "capitulations" became yet another method of gaining one-sided advantage for European subjects in the Ottoman Empire, to be imposed permanently on its ruler. The capitulations gave to European

26

citizens, who resided within the bounds of the Empire, the right to be adjudicated by their consuls, and was used to gain "an increasing number of concessions for the establishment and operation of all sorts of economic enterprises in the Ottoman Empire."[19] In fact, the protection of the capitulations and the energetic intervention of foreign ambassadors in Istanbul and consuls in Jerusalem was on several occasions crucial to override the opposition of the Ottomans to Jewish immigration and land purchase.[20]

Finally, European predominance brought with it the settlement of Europeans in various parts of the Middle East, but mostly in North Africa. While Egypt remained an occupation colony, in which Europeans furnished only a bourgeoisie, in Algeria and Tunisia they made up part of the working and farmer class as well, thus forming an ethnic plantation colony that attracted sizable immigration. This expansion reached its peak in 1926 when Europeans made up 14 percent of Algeria's total population.[21] In the 1880s, Europeans took over the public finances of Tunisia and Egypt, and ultimately France occupied Tunisia and turned it into a "protectorate," while Britain seized Egypt under similarly vague terms. The year of Egypt's occupation – 1882 – was also the first year of spontaneous Zionist immigration to Palestine.[22]

The Ottoman Empire rose to meet political and military encroachment by trying to reform the Empire. The Empire had a long history of attempted reforms, but I will be concerned here only with its most impressive "age of reform," the Tanzimat, noted for its attempted consistency, seriousness, and many-sidedness.[23] This period, customarily dated from 1839 to 1878 (though in many ways continued even in the last decades of the Empire), was called provocatively by P. M. Holt "the revival of the Ottoman Empire."[24]

The aims of the Tanzimat, succinctly, were "to develop strong centralized political institutions capable of fostering capitalist economic growth, and, in turn, drawing further political and military strength from that economic growth."[25] In addition to the replacement of the military with a modern fighting force and the creation of a large and efficient administration, subject to and paid by the Porte, Ottoman reformers were intent on the reintegration of the outlying provinces, and the destruction of the autonomous power groups that had grown up in the days of Ottoman decline. This also included subduing the Bedouins and improving the notoriously wretched internal security conditions. The period called Tanzimat ended about four years before the beginning of self-conscious Zionist immigration to the shores of Palestine.

Land, labor and the origins of the Israeli–Palestinian conflict

Agricultural expansion

European economic penetration and the Tanzimat effected significant economic changes in Palestine during the nineteenth century. Palestine kept pace with Syria, Anatolia, and Iran, the most dynamic economies of the region, partaking fully in the transformative processes of the Tanzimat.[26] In light of recent scholarly work, the view expressed not long ago, for example by Gabriel Baer, that "economic changes [in nineteenth-century Palestine] were extremely small, not only in absolute terms but also in comparison with neighboring areas" is recognized today as erroneous even in regard to the most traditional branch of the economy – agriculture.[27]

Schölch, who compiled an impressive amount of information for the period extending from 1856 to 1882 from the commercial reports of the British, French, German, and Austrian consuls in the port towns of Jaffa, Acre, and Haifa, concluded that:

Palestine experienced a remarkable economic upswing in the two and half decades following the Crimean War. Apart from the building industry, the production of soap, and the manufacture of devotional articles, however, it was mainly the agrarian sector which increased its output on a significant scale. It had already been stimulated by the pull of external markets before the Crimean War, but after the 1850s it became more and more export oriented.[28]

Part of the agricultural product was marketed in the towns, and allowed the purchase of industrial and artisan-made products, in part even imported items, such as textiles, pottery, coffee, sugar, and household items; and average real income and standard of living seem to have risen.[29]

The destination of agricultural exports, which earlier reached mostly Egypt or Lebanon, shifted now gradually toward Europe.[30] In fact, Palestine produced a *surplus* of exports over imports, during the period surveyed by Schölch.[31] The relative share of industrial cash crops, such as tobacco in small quantities, sesame for oil pressing and spices, and olives for soap production, over subsistence crops also grew markedly.[32] The major export crop, however, remained cereal.

Wheat was a typical Middle Eastern crop, which continued to be grown with traditional methods. Due to lack of nature's generosity and man-made causes, Palestinian agriculture followed the by-and-large rigid pattern of the Middle East: cereals, mostly wheat, sown in the winter, rotated on a biannual basis with various summer crops. It was crude (e.g., animal husbandry was not integrated with crop cultivation), and extensive (almost exclusively rain-fed). Such agriculture was highly labor intensive ("dry farming" required frequent, up to four, summer plowings to conserve soil moisture), resulting in the exploitation of its cultivators,[33] but it was neither a subsistence agriculture nor was it a closed one. The yield of wheat stood at 650 kg. per hectare (or 60 kg. per dunam). Though this is only about half the French and German yield, Palestinian yields were exceeded by Argentina by only 10 to 22 percent, and yet Argentina became a major wheat-exporting country.[34] Palestinian wheat was in demand for the manufacturing of macaroni in Italy and France, and its barley was sought after by British beer and whisky brewers.[35] Palestine remained a wheat-exporting country until 1923, when it began importing wheat and flour due mostly to the increase of its population.[36]

Insofar as we find significant innovations in agriculture in Palestine they took place in the villages of the German settlers of the Templar society. The Templars pioneered soil fertilization and an improved crop-rotation method, and introduced machinery, new crops, such as potatoes, and the "mixed farming" method which combined dairy products with the raising of fodder.[37] Only theirs, argues Gross, was a modern agriculture by virtue of its close commercial connection with Europe and other sectors of the local economy.[38] They made their impact, however, not on Palestinian but on Jewish agricultural practices.

To the traditional wheat-growing agriculture one should contrast the rapid growth of orange, and, to a lesser extent, olive groves and vegetable gardens around the townships of Palestine. The *shamuti* or "Jaffa" orange became a prize export item, since its particularly thick skin made it resistant to bruising and drying up during shipment to distant European ports. In the 1880s oranges climbed to second place, after wheat, in the list of main export items from Jaffa, and after 1904 to first place; in 1882 they made up about a fifth of total exports, and after 1904 fully one third.[39] Raising oranges, however, required an outlay of capital since the trees provided commercial yields only after a few years and required irrigation during the dry half of the year. Citriculture also required private land. Consequently, oranges gave rise to a capitalist industry due to their integration into the international market. These plantations, therefore, could not have been an organic outgrowth of the pre-capitalist agriculture. Orange and olive groves were, in fact, financed and owned by urban merchants, and in this sense constituted a separate sector of the economy. It was mostly citriculture that saw slow technological innovation, so that while its acreage grew four times, the quantity of exported crop grew eightfold.[40] Initially shallow wells from which water was raised by an animal-powered wheel restricted the water supply and limited the size of the grove, but in 1897 the internal combustion engine was introduced into the Arab-owned plantations around Jaffa, while depth drilling was the work of Jewish citriculturalists.[41]

Still, citriculture did not suffice to transform local agriculture. In assessing the impact of modernization on Palestinian agriculture, we may safely say that it underwent a remarkable expansion – giving rise to new forms of entrepreneurship, such as partnership between landowner and working partners, necessitating standardizing Islamic contractual and legal patterns[42] – but overall it was not restructured by its integration into the world economy. Issawi, usually very careful in assessing frequently fragmentary evidence, confidently argues that in the whole Middle East in the period 1800 to 1914 "except for the part of the growth which was due to the shift to more valuable crops and increasing irrigation, the expansion in production . . . was almost wholly due to the extension of the cultivated area, and not to greater output per acre."[43] Though Palestinian exports doubled in the twenty-seven years prior to 1882, Schölch concurs by emphatically noting that this "was not caused primarily by an intensification of agriculture, by improved methods of production, by the development of an agrarian infrastructure, or even by a change in the mix of crops produced. Undoubtedly the main factor was the extension of the area under cultivation."[44] Agricultural output expanded as rapidly as it did, according to Issawi, "because the two essential factors of production, land and labor, were available. In all the countries of the region cultivation had shrunk greatly compared with former times, and there were large reserves of unused land."[45]

Even this mode of change – agricultural expansion without modernization – was of sufficient force, together with additional factors, to introduce far-reaching changes into patterns of land tenure and tax collection throughout the Middle East, as well as into patterns of settlement and demography.

Tax reform and land tenure

One of the major consequences of the processes examined so far, was that

the profitability of export-oriented agricultural production and the possibility of extending the cultivated area as a result of the greater rural security after the Crimean War, resulted in a new evaluation of individual landed property, both on the part of the central government and that of the dominant social groups in Palestine.[46]

To comprehend the transformations wrought by the new value assigned to land in Palestine and throughout the Middle East, we have to consider briefly the traditional patterns of land control, and the social hierarchies to which they gave currency. Land tenure is a most complex topic, given the influence of different civilizations and numerous regimes that followed on one another's heels in the Middle East and the effect of local variations in such a widespread area. Luckily, Issawi has provided an admirably simple and straightforward exposition,[47] which, with additions from Kemal H. Karpat's overview of nineteenth-century evolution of land tenure, will suffice for the purposes of our discussion.

Issawi reduced the great diversity into a basic pattern involving the state, the farmer, and an intermediary. Since Muslim conquest in the seventh century, ownership of land (*raqaba*) in the Middle East was vested, with few exceptions, in the ruler or the state, while the cultivator of the land enjoyed the usufruct (*tasarruf*). In the Ottoman Empire, until the seventeenth century, the *timariot*, a cavalryman (*sipahi*), served as the intermediary, paid by taxes collected from the peasants. The *timar* system served a triple purpose: it generated payment to local representatives of the government; provided the sultan with military services; and ensured the urban population and the guilds agricultural staples at fixed prices.[48] When changes in military technology and inflation spreading from Europe helped undermine the *timariots*, they became eclipsed by a tax farming (*iltizam*) system, which was both salable and hereditary, and by the appointment of non-military people as tax farmers.[49]

Tax reform, one of the first innovations of the Tanzimat, replaced all taxes levied on land by one major and reduced tax – the *usur*, 10 percent of the yield[50] – in order to stimulate agricultural production and increase state revenues. At the same time it abolished the tax farms and substituted for them tax collectors directly employed by the central government which was also to pay them a regular salary. This method of state building is well known in the history of early modern Western Europe. In this case, however, *usur* tax revenues fell badly by 1840. The reasons were the shortage of trained bureaucrats, the spreading of those available over too large areas with no knowledge of local conditions, and the passive opposition of the *multazim* who "were basically businessmen who had collected taxes for a profit, and [for whom] the new arrangement certainly was not agreeable."[51] At the end of 1840, therefore, the treasury had to restore the tax farm system, and subsequent tax reorganizations fared no better.

In 1841, in hope of harnessing them to the cart of reform and directing them against the old elites, the reformers appointed members of a group called variously *ayan, ashraf*, or in Turkey *ehali*, to newly established provincial advisory councils (*majlis al-idara*). The advisory roles were infused with real power in direct proportion with the return to the system of private tax farming. Since the provincial advisory council was charged with selling the tax farm to the highest bidder, the wealthy *ayan*, as pointed out for Palestine by Yehoshua Porath, successfully outbid older elites.[52] In the short run, the reformers found out, the replacement of the *multazim* by the *ayan*, "improved the efficiency of provincial government" and tax collection.[53] In the longer run, however, the reform failed ever to give the state a full treasury because the *ayan*, being not just a traditional estate to be used as intermediaries by the state, used their new sources of wealth and power to counteract the state's intention to bolster its power. Now the *ayan* "emerged," according to Shaw & Shaw, "to demand some kind of political influence commensurate with their economic power."[54]

At this point it becomes necessary to extend the canvas and paint the social hierarchy of the Middle East in a few broad strokes. In a seminal article, Albert Hourani has offered an approach to the larger context of Middle Eastern social stratification. Hourani emphasized the prominence of urban "notables," whom he saw not as a social but as a political category, in mediating between government and people. "Politics of notables," or in Max Weber's term "patriciate," emerges, as specified by Hourani, in societies organized according to relations of personal dependence, in which heads of great urban-based families, who dominate their cities and therefore their rural hinterland, are powerful, free, and ready to check the influence of monarchical power. It is in the cities of Hijaz, Syria, and Palestine, which possessed long urban traditions and were neither too far from nor too close to Istanbul, that "we find the 'politics of notables' in their purest form."[55]

For hundreds of years the religious, military, and secular intermediary notables (the *ulama*, the commanders of *janissary* garrisons, and the *ayan* respectively) were prevented from turning into a caste, since they "had no strong, immutable, hereditary property rights, no political or religious posts which were inherited by law, and even hereditary social status was ephemeral."[56] The *ayan*, the most ambiguous category of Hourani's typology of notables, took on clear features only starting in the 1860s, as it came to benefit from "the beginning of a new process of social mobility and economic relations outside the scope of the traditional theory of social estates."[57] The transformation of social stratification was stimulated by the reforms of the Tanzimat, especially in regard to taxes and the enactment of the 1858 Land Code which, according to Karpat, must be seen as "a milestone in the social history of the Middle East . . . from the point of view of . . . its long range effects on social stratification."[58]

In 1858, the reformers turned to land reform which, however, went the way of the tax reform. Indeed, what is so remarkable about Ottoman land reform is the yawning gap between its intent and its results. It is necessary, therefore, to distinguish between two stages in its implementation. The original purpose of the Ottoman government in enacting the Land Code of 1858,[59] was to take into its possession, by reasserting traditional state ownership, tracts of land which, since the decline of the *timar* system, had slipped by one means or another out of its control. By gaining control over land, at a moment when agricultural revenues were on the rise due to increasing export opportunities to Europe, the central authority expected to be bolstered while the influence of the old elites would be further reduced. After all, the expropriation of large land-owners would have increased the number of actual land holders and in this way have created a broader tax base.[60]

What method did the Land Code employ to accomplish this goal? State land, or *miri*, was the most widespread category of land tenure in the Empire, and Doreen Warriner pointed to the registration of title, under the name of the legal enjoyer of the usufruct as a *miri* owner, as the major method for asserting the Ottoman government's rights.[61] Usufructory right, however, was conditional on the continuous keeping of the land in production. Land uncultivated for three years was declared *mahlul* (idle), and reverted to the state. The significance of this qualification is obvious when we remember that the government was intent on raising its revenues from agricultural production. It is enough to mention in brief the other three categories set by the Land Code: *mulk* land, that is private property in freehold, mostly in urban areas, *wakf* land donated to religious foundations while, at the same time, retaining some of the usufructory rights in the cultivator's family, and *metruk* (or *matrukha*), that is, communal land used for road construction etc. The quantity of these three was relatively small in Palestine, and they played almost no role in the story to be told here.

When it emerged that the Land Code did not stimulate agricultural production either, it was altered piecemeal and while each individual step had only limited impact, together they represented the sanctioning, willy-nilly, of a new approach.[62] "Indeed," argues Karpat, "the long-range effects of the Land Code of 1858 must be sought in its failure to reach its original goals."[63] In 1867, for example, new measures were adopted, extending the heritability of land held in *wakf*, and granting, for the first time, permission to foreigners to own land under their own name in most parts of the Ottoman Empire, but outside the capitulatory system and its extraterritorial jurisdiction. The new approach attempted, through the liberalization of the right of succession, to encourage land improvements by promising the possibility of retaining land in the family. "This feature, enhanced further by freedom to rent the land, proved to be the chief means through which much of the *miri* land was eventually converted into private holdings."[64] The cumulative impact of these revisions, in Karpat's words, was that "for the first time in the history of the Muslim world, property rights and control of land by the state was restricted while the scope of private property and its use for commercial purpose increased."[65] In addition, withdrawal of legal recognition of the rights of semi-collective owners involved in share tenancy forms of land tenure, known as *mushaa* in Palestine, also led in this direction.[66] The Tanzimat ultimately continued the process of unofficial land alienation from the state's effective control and laid the foundations for a *de facto* "private land regime."[67] The concentration of land in the hands of large landowners, many absent or even living at great distances, created what Kark called the "fluid inventory of land" in Palestine.[68]

Flexing their economic muscle, members of the rising *ayan* moved quickly to amass agricultural land. They used the available legal methods, and not being satisfied with those, relied on illegal and extralegal methods as well. According to Shaw & Shaw:

as time went on, the new . . . notables were able to use the law to increase their power, using false documents to prove their claims, extending their rights to include the sale of such properties to others, . . . and maintaining their rights whether or not the lands in question were cultivated to the extent required by law.[69]

Not only was the central government more in need of the *ayan* during the Tanzimat, but the centralizing tendencies drove the population more into seeking out the very same group as intermediaries in their dealings with the government.[70] Intensified European economic pressures and the forces of Ottoman centralization, which consolidated the *ayan* into a relatively stable class, also eroded or dissolved the positions of all other classes, and above all of large sections of the peasantry. The peasants, as has been pointed out by all historians who studied this topic, by trying to use the *ayan* as a foil against the threatening growth of state power, indirectly contributed to their influence. Being fearful that land registration was the harbinger of new taxes, or military conscription, the peasants frequently preferred, or even sought, the protection of an urban notable, under whose name they consented to have their land registered.

According to Shaw & Shaw, "far from resisting" the accumulation of land "the men of the Tanzimat encouraged it to promote agricultural productivity."[71] The decline of agricultural production, which was pervasive in the 1840s and 1850s, according to Moshe Ma'oz's report on Syria, was reversed and both the treasury and the *ayan* stratum benefited from this.[72] In the longer run, however, the *ayan* were the real beneficiaries of land tenure reform in the Arab regions of the Ottoman Empire. They became a new class of landowners, "whose economic and political power far exceeded that even of the greatest fief holders at the height of their power."[73]

Private ownership went hand in hand with a new order of stratification. According to Hanna Batatu's massive study of late Ottoman and modern Iraq, and Philip S. Khoury's study of notables in Damascus in the last decades of Ottoman rule, the conclusions of which are largely applicable to Palestine as well, the 1858 Land Code created the conditions for the safe accumulation of private property and with it the circumstances for the formation, gradual and indirect as it may be, of social classes.[74] But, in addition to private ownership of land, control over tax farm allocation and active participation in the provincial advisory councils played an equally important role in the formation of the *ayan* into a social class. According to Khoury:

in the last decades of Ottoman rule . . . urban leaders and their families were to successfully transform their traditional type of influence into a stabler type of power based on landowning and office-holding in the growing secular wing of the state bureaucracy, a base far better suited to turn-of-century Ottoman realities.[75]

He calls, therefore, the *ayan* after the decade of the 1860s a "landowning–bureaucratic class," and insists with historical hindsight, that "this combination made the class virtually unassailable from below, for nearly a century."[76]

The reliance of the Ottoman reformers on the *ayan* in administering their innovations was not any different from the policies of European Absolutist rulers seeking to harness the bourgeoisie to their carriage. The Ottomans also tried to stimulate an "upward cycle" of taxation, described, by Immanuel Wallerstein,[77] as the replacement of feudal decentralization by the raising of taxes, initially through tax farming, venality of office, and coin debasement, and later through direct collection by state bureaucracy, for the purpose of expanding the administration and the military. Like Western European rulers in their respective countries, the Ottoman sultans eventually succeeded in abolishing the *timar* system (and the *janissary* regiments), maybe even more easily than in Europe, since the Ottoman Empire was more centraLized than the European feudal state.[78] But when the Ottomans tried to move to the top of the cycle, namely to direct taxation, they found that they could not and remained stuck in what for Europe had been an intermediary stage: tax farming.

35

Why was the process of reform by and large arrested at this point? By reforming itself, according to Owen,

Ottoman . . . government played an important, if subordinate role in the process of Middle Eastern economic transformation. The attempt to reform administrative structures, to strengthen armies and to bring distant provinces under central control was an authentic local response to fears of further European political and military encroachments into Muslim lands . . . But, in the event, such policies only exposed new weaknesses which increased dependence rather than reduced it.[79]

Increased commercial exchange with Europe brought only limited fiscal revenue because the Ottomans had limited success in bringing about the revision of the Anglo–Turkish commercial treaty of 1838. Also the Ottoman government was reluctant to carry out its drastic plan of abolishing the *wakf* holdings. Thus major sources of revenue were blocked. Ottoman towns could not turn into industrial cities, and their merchants, financiers, and industrialists tended to remain a powerless element.[80] Those involved in merchant and craft occupations were increasingly recruited from minority groups – Greeks, Armenians, Jews, and Christian Arabs – and the concentration of so many financial activities in the hands of European capital facilitated the emergence of these minorities as intermediaries between Europeans and the local population, further entrenching them in their positions. But this stratum's minority status rendered its influence on the Ottoman authorities negligible.[81]

While in Western Europe the cities and the monarchy rose for a long time simultaneously, as production and the urban tax base expanded, in the Middle East the limits set on the expansion of urban production made this alliance short-lived and problem-ridden. In the subordinate relationship of the Ottoman Empire to Europe, the enhancement of the market and international trade freed the notables from political dependence on the state, and magnified their influence over its policies.[82] Most significantly, the administrative, tax, and land reforms of the Tanzimat ended by transforming the *ayan* into powerful officials, tax collectors, and large private landowners at the expense of the state. In encompassing these facts in a broader picture, I may say that the Ottoman Empire never passed successfully through a mercantilist stage, and without autonomous economic nationalism, it could not carry to completion its modernization.

New settlement and demographic patterns

In recent years a number of outstanding works of archival research have brought us to safer grounds as to the estimation of settlement patterns and demographic trends in Palestine. Wolf-Dieter Hütteroth and Kamal Abdulfattah reconstructed the settlement patterns and areas of agricultural cultivation in Palestine and the adjacent areas on the basis of the 1596 Ottoman census of the Arab provinces, and compared them with the maps of the British Palestine Exploration Fund, drawn between 1871 and 1877. For the end of the sixteenth century, they conclude, the census gives "a picture of a prosperous country, with a density of agricultural settlement and a level of agricultural productivity far above that of the period of decline which, up to now, has frequently been attributed to the whole Ottoman era."[83] The size of the population is estimated to be 206,290.[84] It inhabited a network of small villages, arranged in a continuous line, with almost no isolated outposts. There were compact areas of high density: the mountains around Jerusalem and Nablus, the Galilee – where the distance between the villages was small, with hardly any open spaces between them – and the plains around Gaza. This means, of course, that the "Palestine coast lands [were] not generally empty." Only three flat areas – the Jezreel Valley, the northern part of the coastal plain, and the environs of Haifa – had "no villages in their central parts."[85] In addition, there were 1,384 satellite villages (*mazra'a*), engaged mostly in the cultivation of wheat. This would mean that there could not be much more space for the extension of cultivation through traditional methods.[86] The percentage of the nomadic population was low in comparison with the settled population, and the size of the towns was surprisingly small.[87]

The contrast with the settlement and cultivation patterns of the nineteenth century is "striking."

If the villages found on the Palestine Exploration Fund maps are marked on the map for the sixteenth century, many places remain unfilled. The density of settlement is far below that of the sixteenth century, the whole pattern has changed and the decline is significant: the settlement frontier has retreated, the density of villages is lower in most areas, the percentage of nomads is higher, but the towns have grown in number and relative importance, and the average size of the remaining villages seems to be larger.[88]

Most cruelly hit were the flatlands: in the Gaza plain half the villages were lost, while in the mountainous regions of the Galilee, Jerusalem, and Nablus the loss was closer to 20 percent.[89] The growing preference for habitation on hilly land is amply demonstrated in Hütteroth and Abdulfattah's comparative historical work. James Reilly provides a commonly accepted summation of the resultant geographical distribution of the Arab population in Palestine:

in the middle years of the nineteenth century most Palestinian villages were located in the hills and mountains that run like a spine through the middle of the

458269780526327

country, from the Galilee to Jabal al-Halil (Hebron) in the south. This was in spite of the fact that Palestine's plains, such as Marj ibn Amar (Esdraelon [or Jezreel Valley]) and the coastal plain, are more fertile than the hills.[90]

Malaria,[91] excessive taxation,[92] and especially the age-long struggle of the nomad with the sedantary agriculturalist, that weighed more heavily on the latter due to the weakening of state power,[93] are among the reasons listed for Palestinian loss of villages between the mid sixteenth and early nineteenth centuries.

But the agricultural expansion of the nineteenth century went hand in hand with and was bolstered by two major transformations: the growth of the Palestinian population and its resettlement in the plains and alluvial valleys.

In the first half of the nineteenth century, Schölch views Palestine's population as relatively stagnant at about 350,000.[94] But in the second half of the century a clear upswing is detectable. On the basis of Ottoman censuses, Karpat gives the population of the three *Sanjaks* that concern us, and that were counted between 1881 and 1889 (but published in 1893) at 426,566.[95] Justin McCarthy figures the population of the *Sanjak* of Jerusalem in 1914/15 at 328,168 inhabitants (adding an estimate for the *kaza* of Beer Sheba, that was excluded), the *Sanjak* of Acre – 133,877, and the *Sanjak* of Nablus – 154,563, that is the total population of what came to be the Mandate of Palestine at 651,884.[96] Even without tackling the difficult question of the rate of population growth, it is obvious that in the nineteenth century Palestine experienced significant demographic expansion. In this, Palestine kept on par with and even was ahead of the rest of the Middle East.[97] In sum, the major demographic trends of Palestine point to a decline from the middle of the sixteenth century till sometime in the early nineteenth century, after which a prolonged expansion took place. The expansion of the Palestinian population was an important contributing factor to the shift in settlement patterns.

By and large, the reclamation of the coastal zone and the inland valleys for settlement was started by forces that were not local. Settlers were assisted during the Egyptian conquest in the 1830s by Ibrahim Pasha, Muhammad Ali's son, and subsequently by the Ottoman government itself in attempts to strengthen the security in border and other problematic areas and, in general, to increase revenues by expansion of cultivation. Ibrahim Pasha brought settlers, some of them Bedouin tribes, to Jaffa and the surrounding villages, to Hadera and Wadi-Ara, the environs of Acre, the Jordan Rift and the Beit-Shean and Hula Valleys.[98] The Ottomans had on their hands various refugee populations that were expelled following loss of territories by the Empire. For example, they resettled in some areas of the Empire about two million

38

Circassian refugees from Bulgaria and Rumelia, of whom a small number ended up in north-eastern Galilee. Refugees from among Algerians that rebelled against the French occupation were settled in Syria and northern Palestine in 1856.[99] The population of Palestine between 1880 and 1913, according to Owen, was augmented in addition to Jewish in-migration by "smaller numbers of Trans-Jordanians, Druzes, and a variety of agricultural colonists such as Circassians, Sudanese, Persians, etc."[100] In general, when the plains were pacified in the 1860s by Ottoman troops returning from the Crimean War, a long-term westward shift in the population's settlement pattern began.

Owen lists four groups that vied for the flatlands. In addition to inhabitants of nearby hill villages that threw off satellite settlements (*khirab*) in areas where they used to farm in the past, nomads and semi-nomads now became willing to settle and reap the new benefits of cereal cultivation, mostly in the environs of Gaza. The remaining two groups were of a different nature. The third, the group we examined in the previous section, was not made up of cultivators but of city-based bankers and merchants, whose interest in agriculture grew parallel to its commercialization and export orientation. Large landowners actively sponsored colonization by encouraging peasants and semi-nomadic tribesmen to work their land, thus combining in one project all groups mentioned earlier.[101] In Palestine the best known example is the colonization of the Marj Ibn Amir (Jezreel Valley) by the Sorsuq family. The fourth group were foreign colonizers, such as the German Templars, American Protestants, and of course, Jews.[102]

How did the Jewish settlers fit into the general geographical pattern of settlement? As already mentioned, the choice of tracts to be purchased by Jews in Palestine could not have been motivated by primordial reasons, since the areas of Jewish antiquity were almost totally ignored in favor of the coastal areas and inland valleys. The cause of this remarkable shift was that the former were densely, the latter sparsely, inhabited. But instead of addressing the coastal zone as an homogenous unit, it is possible now, on the basis of David Grossman's painstaking research, to begin carefully to examine interregional variations.

In a number of recent studies,[103] Grossman compared three sub-regions of the coastal zone spreading from the coast to the foothills. He found that the southern coastal area proper, between Gaza and Rechovot, manifested a highly stable and large population and experienced the establishment of only a handful of Jewish settlements, and these only after 1936. The same held true for the similarly located Lydda Valley in the heart of the coastal zone: into this triangular area between Ramla, Yahud (Yahudia), and Jaffa, which boasted a relatively stable and

39

continuous Palestinian settlement and very fertile land, Jews were not able to penetrate.[104] The inland plains of Soreq and Ayalon and the adjacent low hills (the lower Shefela) were beset by the most unstable settlement pattern, and immigration of Egyptians during Ibrahim Pasha's time, and Jewish settlers after 1882, "was important in restoring stability to the area." Finally, the more rugged parts of the hilly region, west of Hebron (the higher Shefela), saw a seasonal and cyclical pattern of temporary settlements, inhabited by agriculturalists during plowing and harvesting seasons, and occasionally by nomadic shepherds. The same pattern was found in the Sharon Plain region, where the thrust of new occupation, through the establishment of satellite settlements, was mainly to marginal agricultural land, and not to the fertile land of the plains, which was owned by large landowners.[105] These areas appeared unfit for Jewish settlement, even after 1948, because of the low standard of living they offered. There was, then, a strong correlation between the density of the Palestinian population and the productivity of land and its desirability for Jewish settlement, even in the coastal zone.

It should not be concluded, however, that Jewish immigrants settled solely on vacant and fallow land. While the decline of Ottoman state power is "undisputed" its effects are given to debate. To the widespread view of unilinear decline, claimed to have resulted from the weakening of central authority, Theodore Swedenburg opposes a perspective that emphasizes the emergence of a flexible pattern of social organization and type of cultivation designed to take advantage of statelessness. In regard to the question of settlement, he argues that it is "a mistake to assume that, simply because of lack of state control or because lands were not permanently settled, they were not cultivated." In fact, the plains were cultivated "in a manner that allowed the farmers to avoid control by the state, landlords and the powerful Bedouin tribes." Among its features he mentions the Palestinian cultivators' repeatedly asserted nomadic capacity, the exchange and interaction between cultivators and herding populations to a larger extent than it is usually admitted, the periodical fallowing of agricultural land, etc.[106]

Ben-Arieh argues that the lands of the settlements of the First *Aliya* were "considered by the local Arab population secondary, or marginal, lands. These were lands not cultivated by them, or cultivated in part and intermittently."[107] But, even if that was the case in the past, about a generation or two before Jewish colonization the Palestinian Arab agricultural population also became involved in the search for additional land resources. Improved security conditions, the curtailing of Bedouin marauding, the new economic incentives of commercialized agriculture, and the end of the cycle of plagues, etc., also brought about a demographic increase of the local Arab population and "an acceleration of that process of filling in the empty or sparsely occupied areas on the coastal plains to the north of Jaffa."[108] These were, however, the very areas of sparse settlement where Jewish colonization was possible. Jewish moshavot usually purchased their land from recent, frequently absentee, landowners who took advantage of the Tanzimat's Land Code and, therefore, were received with hostility by Arabs with claims of their own, until the questioning of Jewish buyers' rights became "an inseparable part of the purchase of land and the history of *each and every* Jewish settlement," by the last two decades of the nineteenth century.[109] The same processes which made Jewish settlement possible also strengthened the forces which stood to impede and oppose it, and added a dynamism and measure of urgency to their conflict, making it less avoidable. There was no way for Jewish immigrants to stop or deflect the westward population shift taking place in Palestine; they had to try to turn it to their advantage by participating in it as energetically as possible.

The implications for Jewish settlement

The integration of the Middle East into the modern world economic system, the centralizing and modernizing reforms of the Tanzimat, and the subversion of the latter by the notables, made it possible for Jewish immigrants to purchase land and settle in the sparsely settled regions of Palestine. The combination of these processes permitted the satisfaction of the settlers' "demographic interest," i.e. a sufficiently conclusive land:people ratio, for the purposes of Jewish settlement, though the Ottoman Empire never became a prototypical frontier of European pure settlement.

"From the landowner's point of view, land came to be regarded as an economic means,"[110] as is clear from the examination of the type of landowners who sold land to Jewish settlers and settlement companies. Based on incomplete figures, between 1878 and 1936, for the 681,978 dunams purchased by Jews (about half of the 1.39 million dunams purchased prior to 1945) for which information is available, only 9.4 percent originated in *fellaheen*. Over three-quarters of the land was purchased from *big landowners*, most of whom had acquired their land in the last half of the nineteenth century, that is, not too long before they put it up for sale. Non-Palestinian, that is, Ottoman notables living for example in Beirut, were the major source of purchase (52.6 percent), and Rashid Khalidi's unpublished Palestinian sources indicate that before the First World War, their share was even bigger.[111] But even big Palestinian landowners were not immune, and sold 24.6 percent of the land purchased by Jews (13.4 percent originated in government, foreign owners, or churches).[112] It is also significant that after 1933, when in absolute terms the sale by all sources declined, the absolute share of Palestinian big landowners declined the least, and percentage-wise rose to 62.7 percent.

Among the Palestinian landowners who sold land to Jews throughout the period, we find branches of the al-Dajani family of Jaffa, the al-Husayni, al-Nashashibi, and al-Alami families of Jerusalem, the Abd al-Hadi family of Nablus and Jenin, the al-Shawa family of Gaza, etc., who all belonged to the outstanding families of notables that have also contributed leading members to the Palestinian Arab national movement.[113] The economic incentive of rising land prices – increasing probably as much as fifty times between 1910 and 1944[114] – was so overpowering, emphasized Porath, that land sale to Jews continued in spite of the demoralization it spread in the ranks of the Palestinian national movement. It also supplied the British with an easy excuse not to intervene in the dispossession of Palestinian peasants.[115]

Just how crucial the existence of a land market was for Jewish colonization we may glean from the detailed overview of the colonization enterprise by Menachem Ussishkin, the rising leader of Hovevei Zion, in 1904, at the beginning of the Second *Aliya*.

In order to establish autonomous Jewish community life – or, to be more precise, a Jewish state, in Eretz Israel, it is necessary, first of all, that all, or at least most, of Eretz Israel's lands will be the property of the Jewish people. Without ownership of the land, Eretz Israel will never become Jewish, be the number of Jews whatever it may be in the towns and even in the villages, and Jews will remain in the very same abnormal situation which characterizes them in the diaspora. They will be without a recognized status. But, as the ways of the world go, how does one acquire landed property? By one of the following three methods: by force – that is, by conquest in war, or in other words, by robbing land of its owner; by forceful acquisition, that is, by expropriation via governmental authority; and by purchase with the owner's consent.[116]

The concrete problem at hand was: "which one of these methods will be appropriate in our case? The first method is totally ungodly. We are too weak for it."[117] It was unlikely, Ussishkin believed, that the Ottoman sultan would assist Jewish settlement by providing it with land privately owned by him. Certainly, neither the Ottoman authorities nor the European governments would give Jewish settlers a charter to expropriate land currently owned by either peasants or landowners, since such charter could not deny Muslims the right to autonomy it conferred on Jews. "In sum, the only method to acquire Eretz Israel, at any time and under whatever political conditions, is but purchase with money."[118]

In contradistinction to the political and military means at the disposal of colonial powers, this facet of capitalism, as recognized indirectly by Ussishkin, was the only basis for the possession of Palestine. The historical weakness of a scattered people, and the mental traits which evolved in conjunction with it, also account for the relatively benign character of Jewish colonization, at least until the end of the British Mandate and the War of Independence. Only then did "the original territorial accumulation, during which the Jewish immigrants converted money into land," end, and the settler society, reluctantly, changed its means of accumulation "from money to sword."[119] In a reversal of historical patterns, the period of "primitive accumulation" was less violent than the completion of the "transformation of Palestine."

The second precondition of Jewish settlement was the relative sparseness of the Palestinian population in the coastal zone and the inland valleys. In 1907, Arthur Ruppin, then an employee of the WZO and the future head of its Palestine Office to be established the following year, submitted a memorandum in which he outlined the aims of Jewish colonization in Palestine. Ruppin invoked what in this study is called the "demographic interest," by pointing to the poor people:land ratio of Jews *vis-à-vis* the Arab inhabitants. According to the numbers he possessed, Jews made up only 80,000 of the 700,000 inhabitants of the land, and owned only 1.5 percent of its 29,000 square kms. Under these conditions, he reasoned, Turkey could not grant the privileges that might lead to the Jewish residents' political domination. Ruppin concluded:

I see it as absolutely necessary to limit, for the time being, the territorial aim of Zionism. We should strive to attain autonomy not in the whole of Eretz Israel, but only in certain districts. It is obvious that the two districts most fit are part of Judea [at the time this designation applied to the southern part of the coastal zone, spread out around Jaffa] and the environs of Lake Tiberias . . . It will be possible to join the two areas . . . through the purchase of sufficient land from Jaffa via Petach Tikva, Kfar Saba, Hadera, Zichron Yaacov, Shfeia up to Mescha [Kfar Tavor], until the formation of a narrow strip, all of which is in Jewish hands, and on which a road, leading through Jewish land, may be constructed from Lake Tiberias to Judea.[120]

By connecting Jaffa and Lake Tiberias, via the Jezreel Valley, Ruppin drew the famous N-shaped settlement pattern of Jewish colonization, which remained in force till the "Stockade and Watchtower" settlements of the 1936–9 period. Though Ruppin incorporated into his map the traditional Jewish population of some of the holy cities, it was based on the contours of the already existing modern Jewish agricultural settlement.

Ruppin's memorandum together with Ussishkin's "Our Program" of

1904, are key documents for the comprehension of the Zionist perspective of the era, precisely because they are not ideological proclamations, but rather hard-headed and down-to-earth blueprints. Both programs cast a cold eye on the prevailing conditions with the intention of offering a method for reaching Jewish autonomy in Palestine. Purchase of land on the open market, as Ussishkin insisted, and occupation of the sparsely inhabited coastal zone, the Jezreel and some other valleys, in Ruppin's view, were the essential conditions of late Ottoman Palestine which Jewish settlers could and should use to further their aim. To take advantage of these scanty favorable conditions, Jewish settlement bodies still had to work out a method of state and nation formation.

Chapter three

From land to labor: unequal competition and the "conquest of labor" strategy

I presume that no one's conscience may be clear *vis-à-vis* his own history . . . Whoever has carried the burden of history, must testify, for better or worse, to the causal relationship between events.

Siegfried Lenz, *Homeland Museum,* 1978

Jews wish to maintain a European standard of civilization in Palestine and must yet compete economically with a majority not accustomed to such a standard. [This] contains the root of all the difficulties with which our agricultural colonization has to struggle.

Arthur Ruppin, *The Agricultural Colonization of the Zionist Organization in Palestine,* 1926

It should have been the case that the Jewish bourgeoisie would be chauvinistic, and would demand only Jewish labor. We, the socialists, should have been more moderate. Tending towards internationalism, we should have demanded that workers be employed without regard to national and religious differences. In reality, we see exactly the opposite taking place.

Itzhak Ben-Zvi, Letter to editorial board of *Haachdut,* 1914

The abundance of land on the North American continent, in southern Africa, and Australia made the opening of the land for settlement the first priority for immigrants to these countries and established the major opportunity structure for their social mobility. Only at a later stage, when smallholders in southern Africa were proletarianized and impelled to enter the labor market, by the time the Australian gold rush was over and squatters took firm hold of the extensive sheep runs of eastern Australia, and with the arrival in the United States of massive numbers of poor immigrants who, following the Civil War, were directly employed in industry, did the labor market in these societies become the primary arena of social organization and conflict. Among these settlement societies Palestine was an exception.

45

The accumulation of Jewish territorial assets in Palestine and the establishment of new colonies came to a halt in 1903, barely twenty years after their inception, just around the time when the immigrants of the Second *Aliya* began arriving on its shores. The Zionist movement at the time was at its lowest ebb. The old movement, the Hovevei Zion of Odessa (founded January 1882, recognized by the Russian government under the name Society for the Support of Jewish Farmers and Artisans in Syria and Palestine only in 1890) had never been up to the task of colonization on a large scale, and the new World Zionist Organization (founded in 1897) was opposed to practical colonization prior to receiving political guarantees. The major patron of the First *Aliya*, the Baron Edmund de Rothschild, had already withdrawn his tutelary administration and direct support of Jewish settlement in 1900, the Jewish Colonization Association (the JCA was founded in 1891 by the Baron Maurice de Hirsch), the only non-Zionist worldwide colonization society active in Palestine, was already past the peak of its settlement drive of 1900–3. No privately established colony, however, was known to subsist or be established without the assistance of one or more of the above mentioned bodies. In short, the possibility of becoming a small farmer after temporarily laboring on other people's land, an inspiration common to propertyless immigrants in settlement societies, was out of sight for the Second *Aliya* immigrants.

The emphasis in the immigrants' lives shifted, consequently, to the labor market. The conflict over its control became the major social dynamic of the *Yishuv*. The period of the Second *Aliya* – lasting the ten years from 1904 to the outbreak of the First World War – was coterminous with this struggle. This short period may even be subdivided: from 1904 to 1908/9 the labor market conflict was exclusive, for the balance of the period the renewal of the settlement potential began to overshadow it. This conflict, atypical though it was for a settlement society and short in duration, was nevertheless the central stage for the shaping of the method of Israeli state and nation formation and is, therefore, the focus of our interest.

How has the singularity of this period been understood? Contemporaries, not surprisingly, and subsequent interpreters, whether philosophers, historians, or social scientists, unduly came to transform the attributes of the frontier into allegedly intrinsic characteristics of the immigrants themselves. The impasse in territorial expansion found its distorted reflection in the image of the immigrants as motivated throughout by high-minded idealism. Determinism, then, was dressed up as voluntarism. This is a good point to recall Lukacs's blunt but perceptive observation that "fatalism and voluntarism are only mutually contradictory to an undialectical and unhistorical mind." Indeed the immigrants' idealism did not exist apart from the narrowly constraining social and economic conditions of Palestine at the time. Shifts in access to land, in this as in other settlement societies, lurked behind the immigrant-settlers' ideas, attitudes, and actions.

No lesser person than Martin Buber promoted, starting in 1942, the view of the early Jewish immigrants to Palestine, the subjects of this study, as possessing a unique spirit not shared by later arrivals. According to Buber, since it was well nigh impossible to acquire property in Palestine until the end of the First World War, immigrants who came with the intention of attaining riches were driven away by a "quasi-automatic principle of selection," which, at the same time, retained the dedicated and self-motivated. These pioneers (*halutzim*) transformed the contemporary existential crisis of Jewish diaspora life into an internal revolution in Palestine. During the British Mandate, Buber argued, Palestine gradually became integrated into the orbit of the capitalist world economy. In consequence, the immigrants who arrived at this period were semi-pioneering, motivated in part by material in part by ideal considerations. Some of them, therefore, could be assimilated into the group of the pioneers by way of a "planned selection." Finally, when the rise of the Nazis to power in Germany in 1933 dramatically accelerated the tempo of the external crisis of Jewish life, an unselected mass of refugees, whose inner change could not keep pace with the outer, arrived. The pioneers had no authority over these later arrivals and fell short of assimilating them.[1]

S. N. Eisenstadt took up this thesis and developed it further in a series of writings around 1950. In his perspective, Buber's distinctions were transformed into a hard and fast dichotomy between the *ole* (person "ascending" to Eretz Israel),

a concept indicating mostly a voluntary, conscious passage to Eretz Israel, issuing from a substantial, sometimes even total, rejection of the social reality in which the *ole* resided abroad. The *ole* comes to Eretz Israel for the sake of constructing a new society, an autonomous Jewish society . . .

and the immigrant

who removes himself from one place of residence to another one, not out of the desire to create a new society, but out of a certain partial social impulse, such as an economic, political, or religious impulse, which compels him to leave his social environment, but is not issued out of the rejection of that social reality.

Eisenstadt also shifted Buber's chronology by fixing the main point of demarcation between the two immigrant types in 1948, with the establishment of the Israeli state. Prior to independence, in Eisenstadt's

view, Palestine attracted mostly *olim* while, according to his classifi-
cation, post-1948 arrivals were immigrants, whether of *ashkenazi* (Jews
descending from Europe, or the West in general) or *mizrachi* (Jews
hailing from North Africa and the Middle East) background. At the same
time, almost all *mizrachi* Jews, whether they arrived before or after 1948,
were fitted into the immigrant category.

While the distinctions made by Buber, the philosopher, were rooted as
much in the circumstances of Jewish diaspora life as in the objective
economic conditions prevailing in Palestine, Eisenstadt, the social
scientist, divorced his dichotomy completely from Palestinian conditions
and rooted it exclusively in the dynamic of Eastern European Jewish
society. By applying the classificatory scheme to the immigrants'
characteristics prior to their actual arrival, the voluntary potential of
their actions in Palestine was expanded considerably. Eisenstadt defined
the external framework which propelled Jewish immigration as the crisis
of modernization introduced into Jewish society by the pressure of the
surrounding society. The self-selecting individual *ole*, as part of the
Zionist rebellion against the forces of disintegration which emptied
Jewish communal life of its gratifications and security, was open, in his
view, to assume new vocational roles. But Eisenstadt was in concert with
Buber that "it was not the attainment of instrumental goals that held the
first place [for the *ole*] . . . these goals were largely subordinated to social
and cultural aspirations." On the other hand, immigrants, such as the
mizrachim, came from societies which had not undergone the same
modernization crisis and, while suffering temporary persecutions and
economic vicissitudes, had maintained their communal life. *Mizrachi*
immigration, therefore, involved whole families and communities, and
did not display the same disposition towards occupational transformation that was the *ole*'s hallmark.[2]

The distinction between the *ole* and the immigrant has recently been
subjected to severe criticism by Yaakov Kellner, who argued that it bases
a socio-historical analysis on an ideological assumption. He found easy
proof of this bias in the different periodizations presented by Buber and
Eisenstadt. The former located the turning-point between the dedicated
ole and the pragmatic immigrant in the 1930s, the latter in 1948. "It
seems," pointed out Kellner, "that in the analysis of the different
immigrant waves historical reality was without importance – provided
that the comparison with the period preceding the moment of analysis
presented the new immigrant as endangering the achievements of the
veteran community." Kellner, in contrast to both Buber and Eisenstadt,
suggested that the characteristics of the present should alert us to the

importance of re-examining the spirit of the earlier immigrants, and, of course, of refraining from idealizing them.

In his own brief study Kellner found that the First *Aliya* was construed, for example by Achad Haam and M. L. Lilienblum of Hovevei Zion, as a normal immigration movement, motivated by the aspiration of the individuals involved to improve their economic position. Contemporary observers in Palestine, such as Yehoshua Barzilai, identified the same stages in the dilution of dedication among the new arrivals as did Buber and Eisenstadt, but already within the microcosm of the First *Aliya*. Barzilai regarded the earlier newcomers of this wave as akin to *olim*, and the later ones as "immigrants." Kellner was critical of the idealization of the *olim* by ignoring that "the circumstances of migration and absorption place newcomers of the most varied motivations in the very same situation: that of the immigrant." He concluded, therefore, that the Eisenstadtian dichotomy is a distorted reflection of an "internal tension which is to be found in every wave of immigration."[3]

As immigrants to Palestine between 1882 and 1914 constituted no more than 3 to 4 percent of Jewish immigrants leaving the Pale of Settlement, obviously self-selection played an important role in the direction of our *dramatis personae* to Palestine. Once in Palestine, however, the initial motivation of the immigrants was overlaid by new impetuses, of which the one that proved crucial was their confrontation with the presence of Palestinians in their ancestral land. Old and new factors simultaneously affected the immigrants' subsequent choices. As many of the workers of the Second *Aliya* recognized the loss of their erstwhile "idealism" themselves, we can hardly use it as our single yardstick in accounting for their historical role. If not lost, the Second *Aliya* workers' ideals, as I shall show in this study, underwent the most radical changes in Palestine. At first they wished to be absorbed in the moshava (colony or settlement) of the First *Aliya*; soon after, they became its internal opposition; and, finally, they successfully bypassed it. It therefore borders on the absurd to explain their contradictory actions as motivated by the same ideological commitment to vocational trans- formation. The great German Jewish Romantic poet, Heinrich Heine, reflecting upon the undignified reasons for his conversion to Christianity remarked, in his inimitably witty way: "my principles are not in the least influenced by the thought of wealth and poverty, but my actions unfortunately are." Since I am interested in actions, I cannot ignore their compelling causes.

Kellner's opposition to the idealization of the immigrants was a direct response to its use in stigmatizing new Jewish immigrants at a later time. I find not less troubling Eisenstadt's disassociation of the early immigrants from their own life conditions in Palestine since this serves to render invisible their conflicts with the Palestinian Arab population. In this chapter I will seek to examine the Jewish workers' actions as they took place in, and were circumscribed by the conditions of, the labor market of the Jewish plantations in Palestine, and above all by the competition of Palestinian Arab workers.

The alternative labor forces

The plantation system and its labor demands

The first Jewish moshavot evolved their agricultural system in imitation of the Arab *fellah*'s field-crop, mostly grain, cultivation, with the addition of some plantation products, and through the mixed use of Arab and European agricultural implements.[4] This partial readiness to be acculturated to their neighbors was in large part due to the new immigrants' lack of agricultural experience. But just as they were escaping from the Europe that rejected them, they realized that they could not rid themselves of their own Europeanness. Extensive cultivation methods of field-crops yielded the same appallingly low earnings for the *fellah* and the Jewish farmer, but the latter could not accede to them and clamored for a "European standard of living." Jewish settlements that based their livelihood on grain and other crops, could not carry the overhead expenses of medical, cultural, and religious services, or support rural artisans without an uninterrupted flow of subsidies. Whether built with the settlers' independent means, created under the aegis of Hovevei Zion, or with the assistance of the JCA, both of which were committed, the former for ideal, the latter for economic reasons, to the generation of the simplest form of agricultural life, these settlements were invariably poor, stagnant, and unattractive to potential settlers.[5]

As early as 1882, the settlers turned for help to the Baron Edmund de Rothschild in Paris, whose solution to the problem of low return on field-crops was the introduction of the plantation system (*mataim*), which promised a European standard of living. Rothschild undertook the first borrowing of a European settlement model for application and adaptation to Palestine. New agricultural methods were introduced by agronomists who had gained their experience in southern France and subsequently in French colonial agriculture in Africa, mostly in Algeria. Justin Dugourd, Rothschild's first envoy and director of agriculture, the person who recommended the development of viticulture in Palestine, worked in Algeria and Egypt; Gerard Ermens, the Inspector General of agriculture after 1888, gained his experience in Senegal and Egypt. While subsequently, graduates of the Alliance Israélite Universelle's Mikve Israel agricultural school and other Eastern-European-born agronomists were appointed by Rothschild, the early directors, and in Simon Schama's estimation especially the technical advisors, were "in the mould of the French *service colonial* and imbued with their share of *la mission civilisatrice*."[6] Giladi and Naor point out that "as foreign experts, they considered Eretz Israel to be a colonial domain, in which they had to carry out well-defined technical assignments."[7] Arab agriculture, held in contempt by these experts, was replaced in Rishon Letzion, part of Petach Tikva, etc. by plantations, and these moshavot were in turn imitated in the early 1890s by Rechovot and Hadera, the settlements of the First *Aliya*'s second wave.

The new plantation agriculture was based, first and foremost, on cash crops, primarily the vinegrape. Almonds later became equally important, and orange production grew steadily throughout the period. Secondly, agricultural production was redirected from subsistence or the selling of surplus in the local markets into production *in toto* for the international market. Thirdly, the cycle of field-crop cultivation was replaced by a monocultural agriculture. Though attempts were made to diversify it through the addition of jasmine and other perfume plants, cotton, silk, sugarcane, tea, opium, etc., all of which are also products typical of colonial agriculture, these attempts failed.

The fourth difference is pointed out by Barrington Moore's discussion of vinegrowing in France: "viniculture, particularly in the days before artificial fertilizers, was what economists call a labor-intensive variety of agriculture, requiring large amounts of fairly skilled peasant labor and relatively small amounts of capital either in the form of land or equipment."[8] The vineyard in Palestine was not irrigated and, in consequence, its land had to be plowed four or five times a year to ease the penetration of rainfall into the soil, and had to be deep-weeded to kill off wild growth that might drink away moisture. These characteristics increased the labor intensity and lowered the skill level required in the vineyard. The new agriculture, in sum, required the employment of a large, seasonal, and low-priced labor force. These radical innovations transformed the Jewish settlements: in attempting to emulate the North African colonial economy they also found themselves copying its social structure.

But Palestine did not offer big returns to capital, since land purchase seemed to be too risky, and development costs and investment too high for the returns offered. Furthermore, Jewish plantations developed after the classical mercantilist age of slave-labor plantations which thrived on price differentials and monopolies in trade relations, themselves maintained through political power differences. Consequently, Jewish plantations were capitalist in character and, having to compete in the international market, remained exposed to its fluctuations. In consequence of this outward economic dependence, they did not give rise to a politically conscious and well-organized plantation aristocracy. The small size of the Jewish-owned plantations – the average size of Rishon Letzion's plantation being 83.4 Turkish dunams (18.9 acres) and in richer Petach Tikva 134 Turkish dunams (30.5 acres) with even the two largest estates holding 684 and 906 Turkish dunams (155 and 206 acres respectively) – was a further limiting factor.[9] The character of the Eastern European Jewish immigrants, mostly of petty bourgeois provenance, was also adverse to such development at an early phase.

For a few years in the 1890s it seemed that the enormous sums invested in the plantations by Rothschild would soon make them self-supporting. According to Achad Haam's estimate, Rothschild spent forty million French francs on settlements, and according to another assessment one and a half million francs per year on the 360 families concerned.[10] But the dependence of cash crops on the fluctuations of the international market, the vulnerability of monoculture (for example of viniculture to Phylloxera epidemics), and the large overhead expenses of the supervisory apparatus, turned the scales and proved that colonial agriculture was not viable in Palestine. In 1900, Rothschild transferred his moshavot to the management of the JCA. Under its strict direction viniculture underwent ruthless streamlining. The moshavot started to emerge slowly from their dire straits around the middle of the new century's first decade, and to show signs of prosperity by the end of the decade. But the plantation system as a whole, with the notable exception of orange production, did not fulfil the grand hopes attached to it, and proved to be an ephemeral stage in the evolution of the Palestinian Jewish economy. Already before the First World War, a model of "mixed farming" (*meshek meurav*), integrating crops and fruits with animal and dairy farming, directed to self and local-market consumption, began to evolve slowly from the lessons of the failed experiments. Nevertheless, from the early 1880s at least until the outbreak of the First World War, plantations remained the dominant mode of production and the main source of employment.

One of the central tasks of the Jewish settlers and the Rothschild tutelary administration was the recruitment of a labor force which would satisfy the requirements of plantation agriculture. There were two alternative sources: Palestinian villagers from the environs of the Jewish settlements and propertyless Jewish immigrants who arrived as part and parcel of the First *Aliya*.

In field-crop cultivation, concentrated mostly in the Galilee and modelled in large measure after Arab agriculture, it was easy to extend to Jewish settlements the prevailing Arab custom of the live-in landless *charat*, who was employed on a yearly basis and paid one-fifth of the product. I find no indication in the historical sources of a shortage of Arabs employed as *charats* by Jewish farmers.

In plantations, however, the recruitment of Palestinian laborers was more complicated, and its pattern not so easily discernible. The expansion of the employment opportunities and the supply of workers was in all probability not simultaneous, since the first expanded and contracted in spurts, while the latter expanded at a more leisurely pace, and most likely varied locally. Kolatt's argument that the supply of Arab laborers was limited in the early years of the First *Aliya* seems to be well founded.[11] At the same time, around certain moshavot the population of the Arab villages grew steadily through in-migration,[12] that is, the Palestinian Arab agricultural population seems to have responded to the new demand. Since the labor market was expanding, most labor seekers, whether Jewish or Arab, appear to have found employment.

One advantage on the side of the Jewish workers was that they arrived coterminously with the two large waves of the First *Aliya*, in 1882–4 and 1890–1, and therefore found immediate employment in projects connected with the establishment of the new settlements. From a memorandum of the colonists and laborers of the Rothschild colonies, drawn up in 1900, we learn that: "almost from the inception of colonization in Palestine, and particularly from the introduction of viniculture and the plantation system, a class of Jewish agricultural laborers was formed."[13] At the beginning of the second wave of the First *Aliya*, in 1890, the Jewish moshavot employed about 5,000 laborers, of these 1,200 were Jewish and the rest Palestinian Arab.[14] The Jewish labor force, however, was more heterogeneous: in addition to immigrants too poor to purchase land, it also included landowners whose vineyards were too young to yield, artisans en route to urban employment, and an assortment of eccentric types such as are to be found in and around all movements of social change.

The most important source of Jewish employment was the tutelary Rothschild administration. Large parts of the settlers' plantations were undivided and their cultivation, together with the experimental parcels owned directly by Rothschild, was carried out under the direct supervision of the administrators.[15] It was on these lands that Jewish workers found work, since under the Rothschild tutelage economic and philanthropic considerations were never separated systematically (though the pendulum swung occasionally from one extreme to the other), and the costs of the labor force were not always a major concern. Gradually, as the vineyards matured, they were subdivided and transferred to the control of their owners.[16] This process raised for the first time, on a significant scale, the choice between Palestinian Arab workers and immigrant Jewish workers for the Jewish planters. The planters opted for the cheaper and more pliant Palestinians,[17] and with the transfer of the Rothschild moshavot to the JCA at the beginning of 1900, this tendency was dramatically accelerated.

The JCA aimed to eliminate philanthropy and, in order to make the vinegrowers competitive in the international market, commenced paying them the real market value for grapes. The newly formed Wine Producers' Cooperative Association was forced to uproot as much as 50 percent of the vineyards. The experimental stations were dismantled and together with the undivided vineyards were transferred to the planters.[18] The result of these steps was nothing short of the destruction of the Jewish agricultural proletariat in Palestine.

The inquiry by Ephraim Komarov of the Vaad klali shel hapoalim haivriyim beeretz israel (General Board of Hebrew Workers in Eretz Israel) found that the majority of the 560 families of laborers throughout the country (not counting Sedjra) was already anticipating the termination of their work on the completion of the harvest in October 1900.[19] The wages of the workers in some locations, such as Zichron Yaacov, dropped by 33 percent, that is, to the market level determined by the wages of Arab workers.[20] Shmuel Hirschberg, a merchant from Bialystok travelling through Palestine at the time, recorded that the livelihood of the workers "diminished and dried up" and "they have no hope of making a living from their work anymore." The reason, given by both Komarov and Hirschberg, was that Jewish workers "were unable to compete with the Arab who requires a lower wage."[21] In 1900, the potential threat in a split-labor-market situation – the choice of the employers to replace the higher-priced workers with the lower-priced ones – had become an actuality.

These events sent shock waves through Jewish and Zionist circles in Eastern Europe. In 1901 the *Achiassaf* Yearbook, published in Warsaw, accused the JCA of having decided to solve the *Yishuv*'s problem with a "sharp knife," as it cast "great doubt over the ability of the laborers to survive in Eretz Israel."[22] The *Achiassaf* report was no exaggeration. By December 1902 only 200 of the original 560 families of workers – among them 114 that the JCA consented to employ – remained in Palestine, that is, 65 percent of the workers had left the country. The JCA demonstrated that it saw no future for Jewish agricultural workers in Palestine by actually financing their emigration,[23] while Rothschild ignored their plight,[24] and Hovevei Zion were too impotent to make much of a difference.

Only the employees of the Rishon Letzion vine cellar were able to protect their working conditions, for the inverse reason which had caused the agricultural laborers to lose their jobs. The cellar workers fell in a special category in the labor market due to an extraneous reason: since a large portion of the cellar's wines were sold for religious rituals their production was subject to Judaic laws of religious purity and defilement. Wine touched by a non-Jew became "libation wine" (*yeyn nessech*), and this ban ensured exclusive Jewish employment in the cellars. Fearing no competition from Arab workers, the Jewish cellar workers blocked the way of Feriente, the chief JCA representative in Palestine, in his visit to the cellar until he consented to reconsider and ultimately reverse the decision to reduce their numbers and lower their wages.[25]

The workers-to-be of the Second *Aliya* demanded a re-evaluation of the preference for Arab workers. Obviously, the choice between these alternatives carried far-reaching consequences for the propertyless Jewish immigrants and ultimately for the shaping of the Israeli state and nation. In this chapter I will examine the labor-market conflict born of the encounter between Jewish immigrant workers of the Second *Aliya*, Palestinian Arab workers, and Jewish planters. In the next sub-section, I will present the different initial motivations and resources of the two groups of workers upon entering the labor market, and the reasons behind the Jewish workers' declared aim to "conquer labor," that is, to monopolize the labor market. In the second section, the dynamics of the conflict will be presented, its outcome will be the topic of the third section. In the final section I focus on the impact of the conflict on the Jewish workers themselves, and lay the framework for the examination, in the balance of this study, of the ways in which the Jewish workers used the lessons they learned from the labor market conflict for shaping Israeli nationalism and the Israeli–Palestinian conflict in general.

Cost of labor: resources and motivations

When prospective laborers of unevenly developed regions of the world economy meet in the labor market, the pay for which they are ready to undertake work depends, according to Bonacich, on their "different employment motives and levels of resources." Among these she numbers the length of employment sought, previous standard of living, and extent of organizational experience in the market situation. I will consider, in addition, another factor pertinent to our particular comparison: previous work experience. Contemporary sources dwelt at great lengths on the different characteristics of the Arab and Jewish labor forces. They seem to corroborate one another and, except for minor details, the general picture was accepted by most observers (though they reached different conclusions on its basis).[26]

(1) *Length of employment:* Many of the Palestinian Arab laborers of the Jewish plantations were smallholders seeking a source of income to supplement their returns from the traditional, and in part pre-capitalist, economy. This economy, poor as it was, nevertheless provided its cultivators with agricultural crops for self-consumption, as well as with services provided within the family, such as housing, health care, and food preparation, and in this way indirectly "subsidized" the capitalist Jewish sector of the economy. Jewish workers, on the other hand, had to sell their labor power in order to acquire their only source of income. The cushioning of the pre-capitalist economy differentiated between the types of employment sought by the two groups: temporary work and supplementary income for Palestinians, year-round employment with fixed income for Jewish laborers.

(2) *Standard of living:* "In general, the poorer the economy of the recruits, the less the inducement needed for them to enter the new labor market," according to Bonacich's observation.[27] In the performance of the same task by Palestinian and Eastern European Jewish workers, the latter required significantly higher levels of remunerative satisfaction than the former. Jewish workers hailing from an urban environment and a petty bourgeois background demanded higher wages for the satisfaction of their "cultured" needs.

(3) *Organizational experience:* The Arab laborer, wrote Joseph Vitkin, a teacher in a number of moshavot, "is almost always a submissive servant, who may be exploited without opposition and accepts lovingly the expressions of his master's power and dominion," while the Jewish laborer "guards his freedom and protects his honor, at times, with nervous exaggeration." Even if this description, the likes of which abounded in contemporary sources, greatly magnified the resignation of the Arab workers (who were at times also described in quite different terms), without doubt they could not have possessed the political experience of the Jewish workers of the Second *Aliya*, who came from Russia, the most revolutionary society of Europe at the time. In consequence, according to Moshe Smilansky:

Arab [workers] are distinguished . . . by one virtue that is much appreciated by the Jewish farmers, and it is their lack of development, as a result of which they do not know what to demand from the employers . . . the Arab consents to be working every day of the week, and even continuously for full months without resting for a single day, and he demands no raise for all that [effort] of his regular wage.[28]

Trade-union organization, the expression of the "development" Smilansky points out as missing in Arab society, is significant both in fighting for wage raises and for reducing unpaid labor. In both these respects the labor cost of the Arab worker was lower for the employer than that of the Eastern European Jew.

(4) *Work experience:* Bonacich's comparison of two work forces with differing labor costs assumes that both are equally competent at performing the same work. In our case, not only did the groups issue from unevenly developed regions but were also from different strata of their respective economies. Yaakov Levine, of the Second *Aliya*, wrote: "the Arab performed agricultural labor since his childhood. All his limbs have become skilled in this labor and the whole gamut of tasks is known to him . . . the farmer does not have to teach him the work." On the other hand "the Jewish laborer in Eretz Israel, obviously, was never a toiler of the land, and frequently not even an artisan in his home [land], but rather a semi-intellectual [*hatzi-intelligent*]. A certain length of time has to pass until he becomes accustomed to agricultural labor."[29] Jewish workers, in contrast to their Arab counterparts, frequently lacked the physical strength and stamina required for agricultural labor.[30] In addition, he pointed out, during the training period the value of their work was lower, though the cost of their labor remained the same.

The four comparisons add up to the same picture of unequal competition: an experienced labor force, cushioned by traditional sources of income, and less likely to counter the employers through organized action, side by side with an inexperienced labor force, whose needs were relatively more complex and whose ability to organize for their satisfaction stronger. The reproduction of the former group in the labor market was by far less costly. The first group according to Vitkin's unequivocal statement was "cheaper and less demanding," the other required a salary which was always higher even if it was "not always in accordance with a qualitative or quantitative advantage of its work." The two groups chanced to descend from different ethnic backgrounds, the former was Palestinian Arab, the latter Eastern

European Jewish. Their meeting in the same labor market in Ottoman Palestine, and readiness to seek out available jobs for different wages in the agricultural sector, inevitably pitted them against one another. Had an ethnic, religious, or cultural difference been the source of the conflict the groups standing against one another would have been arrayed differently: the Jewish employers would have closed ranks with the Jewish workers thus excluding the potential Arab competitors from the market. But the conflict was over wages and occurred first and foremost between Jewish workers and employers. Even so the Palestinian workers, standing between the Jewish workers and their ability to attain satisfactory wage levels, became the target of the Jewish workers' struggle and being an ethnically different group, the opposition of the Jewish workers to them was formulated first and foremost in national and ethnic terms even if ultimately it was not national differences that were the formative causes of their conflict.[31]

The dynamics of the struggle

The general parameters of the agricultural laborers' lives were set by the lack of settlement bodies able to provide them with land. Having turned to the option of becoming the permanent laboring mass of the moshava they still had to create conditions to secure that employment, that is, to prevent their displacement by the planters through the employment of lower-paid Palestinian Arab workers. The very combination of the exigencies of profit-making and the availability of cheaper workers jeopardized the employment of the costlier workers. The nature of these constraints limited the higher-paid Jewish workers to three available strategies, which corresponded to three chronological stages, in finding employment and protecting their workplace in the Jewish plantation of Ottoman Palestine.

Downward wage equalization

The first strategy was the *equalization* of their wages with the wage level of their unwitting competitors. It involved an attempt on part of the Jewish workers to "descend to the living standard of the Arab, [that is,] to live in tents and frugally."[32] Various contemporary sources describe such undertakings. Mania Shochat, Eliyahu Even Tov, and Sarah Malkhin tell, in separate stories, of cases in which Jewish workers refused "positive discrimination" on the part of the planters by insisting on working for the same wage as their Arab co-workers.[33] This attempt at *downward equalization* was part and parcel of a general opposition to philanthropic assistance of any sort, asserting that a worker was to live off his or her wages. The oracle of this view was the philosopher Achad Haam, a leader of Hovevei Zion, who argued that the placidity of the settlers of the First *Aliya* and their low morale was caused, to a large extent, by their dependence on philanthropy.

At the end of 1904, more or less simultaneously with the onset of the Second *Aliya*, Menachem Ussishkin, the up-and-coming young leader of Hovevei Zion, offered similar counsel. In his pamphlet "Our Program," he laid down the lessons learned by Eastern European Zionism from its scant achievements in its first generation, in the form of a comprehensive plan for the colonization of Palestine. Relevant to our topic is his proposal for procuring a Jewish working class. Ussishkin demanded that "thousands of youngsters come to the Jewish moshavot and offer themselves as laborers at the very same wage received by the Arabs, and live a life of incomparable hardship, very much as soldiers live in military barracks."[34] Some historians find anti-philanthropy so typical of the Second *Aliya* workers that they detect it throughout the period under study[35] and see it as a main constitutive element of their unique independence of spirit and creativity.

Equalization of pay to eliminate the split labor market is one of the alternative strategies of higher-paid workers listed by Bonacich, but for it to succeed requires raising the lower to the higher-priced workers' wage and not the other way around. Downward equalization, in fact, was abortive and its accompanying anti-philanthropic attitude was equally short lived. In Yaacov Levine's view its brief spell was an immediate response to Ussishkin's call (though more likely they were coincidental), and according to Jonathan Frankel, it was typical only of the period around 1905.[36] Downward equalization failed and the few irresolute attempts it spurred to organize in concert with Arab workers were easily foiled by the planters.[37] Ussishkin, obviously, was well aware of the counsel of despair side of his program, and therefore tried to mitigate its consequences by limiting the sojourn of the "soldiers" of Zionism to a few years. Since the workers of the Second *Aliya* came to Palestine with the intention of staying there, they found this solution unworkable and chose another strategy. The elimination of the split labor market and the danger of a new wave of displacement was not to come from the permanent lowering of the Jewish workers' living standard.

"Conquest of labor"

In 1905, in order to prevent their undercutting and potential displacement, a group of workers set up the Hapoel Hatzair Party with the goal of the "conquest of labor" (*kibush haavoda*). "Conquest of labor" is an overdetermined expression that carries at least three meanings. These denotations corresponded to different levels of historical and social reality, and carry separate implications.

The *first meaning* entailed the struggle aimed by the workers at themselves, also referred to as "self-conquest" (*kibush atzmi*). To overcome the traditional distance of Jews from agricultural work the immigrants had to acquire the work habits and muscular power of the agricultural laborer in Palestine. This goal, which entailed the transformation of the inverted pyramid of Jewish occupational structure, was essentially a physical, and to an extent a psychological, identity formation, and possibly conversion. The *second meaning* of the "conquest of labor" was class conflict: the struggle with the planters and landowners over working conditions and above all over the wage rate. This was a social struggle typical of market relations, to be found in Palestine as in other societies dominated by capitalist relations of production. The peculiarity of this struggle in the moshava was the downward pressure on the Jewish workers' wages caused by the availability of lower-paid Arab workers, and therefore the capitalist dimension of the conflict was overlaid by a third, ethnic or national, level. The *third meaning* of the slogan "conquest of labor" signified the "taking away of the work in the moshavot from the Arab workers and transferring it into the hands of the Jewish workers."[38] This aim, found in a number of multi-ethnic societies, and especially settler societies, was the struggle for the exclusion, or alternatively the caste binding of the Arab workers. This was the meaning Hapoel Hatzair chose to emphasize by decorating its periodical's masthead with the slogan: "A necessary condition for the realization of Zionism is the conquest of all branches of work in Eretz Israel by Jews."

Being interested in the evolution of the Israeli–Palestinian conflict, the third meaning will be the focus of my study. But no matter what the topic of one's inquiry is, these connotations have to be kept apart. In the conflation of the struggle against self and planter with the conflict with the Palestinian Arab worker,[39] the latter is made invisible in the early stages of Jewish settlement, and in consequence the pervasive impact of the conflict with Arabs, as workers, on the character of Israeli nationalism and through it the formative impact of this conflict on central aspects of Israeli society, goes unnoticed.

In Bonacich's terminology "conquest of labor" parallels the aspiration to split the labor market through the *exclusion* of the Arab workers. The formulation of the goal as a "conquest," though one to be accomplished through public persuasion and not violence, signaled a militant intent.

The Jewish agricultural laborers, even if they belonged to rival organizations, followed the lead of the founders of Hapoel Hatzair, and geared up for struggle and conquest. "Conquest of labor" unfolded in two major stages.

Subsidization   The aim of exclusion was to attain "European wages" for Jewish workers, and its realization called for and led through the *subsidization* of the Jewish workers for the performance of work done more cheaply by Palestinian Arab workers. The very first group of Jewish agricultural laborers in 1882, the legendary *Biluim*, were also the first to receive a subsidy at the Alliance Israélite Universelle's Mikve Israel agricultural school.[40] The same *modus operandi* was adopted by the Rothschild administration. In 1894, for example, the composition of the wages paid to the workers of Zichron Yaacov was abruptly changed: hitherto they had been paid ten piasters, henceforth they received six piasters "since that is the wage of the Arab workers," and the additional four piasters were paid out from a charity fund.[41] (See Appendix to this chapter: The Ottoman Monetary System.) Hovevei Zion also followed the same practice.[42]

With the transfer of the moshavot to the JCA, and the land to the planters, the latter discontinued the subsidies paid by the settlement organizations. But subsidization found its way back into the labor market soon after the start of the Second *Aliya*. In November 1909, Joseph Aharonowitz, editor of *Hapoel Hatzair* and one of the most perceptive observers of the period, surveyed changes in the standing of the Jewish workers in the market in the first five years of the "conquest of labor" strategy. He reported: "we began to encounter the following spectacle: on one side stands a group of workers laboring for the daily wage of seven piasters, and on the other side, performing the very same work, stands another group laboring for the price of ten piasters a day."[43] In another place Aharonowitz argued that, in general, the wages of Jewish workers were doubled between 1905 and 1908.[44]

Aharonowitz provides us here with one of the rare descriptions of the *actual* splitting of the market, that is, of different wages paid to the Arab and Jewish workers (the first and second groups respectively) for performing "the very same work" (*ota avoda atzma*). As we recall, Bonacich's definition of the split labor market is the following: "to be split, a labor market must contain at least two groups of workers whose price of labor differs for the same work, or would differ *if* they did the same work."[45] Examples of the "pure" case – two groups that are paid differentially for the same work – are few and far between, hence the *caveat*. We rarely recognize the existence of the conflict behind the formation of a two-tiered market, since we encounter only its end result. When lower-paid competitors are successfully excluded from the market the conflict seems to leave no traces. When they end up occupying the lesser jobs, the division is explained as the consequence of "initial" differences in skills. That the acquisition of these very skills is what the conflict was all about is forgotten. Split labor market theory allows us to reconstruct the conflictual phase, not only as a speculation on the order of Hobbes's and Rousseau's "natural condition," but, as we observe in Aharonowitz's account, as a possible and concrete social situation. A "pure" split market, however, is highly unstable, hence the Jewish workers could not be satisfied with it and continued demanding the total exclusion of Arab workers.

What spurred the planters, fearful as they were of what they perceived to be class struggle between the two groups, to be as generous toward the Jewish laborers, unexperienced, expensive, and militant, as these were? Probably the most important reason was the basic understanding on the planters' side of the shared demographic interest of both groups. The leaders of the First *Aliya*, which itself initially was intended as a pure settlement drive, repeatedly expressed their sympathy with and understanding of the demand for the creation of a Jewish working class.[46] But no sooner had they declared their understanding of the importance of the creation of a Jewish working class, than they would launch into an equally sincere and passionate explanation of their inability to carry out the aforementioned goal. Certainly, the planters did not ignore or treat lightheartedly the national goals but saw them always through the prism of their own interests, the survival and flourishing of the ethnic plantation economy. Consequently we find among them only the smallest number of planters, maybe half a dozen, but certainly no more than a dozen, who employed Jewish workers exclusively. The majority employed solely Arabs, a minority favored "mixed labor," that is, a part Jewish and part Arab labor force.[47]

Two other factors were probably just as important. If the planters tended to forget their shared demographic interest with the workers, then Jewish intellectual circles in Eastern Europe (as well as in Palestine), that were less likely to take a hard-headed view of economic interests, were there to remind them. The workers also effectively wielded their own press: two weeklies, *Hapoel Hatzair*, from 1908, and *Haachdut* from 1911. The planters, who had no organ of their own, often expressed anger and demanded, during mediation attempts, that the workers stop their "campaign" against them in the press.[48] The WZO, though it never underwrote the "conquest of labor" strategy, also supported the workers when the demographic dimension of the struggle was conspicuous. For example in 1908, at the behest of *Hapoel Hatzair*, its executive condemned and effectively halted the attempt of the Petach Tikva planters, under the pressure of lowered prices, to displace their Jewish workers with imported lower-priced workers from Egypt. Both the workers and the WZO were united in opposition to a step which would have increased the Arab population of Palestine, rather than its Jewish *Yishuv*.[49]

But these factors could have exerted their influence only as long as Jewish workers constituted only a fraction of the labor force. The wages paid to the Arab workers made up the major item on the planters' list of expenses. In consequence, planters on several occasions undertook monopsonistic practices to fix[50] or even, in the crisis year of 1900, reduce the wages of their Arab workers,[51] and to anticipate and break their strike attempts when Jewish demand was on the rise.[52] They went furthest in Hadera, where they established the "Order Keepers" organization which was to fix wage levels, anticipate demands for wage hikes, keep tabs of Arab workers, and regulate all other aspects of Arab employment.[53] The planters did not act in such unison, in moments of economic crisis, to lower or fix the wages of the small number of Jewish workers. They were satisfied with invoking the very same "market principle" to do justice between themselves and the Jewish workers, which they were entirely ready to violate when it came to wages to be paid to Arab workers. As long as they possessed the ultimate weapon of displacement, the workers' demand for an exclusive Jewish labor market was as rational as the refusal of the planters to accede to it was economically justified.

How large was the subsidy paid to unskilled Jewish workers? The Jewish workers, idealistically motivated though they were, could not but be acutely aware of the impact of wages on their lives and future and, making my task easy, reported their wages again and again in articles, essays, letters, and even in memoirs written decades later. From these data and the results of a census of 803 Jewish agricultural laborers, conducted in August 1914 by the Histadrut poalei yehuda hachaklaiyim (Federation of the Agricultural Workers of Judea), it is possible to piece together a relatively coherent picture of the wage structure, more consistent than we might expect from an era without elaborate statistical institutions (see Table). Our data cover the major moshavot of the coastal zone – Petach Tikva, Rishon Letzion, Rechovot, Ness Ziona, Zichron Yaacov, and Hadera, and the Ben Shemen and Hulda farms of the WZO – which made up the central labor market of the plantation economy, employing most of the Jewish workers at any one time.

Taking the First and Second *Aliyot* as a single time unit we may draw a number of conclusions. First, among unskilled workers Jews always

*Daily wages paid to Eastern European Jewish and Palestinian Arab
unskilled agricultural daylaborers in the Jewish labor market of Ottoman
Eretz Israel in the coastal zone, in Ottoman piasters, according to
period, and type of moshava*

	1882–1900	1905–1909	1910–1914
Palestinian Arab daylaborers in private and Rothschild-supported moshavot	5–6.5	5–8	5–8
Eastern European Jewish daylaborers:			
Private moshava	7–9	7–12.4	10–12.4
Rothschild-supported moshava	8–12.4	NA	NA
WZO-supported farm	NA	NA	9–12.4

Sources: About 100 independent observations, collected from contemporary
periodicals, letters, protocols, and memoirs.

received higher pay than their Palestinian counterparts. Secondly,
between 1905 and 1914, when the wages of both groups rose, the increase
of wages paid to Jews was greater. These findings indicate that the
strategy of "conquest of labor" had produced a rise in the wages of
unskilled Jewish workers, even if it did not remove the threat of
displacement.

Comparison of the wages of unskilled workers in the sub-periods
reveals equally significant results. First, the wage gap between inexperienced Jewish and Arab workers (see lower end of the pay scale), from
the First to the Second *Aliya*, grew more in the private moshava than the
gap between the wages of experienced Jewish and Arab workers (see
higher end of pay scale). The wage paid to experienced Jewish workers
rose in private moshavot from 9 to 12.4 piasters by 1909, but remained
stationary afterwards, and did not rise at all in comparison with the
Rothschild moshavot. The gap between the maximum wage paid to
experienced Jewish and Arab workers even declined. The experienced
unskilled workers faced, consequently, an *upper limit* on their wages,
which they could not remove, either by relocating to another type of
settlement or by gaining more years of experience.

The 1914 census confirms the existence of an upper limit on Jewish
agricultural wages for the 1910–14 period. The mean wage of 412 Eastern
European unskilled Jewish daylaborers was 12.86 piasters per day, and

their median wage was 10.6 piasters. Only 11.8 percent of this group earned more than 12 piasters. The census also demonstrates the great homogeneity of the Jewish wage labor force on the eve of the First World War, concentrated around the modal value of 10 piasters.

For laborers whose only source of income was their wages, the Achilles' heel of the plantation system was not the upper wage limit but the seasonal character of its agricultural work. With the completion of the harvest in the vineyard around late August, Jewish workers were unemployed until the beginning of the rainy season, sometimes in November, more frequently in December.[54] Daylaborers – who made up 68.9 percent of the 1914 census respondents – also lost pay for idle rainy days during the season, and received no pay during the long Jewish holidays.[55] In addition, about half of the workers in the census reported that they lost workdays due to sickness which, as a result of malaria and insufficient nutrition, was widespread.[56] Altogether 58.5 percent were without employment, for shorter or longer periods, in the year the census was taken.

Monopolization of skills   The upper limit on the mobility of the unskilled Jewish worker, I propose to argue, was the obvious reason for the decision of Hapoel Hatzair to change its strategy for splitting the labor market in late 1908. Instead of aiming at the total exclusion of the Arab workers, ethnic caste construction, that is, the concentration of Jews in skilled work, came to be viewed as a more promising strategy (though the new approach was not officially expected to supplant the earlier one).[57] Accordingly the slogan on the party's periodical was modified in October 1908 to read: "A necessary condition for the realization of Zionism is the proliferation of Hebrew workers in Eretz Israel and their entrenchment (*hitbatzrut*) in all branches of work."[58]

The process of "entrenchment" called for monopolization, as may be observed in the transition from the "pure" form of the split labor market to a more typical caste-based case, for example in regard to the semi-skilled, or possibly skilled, job of deep-weeding. As vineyards at the time were not irrigated, the growth of certain types of weeds with deep roots, such as couch grass, that multiplied rapidly, and sucked up a great deal of moisture, was a grave danger to the vines. Vineyards had to be weeded thoroughly, and it was imperative not to cut or damage vine roots during this work. During the First *Aliya* deep-weeding was performed by Jewish workers and was considered a skilled job, but with the displacement of the Jewish agricultural workers in 1900, this job, together with grafting and pruning the vines was transferred to Arab workers, who were paid lower, probably unskilled, wages.[59] In 1908/9, this task was reinstituted as a skilled job, paying a skilled wage. According to Aharonowitz:

> gradually, certain jobs, performed earlier by the local workers, began to be separated from labor in general (*avoda klalit*) and turned into specialized, Jewish jobs. Earlier, for example, the local people used to deep-weed the field for the same price for which they performed all jobs. Now, there are many farmers who will not give this work but to loyal hands . . . paying a decent wage for it.[60]

The preference of Jewish planters for Jewish workers transformed "pure" splitting based on subsidization into monopolization of certain skills, a social arrangement which gave it permanence.

In transferring skilled tasks to a socially distinct group of workers, Jewish planters in Palestine followed the traditional practices of the French vineyard and its colonial extensions. Grapevine cultivation, as may be observed in France and its North African colonies, involved a clear division between a number of specialized skills and unskilled work. Laura L. Frader's study of the small village of Coursan, in the Languedoc region of southern France between 1850 and 1913,[61] Jean Poncet's study of French colonial agriculture in Tunisia,[62] and H. Isnard's two-volume study of the vineyard in Algeria delineate the hierarchy of tasks, from the simple jobs of breaking the ground, hoeing, etc. to the more delicate ones of pruning and grafting the vines. "Delicate vineyard work: pruning, chemical treatments, and . . . [the] grafting" of the famous French grape varieties on American vine cuttings and root stocks, which were immune to Phylloxera, became essential after the devastation of large areas of vineyards in France between 1865 and 1885. The latter tasks were always better paid.[63]

While the division between unskilled and skilled tasks seems to have been due to the objective requirements of agriculture, we cannot fail to notice that it was overlaid by another, social, reality. In Coursan, specialized tasks were performed by the *colle*, a group of ten to fifteen experienced workers that moved from one vineyard to another, and enjoyed a comfortable income.[64] They were natives of the village, themselves frequently the owners of small vineyards, while the unskilled vineyard hands, called by the skilled workers *gavots* or *gavaches* (meaning careless or crude), "who did the rough cultivation and digging," were initially migrant workers from the mountainous regions.[65] In Tunisia and Algeria all skilled and some unskilled labor was done by various groups of Europeans, mostly experienced migrant workers of *déclassée* small vineyard owners turned workers from southern Italy, Sardinia, Spain or the Midi region of France. Arab workers, whether Sudanese, Kabyle, Moroccan, or native to the region, were invariably restricted to

less skilled tasks, such as breaking the soil, hoeing and deep plowing, or
to seasonal work, such as harvesting the grapes.[66]
We encounter the same agricultural exigencies and corresponding
social hierarchy in the Jewish-owned vineyards of Palestine. What were
the justifications offered for reserving skilled work for Jews? The
memorandum presented by the planters and workers to Rothschild in
1900 detailing the history of vinegrowing in the moshavot reported that
"certain complex and delicate jobs, such as pruning and grafting can be
performed solely by Jewish workers; the Arabs have not proved
themselves at all capable of performing these jobs well."[67] For example,
wrote Barzilai in 1894, the planters of Rishon Letzion "realized that
scholarly (*yodei sefer*) workers are more capable of certain tasks than
simple workers, and in the grafting season wished to give many of their
workers five francs a day instead of the nine piasters they generally
receive."[68] Zeev Smilansky repeated the same idea more eloquently in
describing "the more cultured jobs, such as grafting, pruning, etc. that
require more intelligence, attention, and a distinguishing eye from the
laborers," and "the analytical tasks (*avodot iyuniot*), which demand
special devotion and spiritual training (*imun ruach*)."[69] During the
Second *Aliya* the avowed higher skill level of Jews was supplemented by
a political justification: Aharonowitz, a major articulator of the Second
Aliya's experience, already described the advantage of the Jewish
workers in being "loyal hands (*yadayim neemanot*)."[70]
But while the *colle* members in the Languedoc, and the small vineyard
owners of the Midi, Spain and southern Italy could justly claim to be the
"artisans of the vineyard," or at least the most experienced of the labor
force of which they were a part, the Jewish workers could hardly do so.
Only thirteen persons, of the 686 who reported their pre-immigration
profession in the 1914 census, had been farmers before their immigration, while 30.5 percent were merchants or shopkeepers, 27 percent
studied in a variety of schools, and 19.6 percent were artisans.[71] The
overwhelming majority of Jewish workers thus had no prior exposure to
agricultural work of any sort, and whether their educational background
was in any way relevant to the acquisition of certain agricultural skills
seems far from certain. Furthermore, contemporary observers were
unable to agree whether the productivity of the Jewish workers was
higher or equal to that of their Arab counterparts. Barzilai, on the one
hand, argued in 1894, that in skilled work the advantage of the Jewish
workers was obviously greater and therefore their higher wage was
justified.[72] Levine, on the other hand, wrote close to twenty years later,
that "concerning [productivity in] the jobs . . . that are not so simple . . .
it is difficult to decide since there is no sufficient accumulation of

evidence."[73] Moreover, grape cultivation, even if not intended for wine production, but for table consumption, raisins, and juice, and therefore less delicately attended to, was second only to olives in unirrigated Palestinian Arab agriculture. But Palestinian Arabs, though experienced in the art of raising grapes, including some of its skilled tasks such as pruning and the use of special tools, such as the jagged knife (*shurshara*) and before the First World War the pruning-hook, were excluded from such work in the moshava.[74]

In Languedoc, Tunisia, Algeria, and Palestine, the labor market came to be split and the lower castes of French "hillbillies" and Tunisian, Kabyle, Moroccan, Algerian, and Palestinian agricultural proletarians, were effectively debarred from the performance of skilled tasks. This division was made possible through the monopolization of specialized skills by the higher-priced workers. The basis of their monopoly was not always an exacting technical knowledge, or extended education, but *access* to the acquisition of the skills and experience through using them.[75]

Towards the end of 1909 the Eretz Israeli plantation economy evinced a number of discontinuities in the labor market which indicated that it was well on its way towards the recovery of its character, lost in 1900, as a split labor market. Aharonowitz distinguished three separate tiers in the structure of the market, according to the ability of the Jewish workers to establish themselves in each one.

in some of the moshavot of Judea three categories of labor developed:
(1)   One category is almost completely in Jewish hands, for example, the pruning of vines, grafting the trees in the orchards and vineyards, and other specialized jobs.
(2)   The second category began to be transferred gradually to Jews, for example guarding the vineyards, deep-weeding the soil, tying the trees to supporting poles, etc.
(3)   And the third category, which includes the simplest jobs, remained almost exclusively in the hands of the locals, since its price is still low and Jews cannot compete in it.[76]

This categorization, measuring the relative success of the campaign for the "conquest of labor," or the conquest of the labor market in our nomenclature, indicates that in the five years between 1904 and 1909 Jewish workers made obvious headway. This progress did not however, signal the *exclusion* of the Arab workers as Aharonowitz surmised, but their binding into a lower *caste*. He was also wrong, therefore, in regard to the third category: the rise in the price of simple work could only have taken place if the Arab workers had been excluded from it.

An examination of the wage structure of skilled Jewish workers is now in order. Wages paid for grafting and pruning, like the wages of experienced unskilled workers, did not change much during the Ottoman period, and ranged from three to six French francs per day.[77] We are immediately struck by the wide wage gulf that separated skilled and unskilled Jewish workers. A skilled person could earn up to three times more per day than an experienced unskilled worker.

Skilled workers, however, labored under an even greater disadvantage than unskilled workers due to the seasonal nature of their work. The grafting of quality vines to sturdy American root stocks is done only once in the lifetime of a vineyard, while the pruning of the vines is gradually reduced, after the final shape of the vine is determined in the first three years of its growth, from three times to once a year. According to a chart of the cycle of agricultural tasks in the plantations, prepared by Barzilai, winter pruning usually took a month at the end of each calendar year. Deep-weeding was also carried out only in the first year, for a month, in January or February after the harvest.[78] Similarly, in orange groves, irrigation, the only mechanized act of the plantation economy, which was done by a steam-operated wheel, was required for the five hot summer months, and even then only intermittently. According to Barzilai's chart, only thirty full working days were required to irrigate a mature orange grove, a job which paid forty to eighty francs.[79]

In fact, year-round employment was better paid overall even at the price of giving up the performance of skilled jobs for a number of weeks each year. Komarov reported that Jewish laborers of the Menucha Venachala plantation company in Rechovot preferred to be employed nine months a year at the daily wage of seven to nine piasters "even at the time of pruning and grafting – a job that pays four to five francs – as it is better for the workers to have regular work for the year at a fixed wage than to work intermittently."[80] Being a skilled worker was only a temporary employment, and therefore offered no real solution to the majority of the Jewish workers.

The effects of the "conquest of labor" strategy

We may trace the results of the failure of Jewish workers to conquer the labor market of the Jewish plantations in Palestine on three levels. On the most immediate level, I will inquire why the living standard the Jewish agricultural workers were able to attain in the decade between 1905 and 1914 did not make possible the reproduction of this class. Subsequently, I will examine the consequences of that low living standard on the employment pattern and on the demographic expansion of the Jewish agricultural proletariat. Thirdly, in the concluding section to this chapter, I will inquire as to the legacy of the failure to attain a European standard of living and expand in numbers for the formation of Israeli nationalism and the Israeli–Palestinian conflict.

Standard of living

The major expenses of the Jewish agricultural workers were housing and food. On the basis of the 1914 census we can estimate the relative shares of these expenses in the workers' budgets. The average monthly expense, as reported by 381 respondents, was 6 francs for housing, and by close to 500 respondents, 37.3 francs for food. The share of expenditure on food is staggering. Most of this information was provided by unmarried workers.

What was a typical meal partaken by the Eastern European Jewish worker? Levine provided us with the following colorful description:

> should you look into the basket of the Jewish worker on his way to work – in Petach Tikva, for example – you will not find a royal repast, but a slice of bread, a bit of *chalva* [a honey and sesame-based oriental sweet], a piece of sugar, occasionally an egg, a tomato, and at most – a piece of cheese . . . [I]n the evening, returning from work, he frequents a workers' hotel and devours a dish of soup or occasionally even a piece of meat. All this food costs no less than 25–30 francs a month . . . [T]o eat at a private home – as the cooking of the workers' hotel causes stomach diseases and therefore it is not possible to partake of it in the long run – costs 40 francs per month.

While not a royal repast, it seems that the Jewish workers were used to a varied and well-balanced diet. Performing unfamiliar physical labor demanded that they replenish their strength and made it difficult, if not impossible, to save on food. In reading this description of the Jewish worker's diet, we again recognize that we are inquiring into the life and habits, needs and wants of Europeans. Ben-Gurion, comparing Russian and Palestinian diets, complained that in Palestine "there is no milk in the summer, it is almost impossible to find butter, bread is not the choicest, meat is a bit more expensive." Palestine also has its good foodstuffs that were even cheaper than in Russia, but one had to learn to cook them and get used to eat them, but "the plight (*asson*) of the workers is that they don't know how to cook nor do they have the leisure to cook."[81] Levine gave us another list, probably less reliable than the first, but nevertheless indicative of the difference between the standard of living of the Palestinian Arab agricultural proletarian and the Eastern European immigrant. According to Levine "the needs of the Arab, as is well known, are far and few between: a few pita-breads, an onion, a handful of dates, a bunch of grapes – make up his own, his wife's and offspring's daily meal."[82]

In 1901 Hirschberg reported that the average Jewish family consumed goods and services at nine piasters a day, and Katznelson repeated the same figure for 1904/5.[83] This seems an absurdly low sum, unless we remember that according to Nawratzki's account between 1904/7 and 1907/10 a family's food expenses rose from thirty to forty-five francs,[84] and even this seems an underestimation. This significant inflation in food prices was caused, according to Treitsch, by the wave of immigration and the growth of monetary circulation.[85] The estimate of *Hapoel Hatzair*, of May/June 1909, already put the necessary monthly expenses of a single worker at forty francs, that is, slightly less than the expenses of an entire family in 1901–5.[86] Arthur Ruppin concluded at the end of 1911 that "the minimal wage required for the subsistence of an *ashkenazi* worker is about 40–50 francs a month."[87] Finally, in 1910, the WZO's Palestine Office published the following estimate: forty francs are required for the overall expenses of a single worker, and seventy-five francs (fifteen francs for housing and an additional sixty francs for food) for a family.[88]

I am ready now to examine whether the wage paid to the Jewish experienced unskilled agricultural laborers was enough to maintain their standard of living. On the eve of the First World War the average monthly income, counting twenty-five working days, stood at fifty francs. The contemporary estimate of Kaplansky of the average Jewish daylaborer's yearly wage at 400–500 francs is similar.[89] This is just about what Ruppin considered to be the minimal sum required for the expenses of a single person. But as we have seen, the income of 400–500 francs was conditional on not losing working days. In addition, alongside housing and food expenses we have to count all those expenses which the Jewish workers invoked to explain their more developed "cultural" needs: such as laundry, mail, books and newspapers, dues to workers' organizations, etc. The novice worker was in even more dire straights. Under such conditions it is not surprising that the opportunities of the Jewish agricultural laborer seemed bleak.

If the single worker at least could make ends meet, this was not possible for a family. The plight of the workers was summarized in the complaint that it was impossible to establish or maintain a family or save money for settlement from their wages.[90] These two aims, however, were not unconnected. Without owning a piece of land, it was possible only for the smallest number of skilled workers, mostly supervisors of large plantations, to meet the financial needs of a family. Lacking the possibility of settling on land, agricultural workers were doomed. The life of the Eastern European Jewish agricultural worker was a dead end, and its objective difficulties and the lack of foreseeable mobility combined to make this path unattractive and after a few years of futile attempts many found it unacceptable.

Lack of commitment and failure

It should be clear by now that the results of the Jewish agricultural workers' struggle for the "conquest of labor" were mixed. On the one hand, the labor market came to be split at each skill level: all skilled labor in the plantations was monopolized by Jewish workers; when tasks traditionally performed by Arab workers were transferred into Jewish hands, they were transformed into skilled and better paying jobs; and when unskilled tasks were performed by Jews their pay was higher than that of the Arab workers doing the same work. To the question, suggested by Bonacich's theory, whether Jewish workers succeeded in splitting the labor market we will perforce answer positively. At the same time, a broader question presents itself: did the Jewish agricultural workers of Palestine succeed in acquiring "civilized wages," that is, wages which would enable them to attain a European standard of living, and provide for a family? The answer to the second question, as we have seen, must be negative. The monopolization of skilled and semi-skilled tasks did not provide the workers with the economic security and standard of living they required, since wage levels were only one cause of their distress. Lack of social services and the seasonal nature of their work counter-balanced the advantage of higher wages. Unskilled workers were in an even less advantageous position. Jewish workers split the market but failed to conquer it.

Conquest of the market would have succeeded only had their most ambitious goal, the complete exclusion of Arab workers from the Jewish-owned plantation, been realized. Such exclusion would have homogenized the labor force, and made possible the raising of the wage level of unskilled workers. In the absence of such a radical solution, a permanent Jewish working class, capable of reproducing itself, was not created, and Jewish unskilled workers suffered from "considerable unemployment" right down to the Second World War.[91]

As a result of a split but unconquered market various anomalies developed in the labor market. Many an historian has been puzzled by this seeming paradox, pointing to the fanatical attachment of the workers to their maximal goal when, in fact, there was a persistent shortage of laborers for the jobs available. The explanation is always the same: the workers' ingrained militant ideology. The workers' attitude, however, is better understood by its correlation with the imbroglio dominating the market. Let us follow up this line of thought.

Planters complained that newly trained workers often left work after only a few weeks or months,[92] and settlement bodies and even workers' organizations failed to supply sufficient numbers of Jewish workers for available work.[93] The first issue of *Hapoel Hatzair* from 1908 already reported from Petach Tikva that while new orange groves were being planted, only a few of the new jobs created there had been taken up. Most workers were described as either planning to emigrate or "are not striving to become acquainted with the place and the working conditions."[94]

One facet of this problem became known during the Second *Aliya* as the "wandering" of the workers. Jewish agricultural workers exhibited a marked tendency to move from one locality to another, from one employer to another. This phenomenon of roving was especially impressive considering that frequently they walked long distances, since mechanized transportation was expensive. Sometimes the workers left Palestine for shorter or longer periods, visiting their families abroad, or taking care of pending business with the authorities in their country of origin, etc. This cavalier attitude to work naturally did not endear them to the planters.

But lack of persistence and frequent vagabondage, it seems to me, were due to the hardships experienced in most workplaces and the hope of finding a better job elsewhere. As very few moshavot supplied the workers with social services, and they very rarely owned a house or land, there was little to attach them to any one place. The seasonal nature of the work also provided them with opportunity for travelling and satisfying their urge to know their chosen land. Their peregrination, therefore, seems to have been motivated above all by their lack of roots due to their imperfect domination of the market.

The planters and representatives of settlement bodies felt, in view of the workers' limited commitment to their place of employment, that Jewish agricultural laborers were only transient workers en route to other occupations, destinations, or more secure forms of existence. Most significantly, the workers themselves arrived at a similar conclusion. Zeev Smilansky, in his historical account of the Jewish workers of Palestine, already detected such inclination among the 1890 wave of workers. It was a common occurrence that after the first "honeymoon" only a small minority of the workers stayed on, while in the majority "the sparks of love for the Holy Land are gradually extinguished from week to week." In consequence, "some have become farmers and remain in the moshavot; of the others the majority have left the country and the minority have moved to the cities and taken up other ways of making a living."[95]

Two of the leaders of the Hapoel Hatzair Party expressed the same conclusion in regard to the Second *Aliya.* Joseph Vitkin said the following in a lecture delivered at the party convention in 1908:

to our grief, a number of years have passed, and reality has not justified our hopes . . . Many of the workers have begun to abandon the work: both those who possessed the physical vigor required for the work, and those who excelled in their work on account of their dedication to the ideal. Stealing away ashamed, they have begun to give way. Most of the former have left work and country simultaneously, and the latter began to search for intellectual work, and have become teachers, writers, secretaries, etc. . . . and even those who are continuing their work for the time being aspire, secretly or openly, to be extricated from it either by becoming supervisors and foremen oppressing other workers, or by settling. The workers have ceased to think about remaining mere agricultural workers for ever.[96]

When Vitkin expounded his interpretation in 1908, he was opposed by Aharonowitz, the major oracle of the Hapoel Hatzair. Two years later Aharonowitz reached the same conclusion. As the early immigrants in the Second *Aliya*, that "came to the hoe,"

could not summon their strength to create something tangible due to their small numbers and the lack of succor and help by the [World] Zionist Organization, they gradually degenerated, gradually despaired, and all, or many of them, are wandering now, like shadows, from moshava to moshava, from Judea to the Galilee and back, and the whole subject is but a bone stuck in their throat – they can neither swallow nor retch it: they cannot leave the country as they have no place to go, and they cannot stay as they find no more interest in it, their whole being only arousing pity.[97]

By the end of 1909 even the most dedicated and optimistic of the idealist workers (the pronoun "they" means here "we"), could not but admit that the conquest of the labor market in the Jewish moshavot of Ottoman Palestine, was an abysmal failure. Vitkin's carefully chosen and nicely stylized words, and Aharonowitz's dramatic style, relating the experience of the agricultural laborers of the Second *Aliya*, the most outstanding in their idealism, was but an echo of Zeev Smilansky's brief summary of the experience of their predecessors, the First *Aliya* workers. The philanthropic economy of the First and the capitalist economy of the Second *Aliya* ultimately yielded similar results. "In the last two years," wrote Aharonowitz in the same article, "an idiom began to be circulated in the workers' camp and 'despair' is its name." There was no immediate cause of the crisis of 1908/9, it seems to have been the expression of an accumulation of disappointments and the final realization that the path to the creation of a Jewish agricultural proletariat would not lead through private, capitalist agriculture.

Of all the waves of immigration to Palestine, the Second *Aliya* had the largest percentage of emigration. Of the 35,000–40,000 immigrants who arrived in Palestine between 1904 and 1914, in certain years the number of emigrants was a quarter to a third of the immigrants of the same year.[98] Yosef Gorny calculated, on the basis of the survey of the WZO's Palestine Office during the years of the First World War, that there remained only 5,965 Second *Aliya* immigrants in the moshavot and towns, not including Jerusalem.[99]

The 1914 census makes it possible to break down the agricultural labor force of the southern coastal zone according to its length of stay in Palestine. Of the 733 respondents who were born abroad we find that 53.9 percent arrived during the twelve months before the census was taken, 18.7 percent arrived twelve to twenty-four months before the census, and an additional 7.1 percent twenty-four to thirty-six months earlier. Of the respondents 98 percent were Second *Aliya* immigrants, but 80 percent of them came to Palestine in the three years preceding the census, and over half in the preceding year. We may infer that the overwhelming majority of the immigrants from the earlier years returned to their country of origin or left for more promising destinations. This conclusion is borne out by the fact that only 13 percent of the 1914 labor force arrived between 1904 and 1909.[100] Finally Ben-Gurion estimated that 90 percent of the immigrants of the Second *Aliya* (most likely the reference is only to the agricultural workers) left Palestine. From Ben-Gurion's estimate of 90 percent emigration and the Palestine Office's census which found that during the First World War there were 1,297 agricultural workers in Palestine, we may conclude that the *total population* of the agricultural workers of the Second *Aliya* examined in this chapter was about 10,000 individuals.[101] In comparison with the low rate of those remaining in Palestine from the Second *Aliya*, Ben-Gurion reported that the overwhelming majority of the immigrants of the Third *Aliya*, arriving between 1918 and 1923, stayed.[102] By then, of course, the WZO, encouraged by the Balfour Declaration and the British Mandate, was fully committed to land purchase and to settlement activity. Moreover an organizational structure intended to circumvent the market, based on the experience of the Second *Aliya* between 1908/9 and 1914, and shaped during its years of trial, was already in place (this is the topic of Chapters Seven and Eight).

Another comparison is equally valuable. The years prior to the First World War were also the years of the development of French colonial agriculture in Tunisia and Algeria, based mostly on vinegrowing. Tunisia saw the introduction of viticulture in 1882, that is, in the same year as in Palestine. An official census, taken in 1912, found 637 French and 1,128 Italian and other European workers, and 10,289 Tunisian workers in the vineyard labor force. Of the workers 17 percent were

European and in a regional breakdown their proportion varied from 5 to 27 percent.[103] This low proportion derived from the same reasons as in Palestine. An observer concluded that: "we cannot hope that a French colonist will be patriotic and rich enough to employ his fellow citizens in preference to foreign workers who cost half the price and even less."[104] For the capitalist colonists, in Poncet's view, the small peasant and rural worker of French origin were "absolutely undesirable," since "they were poor but nevertheless accustomed to a high standard of living." French colonial vinegrowing in Tunisia, similar in its backwater character to Palestine, also preferred a large local work force with "as few demands as possible"[105] combined with a small European work force for the skilled and supervisory tasks.

Algerian colonial agriculture, though larger in its size and import than its counterparts in either Tunisia or Palestine, had the same fate, and in some ways its history is even more instructive than the Tunisian case. French colonists in Algeria relied on a European labor force, of changing composition, for a longer period than either the vinegrowers of Tunisia or Eretz Israel. In Algeria, according to Isnard, initially "the major share of the labor force that the colonist needed for the creation and exploitation of their plantations was furnished first and foremost by Europeans."[106] Skilled and semi-skilled work was carried out by seasonal workers from the European mainland, who arrived in November of every year and returned to their homelands around May. But the composition of the labor force and the tasks undertaken by it changed throughout the period under discussion and also varied regionally. A work force, composed in the 1870s, predominantly of Europeans, had been transformed in the span of fifty years until "in 1914, wine production used an abundant labor force, of which natives constituted the principal element."[107] Cyclical marketing crises affecting Algerian wines was the dynamic behind these developments. "This substitution," according to Isnard, "beginning in 1893, accelerated during the first years of the twentieth century with the aggravation in the crisis of marketing."[108]

In 1894 an agronomist by the name of Paul Perrenoud, published an article entitled "The Situation of the Agricultural Laborer in Algeria" which is reminiscent of the descriptions and complaints of Komarov, Aharonowitz, and their associates. With the marketing crisis, wrote Perrenoud, "the fate of the metropolitan worker in Algeria has become very problem ridden, very miserable and very precarious." Nine-tenths of the French, Sardinian, Italian, and Spanish workers, who had been employed in the vineyards just a few years earlier, either returned to Europe or renounced agriculture altogether and moved into the Algerian towns in search of construction or administrative work. Those who stayed agricultural workers "vegetate miserably." The advice given by Perrenoud to propertyless European workers planning to immigrate to Algeria, was not to do so unless they had the promise of a job.[109]

Though in the Algerian vineyard the employment of European workers was attempted on a larger scale than either in Tunisia or Eretz Israel, and in comparison with them for a longer period, it was proven that the vineyard and vinegrowing were not capable of providing "civilized" wages to a European labor force. Its monocultural character, vulnerability to plant epidemics and susceptibility to alternating market forces demanded the lowering of wages paid to its workers. Hence, in the majority of cases, vineyard planters came to rely exclusively on local unskilled workers, leaving the skilled tasks alone in the hands of a small contingent of European workers.

The Algerian case is instructive on another count, since Algeria was planned to become a settlement colony. The French government of the Third Republic "set the population of Algeria with French European elements as a constant goal for its efforts."[110] According to Isnard:

one would have thought, in the beginning of the great work of plantations, that French viniculture would favor the constitution of a new social class in Algeria, that of agricultural workers, who will strengthen the European settlement drive. This [thought] had to be abandoned fairly quickly: the role that devolved on the European was, more and more [only] that of technician or supervisor.[111]

Not only was the European laboring mass needed by the vineyard in the second decade of our century insignificant, but also the population of planters grew extremely slowly. In 1880 viniculture was viewed by many in France as possessing "a most considerable colonizing influence." Surveying the various vinegrowing regions of Algeria, Isnard concluded that either they were populated sparsely by Europeans, or that their European population was confined to small areas. In 1914 the number of European vineyard planters was inferior to their number in 1885, though their cultivated area rose two and a half times. Only the administrative district of Algiers, where the creation of viniculture coincided with massive development works undertaken by the government, showed a significant gain in its planter population, but even here the latter expanded at a much slower rate than the urban population. On the whole, French immigrants preferred the Algerian town to rural life.[112]

Vinegrowing did not prove its colonizing potential in Algeria, Tunisia, or Palestine. The First *Aliya*, resembling other contemporary settlement drives, had to settle for a weaker colonization drive in the form of an ethnic plantation colony. How limited the choices faced by Jewish planters and workers in Palestine were, becomes more obvious in light of the limited success of the Third Republic in pursuing this aim despite its massive commitment of military and financial resources. It seems that the choice of the appropriate agricultural plant is significant in determining the extent of a colony's population by European immigrants. Orange growing, for example, was more "population producing" than the vineyard. Even so, monoculture generally engendered only a weak colonizing impetus. A more substantial key to the growing Jewish agricultural population of Palestine became the mixed farm (*meshek meurav*). Though the wrong crop could check the growth of the colonizing population, ultimately, increased European population was not only the corollary of a successful agricultural decision but the result of a more comprehensive method of state and nation formation.

"Conquest of labor" and the foundations of Israeli nationalism

During the Ottoman period, on the basis of contradictory material interests and settlement models two fundamental views of future Israeli state formation crystallized in Palestine: one the planters', the other the workers' view. The respective nationalisms of the two *Aliyot* were not determined by their territorial aims, which were uniformly maximalist. Given the unbridgeable gap between the desire to possess all of Eretz Israel, itself a vague geographical concept at best, and the restrictive means at the disposal of the First and Second *Aliyot*, neither of which enjoyed state or military power and consequently was dependent on piecemeal accumulation of land purchased on the market, the dimensions of their ideal territorial aspirations remained immaterial for their immediate national concerns. In fact, as long as the question of political sovereignty over land did not come up, conflicts over national strategies could hardly have been derived from interests related to land. Hence, their respective positions *vis-à-vis* the labor market formed their vistas and national strategies. Antithetical in their methods, they shared, nevertheless, the basic dimension: both strategies had to respond to the problems posed by a third group, the Palestinian Arab workers, and through them by Palestinian society at large. They were two versions of Israeli nationalism, since both classes presented their particular interest as identical with the interests of the "nation."

The planters advocated a *moderate Israeli nationalism*. Their attitude toward the Palestinian Arab population was measured and circumspect in consequence of a number of factors. Above all, the planters needed the Palestinians as a low-paid labor force, which was the basis of their prosperity. The "major motive force" in the construction of the Jewish community, according to one of the leaders of the planter class, was the "economic base." The refusal to employ Jewish workers, in this leader's mind, was less likely to cause the bankruptcy of the Zionist enterprise than their employment.[113] The profitability of the plantation system was the foundation of Jewish life in Palestine and had to be preserved. The planters were quick to forget that they too had been established on philanthropic foundations; furthermore, while opposing the Jewish workers' attempt to circumvent the market mechanism, they were always willing to engage in monopsonistic practices *vis-à-vis* the Arab laborers. Theirs was not the struggle of a pure capitalist principle, which no group in Eretz Israel was ever strong enough to adopt to the full, but of a vested interest.

The planters supported their demand for consideration of the Arab population and its potential strength by a number of additional arguments, of which I would like to mention two. In the first important article on the labor market conflict published during the time of the Second *Aliya* in the independent press in Eretz Israel, Meir Dizengoff, speaking the planters' mind, asked:

How can Jews, who demand emancipation in Russia, rob rights and act selfishly towards other workers upon coming to Eretz Israel? If it is possible for many a people to hide fairness and justice behind cannon smoke, how and behind what shall we hide fairness and justice? We should absolutely not deceive ourselves with terrible visions. We shall never possess cannons, even if the *goyim* shall bear arms against one another for ever. Therefore, we cannot but settle in our land fairly and justly, to live and let live.[114]

Consideration of Jewish interests abroad, and the lack of a militarist posture were two factors that contributed to the articulation of a moderate Israeli nationalism.

The planters' established circumstances permitted them to assume their role as a landowning class, that is to undertake, according to Issawi's distinction, "economic colonization,"[115] or in the classificatory scheme used in this study, to create an ethnic plantation colony. (This is the nineteenth-century variant of a plantation system based on local rather than on imported labour, but without intermarriage with the local population.) Jewish planters did not carry this aim from Europe, but adopted it only under the tutelary Rothschild administration. Initially, even then, they believed themselves to be in the vanguard of massive Jewish immigration to Eretz Israel, which the North African model of plantations and vineyards that they came to employ was understood at the time to facilitate.

In practical terms, the planters' "demographic interest", i.e. their preferred settler:land ratio, continued to be based on the *maximalist* territorial aspirations shared by all Jewish immigrants in the Ottoman era, while their expectation of the size of Jewish immigration was *moderated*. In consequence, the planters were not opposed to the departure of a large segment of the Jewish workers and, in general, failed to develop a strong sense of the demographic side of their colonization. Stamper put this in the following way: "whoever wishes to work will find work and remain in the country, and anyone who does not want [or] cannot work, will shout a bit until he leaves."[116] Aharon Eisenberg added: "If the community decides that somebody incapable of performing the work should not become part of it, then he should heed the decision."[117] In the "natural way," according to Dizengoff, the *Yishuv*'s development was to be "work for generations."[118] And Aharon Aaronshon presented the planters' viewpoint in the most general terms: Wakefield's political economic principles of colonization are not applicable to Palestine; here the course of colonization could not be shortened and propertyless settlers would become successful colonists not through public assistance but through self-selection.[119]

Basing Jewish revival in Palestine on an ethnic plantation economy meant, so the planters believed, not the abandonment but the postponement of the realization of the national goal of the alteration of the demographic balance between Jews and Arabs to the former's benefit. While the settlement method of the First *Aliya* was overtaken by the Second *Aliya*'s method, and therefore it is impossible to evaluate the realism of the planters' perspective with direct evidence, comparative data from the European ethnic plantation type settlements established around the same time in the African continent, whether in its northern, eastern or southern regions, has not borne out these expectations.

As far as their future relationship with the Palestinian Arab population was concerned, the Jewish planters of the First *Aliya* came to view favorably the co-habitation of the two groups under the existing hierarchical arrangement. Their major arena of conflict with the Palestinian population was to be restricted to the purchase and possession of land, hence the national confrontation between the two groups would be moderated. Indeed some observers, Jewish and British, viewed the period of the relations during the ethnic plantation phase as one of limited conflict, that was subsequently exacerbated by the demand for "Hebrew Labor."[120] While the impact of the Second *Aliya* on Jewish–Palestinian relations will be explored later in this chapter, it seems, on the basis of comparison with full-scale European ethnic plantations or ethnic plantation segments of larger colonial drives in Africa, that even the hostility generated among the African or Arab populations by employment on expropriated land was powerful enough to undermine moderately dense European populations that relied on native labor forces to do their work, during decolonization. And if the local opposition was limited, plantation colonies were habitually taken over from the outside by competing, usually pure settlement, types of colonization.

What was the character of the worker's nationalism, and what were its roots? We may distinguish between the answers of three schools to these questions. The *mainstream position* adopted by Gorny, Kolatt, and other historians close to the labor movement, is that "as a matter of a priori Zionist and socialist principle, the worker-pioneers were opposed from the outset to the hiring of Arab labor by Jewish employers."[121] Socialist principles, however, hardly explain Jewish opposition to Arab employment since Jewish workers were not opposed to the capitalist system of wage labor itself, provided the employees were Jewish. And the definition of the workers' national interest varied in direct relationship with the conditions of the labor market conflict: "conquest of labor" was consistent with the aim of pure settlement but the downward wage equalization strategy of 1904/5 also contained the seeds of class solidarity. The opposition to joint organization was fundamentally practical, though clothed, as time went on, in ever stronger ideological armor.

But even on its own terms the ideological explanation is misleading. One of the fundamental principles of Zionism as a "national movement," according to Yosef Gorny, was "the idea of the productivization of the Jewish masses, from which grew the ideology of Hebrew labor as a condition for the . . . independent existence of the Jewish society in Eretz Israel,"[122] "even *before* encountering the realities of Eretz Israel."[123] The roots of the aspiration of Jewish productivization are to be found in the movement of Jewish Enlightenment during the second half of the nineteenth century. The concept of productivization (which, by the way, itself was a mirror image of the anti-Semitic portrayal of Jews as parasitic on society) was born of the conditions of Jewish diaspora life and its continuity with the struggle for "Hebrew labor" in Palestine was far more complicated than Gorny lets us understand. The drive for productivization, that is entry of Jews into the primary branches of the economy, above all agriculture and industry, was a struggle against the exclusion and displacement of Jews from various industrial occupations in modernizing Eastern Europe as soon as they had a foothold in them. It carried no reference to the displacement of non-Jewish workers, nor was it aimed, by and large, to evolve into an ethnic conflict. "Hebrew labor," or "conquest of labor" on the other hand, was born of Palestinian circumstances, and advocated a struggle against Palestinian Arab workers. This fundamental difference demonstrates the confusion created by referring "Hebrew labor" back to the productivization movement and anachronistically describing it as evolving in a direct line from Eastern European origins.

A *"revisionist" interpretation* accepts the economic foundations of "conquest of labor," but argues that "the labor market conflict became closely intertwined with the national struggle between Arabs and Jews" as the labor movement elite recognized the intercommunal political benefits of championing "Hebrew Labor" even autonomously of labor market exigencies. This version has few distinct devotees, one of whom is Kimmerling,[124] and is usually the fallback position of others, such as Anita Shapira,[125] who, in principle, profess adherence to the first view. But this position is already a weaker version of the next perspective, and need not contradict it.

The *third view*, presented in these pages, is that the Jewish labor movement was launched into national conflict as part and parcel of the pursuit of its interest in economic survival. Neither Palestinian hostility, which varied according to the character of Jewish colonization, nor Zionist labor's national militancy towards the Palestinians were exogenous factors superimposed upon the market nexus.

The workers' position – summed up in the "conquest of labor" strategy – which they opposed to the planters' moderate nationalism, is best described as *militant nationalism*. According to Walter Preuss, an early historian of the Jewish labor movement, "the Arab question . . . became the focal point on which depended the whole existence of the Jewish working community. If they accepted matters as they were, they would not be able to stay in the country."[126] Unable to ignore or underrate the importance of the Palestinian population with which they competed daily in the labor market, the Jewish agricultural workers' intolerable position in the labor market rendered them more militant.

The Jewish agricultural workers' position towards the Arab competitor matured under the force of Palestinian circumstances. Strategies similar to theirs evolved in other settlement societies where workers encountered similar circumstances, and Jewish workers in Palestine shared with workers in such places the struggle "to conquer" labor, or in our terms to split the labor market by either excluding or caste binding lower-paid workers. In aspiring to split the labor market European workers were, especially in the early stages of the conflict, not motivated by any inherent racism, but by a desire to protect their European standard of living and to prevent their potential displacement. For example, in the view of a representative of the South African Mine Workers' Union we find such statements as this:

The real point . . . is that whites have been ousted by coloured labour . . . not because a man is white or coloured, but owing to the fact that the latter is cheaper. It is now a question of cheap labour versus what is called "dear labour," and we consider we will have to ask . . . to use the word "colour" in the absence of a minimum wage, but when that is introduced we believe that most of the difficulties in regard to the coloured question will automatically drop out.[127]

Ben-Zvi argued the same:

we have embarked on our course not against the Arab worker but to protect ourselves and our weak positions . . . in general, we have to be careful, that the question of labor will not assume a chauvinistic character, which is not only reactionary but is ridiculous at a place and time in which we are but a weak minority and we cannot move hand or foot without coming up against the strength of our more numerous and powerful neighbors.[128]

But while workers of European descent usually succeeded in other settlement societies in lessening threats of displacement and in maintaining a European standard of living, the Jewish workers of Palestine did not. Their history begins diverging from that of other European working classes in settlement societies upon their failure to accomplish this goal.

To appreciate the necessary new starting point of Jewish workers after their failure "to conquer labor" and the legacy with which that experience left them, a brief comparative inquiry into the conditions of such struggles and the reasons for their success outside Palestine is in order. Australia may serve as an example of a pure settlement society in which the white working class had its way in preventing the owners from undercutting or displacing them by the employment of lower-paid native and imported laborers, through the total exclusion of lower-paid imported workers.

The demand for restrictions on the entry of various types of lower-paid workers – coolies, convicts, and poor immigrants, mostly Chinese and Kanaka – into the Australian labor market, was one of the central factors in the mobilization of Australian workers of European descent. The Australian working class therefore emerged militant from its inception,[129] and subsequent to large-scale intermittent unemployment of unskilled workers from 1857 onwards in all three eastern provinces, opposition to immigration became "a more or less settled policy written into union programs."[130] This process culminated in the formation of the Labor Party, espousing the identity of class and national interests, and notably abstaining from "any idea of the internationalism of the working class."[131] Its attitude has been described as one of constructive pragmatism, as "[Australian socialism] has been called a 'socialism without doctrines' . . . It seeks tools rather than proclaims theories, and does not try to harmonize practical attainments with a preconceived ideal of society."[132] In 1905, the Federal Labor Party stated as its objectives "the cultivation of an Australian sentiment based on the maintenance of racial purity and the development in Australia of an enlightened and self-reliant community," and the extension of state and community owner-ship of economic resources.[133]

Though, under the pressure of the Labor Party and its forerunners, Chinese workers were effectively excluded from Australia in 1888, the importation of Pacific islanders into the sugar plantations of Queensland continued and even increased.[134] The first policy legislation of the independent Australian government in 1900 was the closing of every legal gap permitting the entry of unwelcome immigrants, bringing Australian historians such as Myra Willard to argue the decisive impact of the demand for "White Australia" on the movement for Australian independence from Britain.[135] R. Norris has shown the exaggerated character of this conclusion, but also admits the popularity of this issue for uniting the majority of Australians at a critical moment in their history.[136] The Immigration Restriction bill was the victory of the relatively minor Labor Party, but its adoption was due to Australia being a "pure settlement" colony, in which the midde class was also in favor of ethnic homogeneity and willing to make sacrifices for its realization.

The success of this policy was due to the linkage of the Immigration Restriction Act of 1901 with the protection of the profits of the sugar industry, jeopardized in the competitive international market by higher wages paid to white Australians, by an elaborate tariff system.[137] Sugar produced with the labor of white workers was subsidized in the local market, while the price of foreign sugar was artificially raised. Further acts extended the Sugar Bounty Act to other agricultural produce and to the steel industry.

The white workers' struggles to split the labor market were successful in Australia, where they yielded an exclusionary labor market, and further ensured Australia's "pure settlement" character. (In South Africa a similar struggle was waged in the gold mines and later in the political arena to extend the dominant racial state apparatus that was built up in the initial "mixed settlement" phase of the colony. The white workers' efforts, initially aimed to lessen a threat of partial displacement in 1921–22, yielded a political alliance with the Afrikaner Nationalist Party and culminated in the explicit legal enshrinement of the colour bar and the effective foundation of so-called apartheid[138] which, in actual fact, is a white supremacist regime.) The market was split only through the direct political influence of the white workers on the state apparatus, since the latter alone could *reallocate* the costs of what in effect amounted to a subsidization of the white workers across the society. Consequently, the white working class came to rely on and developed strong bonds with its state which, by reaffirming the workers' privileged place in the nation, decisively contributed to the formation of the nation itself. Furthermore, subsidization enhanced the harmonization of social relations within the dominant ethnic group by disguising the responsibility of the capitalist class for indirectly formenting ethnic conflict between groups of workers by trying to undercut the higher-paid workers, and reaffirmed the white group's shared demographic interest, while it attenuated the Labor Party's socialism and enhanced its national consciousness.

The implications of the absence of a state or state type organizations which would spread the costs of subsidizing the Jewish working class was well understood by both workers and planters in the *Yishuv*. Yaacov Rabinovitch, of Hapoel Hatzair Party, concluded that "since we do not have a government, which would use its resources and institutions on behalf of its workers" as do the Australians, everybody and all the public institutions had to use all means possible for "the protection of national labor and the national worker."[139] Some planters called for "the nationalization of labor" as a "solution to the problem of the workers," through the imposition of a "labor tax" on everybody in order to make the payment of a "minimum wage" possible. Jewish workers and planters both sought an Australian type solution; Rabinovitch directly invoked it, while a similar one was described in uncanny detail by the agronomist M. Zagorodski, who was sympathetic to the planters' views:

Work is done with the assistance of the entire people. The people are interested in seeing that their sons work the land, and are also interested that their employer sons will not go bankrupt. The people therefore enter as a mediator between worker and employer. The people collect the wage the employer is capable of paying the worker according to the situation of the labor market, and pay the worker the wage he needs for his living according to his needs.[140]

But the planters were only indirectly interested in "nationalization," since their position was assured under the prevalent conditions of capitalist development as well, while among the workers a new two-pronged approach emerged. As we shall see in Chapter Seven, a call for the abandonment of the capitalist path of Zionist colonization in favor of nationalist colonization, as the only solution to their plight, began to gather momentum. In the area of the national conflict, the labor movement chose a confrontationist approach.

The strong connection between labor-market position, views on the Palestinian–Israeli conflict, and type and intensity of nationalism, are

85

forthrightly presented in two important articles: in Zerubavel's succinct 1911 article "The Two Methods," and Ben-Zvi's January 1913 essay: "National Protection and Proletarian Perspective." In presenting their arguments I have to run ahead in our story to the period after 1908/9, when Hashomer, the Jewish guard organization (the topic of Chapter Six) was already established and had suffered its first casualties, and the WZO had already set up its training farms (see Chapter Seven), but these subsequent developments were still being interpreted in terms of "conquest of labor."

Zerubavel's article was written in response to news of Arab attacks in Lower Galilee and proposed to examine "the causes of the conflicts, the clashes, and the tense relations" in this region, in comparison with the relative calm of Judea, the southern coastal zone. The prosperous and large Judean moshavot, though they might have aroused the cultural jealousy of the Arab intelligentsia, had not provoked the enmity of the *fellaheen* who were less concerned with the identity of the landowner than with the availability of employment opportunities and, therefore, had no reason to oppose Jewish land purchases. But, concluded Zerubavel, "while, on the one hand, this method does not incite our neighbors in Judea, on the other hand – and this is the crucial point – it is also not the right method for our work of national revival." It furthered only the cause of individuals and of property, but not of the masses and of labor. A different method was implemented in Lower Galilee. In the Galilean moshavot the Jewish workers had assumed guard duty, and in the WZO's training farms also all tasks of labor, hence it was "unavoidable that here clashes will result between the Jews and their neighbors." Zerubavel pointed out that "the first method ensures peace and quiet but it does not provide a comprehensive solution to our complex existential question." He concluded that "we will not accomplish our aim, unless we espouse the direct, consistent, redeeming, second method."[141]

Ben-Zvi, in evaluating the relationship between national and working-class solidarity, presented a similar conclusion in his essay, very likely the most important statement and summary of the period of the Second *Aliya*, of which I can only present a small portion here.[142] Jewish workers were struggling for a place of employment, hence their struggle was nationalist, and only when they could be securely employed would they commence the struggle for working conditions, which would bind them in an international struggle with workers of other nationalities.

As long as nature and society have allied themselves against us, as long as we are a weak minority . . . as long as employers from among our people contracted, explicitly or implicitly, with the *fellaheen* and the natives to reject and restrict the Jewish worker, as long as we are employment seekers even within the Jewish economy, we cannot enact the international solidarity upon which we set our heart.

At present (because in the future Ben-Zvi expected such solidarity to become possible) "we have no alternative but to pave our way with the dead and the martyrs (*halalim vekorbanot*), with our fallen brethren, who are fighting for the happiness of the Jewish proletariat and its future, and the dead of our foes. And we cannot turn away from our radical goal (*matratenu hakitzonit*) until we accomplish it." The radical aim, in Ben-Zvi's words was "the struggle for survival and the struggle for the future of the Jewish proletariat."

The labor movement's attitude towards the national conflict with the Arab population not only in the labor market but also over Jewish possession of land was, surprising though it may sound in retrospect, welcoming. Again moving slightly ahead of our story, let it be related here that the major leaders of the two workers' parties expressed this view clearly and unabashedly. Ben-Gurion declared in 1910, during the Sixth Congress of Poalei Zion: "[Arab] national hatred is the reason that will force, and bit by bit is already forcing Jewish farmers to take on Jewish workers, whom they hate so much." This "important reason" convinced Ben-Gurion "that the Jewish worker will penetrate into the Jewish moshava."[143] Joseph Aharonowitz, editor of *Hapoel Hatzair*, already in 1908 listed "the fear of the farmer of the foreign worker" as the most important reason for the potential success of the struggle for the conquest of labor. In his words: "the more the Arab goes on developing, such incidents [of attacking Jews] will repeat themselves, or will stop being mere incidents and will assume the permanent form of national hatred and jealousy. And this thing, which frightens us so much, is the safest guarantee of the Jewish worker."[144] National conflict was not seen by the workers as a danger, as it was viewed by the property owners, but as the lever to the workers' own interest. The leaders of the Jewish workers were ready to live with national hatred, and also to protect themselves and all other Jews against it in the moshava. As long as no Australian type solution was found, the workers remained militant, though Ben-Zvi's words should remind us that their weakness was a powerful incentive against the transformation of that militant "defensive aggression" into racial prejudice.

It is important to note with Gorny that "not with closed eyes or unwittingly did the [Poalei Zion Party, but the observation fits Hapoel Hatzair Party, if to lesser extent] go towards this contest, but on the contrary, from a keen understanding that the road chosen by her is the only one leading to national liberation," and that the expectation of "a test of strength between the Jewish and Arab populations" emerged from a "sober and realistic perspective."[145]

What, if any, was the direct addition of the Second *Aliya*'s distinct demand for "conquest of labor" to the Jewish–Palestinian conflict in the land market? There were a number of protests against "Hebrew Labor," for example by leaders of Jaffa's Arab community, its Rusian consul, by Arab national leaders "all of whom complained" to Kalvarisky "of the Jewish boycott of Arab labor," etc.[146] The modification of the slogan on the masthead of *Hapoel Hatzair* from "conquest of all tasks of labor" to the "proliferation" of Jewish workers, perhaps was also changed, in part, due to the wish to reduce conflict with Arabs.[147] In 1914, Dr. Jacobson, the Zionist representative in Istanbul, asked Ben-Zvi to use his influence to terminate a major strike aimed at displacing Arab workers, in view of the pending opening of the Parliament.[148] "The Russian Jewish laborers, together with the principle of exclusive Jewish labor" – Ro'i sums up the conventional wisdom – "were considered by a number of Zionists and members of the *Yishuv* to constitute a major factor in arousing the hostility of the Palestinian Arabs."[149] But Ro'i's major source was Levontin, the director of APAC, the staunchest partisan of private enterprise and consequently one of the strongest opponents of "conquest of labor."

While it seems from this evidence that exclusionary intents in the labor market had a significant impact on the worsening of the relations between Jews and Arabs, this view requires closer inspection. The displacement of Arab workers, after all, was by and large unsuccessful in the moshava, and the size of the settlements and later of the WZO's farms was still very limited in this period. Furthermore, violence was rarely used by the numerically much smaller Jewish labor force, who, unlike land purchasers, could not count on the intervention of foreign consuls on their behalf or on the defense of their legal rights by the Ottoman authorities. Finally, the interests of the Palestinian notables, either the modern or religious leaders, were not affected by this campaign and, except for some verbal support, they did not lend a hand to the peasants affected by it.[150] There is also little evidence that the Palestinian Arab agricultural workers were involved in political or other opposition to Jewish workers. They, like the Jewish plantation owners, were favored by their position in the market, hence they did not need to organize or be particularly innovative. The exception to this pattern, as we shall see in Chapter Eight, were the discharged guards of the moshavot and farms, but their violent opposition was limited in scope, and they had no more outside support than the peasants. The indirect character of the impact which the "conquest of labor" had on the Arabs is the likely cause of their muted response to this strategy, which generated less opposition than the more direct clashes over possession of land. Only during the economic crisis of the mid 1930s did serious open confrontations take place in Jewish-owned orange groves. The impact of "conquest of labor," therefore, was more indirect: it affected Israeli–Palestinian relations in its potential long-term structural contribution to state formation, and only minimally affected the relations between Jews and Arabs before the First World War.

While the planters identified the "economic base" as the key interest of the *Yishuv*, the workers viewed the creation of a large Jewish presence, that is, the "demographic base," as the national interest. The Jewish workers, like the planters and all other Jews before the British Mandate era, were territorial *maximalists* seeking to settle Jews everywhere in Eretz Israel,[151] and this aim, combined with the *exclusionary* intent of "conquest of labor" which envisioned Jewish employment everywhere on Jewish-owned land, ensured their *maximalist* view of Jewish "demographic interest." But the largely unsuccessful struggle to find appropriate employment and the subsequent transition from exclusion to caste binding cast doubt on the potential of massive immigration.[152] In fact, throughout the "conquest of labor" phase the distance between the theory and method of demographic expansion grew steadily and kept haunting the workers. Even so, the workers, in contrast to the planters, could not forgo pure settlement colonization, as this aim, termed by Issai "demographic colonization," remained their only chance of survival and settlement in Palestine. They opposed, therefore, the imposition of a Jewish upper class on the masses of the local population, and in their public pronouncements continued to demand that both Jewish worker and farmer be part and parcel of the settlement movement, seeing in a highly dense Jewish colonization effort the key to the employment of Jews without property. Berl Katznelson presented the fundamental attitude of the workers: "If it is impossible to increase the working multitude then it is impossible to create a large *Yishuv*, and therefore impossible to realize the goal of the Zionist national home."[153] The agricultural workers did not have a fall-back position as did the planters and continued to aim fairly consistently for the highest settler:land density. Around 1908/9 when it became obvious that the "conquest of labor" strategy would not yield its hoped-for results, they began casting around for an alternative method for realizing their *maximalist* "demographic interest."

Jewish agricultural workers in Palestine developed a *militant nationalist* approach to Palestinians during their struggle to displace them and conquer their jobs in the Jewish plantations. This strategy was militant but not racist – or effective. They carried over from that failure the conviction of militant nationalism, lack of internationalism, emphasis on demographic colonization, and a strategy of exclusion. They gradually transferred their hopes from capitalist processes that operate through the market to political solutions that circumvent them, and sought to be the footsoldiers of a national public institution, such as the WZO or one of its organs, that would serve as a quasi-state, willing to subsidize or provide "national protection" to them.

Appendix: The Ottoman monetary system

The official exchange rates of Ottoman currency are to be found in the *Encyclopedia Britannica, 11th Edition*, Volume 18: 706, but they mean little in real economic terms. Since Ottoman silver coins were debased, the hard currency in the *yishuv* was the French franc. The French franc's commercial rate of exchange was 4.5 piasters (called the *grush* in Eretz Israel); its Jaffa commercial exchange value from at least 1891 was 6 piasters. Two additional coins were used by the Ottomans: the *medjidie* was worth 26 piasters in Jaffa, and the *bishlik* 3.15 piasters. Around 1907 the French franc gained slightly and was worth 6.2 piasters. For a contemporary comparison: in 1891, according to Luncz, one paper dollar was worth in Jaffa 30.2 piasters, that is, 5 French francs, while according to Achiassaf, from 1895 /6, one gold dollar was worth 4.9 French francs. One piaster, then, fetched 3.3 cents during our period. We might find these commercial exchange rates in at least three sources: the Luncz (Hebrew), and Trietsch (German) tour guides, and the *Achiassaf* (Hebrew) literary year books.

To yield the present-day US dollar value the effect of inflation has to be deducted. The rise in the US consumer price index, which is available to us only for urban wage earners, was from 27 points in 1891 to 246.8 points in 1980, that is 9.14 times. To calculate the 1980 dollar equivalent of the 1891 dollar value we have to multiply the piaster by 30 and the French franc by 1.86. The information concerning the US consumer index is from tables E-135-166 and No. 779 in *The Statistical History of the U.S.: From Colonial Times to the Present*, NY, Basic Books, 1980, pp. 210–211, 467.

Chapter Four

The failed experiment: "natural workers" from Yemen, 1909–1914

There are people who just "live" and are forced to undertake servile and exhausting labor without which others would not have the chance to be exonerated from economic activity in order to philosophize. To back "quality" against quantity means simply this: to maintain intact specific conditions of social life in which some people are pure quantity and others quality.

Antonio Gramsci, *Prison Notebooks*, 1927/37

We are faced in this case with Jews of two stations: in first standing – Jews in general with no adjective attached, and in second standing – Yemenite Jews.

David Ben-Gurion, "A Single Constitution," *Haachdut*, 1912

The organized workers' movement in Eretz Israel is not the movement of the "proletariat." The [General] Federation of Labor is a settlement aristocracy. If a proletariat, which views itself as lacking public influence, is to be found here, then it is among Middle Eastern and North African Jews . . .

Haim Arlosoroff, "Class Struggle in the Context of Eretz Israel," 1926

The practical failure of the "conquest of labor" strategy generated in the New *Yishuv* two alternative, though not unconnected, paths of innovation. The first was the transformation of the plantation's labor force through the introduction of Jews from Yemen. The second was the bypassing of the labor market altogether through various organizational innovations. The former failed, though not without leaving a powerful imprint on the structure of Israeli Jewish society, i.e. on Israeli *nation formation*, as we shall see in this chapter, while the latter, as we shall see in Chapters Five, Six, and Seven, evolved the method of Israeli *state formation*.

The attempt to insert Yemenite Jews into the labor market was, according to David Ben-Gurion, a "radical" attempt to solve the problem of the labor force's composition in the Jewish settlement of

Palestine.[1] Arthur Ruppin, the head of the Palestine Office of the WZO, anticipated that "this experiment (*Versuch*) might contain the most far-reaching (*den weitest gehenden*) consequence for the overall colonization of Palestine."[2] This then was recognized at the time as a major undertaking though, due to its failure, and the alternative course taken by history, it has subsequently been relegated to the margins of that history and rendered an obscure episode. By studying this radical experiment not apart from, but as part of, the state- and nation-building efforts of the First and Second *Aliyot* I hope to restore its proper historical dimensions and significance.

I will seek to answer, in this chapter, the *question*: why did the Eastern European immigrants of the Second *Aliya* make history, while their Yemenite co-religionists remained on the margins of history? This is particularly puzzling since both groups arrived early in the process of nation formation and state building, and since both failed in the same endeavor: displacing the Arab laborers and providing the bulk of the plantations' labor force.

The Yavnieli mission

Jews from Yemen had arrived in Palestine continuously, parallel to, and independently of, the Eastern European stream, during the whole period of the First and Second *Aliyot*. Some of the reasons for their migration, which also strengthened the Jewish community of British Aden, were the opening of the Suez Canal in 1869, and the reconquest of Yemen by the Ottomans in 1872, which integrated Yemen into world commerce and exposed the Jewish artisans to the ruinous competition of European industrial products. The choice of Eretz Israel was also dictated by religious reasons, rooted in spiritual bonds with the Holy Land.[3] Most of these immigrants, like a large portion of the Eastern European immigrants, settled in the towns, and became part of their traditionalist Jewish communities. The connection between the Old and New *Yishuv* was, by and large, limited, and people from Jerusalem, Tiberias, and Safed, made up but a modest fraction of the seasonal labor force in the moshavot.[4]

An exceptional event, in this context, was the decision of about seventy-five families of mostly *déclassé* and unemployed artisans and poor merchants from the community of Yemenite Jews in Jaffa to set up, in 1903, the Peulat Sachir (Wage-Earners' Endeavor) organization. Its aim was, as expressed in its appeal to Rechovot's Board, "to reduce the number of Arab and Muslim workers, and put ourselves – we that are children of one father – in their place in cultivating the land."[5] This request happened to coincide with an anticipated pay hike demand by Arab workers on the eve of the intensive agricultural season, and the General Assembly of Rechovot's Jewish farmers hired some of the Yemenite Jewish applicants in order to forestall these demands. Especially positive in his response was Aharon Eisenberg, the general manager of the Menucha Venachala (Rest and Estate) company, which colonized Rechovot and cultivated the plantations of many of its absentee landowners. In addition to Rechovot, some members of Peulat Sachir were also employed in Petach Tikva and Rishon Letzion. Shortly, however, most Yemenite Jewish workers were found to be unfit for agricultural work and were fired.[6] This attempt, short-lived and pathetic as it was, foreshadowed the fate of subsequent Yemenite Jewish immigrants.

The issue of the place of Middle Eastern and Yemenite Jews in the plantations was occasionally raised in the next few years. The question was not whether they should be employed, since small numbers of *mizrachim* were in the habit of coming to the moshava as seasonal laborers, but rather how to expand their share in the Jewish labor force, as their demographic value for the *Yishuv* was obvious. For example, one of the early congresses of Hapoel Hatzair in September 1907, resolved to call on *mizrachim* as well as on the "non-productive youth" of the traditional Old *Yishuv* to seek employment in the moshava. In fact, nothing concrete was done in this respect.[7]

Jewish organizations came to be seriously interested in the possibility of creating a Yemenite Jewish laboring force only in January and February of 1909, when a spontaneous immigration movement brought to Rechovot nine families, some of whose members were successfully employed in agriculture. This group was extended with the arrival of additional families to Rechovot, Rishon Letzion, and Petach Tikva, altogether about 300 people, throughout 1909 and 1910. Another new element during the period of the Second *Aliya* was the active presence of Eastern European Jewish agricultural workers' organizations, and it was the Workers' Employment Bureau which placed the new arrivals, promising the planters that they would compete successfully with the Arab laborer.[8] Demand exceeded supply at first, as the Board of Rechovot decided that "it is sound and proper to employ them and their wage will be paid to them the same as to Arabs – 6.2 piasters per day."[9]

There is general agreement that the successful employment of the spontaneous immigrants in Rechovot gave rise to the Eretz Israeli initiative for the encouragement, better said catalysis, of further immigration by means of sending a special emissary, Shmuel Yavnieli. Retrospectively, the mission came to be interpreted as an act of moral concern by the *ashkenazi* community, intended to express and promote the solidarity of the Jewish people within Zionism. Not surprisingly, two major versions emerged among the *dramatis personae* as to the authorship of the Yavnieli mission, thus leaving a trail of considerable historical mystification in its wake in regard to *ashkenazi–mizrachi* relations.

The version favored by the labor movement points to an article published by Yavnieli in *Hapoel Hatzair* in June 1910, as raising the possibility of actively approaching the Yemenite Jewish community with the idea of immigrating to Palestine. These articles are supposed to have aroused the interest of either Rabbi Benjamin, the *nom de plume* of Yeshaya Redler-Feldman, an official of the WZO's Palestine Office, or of Joseph Aharonowitz, the editor of *Hapoel Hatzair*. One of these arranged, with the blessing of Arthur Ruppin, the Office's director, a meeting, from which the idea of sending Yavnieli himself to Yemen, preferably with a Yemenite Jewish companion, emerged.[10] Subsequently Yavnieli left for Yemen on December 16, 1910. Some elements of this account, however, are unconvincing. First, Aharonowitz was one of the earliest and staunchest opponents of the introduction of Yemenite Jews, as agricultural workers, into the Eretz Israeli settlements. Secondly, Yavnieli did not suggest in his articles the displacement of the Arab labor force in Palestine through the employment of Yemenite Jews in agriculture. His purpose was to counter the assimilationist influence of the Paris-based Alliance Israélite Universelle's schools among the Jews of Northern Africa, Persia, and Turkey, by calling for a network of Zionist *bookstores*, that would spread Hebrew literature in these countries![11]

Ruppin's own version is that the initiative was born in the Palestine office when Redler-Feldman thought up the idea of sending a messenger to encourage further immigration. Yavnieli's articles appeared just at the time the Office was already looking for the right person to be dispatched.[12] This interpretation also suffers from a number of inconsistencies. First, as late as November/December 1910, the Palestine Office still intended to send on this errand the *hacham* Avraham Nadaph of Jerusalem.[13] Even more surprising is the claim in the memoirs of Zecharya Glusska, a member of the first group of spontaneous immigrants, that the Palestine Office offered the mission to a number of Yemenite Jews, for example to his uncle David Nadaph, then in Rechovot, and only when all those turned down the offer was Yavnieli chosen.[14] Secondly, and even more damaging to Ruppin's version, Redler-Feldman claimed in his memoirs to have been introduced by Ruppin into the plan, which, until then, was kept secret from him. At the same time, Redler-Feldman repeated the other version which made Yavnieli into the initiator of his mission,[15] a line of development we already saw as unlikely. Thirdly, the Office invariably answered queries of Eastern European Jews with no means that they would be able to make a living only as agricultural laborers, but would not be able to support a family from their income, and advised them to arrive with no less than 100–200 francs.[16] Hence, the Palestine Office, on its own, never encouraged potential *ashkenazi* immigrants to "make *aliya*," and such initiative in regard to Yemenite Jews would have constituted a serious deviation from the Office's common practice.

Neither the labor movement's nor Ruppin's version, self-serving as they are, carry conviction, but up to now all historians of the labor movement and early Zionist immigration have subscribed to one or the other, or some combination, and this is true even of historians of the Yemenite Jewish community, including Nitza Druyan's admirable study of the Yemenite Jewish immigrants in Eretz Israel between 1882 and 1914.[17] I would like to offer a novel interpretation, which would explain the involvement of *both* Hapoel Hatzair Party and the WZO's Palestine Office, but locate the initiative for the mission elsewhere.

The clue to an alternative line of reasoning is provided by Yavnieli's own version as to who was involved with his mission. His account finds confirmation in new historical sources and documents which will be presented. Yavnieli argued that his mission was the result of

combined efforts of the representatives of Zionism in Eretz Israel with the workers' movement, especially members of Hapoel Hatzair [Party] and Joseph Aharonowitz at their head, with certain circles of the farmers and public figures in the moshavot, such as Eliyahu Sapir and Aharon Eisenberg, and with the representative of the rabbinical circles, the Chief Rabbi of Jaffa and the moshavot, Rabbi Abraham Itzhak Kook.[18]

Of the three new names, Sapir was the deputy director of the Anglo-Palestine Co. and therefore another representative of the WZO, while Rabbi Kook was involved in the mission only in a minor way by supplying Yavnieli with the cover of his journey as a religious emissary. It is the name of Aharon Eisenberg that offers the necessary fresh clue. An effort to trace the so-far ignored part of the third group – the farmers, or what is a more appropriate term, the planters – in the Yavnieli mission is required on theoretical grounds as well. In all comparable cases, in the Chesapeake colonies of northern America, in California, in eastern Australia, and in southern Africa, the cotton planters, fruit growers, sugar-cane growers, and mine-owners, respectively, were behind the demand for the "importation" of low-cost laborers. They all sought a new type of laborer since native populations could not supply an adequate labor force and "poor white" workers were too expensive and militant.

In order to present this alternative view of the Yavnieli mission's genealogy and its implications, I will examine in subsequent sections of this chapter the interests of the three groups and /or organizations listed by Yavnieli: the planters and the organizations of free enterprise in the second section, the "poor whites," that is the Eastern-European agricultural workers, in the third section, and the WZO, its Palestine Office and its head Arthur Ruppin in the fourth section. Though *ashkenazi–mizrachi* relations are obviously intra-Jewish concerns, their particular shape during the Second *Aliya* and possibly later as well, I will argue, emerged in the broader context of the Jewish–Palestinian conflict, and therefore they form one dimension of the evolution of Israeli nationalism. In the final section, therefore, I will endeavor to present, through the use of the relatively scanty memoirs, contemporary letters and documents, and conversations quoted by observers, some of the demands and plaints of the Yemenite Jewish immigrants themselves. I will focus my query, above all, on the connection between the formation of the identity of the Yemenite Jewish immigrants in Eretz Israel and their place in its labor market in the context of the formation of an Israeli nation.

Agudat Netaim and the planters' interests

My thesis is that Aharon Eisenberg, the general director of Agudat Netaim (The Planters' Society) – the largest capitalist enterprise during the Second *Aliya*, was the first one to suggest the catalysis of Jewish immigration from Yemen through propaganda initiated from Eretz Israel. Though the contours of his role may be established with a satisfactory measure of clarity, it has to be acknowledged that some uncertainty, as we shall see, still shrouds the specific details surrounding the Yavnieli mission. The reasons for Eisenberg's interest in the employment of Yemenite Jews, it will be argued, had to do with the hybrid character of the Planters' Society, expressed both in its origins and aims.

Eisenberg was the director of Menucha Venachala, the founding company of Rechovot. Hadera and Rechovot, the two moshavot created by the second wave (1890/1) of the First *Aliya*, were based on a new and synthetic colonization method. They were established by colonizing companies from Eastern Europe that were organized by two groups of people: some who planned to make the move when their vineyards became profitable and others intending to move to Palestine and cultivate their land right away. From among the latter group the directors and supervisors of the future colony were selected. These two moshavot remained organizationally independent of the Rothschild administration – though the latter consented to buy their grapes at the same inflated prices paid to other First *Aliya* moshavot – and, in consequence, their aim as pure settlement colonies was less corrupted by the wholesale reorganization of the first wave of colonies (1882/4) along the North African plantation model. Due to the favorable proportion between its absentee and present colonizers, which made Rechovot the only relatively successful colony set up by private enterprise before the First World War, and the economic advantages accruing to its large size and more efficient cultivation methods,[19] Menucha Venachala was able to employ a substantial percentage of Jewish workers.[20] In December 1903, Eisenberg was the one to employ on the lands of Menucha Venachala thirty-two Jewish immigrants from Homel – who, in fact, were the first group of arrivals of the Second *Aliya*. He was able to state in 1904 that "a large part of our workers are Jewish, and most Jewish workers in Eretz Israel worked or even now are working in our company,"[21] in contradistinction to private planters who refused to employ new Jewish workers and ignored their plight and hunger. Menucha Venachala, however, never espoused a policy of employing an exclusive Jewish labor force.

In August 1905, recognizing the lull in settlement after the end of the JCA's 1900/3 settlement drive in the Lower Galilee, Eisenberg established a new colonizing company, to be called Agudat Netaim. The decline of the North African model that informed Rothschild's effort invited further innovation and importation of other models, and the first attempt emerged from Rechovot, which had been furthest removed from the Rothschild system. Agudat Netaim embodied some of Menucha Venachala's principles but a number of new and more ambitious factors were also evident in its design. Eisenberg explained the need for such an organization in the following way:

colonizing work is difficult all over the world, especially in [deserted] places where new colonization has to be instituted from [scratch]. Such work is generally directed by large colonization-societies which obtain material and moral support from the governments by which they are authorized. Even then the full development of a new [colony] requires much labor, money and energy. If that is the rule in all the countries it is much more true in Palestine, where the laws of the country and especially the land laws have not yet attained the stage of full development.[22]

According to Joseph Katz's study of private Jewish colonization, Eisenberg, with some others,[23] was also influenced by a Californian rural settlement method which received wide exposure in Eretz Israel.[24] In Maywood Colony between Corning and Red Bluff in Northern California, the company of Foster & Woodson offered a five year installment payment plan for the purchase of an already producing fruit orchard, to which its owners could move and cultivate it themselves if they so inclined.[25] Probably just a scheme of clever developers, whose pamphlets travelled far, Maywood Colony left few traces in California, but this plan appeared to have been ideally suited to European Jews wishing to return to the soil.

The original plan of Agudat Netaim was to purchase plots of land, turn them into plantations and orchards, and manage them until they produced crops, and then resell them at a profit. To raise funds the company planned to sell a hundred shares at the high value of 10,000 francs each, payable in sums of 500 francs twice a year for ten years. In addition, the company planned to use its expert knowledge to manage plantations of absentee landowners, both shareholders and others, in return for a 10 percent commission. At first Eisenberg and the Board raised the money in Eretz Israel, then they turned to Jews abroad.[26]

A special plan was offered for preparing a Jewish labor force suitable for the company. Agudat Netaim promised "to make it a rule to employ new immigrants ignorant of agriculture, who would find it very difficult to obtain work elsewhere." In this way a Jewish class of experienced and skilled agricultural workers, at the disposal of the landowners upon their immigration, would be trained. Permanently employed Jewish workers, found to be industrious, would be offered by Agudat Netaim small plots at cost price to be paid by installments in ten years. On these plots, located near the plantations, the workers would construct their homes and would use the revenues from their auxiliary farms to augment their income. The creation of "workers' colonies" was viewed by Eisenberg as "a general method for the solution of the problem of the Jewish worker."[27]

Agudat Netaim's grand colonization scheme, in sum, gave preference to private funds and free enterprise methods, to plantation agriculture, to large size combined with gradual investment, and the tying of Jewish workers to the colonies by providing them with housing and small plots. In coming to offer a general colonization model, Eisenberg could not afford to ignore the "worker's question," as did the farmers of the First *Aliya*. The national ambition, expressed in the goal of pure, or at least demographically dense, settlement, played an equal role in his colonization model.

Due to the refusal of the Ottoman authorities, fearful of Jewish colonization, to register Agudat Netaim officially, its initial growth was slow. By January 1908, only thirty of the planned 100 shares were sold, and shares of lower nominal value were also made available to potential purchasers.[28] The sale of shares grew very slowly and picked up only after 1912, reaching 183 on the eve of the First World War. While Agudat Netaim never became the tool of colonization it set out to be, and in 1917 it went into the receivership of the Anglo-Palestine Co., during the period of the Second *Aliya* it remained the largest employer in the Jewish plantation economy. By 1914, it employed close to 20 percent of the Eastern European Jewish labor force in Eretz Israel.[29] As such it had distinct interests in regard to the composition of the labor force, and will be the focus of our attention together with a number of similar bodies.

Examining the financial accounts of Agudat Netaim and Eisenberg's letters it becomes obvious that the capitalist and nationalist aims of the company found their concomitant expression in the division of the company's clients into two distinct congeries. The first was composed of European Jewish shareholders, who usually were among the prominent members of the WZO. The second was made up of Eretz Israeli Jewish owners, members of the First *Aliya*, who hired the company to manage their plantations. The former were more interested in the *national* side of the company's work,[30] and therefore found less objectionable the employment of higher paid Jewish workers, while the latter were above all concerned with the profitability of their plantations and, in consequence, were more inclined to favor the employment of Arabs.[31] Neither initially, when the company was too slow in developing, nor subsequently, when it expanded more rapidly but its debts to the Anglo-Palestine Company and its members rose steeply from 70,000 francs in 1911 to 275,000 francs in 1914,[32] could it afford to alienate either of the two groups. Yemenite Jews were ideally suited to satisfy both nationalist and capitalist interests since they were Jewish workers who were to be paid Arab wages.[33]

Eisenberg, who already responded positively to Peulat Sachir in 1903, and employed most of the spontaneous immigrants of Yemen in 1909/10, explained his preference for Yemenite Jewish workers, in a letter written on March 21, 1909 to Menachem Ussishkin.[34] The reasons he gave were two. First, the 10,000 *ashkenazi* workers he had known during his twenty-three years in Eretz Israel, were an "artificial" labor force: most had left the country after three years, their one or two years' training coming to naught. Secondly, and more significantly, he concluded that "in no way will the conditions of the Jewish community accord with the necessary needs of the [*ashkenazi*] Hebrew worker." Eisenberg transferred his hopes to a new alternative:

there is but one element capable of being a loyal Hebrew worker who may be trusted to stay in the country, even better – who has to stay and cannot leave the country due to his nature, language, and manners, and who gives hope to ridding us of the Arab worker: and he is the Yemenite Jew!

The second adversity that plagued Eastern European Jews also did not affect the new element, as he had learned from employing "the majority" of the spontaneous Yemenite Jewish immigrant workers:

these brothers of ours are contented with little (*chayim bemidat hahistapkut bemuat*), at the level of the Arab, so that they are satisfied with five francs per week, and they are endowed with supreme moral qualities, are very religious, well-versed in the *Tora* [Pentateuch] and speak Hebrew and Arabic.

Having laid down the general reasons for the preference of Yemenite Jews as the laboring force of the Jewish moshavot, Eisenberg suggested a two-part practical plan to secure this labor force. Essentially, Eisenberg believed, all that needed to be done was to settle the immigrants in villages neighboring the moshavot, as was the case with the Arabs, and provide them with "small and cheap houses, that will cost together with the lot no more than a thousand francs." These houses, and the vegetable garden, goat, and chicken on their plots would tie the Yemenite Jews to the moshava, and would enable them to repay their debt. This part of his plan, wrote Eisenberg:

I have already submitted to the Anglo-Palestine Co. Bank and to Dr. Hissin [director of Hovevei-Zion's Jaffa Office], and promised to take on, for a start, fifteen families under the following conditions: permanent employment with us, small houses for dwelling, small plots, and payment in installments for fifteen years, us assuming responsibility for these payments, and later we will take more [families].

In his earliest written reference to the topic, on February 14, 1909, Eisenberg also sought assistance for this part of his plan from the Esra philanthropic association of German Jewry, by reinterpreting the latters' offer of housing assistance to workers in such a way that it would fit "families content with little."[35] (It should not be surprising that Eisenberg approached Esra, Hovevei Zion and APAC, while he ignored Ruppin, since the Palestine Office in early 1909 was a relatively new and untried organization.)

Once his plan was adopted, its success would depend on its second part, namely:

we will begin in its implementation by turning things in such a way (*lesovev pnei hadavar*) that an awakening (*hitorerut*) will come into existence there in their place, in Yemen, and 10,000 of them, as I have been told by their leaders and sages, will be ready to come to Eretz Israel.

Eisenberg wished to keep his idea of a "propagandistic awakening" secret. His reason was that if the awakening was too formidable "and they will only know that there is some hope in store for them in Eretz Israel, then they will come here in thousands, and therefore it is necessary and obligatory that no responsibility whatsoever shall ever fall on us." To prevent this danger, the "propagandistic awakening has to come indirectly from the side (*mihatsad shelo beorach yashir*) [*sic*], and it is the thing that has to be kept in utmost secret that is not revealed but to a few," such as Ussishkin himself.

Having imagined both parts of his plan realized, Eisenberg was already carried away by

the spectacular sight of 10,000 workers from among our brethren, who are natural workers, family men, religious people, and local [i.e. Ottoman] citizens. Then we will be able to say safely that we have been worthy of a great destiny [*sic*] in regard to the difficult and complicated question [of Jewish labor] that has been burdening us so many years.[36]

Ussishkin was not as enthused about the project as Eisenberg, and gave him a non-committal answer.[37] Obviously, as the head of Hovevei Zion, and as such the most prominent leader of Eastern European Zionism, he could hardly have accepted the idea of removing the poorer *ashkenazi* elements from the labor market of the Eretz Israeli moshavot. Though Ussishkin showed reserved interest in the housing project, he completely ignored the propagandistic awakening proposal. Levontin, APAC's director, and Ruppin, in their subsequent negotiations with Esra and the JNF, sought housing allowances for *both* Eastern European and Yemenite Jewish workers. Eisenberg's housing plan for Yemenite Jews was adopted by Levontin and Ruppin with some modifications (such as Ruppin's request for 2,000 francs for Eastern European and 1,000 francs for Yemenite Jewish workers), and his influence on their thinking is obvious.[38]

Eisenberg's plan, accordingly, preceded Yavnieli's article in *Hapoel Hatzair*, called directly for the employment of Yemenite Jews in the plantations, and was communicated to APAC, Hovevei Zion, and Esra, and influenced both Levontin and Ruppin. The surprising fact in the history of the Yavnieli mission is that close to two years passed between the successful employment of the Rechovot group, and the dispatching of a messenger to Yemen. What could have been the reason for the delay?

As far as the second part of his plan, its propagandistic aspect, was concerned, Eisenberg, as he testified in his letter to Ussishkin, initially did not dare involve APAC and Ruppin at all, since he saw the "propagandistic awakening" as a cause to be concealed. The cold shoulder turned by Ussishkin on this idea probably reinforced his natural caution. The first time this theme reappeared was in the form of a reference to the sending of an emissary to Yemen in Ruppin's letter to the head of the Zionist Executive only on November 9, 1910. In that letter Ruppin justified the Office's decision to take on itself the mission, by the commission (*Auftrag*) received from the estates (*Gutswirtschaften*) and colonies, to find up to a hundred Yemenite families for agricultural employment.[39] Ruppin's letter, contradicting his subsequent recollection which credited Redler-Feldman with the initiation of the mission, indicated clearly that he acted on behalf of the planters' interests, and I would speculate at Eisenberg's behest. It should also be mentioned that in the meantime Eisenberg and Ruppin evolved contacts growing in their cordiality and significance. Eisenberg was asked to assume various duties and assist the Office, e.g. by serving on the Office-sponsored Court, by consenting to have land purchased by the Office or the JNF registered in his name as an Ottoman subject, etc., that is in ways which presupposed that Ruppin trusted him thoroughly.

It is certain also that the ideas expressed in Eisenberg's letter to Ussishkin were not just the result of a momentary explosion of enthusiasm. In a letter written by Eisenberg, four years later, to one of the shareholders of Agudat Netaim, he took the role of the initiator of the Yavnieli *Aliya* on himself:

on the basis of a number of years of preparation and work, four years since the idea was born in my heart, we prevailed on (*lipheol al*) the Jews of Yemen to leave their residences there and come to Eretz Israel. And now hundreds of families arrive and we settle them in the existing moshavot as workers.[40]

There is also a great deal of evidence of his continuous involvement with the immigration and absorption of Yemenite Jews in Rechovot and Hadera. For example, he was able to anticipate the arrival of the first group about a month ahead of time, and repeated Agudat Netaim's interest in employing fifty families.[41]

Once the Yemenite Jewish immigrants arrived, we learn from the memoirs of Saadia Masswari,[42] the oral history of Jephet Masswari,[43] and contemporary accounts[44] that Agudat Netaim's five plantations: Heftziba (est. 1905), Birkhet Ata (1905), and Zeita (1913) adjacent to Hadera, one nearby Rechovot, and Sedjra (1913), and Menucha Venachala in Rechovot, were their major employers. In both Rechovot and Hadera, the Yemenite Jewish arrivals eventually exceeded the planter population.[45] Even when not employed by Agudat Netaim and Menucha Venachala Yemenite Jews usually did not find employment on the open market, but in some very unique niches, all of which resembled the companies run by Eisenberg in being restricted, for one reason or another, to employing a large or exclusive Jewish labor force. In Rishon Letzion, the major employer was the winery, which could employ only

Jewish workers, since a large portion of its wine was intended for ritualistic use, and Jewish laws of defilement and purity banned wine touched by non-Jews.[46] In Zichron Yaacov, the institutional employers included the winery, and the orchards managed by the JCA.[47] The JCA also sought to employ Yemenite Jews in some of its settlements, such as Yavniel, in the Lower Galilee.[48] Two of the private *achuzot* – Migdal and Poriah – established in imitation of Agudat Netaim, also numbered Yemenite Jews among their workers.[49] In sum, as Druyan makes clear. "in most cases, Yemenites were not the workers of this or that farmer, but were employed by the foremen of various societies: Menucha Venachala in Rechovot, [Agudat] Netaim in Hadera, JCA in the Galilee, etc."[50] Finally, at the risk of running ahead to a part of our story to be related in detail only in Chapter Seven, mention should be made of "the Yemenites [of Petach Tikva] who, charging 8/9 piasters, moved to Ein Ganim and inherited the places of the *ashkenazim* that worked for 12 piasters per day . . ."[51] Ironically, Ein Ganim was a workers' settlement set up by Hovevei Zion, and being committed to the exclusive employment of Jewish workers also found Yemenite Jews attractive.

Let us turn now to the place occupied by Yemenite Jews in the plantation's labor force. Being hired explicitly to displace the unskilled Palestinian Arab labor force of the plantation, Yemenite Jewish workers were usually relegated to the same menial or unskilled work – the major one being the hoeing of the soil in between and around the trees to allow the penetration of rain into the soil – which was the lot of the Arab workers.[52] The upper limit of the Yemenite Jewish agricultural worker's mobility by and large was the semi-skilled task of deep-weeding (*injil*).[53] One of them, David Madar-Halevi, described their "employment opportunities," in a letter rich of Biblical allusions, as follows:

[we] are hoping and waiting for hope, [asking] whence will our help come, but only the hoe is [our] friend in need . . . we were truly forced to work with the hoe, and to suffer lifeless anguish and the cursing of the foremen who came to supervise our hands' work. When someone is erring, the foreman calls him: "jackass," "some Arab," "savage." . . . we loathed this situation, but what to do? . . . we went to the [companies] to work there and learn deep-weeding. Whoever was trained – worked in deep-weeding, and those who did not know the intricacies of deep-weeding continued to hoe by the trees, their work going on until all became qualified in agriculture, worked, suffered, ate bread with curses, with the sweat of their brow and their soiled bodies.[54]

But even in performing semi-skilled or even skilled work, they frequently received unskilled wages, or at least wages lower than that of their *ashkenazi* co-workers.[55] Not only did Yemenite Jews perform less skilled jobs but sometimes they were also employed in the declining vineyards rather than in the expanding orange groves.[56]

One of the many tragedies of the Yavnieli immigration was the rapid disillusionment of the farmers and the capitalist or institutional employers with their new laborers. It is obvious that this turnabout was caused by the failure of the Yemenite Jewish immigrants to replace the Palestinian Arab villagers in agricultural work.[57] The most likely reason, pointed out by both Joseph Meir and Nitza Druyan, was that "the Yemenite does not work all that cheaply and refuses to be a submissive slave of his Jewish brother."[58] The average wage, paid between the years 1905 and 1914 to unskilled Arab day-laborers by private Jewish farmers, was 5 to 7, occasionally 8 piasters. Yemenite Jews received, on the average 6.2 to 8 piasters, sometimes going up to 9 piasters. The average wage of the Eastern European agricultural worker in the plantation economy of the southern coastal zone was 2 francs (12.4 piasters). Yemenite Jews were located, then, in-between the *ashkenazi* and Palestinian Arab workers, adding a new tier to the labor market rather than occupying the lower one as they were expected to.

According to the combined impressions of Joseph Shprintzak, a member of Hapoel Hatzair Party serving as the main representative of the Palestine Office to the immigrants, Ben-Zvi of Poalei Zion, Yavnieli, and David Madar-Halevi, a leader of the Yemenite Jewish community of Rechovot, even a stable income of 9 piasters per day "does not suffice for the livelihood of the Yemenite family." Food prices in the moshavot were high, especially in comparison with Yemen, and therefore "their meager wages do not suffice even for the satisfaction of their minimal needs." In addition to food and clothing, the Yemenite Jew had expenses connected with the life of the community and with religious tradition, such as festive Shabbat and holiday meals, and "had to improve and decorate his house, [have a] bed and table, chair and lamp, pillows and covers." Obviously Yemenite Jews "easily adopt new needs, but the means for their satisfaction do not grew adequately." In sum, "although the Yemenite is content with little, even his frugality has its limits."[59]

Under such conditions the Yemenite Jewish immigrants led a desperate struggle for everyday survival. Not being able to sink roots in the capitalist market of the plantation colony, for which they were intended, Yemenite Jews frequently became a lumpenproletariat which lived on the margins of the plantation economy. Shprintzak summed up their experience during the First World War in the following way:

this community serves our *yishuv* like Gibeonites "drawing water and cutting wood." . . . The Yemenite quarter served as the reservoir of workers foreordained to work solely with the hoe. If anybody needs a messenger, to walk a short or long distance, it is obvious that he is to be looked for in the Yemenite quarter . . .[60]

Many of the Yemenite Jews were employed in whatever jobs they could find at any time, whether menial tasks in agriculture, or as porters, construction workers, messengers, etc. In their memoirs, the immigrants remembered fondly the work of their wives, and in general Yemenite Jewish women and frequently even children, working in the fields, picking fruit, hauling baskets of oranges, grapes, and almonds, or working as housemaids and servants, were the main breadwinners of their families.[61] The phenomenon of begging, not known among Yemenite Jews in their country of origin, also appeared, arousing the fury of the planters.[62] Violence directed by planters at trespassing immigrants was not unknown, for example, to forcibly prevent women from gathering branches and vine-twigs for firewood in the vineyards.

Another major difficulty that beset Yemenite Jews in Palestine was the housing situation. Prior to the arrival of the immigrants, no preparations were made to ensure suitable housing for them. Upon their arrival, Yemenite Jewish immigrants could "choose" to live in either cow-sheds or stables, under the open sky, to erect wooden huts or, if they were lucky, to move into temporary shelters such as cellars, depots, etc. Between 1912 and 1914, the JNF, in cooperation with the Palestine Office, financed the construction of more durable homes. These consisted, according to Druyan's painstaking research, of either tiny single-dwelling houses, some in fact built by the immigrants themselves, or of long wooden barracks, that contained eight to ten rooms. All of these accommodations, Druyan sums up, sufficed for no more than 30 percent of the Yemenite immigrants in the colonies. The houses were built in separate quarters, at some distance from the existing moshavot: Shaarayim near Rechovot, Machane Yehuda near Petach Tikva, Nachliel near Hadera, Nachlat Yehuda near Rishon Letzion.[63] These quarters, or shall we call them slums, were built either from the donations of various philanthropic bodies, or with the monies of a special drive for the construction of the *Jemenitenhäuser*. Some of the money collected for the express purpose of building homes for the Yemenite Jewish workers, was diverted to other purposes for both Yemenite Jewish and *ashkenazi* workers though, occasionally, Ruppin also spent money on construction prior to its authorization from Cologne. The Yemenite Jewish residents were to pay either monthly or yearly rents.[64] When the dimensions of the housing shortage were revealed, the heads of the WZO in Germany refused to spend much of the very limited budgets of their, at the time, objectively poor movement on philanthropic aid. They were willing to spend money on the Yemenite Jews only commensurate with their "value" for the overall colonization goal of the Zionist movement.[65]

Finally, Yemenite Jews, and particularly their children, suffered from a tragically high mortality rate. According to Yavnieli's count, between 1912 and 1918, 124 of the Yemenite Jewish residents of Petach Tikva, that is a staggering 40 percent of their total number, died. Of the dead 73 were children, while only 45 boys and girls survived. The treasurer of Petaḥ Tikva's *chevrat kaddisha* (burial society) remarked with bitter irony that "the burial of a Yemenite costs us 50 francs, at such rates it would be better to have them cured." While it is true that the Jewish community in general suffered from the ravages of the First World War during that period, the war cannot explain the great difference in the mortality rate between the *ashkenazim* and Yemenite Jews of Rechovot, for example. Among *ashkenazim*, 75 of the 900 residents there died, among them 11 children, of the 237 Yemenite Jews 101 died, and among these 76 were children.[66]

The inability of Yemenite Jews to displace Palestinian Arab villagers from the unskilled work of the plantation, and in consequence their transformation into a marginal and burdensome social and economic element, was almost universally recognized at the time. The planters, in Druyan's assessment, put up for lack of an alternative with the presence of Yemenite Jews in their settlements, but "had they been asked in the years [prior to the First World War] what was their wish, would have admitted that they preferred that the Yemenite immigrants leave the settlements, and have openly talked to them on various occasions in a similar vein."[67] One of the workers' papers wrote in October 1912, under the heading "Illusory Victory":

The arrival of the Yemenites has virtually frustrated all hopes attached to them. Instead of a solution to the old and accursed question of the Hebrew worker, a new problem arose: the question of the Yemenites. Instead of a new and fresh social wave of Hebrew economic work of creation – new confusion, a difficult and depressing confusion . . .[68]

The meeting in the labor market

Starting in 1908/9, a growing sense of their ineffectiveness in monopolizing the labor market evolved among the *ashkenazi* workers. They conceptualized and analyzed this inadequacy with the help of a distinction drawn between "idealistic" and "natural workers." By the term "idealistic workers" they referred to themselves, since they had chosen to migrate to Palestine and not, say, to the US, and since they were ready to move from the more developed city life to the country. "Natural workers" meant not experienced agricultural workers, because there were none in any significant number among Jews anywhere. Nitza Druyan conjures up vividly the characteristics attached to the concept during the Second *Aliya*: "a person capable of performing hard work, living in uncomfortable circumstances, somebody obedient who does not challenge the yoke of the employer, and above all – content with little."[69] Her picture is analogous to the description of the person who comes from a less developed region, and therefore as Bonacich indicated, will be satisfied with lower wages. Early on it was frequently argued that the "idealistic workers" alone had the tenacity to stay in Palestine in spite of all adversity, but gradually the view that only "natural workers" could sink roots in the labor market gained ground. After the spontaneous immigration of the Yemenite Jews this dichotomy was extended to *ashkenazi–mizrachi* relations.

In considering what their position should be toward the employment of Jews for Arab wages, Joseph Aharonowitz, *Hapoel Hatzair*'s editor, demanded of the *ashkenazi* workers, in November 1909, that: "first of all, we ask ourselves, which tasks do we mean?" If the intention was to introduce the Yemenite Jewish immigrants into the skilled and semi-skilled tasks, that were relatively better paid, then "we are creating a *competitor* more dangerous than the previous one . . . Against [the new] competitor we have neither the permission nor the ability to fight . . . and he renders the existence of youngsters from [Eastern Europe] completely impossible." Even the Eastern European workers already in Palestine would have had to leave if they were replaced in the performance of these tasks by Yemenite Jews, since they could not acquiesce in the reduction of their wages. If, on the other hand, the newcomers were intended to be the unskilled and low-paid laborers who were to compete with the Arab workers, then "we are sinning against the Yemenites, whom we are using as the [raw] material for the realization of our ideals."[70]

Aharonowitz's fears of displacement of Eastern European by Yemenite Jewish workers were well founded. Agudat Netaim used Yemenite Jews mostly to replace unskilled workers, but since their wage level eventually stabilized somewhere between the Arab and *ashkenazi* wages, in many places they ended up driving out the latter. Already at the time of Aharonowitz's article it was reported from Rechovot that "the Yemenites [of the spontaneous wave of immigration] always have work even when the *ashkenazi* workers are unemployed."[71] A year later, when the first immigrants of the Yavnieli *Aliya* arrived, the Menucha Venachala company stopped hiring new *ashkenazi* workers, and began taking "in their stead" Yemenite Jews.[72] In Rishon Letzion "the Yemenites took the place of the *ashkenazim* in the winery,"[73] and in the workers' settlement of Ein Ganim, the lower-paid Yemenite Jews "inherited the place of the *ashkenazim*."[74] Especially in remote colonies in the southern coastal zone we find that "*ashkenazi* workers are frequently rejected in favor of Yemenites since the latter are cheaper." According to another source the wages of the Eastern Europeans still employed were reduced to the customary level of wages paid to Arab workers.[75]

Which of the strategies enumerated by Bonacich were chosen by the *ashkenazi* workers *vis-à-vis* their Yemenite Jewish competitors? To safeguard their employment opportunities, the Fourth Congress of the Federation of the Agricultural Workers of Judea, as the southern coastal zone was called at the time, adopted a resolution in December 1913 stipulating that "it is the duty of the [local] workers' boards to try and bring Yemenites everywhere into all types of work and equalize them in price with the *ashkenazi* workers."[76] Zerubavel, one of the leaders of the Poalei Zion Party, in explaining the background to this unique resolution, wrote that

only recently has the attitude [of the *ashkenazi* workers] toward the Yemenites begun to change. And the reason is obvious: what in fact happened is that the cheap and pliant Yemenite competes not with the Arab, but with the *ashkenazi*. The farmers understood this very well, and they began to introduce the Yemenites to occupations that were always in Jewish hands, but in result the [*ashkenazi*] workers' wages were also reduced. Hence the necessity of equalizing the Yemenites with the *ashkenazim* in work, and following this reality came also the decision of the congress.

But even in this case I suspect that the initiative came not solely from the *ashkenazi* workers' Federation; an equally important inducement was the participation of a delegation of Yemenite Jewish agricultural workers from Rechovot and Rishon Letzion, who, without being invited, attended the Fourth Congress.[77] Though we find in the agricultural workers' papers numerous expressions of deep concern for the abject situation of the Yemenite Jewish workers, and anger at the planters' demeaning attitude toward them, as well as reports of organized attempts to help them improve their living and health conditions, this concern was not matched by plans for wage equalization, and I found no proof that even the Fourth Congress's resolution was ever acted on.

Small numbers of Middle Eastern Jews, mostly from the urban Old *Yishuv*, participated in agricultural or semi-agricultural work already during the First *Aliya*. Why then do we find the drive for equalization of working conditions between Jewish workers only as a consequence of the Yavnieli *Aliya*? One likely answer is that in the past the number of non-*ashkenazi* workers was so small that they constituted no threat to the

Eastern European Jews' wage level, which anyway was frequently determined by philanthropic considerations. Another, admittedly more speculative, possibility is that there was no wage differential between *ashkenazi* and *mizrachi* Jews prior to the spontaneous immigration of Yemenite Jews in the winter of 1908 and the subsequent Yavnieli wave. Nitza Druyan, for example, argues that the few Yemenite Jewish workers in the moshavot during the First *Aliya* "were integrated in general with the rest of the moshava's workers, and their living and working conditions were not different from theirs."[78] One of the sources she relies on, however, seems to contradict her by indicating that Yemenite Jews from Jerusalem used to work together with Arab agricultural laborers during the harvest in Gedera, while *ashkenazi* workers preferred to stay away due to the low wages.[79] Her conclusion is corroborated, however, by a list of wages paid to quarantine guards in Rishon Letzion on October 31 and November 1, 1902. This document, rare in that it listed not just bulk wages but also the names of the payees, was preserved as part of legal proceedings. By dividing the names of the twenty-two guards by ethnic origin we get nine Arab, seven *mizrachi*, and six *ashkenazi* guards. We find the already known fact that the wages of all Jewish workers were about 50 percent higher than the wages paid to Arab workers (9 piasters versus 6.2 piasters), but we also discover that the wages of *mizrachim* and *ashkenazim* were identical.[80] It seems then that the differentiation of wages between Jewish workers was not yet a clearly established practice. Of course, we cannot reach definite conclusions on the basis of such scanty and mixed evidence. Nevertheless, it is intriguing to contemplate the possibility that the wage gap between Jews of different descent opened up, or at least was institutionalized, only as a consequence of the introduction of the non-*ashkenazi* Jews into the struggle for "conquest of labor." If this indeed was the case it is less puzzling that wage equalization remained a marginal strategy during the Second *Aliya*.

The dominant position was expressed, in a rebuttal to Aharonowitz, by Zeev Smilansky another leader of the *ashkenazi* workers, who argued that: "the Yemenite workers are less capable of performing cultured tasks (*avodot kulturiot*) than the young [*ashkenazi*] workers, most of whom are educated and quick to grasp the tasks which require intelligence (*tvuna*) and attention more than physical strength."[81] Another fairly typical article presented the distinction in the following way: "where the young *ashkenazi* worker introduces life, ideals, and culture . . . the *mizrachi* introduces nothing." Yet another way in which this shift was articulated was by describing the *ashkenazi* workers as a vanguard of pioneers – as "quality," and the Yemenite Jews as "quantity" or "rearguard" in Zionism.[82]

In these articles we find an interesting transition among the *ashkenazi* workers: no more just acquiescence to or regret for the lower wages paid to their Yemenite co-religionists, but its justification by reference to their allegedly being less "cultured" or "civilized." In all probability this transition corresponded to the shift in the strategy of splitting the labor market from exclusion to caste division. This may be observed, for example, in Rachel Yanait's assertion that Yemenite Jews were solely apt to "conquer" the simple tasks, while the Eastern European workers alone were capable of becoming "entrenched" in the skilled tasks that lift their standard of living.[83]

This perspective was the corollary of the *ashkenazi* workers' self-portrayal as representing a higher level of culture, a perception which, undoubtedly, they evolved in comparing themselves with, and guarding themselves against the competition of, Palestinian Arab workers. For example, when Menachem Shenkin, the director of the Information Bureau of Hovevei Zion in Jaffa, raised the specter of the displacement of *ashkenazi* workers at the General Assembly of Hovevei Zion, an editorial of *Hapoel Hatzair* reassured him that

we do not think that in order to employ Yemenites, the young [i.e. *ashkenazi*] workers will have to be driven out, since in those [skilled] tasks in which the latter are entrenching themselves – the Yemenite will not be able to dig in so quickly, similarly to the Arab who is also incapable of these tasks.[84]

Thus the Jewish–Arab conflict in the form it assumed during the Second *Aliya* in the labor market prominently influenced both the "importation" of Yemenite Jews into Eretz Israel and supplied the distinctions and labels which could be applied to them.

Ironically, however, not only the concept of "natural worker" but also the term "idealistic worker" underwent a mutation. As part of his comparison Zeev Smilansky dismissed the designation of the *ashkenazi* workers as "idealistic," since, in his estimation, it was "hard to find a person whose idealism will persist." "The pioneers," he argued, "end up shirking work, sooner or later, and turn to more comfortable and pleasant ways of making a living" – outside of agriculture. As a matter of fact, the consensus at the time was that a person might persist in being "idealistic" at most for five years.

Zeev Smilansky's conclusion was that *ashkenazi* workers had abandoned the menial jobs, while the Yemenite Jews were only capable of performing unskilled jobs, and therefore without anyone's intervention a natural caste system was emerging. This view served to legitimate the dominant strategy favored by the Eastern European Jewish workers – the segmentation of the labor market into two castes: skilled work being their preserve, while the unskilled tasks, performed by the Palestinian Arab villagers, were to be passed into the hands of their Yemenite co-religionists. It is more understandable therefore why the *ashkenazi* workers were not dead set against Agudat Netaim's plan and why Yavnieli concurred with the WZO's Palestinian Office by going on his mission.

It has to be made clear, at the same time, that there was a great deal of reluctance on the part of the Eastern European workers to accept the implications of their defensive strategy. A consequent mixed consciousness, present especially among the leaders of the *ashkenazi* workers, may be detected, for example, in the decisions of Hapoel Hatzair Party's Eleventh Congress, in April 1912. The Congress expressed its joy at the arrival of the immigrants, and greeted them as realizing its own aspiration to attract *mizrachi* Jews to agricultural work in the colonies. They also viewed the Yemenite Jewish immigrants as desirable comrades in the efforts for the expansion of the number and entrenchment of the status of the Hebrew worker in Eretz Israel. These resolutions were explained to the readership in the following way:

we do not view the Yemenites as competitors, and not as "blacks" who have to come and do the work that the "whites" are incapable of performing, but as comrades equal to us. Our work in Eretz Israel is national work, and we have to attempt to attract to it all parts of the nation without any difference.

But while the preamble and its interpretation presumed to state the inherent equality of all Jews, the six subsequent resolutions were worded in the most general terms, and made no mention of equalization of wages or tasks, of the kind adopted by the Federation of the Agricultural Workers of Judea.[85] I have to agree, therefore, with Israel Kolatt that Hapoel Hatzair Party, and in this respect Poalei Zion were no different, reached no "clear conclusion" on their position *vis-à-vis* the Yemenite Jewish agricultural workers.[86]

Finally, it has to be understood, that not the *ashkenazi* workers but Agudat Netaim determined who would perform which work. The only leverage over the planters the *ashkenazi* workers possessed was contingent on the good will and national sentiment of the planters, and given the latter's more moderate nationalism this was rather limited. But, there was one area in which the *ashkenazi* workers had overriding influence on the Yemenite Jews' social position, which they used to the fullest, and I will turn to it now.

The Palestine Office and conflict over access to land

At this point it becomes possible to sharpen the initial question concerning the different historical role and significance of the Eastern

European and Yemenite Jewish agricultural workers in Israeli state formation by asking: how was the segmentation effected between the two groups in spite of the fact that *both* made only minimal headway in conquering the labor market? This question brings us to the WZO, its Palestine Office, and the latter's director Dr. Arthur Ruppin.

The different bodies of the WZO never intended to support Eisenberg's plan to totally replace *ashkenazi* with Yemenite Jewish workers. They were interested, however, in assisting the farmers of the First *Aliya* and saw benefit in encouraging some Yemenite Jews "to make *aliya*" and work in the colonies as agricultural workers in order to displace the Arab labor force.[87] Most of their design fitted in with Eisenberg's plan, to have most Yemenite immigrants settled in separate neighborhoods, near the existing agricultural settlements. But there were two additional initiatives embarked on at the time that impinged on the future of Yemenite Jews in Palestine.

The first, undertaken in partnership between Hovevei Zion and the WZO, was to set up a new type of colony: the workers' settlement (moshav *poalim*). The aim was to make the workers more competitive by providing them with auxiliary farms and homes in order to compensate them for the very advantages the Arab workers had. The WZO, operating in this context as a truly international Jewish body, intended to turn the moshav *poalim* into a mixed *ashkenazi*–Yemenite Jewish settlement, with the obvious intention of viewing the latter as potential settlers and not solely as a demographic cushioning. Three such workers' settlements were constructed between 1909 and 1914, Ein Ganim, established before the Yavnieli *Aliya* in 1909, Nachlat Yehuda in 1913, and Ein Hai (later renamed Kfar Malal), established in 1914, nearby Kfar Saba. It is the last one I will examine.

Since the attempt at mixed settlement in Nachlat Yehuda ended with an inconclusive struggle over the respective size of lots and/or the number of *ashkenazi* and Yemenite Jewish settlers, at Ein Hai a deliberate attempt was made to provide equal resources to members of both groups. But in June 1914, *Hapoel Hatzair* published an article according to which the Central Zionist Office in Cologne decided to exclude Yemenite Jews from Ein Hai, since they were not expected to find employment in nearby Kfar Saba. In fact, the reasons of the cancellation were related most likely to anxiety aroused in the leadership of the Jewish National Fund, traditionally very protective of its assets, by the opposition of the future *ashkenazi* settlers of Ein Hai to the project. We can learn of their views from a letter written by the Palestine Office to the Federation of the Agricultural Workers of Judea:

we had another opportunity to meet members of the workers' moshav Ein Hai and we came to recognize that the *ashkenazim* are unhappy with the association with the Yemenites, and they see no benefit from such partnership, and only their respect for the Board of the Workers' Federation restrains the expression of their opposition.

The opinion of the Palestine Office was that "forcing both sides, the *ashkenazim* and the Yemenites, to make concessions above the ability of both[!]" might endanger Ein Hai. Though Yavnieli and the leadership of the *ashkenazi* Federation, especially Berl Katznelson, wished for equal distribution of land resources between *ashkenazi* and Yemenite Jews and expressed apprehension about discriminating against the latter, the rank and file would not have it.[88] Fearing the abandonment of Ein Hai by its *ashkenazi* worker-settlers, the Palestine Office concluded that the Yemenite Jewish candidates should be given generous plots and be moved to another workers' settlement.[89] Because of the outbreak of the First World War the part of the plan concerning the Yemenite Jews was not realized.

The second project, undertaken directly by the Palestine Office, in the period under study, involved the founding of *training farms* for agricultural workers in Kinneret (est. 1908), Ben Shemen (1908), and Hulda (1909). While the story of these farms belong properly in Chapter Seven I will present a few of their features that are necessary for highlighting their significance for the structuring of *ashkenazi*–Yemenite Jewish relations. First, the training farms proved to be an attractive place of employment for many of the *ashkenazi* workers, since they almost exclusively employed Jewish workers and paid them year-round wages. Secondly, the training farms, especially Kinneret, served as the cradle of a new, and collective, form of settlement – the kibbutz, the cornerstone of the exclusive Jewish sector of the economy, established on land purchased by the JNF. In this fashion the JNF, and its parent organization, the WZO, assumed the mantle of the major settlement body in Palestine.

Israel Bloch, a founding member of Degania, the first kibbutz, set up in 1910, viewed the problem of the Yemenite Jewish workers in the context of the new venue opened up by settlement. He said in the Second Congress of the Federation of the Agricultural Workers of the Galilee that:

no one thinks here anymore about *conquest of labor*. The question of the *conquest of land* is our main object at present. If we conquer the moshavot, but have no new locations, we will have another thousand or two thousand workers. But that is not our national goal. The question of labor in Petach Tikva will be solved by the *mizrachim* or will not be solved at all.

Joseph Bussel, the ideologue and leader of Degania, painted this new division of labor between *ashkenazi* and *mizrachi* workers in more psychological colors:

the *ashkenazim* cannot compete with the Arabs and work for the farmer under difficult conditions. The *ashkenazi* worker that comes from abroad will not remain a lifelong worker and will not work for ever for the farmer. The reason is that he aspires to become free and refuses to be enslaved. The above mentioned role will devolve on the *mizrachi* Jews who after a year of learning, will stay in the moshavot and do all the "inferior" tasks. We have to divert our energy from the moshavot and not lose our strength in vain.[90]

"Conquest of land" basically solved the workers' problem by eliminating the worker altogether. Having excluded Arab competition from the training farm and the new settlements, the workers saw no point in introducing Yemenite Jews into them. The Palestine Office, therefore, met in the Galilee with the adamant opposition of both the workers and their leaders to attempts to mix the two groups.

An examination, in this context, of the predicament of a group of Yemenite Jews at the Kinneret training farm will illustrate this point. In February 1912, a group of eight Yemenite Jewish families was sent by the Palestine Office to Kinneret. In reconstructing the events that transpired subsequently I have to rely on only two available memoirs and a few contemporary articles in the workers' papers. In April the agricultural season was over, and according to the memoirs of the local nurse, Shoshana Blubstein, Joel Golde, the agronomist-manager of the farm, announced to the Yemenite Jewish families that they had to leave. In her account, most of the *ashkenazi* workers remained passive and the Yemenite Jewish families were "expelled" in May 1912.[91] (The *ashkenazi* workers' indifference is especially striking against the background of the refusal of non-*ashkenazi* Jewish workers from Tiberias to be used to break their strike against the farm's previous director, Moshe Berman.[92]) In the memoirs of Moshe Smilansky, we read that the Palestine Office sent the Yemenite Jews to Kinneret with the intention of turning them into members of the farm's labor force, but the *ashkenazi* workers maltreated them, and the two mediators sent out, seeing the extent of the hostility and fearing bloodshed, decided to have the Yemenite Jewish families removed from Kinneret.[93]

Which one of the versions is more reliable?[94] Moshe Smilansky was a planter, initially and atypically friendly to the workers, subsequently their bitter foe, and hence had an interest in defaming the workers in his memoirs. But in this case it seems to me that there are four good reasons to conclude that his version is closer to the truth.

(1) We already saw in the case of Ein Hai that the *ashkenazi* workers raised obstacles in the way of an ethnically mixed settlement but passed off the responsibility for withdrawing the Yemenite Jewish candidates to the WZO.

(2) In the middle of the contention at Kinneret, in April 1912, the Third Congress of the Federation of the Agricultural Workers of the Galilee took place in Sedjra, and decided to set up a special committee which, in addition to assisting Yemenite Jews in improving their living conditions, would work toward "their concentration mostly in the moshavot."[95]

(3) The Palestine Office did not give up trying to mix the groups and in its 1914 building program for Yemenite Jews included houses at Kinneret, Degania, and two more locations in the Galilee. The Committee for Yemenite Affairs, which advised the Palestine Office, decided, however, to concentrate all but two houses in Judea. And on that committee, in addition to the Palestine Office's official, there were only representatives of the *ashkenazi* workers' parties.[96]

(4) The same debate between Blubstein and the other workers of Kinneret repeated itself at kibbutz Degania a few years later, probably during the First World War. By then, Yemenite Jews were viewed by the majority in their role as wage workers, but a small number of kibbutz members demanded that Degania's Yemenite Jewish wage workers be allowed to participate in its decision-making process. They were opposed by the majority of the kibbutz and "not one" of the supporters of the integration of Yemenite Jews, and maybe of *ashkenazi* wage workers as well, "remained in Degania or in the kibbutz movement."[97]

Could it be that the *ashkenazi* workers preferred to exclude the Yemenite Jews because they were not seen as ready to be part of the close-knit kibbutz, based on principles bearing an affinity to socialism? I would think this but a small part of the reason. Yemenite Jewish settlers were excluded not only from the kibbutz but also from Ein Hai, which was a private smallholding colony, and from the training farm at Kinneret, which was not yet a permanent settlement. The kibbutz, at the time, was not based on preconceived principles, as we shall observe in Chapter Seven, and its organization remained in the making at least for a decade, and some sort of affiliation between the Yemenite Jews and the kibbutz members might have been attempted. The key to the opposition to integrate Yemenite and Eastern European Jews must have been connected with what all these forms of settlement and life had in common, namely, that they were involved no more in the struggle for "conquest of labor," and, therefore, they were exclusively Jewish. To ensure that exclusivity, the *ashkenazi* workers monopolized the precious and new but limited land resources of the JNF. The place of the Yemenite Jews was seen to be only in the moshavot where the displacement of Arabs was possible. The Kinneret incident then may be viewed not as exceptional, but rather as paradigmatic of the relationship between the *ashkenazi* workers and leaders of the Galilee and the Yemenite Jews.

Gorny views the reliance on the Yemenite Jewish agricultural laborer as the illustration of the end of the old road of "conquest of labor" taken by the Eastern European workers. I agree, however, with Israel Kolatt who, in contrast, treats Yemenite Jews as removing an obstacle in the way of the Eastern European group. The agricultural workers of the Second *Aliya*, who "rejected" settlement in favor of becoming lifetime laborers, regained their freedom of choice when the option of settlement reappeared, in consequence of the entry of Yemenite Jews into the moshava. In his words:

the return to the idea of [settlement] was made easier for its supporters, and not only its supporters, by having found a new solution to the problem of the Hebrew labor in the moshavot – the labor of cheap Jewish workers – the Yemenites. The sharp negation of Jewish settlement based on cheap local labor could not persist in face of cheap Jewish labor.[98]

Having found in the Yemenite Jewish workers substitutes – even if more apparent than real – for themselves, justified the *ashkenazi* workers' decision to turn their energy away from the moshava and to the farms, and more significantly to cooperative settlements: to the future kibbutz. Yemenite Jews, and I would like to add Palestinian Arabs, though both excluded from the kibbutz, were an invisible link in its genealogy. Discontinuities in the labor market, then, not only hide aspects of the social structure but also split our consciousness.

Demands and identity of Yemenite Jews

It is not particularly hard to ascertain that the central demands of the Yemenite Jewish agricultural workers themselves were equal pay and a plot of land. Yemenite Jews in Petach Tikva told one of their visitors:

One thing we have to comment on is the difference in the price of labor. We are one people and one language, and why is it that the smallest of our *ashkenazi* brethren receives 2 francs, some $2\frac{1}{2}$, and some 3, while we – even the biggest [*sic*] among us – receives 9–10 piasters [one franc equalled 6.2 piasters] per day?[99]

David Madar-Halevi, one of the Yemenite Jewish agricultural workers, wrote to the Palestine Office, that "we demanded of the farmers the raising of the price [paid] to Yemenites to the same [level] as to the *ashkenazi* workers."[100] Not only did the Yemenite Jews complain about their lower wages, but they suffered, as Ben-Zvi wrote, from the favoring attitude of the farmers to the *ashkenazi* workers.[101]

An even more persistent demand of the Yemenite Jewish agricultural workers was "one small corner and 'a bit, only a bit, of land.'"[102] Ben-Zvi also admitted, in a later period, that the Yemenite Jews' motive for immigration was not a desire to become wage laborers for other farmers, but the aspiration to "reach the level of secure existence from *autonomous labor (avoda atzmit)* like their *ashkenazi* brethren who immigrated from Europe."[103]

The secondary status accorded to Yemenite Jews in the labor market and in the denial of access to land was a major factor in defining their separate identity in the emerging Israeli society. There were obvious cultural differences between the *ashkenazi* and Yemenite Jewish agricultural workers, and Nitza Druyan, for example, emphasizes that given their separate prayer versions "it was clear from the outset . . . [that] Yemenite Jews would pray separately,"[104] and we also find references to the desire of the immigrants to insist on their traditional rules of ritual slaughtering. In their first years in Palestine, Yemenite Jews, she concluded, remained "a separate social unit, whose values and culture were based on the tradition brought by them from their homeland. They were almost unaffected by the Eastern European environment."[105]

While keeping in mind the importance of the "primordial" differences, I wish to argue that the segregation of Yemenite Jews from their environment was not just the result of their unique cultural heritage. We may assess the significance of cultural distinctions by examining the different relationships between and within the three language groups – Eastern European Jewish, Yemenite Jewish and Palestinian Arab – that lived or worked in the Jewish moshava. The most obvious language barrier was the Arabic spoken by the local population which was mastered only by a relatively small number of Jewish immigrants. Nevertheless, conflicts between Jews and Arabs in the moshava due to disagreements over employment were rare. Yemenite Jews occupied a middle position in terms of their ease of communication: they spoke among themselves a "special Arab-Yemenite-Jewish language," and the men also knew Hebrew which served them in Yemen as the language of ritual, and "in spite of their different pronunciation the inhabitants of the moshavot understood them well."[106] But the two subgroups sharing at least one language – Yiddish, but frequently also Hebrew, and sometimes even Russian – that is, the *ashkenazi* planters and workers, were the ones locked in the most intense conflict. I would argue, therefore, that the impact of cultural differences and similarities needs to be examined in light of other relevant aspects of social relations, which might either strengthen or weaken them, thus giving these their true significance.

Side by side with the Yemenite Jews' desire to preserve some of their traditional cultural heritage, there were also signs among them of a tendency favoring integration into the Eastern European environment. Their condition for diluting their "primordial" characteristics, however, was to be accepted and treated as equals.

In an undated document, but one certainly originating in the Ottoman period,[107] that presents the resolutions of the "Assembly of all the Agricultural Yemenites from all the moshavot of Judea" (in fact, they were from the three largest ones: Rechovot, Rishon Letzion, and Petach Tikva), we find a vigorous expression of the aspiration for integration combined with equality. The Assembly elected two bodies: a court of justice, and, more significantly for our topic, separate "representatives for material matters (*dvarim gashmiyim*)": Israel Ovadia, David Nadaph, Shalom Glusska, Tabib, Saadia Aphuyi, to carry out the following:

(1) It was decided that every Yemenite will have at least one *ashkenazi* friend.
(2) Decided that for every house not less than 2,000 francs, that is, for construction [*sic*].
(3) Every house not less than a six dunam plot.
(4) A well for every settlement with pipes to and faucets in every house.
(5) A settlement has to be a Yemenite–*ashkenazi* mixture (*bilul*).
(6) Schools and synagogues, and bath-houses, houses for pupils and teachers should be together (*sheyihyu beyachad*).
(7) Not less than ten Yemenites in every settlement.
(8) Given the small scale of present Yemenite settlement . . . if land should be purchased nearby Rechovot, its Yemenite residents should be entitled to settle on it.
(9) It was decided that Yemenite workers will be organized together with *ashkenazi* workers, and the Boards will work together, and that there will be one Yemenite together with the central Board.

For further emphasis the document ends with the assertion: "all of the Yemenites of Judea have rendered their opinions to their representatives."[108]

Paragraphs (2), (3), (4), (7) and (8) of the Assembly's decisions speak to the topic of equality: the same resources should be committed to Yemenite Jewish settlement – for example 2,000 francs for a house, in contrast to Ruppin's original plan to spend 2,000 francs for houses intended for *ashkenazi* workers, and only 1,000 francs for Yemenite Jews.[109] Similarly, a demand for equal shares of land is prominently displayed. Other paragraphs – (1), and especially (5) and (6) – point to a remarkable readiness of the Yemenite Jews of the Yavnieli immigrations to weaken those cultural aspects of their identity which stand in the way of becoming one with their *ashkenazi* brethren. This readiness extends to bring "together" schools and places of worship, and while the term used does not speak clearly of amalgamation and the creation of a synthetic Israeli-Jewish identity, it certainly goes a very long way towards implying its desirability from the viewpoint of the Yavnieli immigrants. The demands of equality and assimilation were closely juxtaposed in this document.

The Yemenite Jewish immigrants of the First *Aliya* who took up residence in Jerusalem also evinced similar readiness to be amalgamated with the traditional *sephardi* (originally, Jews of Spanish stock, but by the nineteenth century the differences between most *sephardim* and *mizrachim* were not particularly significant) community organization (*kolel*) of Jerusalem. In that case, the two dimensions of integration are also to be found, as joining a *kolel* meant both participation in the charitable funds (*haluka*) distributed by it to the needy, and the sharing of an organizational framework. Equally significantly, the *sephardi kolel*'s leadership demanded and received "certain concessions in the religious sphere," from the Yemenite Jewish members. Only when the leaders of Yemenite Jews felt that they were short-changed did they decide to establish a separate community organization.[110]

As indicated in paragraph (9), the modus operandi for the realization of these goals was seen to lead through shared organizational activity with the *ashkenazi* workers in joint Workers' Boards. As we have seen, Yemenite Jewish agricultural workers did participate in the Fourth Congress of the Federation of Agricultural Workers of Judea of their own initiative. They also repeatedly responded to invitations of *ashkenazi* workers from the moshavot of the southern coastal zone to cooperate, even though, having been let down a number of times, they harbored suspicions of the *ashkenazi* workers' commitment to cooperation.[111]

Yemenite Jewish agricultural workers, without any public backing or resources collected abroad, were not able to create any viable organization. Lack of organization was one of the major sources of their weakness, as they themselves and contemporary observers were quick to recognize. The response to economic grievances was usually spontaneous and short-lived.[112] Though powerless, Yemenite Jewish workers seem to have been determined to demand their due. They were involved in a number of strikes between 1911 and 1914. For example, they launched a strike in protest against a foreman in a plantation of Menucha Venachala in Rechovot, who beat one of them.[113] The goldsmiths in the Bezalel colony at Ben Shemen struck twice, first in February 1911 for improved wages, and a year later demanding to be allowed to buy their houses instead of renting them.[114] Finally, in Hadera, the Yemenite Jewish workers struck in the orchards of Agudat Netaim, demanding improved wages, better treatment and a shorter workday on Friday.[115] In other places demands and threats were also raised.[116] These strikes were of little avail and never lasted for more than a number of days. This could barely have been otherwise given both their lack of bargaining power and resources.[117]

Israeli nation formation

The study of the Yavnieli *Aliya* teaches us that the process of nation formation or its results were not preordained by the shared religion of Eastern European and Yemenite Jews, any more than state formation was predetermined by imported ideas. The status and class position of Jewish groups in early Israeli society was bound up, and maybe for some groups and strata still is, with the broader national conflict between Jews and Arabs, hence the dominant criterion of differentiation between *ashkenazim* and *mizrachim* turned on their respective "national value."

Thus we come back to the initial question, concerning the cause of the different fate that befell *ashkenazi* and Yemenite Jewish immigrants of the Second *Aliya*, and observe that this "value" did not arise from the two groups' respective levels of Zionist ideological preparation but of their dissimilar labor market location. Yemenite Jewish agricultural workers were expected to fill a unique category in the labor market which determined their potential "national worth." They alone, it seemed, could simultaneously carry out the national aim of colonization by replacing Arab workers while being paid Arab wages, that is, make possible a plantation-based demographically dense settlement.

Not surprisingly, Yemenite Jewish agricultural workers felt hemmed in between the Arab and *ashkenazi* groups in the labor market. In a letter from Ness Ziona, described as typical of their feelings, they wrote that: "you gave us work like to the *goyim* [Gentiles], and meager wages . . . And now we demand of you work for men and women in wages that will be sufficient for eating and drinking . . . We are contemptible and abject in your eyes; and you say to us: dogs, *goyim!*"[118] The comparison made by the *ashkenazi* employers and workers between Yemenite Jews and the Palestine Arabs (the *goyim* of the letter) was, I would like to argue, the *major* source of the Yemenite Jews' bitterness. Obviously, the association of the two groups, presenting them as "Arab-Jews," was first the source and later the consequence of the wages, lower than paid to *ashkenazim*, that they received. The initial difference between the *ashkenazi* and the Yemenite Jewish workers, which determined their differential wages in the "conquest of labor" phase, persisted even after the Eastern European immigrants ceased being "idealistic workers," and it became obvious that the Yemenite Jews were never the "natural workers" they were expected to be. The failure of *both* groups to replace the Palestinian Arab worker did not change their relative positions.

The gap between the employment conditions of the two groups in the moshava's labor market was not the making of the *ashkenazi* workers, who were powerless to impose on the employers the institution of a caste solution, either in regard to Palestinian Arabs or Yemenite Jews, and insofar as it existed it was the doing of the planters. The Yemenite Jewish workers remained employed in the mixed private sector of the economy still engaged in the hopeless struggle for "conquest of labor," and were cast as "quantity," while those of the *ashkenazi* workers who were set up in the exclusive Jewish sector of the economy, as settlers on the JNF's land, were transformed into "quality."

With the renewal of the path of settlement, the organized *ashkenazi* workers gained an effective veto power over the modest attempts of the Palestine Office to mix the two groups and, for all practical consequences, brought about the splitting of the Zionist movement. *Ashkenazi* immigrants of later waves, who entered the private agricultural labor market, could look forward to settlement with the assistance of the WZO, while the first Yemenite Jewish settlement – Kfar Marmorek – was set up only in 1930. The preservation of the Yemenite Jews' initially low price of labor ensured that they were excluded from both the privileges of the split labor market (such as skilled work) and those of the training farms and settlements (such as safe employment) that accrued to the *ashkenazi* workers. The exclusion of Yemenite Jews from these privileges signalled the formation of a *split national movement*.

Only very few people rose above the reality of the split labor market, and the interests of the Eastern European workers determined by it, and defined the interest of Israeli nationalism as non-exclusionary *vis-à-vis* Yemenite Jews. One of the "Jewish internationalists" was Zerubavel of the Poalei Zion Party. In the October 1910 meeting of the Party's Council he said the following:

A few years ago everybody was excited by the arrival of the Yemenites to Eretz Israel and now, on the contrary, it is argued that the Yemenites are pushing out simultaneously the Arab and the *ashkenazi* workers, and virtually a propaganda campaign is conducted against them. The source of the error lies in the desire to solve nothing but the question of the Jewish worker from Russia . . . But, according to our world view, the fundamental task is to solve the Jewish national question in general, and for us there is no difference between the *ashkenazi* and the *sephardic* element. The fundamental task is to create here an autonomous Jewish society, and if the Yemenites are capable of realizing it – let it be.[119]

Zerubavel, however, found himself isolated in the Council of his Marxist party. A similar position, motivated by a purely humanist ethic, was expressed by A. M. Koller in the context of the debate over the size of plots accorded the *ashkenazi* and Yemenite Jewish groups in Nachlat Yehuda, on the pages of *Hapoel Hatzair*. In his words:

if the *yishuv* will develop and flourish only an account of the Yemenites' ignorance and abjection, if the idea of our redemption and renaissance is capable of realization only on their account, and only through them will our fondest hopes and aspirations come true, then – it is better that we shall not be redeemed and revived. It is better for us that the wind will carry all, and we will not build the house of our freedom on a basis of slavery and degradation![120]

Needless to say, Koller's cry of *"fiat justitia et pereat mundus"* had just as little impact as Zerubavel's internationalism.

Without the possibility of joining their interests with the *ashkenazi* workers and organizing jointly with them, Yemenite Jews had no access to the new Israeli identity – based on political organization, guard organizations, and cooperative settlement, all mechanisms for bypassing the inhospitable labor market – that was forged by the latter. The Yemenite Jews of the moshavot were left either to cultivate their traditional religious distinctiveness or to indulge in petty jealousies and quarrels. Among themselves, they stopped even being just Yemenite Jews and instead, rendering now irrelevant divisions based on their origin in particular regions of Yemen into a foundation of present divisions, became *émigrés* of Saana, Heidan, Sharab, etc.[121] Short of becoming "Israelis," they remained traditional Jews.

The *ashkenazi* workers assumed a modern national Israeli identity while the Yemenite Jews remained restricted to their traditional religious Jewish identity. The *ashkenazi* workers, enjoying the land resources of the Zionist movement and the mobilizing lever of their modern identity, evolved into the makers of Israeli history, while the Yemenite Jewish workers, cut down to a lumpenproletariat and defined by a pre-modern identity, remained on the sidelines of that history.

Chapter Five

Between trade unions and political parties, 1905–1914

The closing off of the route to settlement and the dead end to social mobility encountered in the Jewish plantation economy of Ottoman Palestine encouraged intensive organizational creativity on the part of the Eastern European Jewish agricultural workers, while the introduction of Yemenite Jews freed them further to experiment with these organizational forms. Chapters Five to Seven will examine three central metamorphoses that developed during different years. The two political parties, Hapoel Hatzair and Poalei Zion, were formed in 1905; the first guard organization, Bar-Giora and its extension Hashomer, in 1907 and 1909 respectively; while Degania, the first kibbutz, officially began its life in 1910. These organizational experiments were developed by different individuals and in relative isolation from one another, but nevertheless followed a similar logic – they were all attempts to bypass the dynamic of the labor market. It was only after the First World War that they were interconnected under the umbrella of the Histadrut, and together became the dominant method of Israeli state formation.

The examination of the political organization of the *Yishuv* discloses a remarkable puzzle. While social groups usually evolve their distinct identity, organize themselves, and amass power as the result of two-way conflicts between them, the *Yishuv* saw a lopsided intra-Jewish balance of political power. The workers organized in political parties already in 1905, established their all-encompassing Histadrut in 1920, united their factions in 1930 in the Mifleget poalei eretz yisrael (Party of Eretz Israeli Workers, in short Mapai) and, in 1933, came to dominate the WZO.[1] Labor's formidable organizational weaponry and subsequent hegemony, however, faced no comparable organization of the planters or of the middle class iN general. If engagement in socio-economic conflict is the key to political organization, then the planter–worker conflict was not the foundation of the workers' political might. For its sources we have to look elsewhere: to the Jewish–Arab conflict in the labor market to which the Jewish groups were dissimilarly exposed.

123

It is a central thesis of all Israeli functionalist sociologists and most modern Israeli historians, with the notable exception of Jonathan Frankel, that the central standing of the workers' parties and organizations resulted from their ideological dedication and clarity, a phenomenon not shared by the bourgeois strata. It is, furthermore, a generally accepted sociological observation that political parties, especially socialist parties, are the site of ideologically inspired politics, while trade unions pursue more mundane bread-and-butter issues. The search for ideological prowess then naturally leads us to the workers' Hapoel Hatzair and Poalei Zion parties. Nonetheless, it is impossible, in the case of these two parties, to sustain such division between parties and unions. Hapoel Hatzair and Poalei Zion vacillated a great deal between these two roles. In many ways, so did most other Israeli "parties." In a 1959 study, Amitai Etzioni pointed out that most Israeli parties controlled stable cores of supporters, Mapai more than the others, through their partisan mastery of employment and health plans, housing projects, vacations, and recreation services.[2] In this chapter, I will attempt to demonstrate that the workers' parties, though not devoid of ideological or general content, were essentially practical-minded and concerned with the mundane aspects of everyday life already during the Second *Aliya* – supposedly their most intensely ideological period.

Significantly, even though many of the new immigrants were involved in political work in the Pale of Settlement, initially they remained unorganized in the plantation colonies.[3] The first organizational creation of the agricultural workers of the Second *Aliya* was Hapoel Hatzair Party. The party evolved, as we can piece together from memoirs, out of the rejection of a manifesto calling for the self-selective immigration from Eastern Europe of "embittered heroes, who will fight desperately for their ideal without any hidden thought of ever considering retreat," published by Joseph Vitkin, a teacher in the Galilean moshava Kfar Tavor.[4] A small group of workers, Shlomo Tsemach, Eliezer Shochat, Nathan Shifris, and others, from a number of moshavot and Jaffa, met in July 1905 in Jaffa, and evolved an alternative perspective, opposed to Vitkin's on three grounds.

First, Vitkin's approach, born of the experience of the First *Aliya*, saw the aim of the immigrants as eventual settlement on land of their own. This goal was not realizable at the time, as we have seen, and the immigrants expected to remain lifetime workers. Secondly, the first wave of Jewish workers attempted to lower their standard of living in order to find safe employment in the moshava's labor market while the foundation of Hapoel Hatzair is connected with the abandonment of this strategy. After all as long as the workers hoped to make their way through the

market, they did not need to organize themselves. Now in the first
creative organizational response in the labor market Tsemach offered the
new vision of "conquest of labor," and the founding of a political body to
carry it out.[5] Furthermore, Vitkin sought support for promoting his
manifesto from Ussishkin,[6] whose own "Our Program," published in the
meantime, advocated the strategy of downward equalization; this
association was also a likely reason for the workers' objection to Vitkin's
summons. Thirdly, Vitkin's summons for the immigration of "heroes"
obviously would have restricted immigration, while the goal of "conquest of labor" opened again the vista of demographic, i.e. large-scale,
colonization.

The organization was publicly launched in October 1905, and in
August 1906 a draft program was prepared by Zeev Smilansky. It stated:
"the role of Hapoel Hatzair in Eretz Israel is the realization of Zionism in
general, and special concern for the conquest of labor by Jews." Among
the means intended for assisting in conquering labor were labor
exchanges and cooperative consumer services, such as kitchens, savings
and loans, stores, sick funds, etc., that is some of the traditional
instruments of the First *Aliya* workers.[7] This narrowly focused draft did
not satisfy Hapoel Hatzair's small urban wing, which repeatedly
demanded a full-fledged political program. The party, however, never
adopted a program and made a virtue of its lack. One of its founders
commended it: "Hapoel Hatzair does not create programs. It is life itself
that at any given moment raises programs for action. This mood
permeated the party at all times."[8]

Hapoel Hatzair is recognizably a product of the Eretz Israeli labor
market, but its lack of ideological disposition, in Kolatt's view, may be
traced to the inspiration of the supra-class Zionism of Hovevei Zion,
which earlier animated the First *Aliya*. Given this influence, Hapoel
Hatzair was not opposed to "property," but saw in labor and property the
dual bases of Jewish colonization. It expected to generate support among
the planters for "conquest of labor," since the entry of masses of Jewish
workers into the labor market alone could provide the "demographic"
foundation of colonization. In a memorandum calling on the Boards of
the moshavot to do more for the employment of Jewish workers, Hapoel
Hatzair accepted the ultimate aim of the "redemption of the land," but
added that "for us to become the rural majority . . . it is required that the
laborers . . . be Jewish." Expecting cooperation with "property,"
Hapoel Hatzair's majority was opposed to class struggle, viewed strikes
as a means of last resort, remained ambiguous, even hostile, toward
socialism, and preferred persuasion, propaganda, and example-setting to
achieve its aims.[9]

In order to influence the planters, the sympathies of other social strata and the WZO were deemed essential. Its supra-class nationalism allowed Hapoel Hatzair to attract a number of writers, teachers, and clerks, though initially it expected even employers and planters to join its ranks.[10] In consequence, Hapoel Hatzair oscillated between the general public concerns and ambition of its urban and intellectual periphery to broaden the party's basis, and the "special concern for the 'conquest of labor'" typical to its core of agricultural workers.[11] Nevertheless, even when it became obvious that no conditions were being created for gainful employment of the Jewish worker, and the party entered a sustained crisis that reached its peak in 1910, the agricultural workers remained in firm control of the party and did not abandon the non-ideological focus on the generation of employment. This concern, after all, was behind the foundation of Hapoel Hatzair.

While Hapoel Hatzair was born in the labor market and remained the party of "conquest of labor," Poalei Zion – the Palestinian branch of an international Jewish working-class party, that was born in Russia – appears to contradict my explanation which roots Jewish political organization in Palestine in the labor market. In fact, the fate of Poalei Zion is the best acid test of the close association between the two.

Poalei Zion was the child of the second wave of Jewish nationalism in the Pale of Settlement. While the generation of Hovevei Zion viewed Jewish national auto-emancipation in terms of the acquisition of legal and political rights, the emphasis shifted at the turn of the century, as a result of the rapid industrialization of Russia and the penetration of Marxist ideas, towards the economic and social content of national existence. It was recognized that the industrialization which destroyed traditional Jewish middlemen occupations, instead of providing the massive numbers of the Jewish poor with entry into the great mechanized factories and integrating them into society, was bringing about their displacement and unemployment.[12] There was, however, a deep disagreement as to the proper response between the vigorous revolutionary socialist party of the Bund, which sought a combination of equality with national cultural autonomy through the transformation of Russia, the Sejmists who wished to nurture Jewish national life in the Pale until the time was ripe for a territorial solution, and the much weaker socialist Zionists who sought a solution in territorializing the Jewish people outside the Pale of Settlement. Among the latter, a debate raged between the Zionist Socialist Workers' Party, which was not committed to a predetermined settlement territory, and the Poalei Zion, and its major theorist Ber Borochov, who envisioned Palestine as the ultimate territory of settlement.

But to Borochov's rigorous Marxist analysis which based the choice of Eretz Israel, "the land of memories," as the destination for colonization on the economic necessity of colonizing pre-capitalist regions, there was an obvious element of "wishful thinking." This incongruence created two factions among Poalei Zion's members. The left wing, hailing from Poltava and Rostov in southern Russia, and led by Ben-Zvi after his immigration in early 1907, insisted on the primacy of socialism, while the right wing, originating from Lithuania, Poland, and White Russia in the north, articulated by Ben-Gurion, insisted on the precedence of nationalism. A third group, around Israel Shochat, representing a "popular-romantic" tendency rather than an ideological one, derived from the experience of Jewish self-defense during the 1903 pogroms.[13] Poalei Zion, consequently, was a brittle conglomeration of tendencies, rather than a clear-cut expression of Borochovian Marxism.[14]

Even though the two parties had divergent starting points – the general and inchoate nationalism of Hovevei Zion for Hapoel Hatzair, and the Borochovian synthesis of Zionism and Marxism for Poalei Zion – the lesser importance of ideological convictions for both is obvious from the actual similarity of their social analysis. Jonathan Frankel's poignant conclusion is illustrative in this respect:

> what impresses the observer most is the extent to which the leading theoreticians of the two parties shared a number of underlying and centrally important assumptions . . . Differences of philosophy, conflicting self-images, and organizational competition kept the parties apart, but in their socioeconomic analysis and their overall political strategy the degree of convergence was remarkably high.[15]

The two most important similarities were the conviction that the key to Zionist colonization was the capitalist path, and the expectation of expanding Jewish immigration to Palestine as a result of that development.

Achad Haam already in the early 1890s, and Hapoel Hatzair subsequently, concluded the necessity of the capitalist path of development in view of the failure of the paternalistic and philanthropic Rothschild administration. Poalei Zion anticipated the capitalist phase of development on general theoretical grounds. The Second *Aliya* began arriving in Palestine in the twilight period between the termination of the Rothschild tutelage and the onset of the WZO's patronage. This was the period of the JCA's market-based approach, and the immigrants of the Second *Aliya* could hardly have expected non-economic interests to buttress Zionist colonization.

With regard to Jewish immigration, both parties took a passive and non-interventionist position, in spite of the fact that they claimed to represent the demographic basis of Zionism. Though "conquest of labor" offered the hope that, in their estimation, 4,000 new immigrants would find employment, in fact, Hapoel Hatzair's founders opposed Vitkin's own call for such immigration. Instead, they presumed to find new recruits in the Old *Yishuv* and among the young generation of the moshava.[16] Though Vitkin's call for the "embittered hero" was rejected, soon Hapoel Hatzair came to expect that as long as the economy was not transformed along capitalist lines, only the self-selected "idealist" worker, sometimes also referred to as the pioneer (*halutz*), would be able to persist in Palestine. Borochov postulated that immigration could be only a spontaneous, or stychic, phenomenon, resulting from objective forces, and not from a series of individual acts of will. Hence Poalei Zion also opposed the encouragement of voluntary immigration.

Why then, in October 1905, did followers of Poalei Zion demonstratively walk out of the founding meeting of Hapoel Hatzair in Jaffa to establish their own party in December?[17] While the contemporary sources are few and far between and strewn with legend, one of the major stumbling blocks, if not the central one, was obviously connected with the issue of internationalism, i.e. whether the nationalism of the "conquest of labor" strategy was justified.[18]

The difference between the two parties was not over the need to create a split labor market in order to furnish employment to Jewish workers, but over the specific strategy to be implemented in the realization of that aim. Hapoel Hatzair was in favor of the total exclusion of Arab workers from the Jewish-owned economy. Poalei Zion, in the non-theoretical paragraphs of its first and most Borochovian-Marxist program of October 1906, expected Jewish workers not to replace Arab ones but to find employment in the new capital intensive branches to be developed by the penetration of Jewish-owned capital. The proletarianized farmers and low income Arab workers were expected to find employment in the less intensive branches of the economy, while the capitalist branches that needed "educated and energetic" workers were foreseen to be dependent on the immigration of Eastern European Jewish workers.[19] For practical purposes, this approach envisioned a segmented economy accompanied by a caste system in the labor market which would eliminate the basis of a potential Jewish–Arab conflict. But in neither party was a strategy of international working-class solidarity – pursuable, in a split market, through wage equalization – seriously contemplated. When in its First Congress in the summer of 1906 Poalei Zion debated whether the trade union which the party sought to establish would enroll both Jewish and Arab workers, or solely Jewish ones, it was the latter position, put forward by Ben-Gurion, which was adopted.[20] "Hebrew labor" was, as Anita Shapira asserts, "the common denominator of the immigrants of the Second *Aliya*."[21]

In practical terms, even the divergence between the appropriate strategies deemed necessary for splitting the labor market did not amount to much. In 1907, Poalei Zion's attempt to organize an *artel* of Jewish construction workers "in order to conquer on behalf of Jews all the branches of labor and industry that already have been established here," sounds as if it was lifted *tout court* out of Hapoel Hatzair's vocabulary. The correspondent of the latter pointed to this similarity, in that Poalei Zion also sought to conquer labor and not the means of labor.[22] And in May 1910, the representatives of *both* parties jointly demanded that Ruppin replace the Arab workers employed in the Palestine Office's national farm in Hulda. They based their complaint on a demand addressed by Jewish workers in Lydda to *both* parties to move against this "shame."[23] Ben-Zvi's retrospective view that "in fact, the Poalei Zion was just as interested as Hapoel Hatzair in conquest of labor"[24] is therefore well founded and should not be seen solely as an attempt to purge from the party's history its Marxist phase.

As we already know, none of the strategies employed by either of the parties in the labor market itself had any meaningful impact during the period of the Second *Aliya*. Hapoel Hatzair's "conquest of labor" produced the splitting of the labor market without, however, permitting the reproduction of the Jewish working class. Since both entry of capital and labor were slow to materialize, Ben-Zvi looked for new fields of expansion among the Jewish workers of the Old *Yishuv* in Jerusalem, and Jewish workers throughout the Ottoman Empire. Poalei Zion, however, had not recorded genuine success in either arena.

But where the parties failed, their veteran members looked for new ventures. "The limited role played by the parties," concluded Jonathan Frankel, "meant that the actual attitudes and behavior of the young immigrants can hardly be described or explained in ideological terms alone."[25] Hapoel Hatzair members questioned the centrality of "conquest of labor" and wished to find new ways of settling on the land. The deviations of Poalei Zion's members from party ideology were even more dramatic. Many ended up in agricultural work rather than seeking out potentially more class-conscious urban and industrial places of employment and, instead of trying to consolidate a foothold in the capital intensive plantations of the southern coastal zone, left for the field-crop colonies of the Galilee. In the Galilee, the "popular-romantic" tendency found a wide open field for its activities and Shochat and others established the para-military organizations of Bar-Giora and Hashomer that, again contrary to party ideology, sought to protect private, if only Jewish, property. There was no room in the Galilee for "ideological or political activity" and the partisan differences "were almost non existent."[26] The members of both parties were among the initiators of the non-partisan and non-ideological Federations of the Agricultural Workers of Judea and the Galilee.[27]

It was in these unions, especially the southern one, that a major turning point was reached: the acceptance of the WZO's land settlement policy (see Chapter Seven). The focus of decision-making in the trade union, rather than in the political party, was seen as a "paradoxical" development only by the Israeli historians, whose idealist version it had now shown to have been standing on its head. The creativity of the trade union evoked Kolatt's wonderment: "the miraculous and bizarre thing that happened in a movement as saturated with ideas as the Eretz Israeli labor movement, is that an organization based on the needs of reality became in fact and in theory the major organization and drove back the proper ideological bodies and parties."[28] The aspiration to gain access to land, after all, ran counter to the ideologies of both parties: it would do away with Hapoel Hatzair's "conquest of labor" strategy while reducing the proletarian character of Poalei Zion, and making its members the recipients of "bourgeois" resources, and, in Borochov's own view, was certainly not a method intended to achieve socialism.[29] This transition was prepared by the very early, but nevertheless piecemeal, metamorphosis of Poalei Zion's imported Borochovian socialism.[30]

Ben-Gurion reformulated the meaning of class struggle beginning in the Third Congress of Poalei Zion, that took place in September 1907.[31] Both Borochov, in Russia, and Ben-Gurion, in Palestine, pointed to the identity of Jewish national interest and socialism, but while for Borochov the relation of national and socialist goals was based on objective identity and the bond between them was organic, in Ben-Gurion's view it was founded on the fact that only the workers were able to realize the national goal, i.e. pure settlement. When Borochov regarded the national interest as being served by class struggle, Ben-Gurion expected the participation of the Jewish worker in the program of national renaissance to ensure the realization of the social aims of the worker. The difference, of course, was that the second way of formulating the "identity" of socialism and nationalism ruled out the need for class struggle. In Ben-Gurion's words:

the first and foremost of the builders and fighters for the Hebrew renaissance is the Hebrew worker, and everything that brings about his entrenchment, development, the extension of his social and political rights, the increase of his material and mental strength – simultaneously benefits the nation in general.[32]

In the Fifth Congress (October 1908), the paragraph proclaiming class struggle as the way of constructing a socialist society in Eretz Israel was eliminated.[33] Gradually, Ben-Zvi himself, the party's ideologue, was eclipsed in the party's leadership by the practical-minded Ben-Gurion.[34]

The early resolution of the debate between the primacy of socialism and nationalism within their "identity" is sometimes obscured by the fact that the strength of those favoring the preeminence of "socialism" was renewed by new immigration.[35] Drawing away the new immigrant members from the socialist formulations current in the Pale and socializing them to the urgency and precedence of Eretz Israeli nationalist practices, was not a once and for all event, but remained a permanent feature of Eretz Israeli party life. The tendency to practicality and the parallel decrease in Marxist terminology, to which new immigrants were socialized, grew gradually from Congress to Congress, and in this way, in Gorny's telling expression, "socialist teachings," were created "in which practical thinking becomes a quasi-ideology."[36] Ben-Zvi himself described the years before 1910 in the following way: "After . . . the creation of the theory – there came a period of deeds with no theory. We undertook many experiments . . . This proves that we still possess an important force – the force of life."[37] The unconnected experiments, carried out under the pressures of "life," signaled a cultural destructuration, that is, the disintegration of a coherent ideological worldview. In Kolatt's words, "the dilemma of the relationship of Jewish labor to socialist ideology . . . engendered a shift in the whole ideological basis, and even a total doubt of the validity of the ideological formulation itself."[38] But it was as early as the Sixth Congress of April 1910, with the acceptance of the WZO's cooperative settlement plan (the topic of Chapter Seven), that, in Gorny's view, "the decision concerning the party's practical path in Eretz Israel already was taken."[39]

Cooperative settlement, combined with political organization and the assumption of the *Yishuv*'s protection by the workers, gradually laid the foundations for their ascent to hegemony in the 1930s. While the brief portion of this story that will be told in this study will have to wait till Chapter Eight, at this point it will suffice to chart the subsequent expansion of the workers' political organization. After the First World War the prominence within the labor movement accrued to Poalei Zion – its Borochovian and Marxist perspective better preparing it to view and implement social change in the political and organizational terms that became feasible after the transfer of government to the British Mandate – and in spite of the "foreign" import of Poalei Zion's ideology, its leaders, Ben-Gurion, Ben-Zvi, Tabenkin and many others, occupied the first rank of the leadership of the workers' movement, while Hapoel Hatzair lagged behind. In 1918/19, Poalei Zion united its forces with a large group of unaffiliated Second *Aliya* workers led by Berl Katznelson. In the elections to the Histadrut, the new Achdut Haavoda (United Labor) became the majority party, and was subsequently joined by many of the Third *Aliya* immigrants under Elkind's leadership. Hapoel Hatzair united with it in 1930 to form Mapai, which became the hegemonic party of the *Yishuv*. Under Mapai's influence, the religious Mizrachi and the petty bourgeois General Zionist political parties – in other societies not usually sympathetic to workers' parties – split between factions that supported and ones that opposed the labor movement, and the latter's central faction led a ruling political coalition, of which it always remained at the center, in Israeli society until 1977.

Given that the political organization of the workers took place in the labor market and its extensions, can we explain the inability of the planters, or the bourgeois strata in general, to crystallize their counter-vailing political center by reference to the same arena? This question was addressed by Dan Giladi in a brief but eye-opening study that spans the period 1882–1939.[40] Using the total Jewish capital import into Palestine as an indication, he reports that, between 1882 and 1921, of a total of 19.4 million Palestinian Pounds, 11.5 were private, 5.1 philanthropic (mostly from Rothschild and the JCA), and only 2.8 million belonged to the WZO (furthermore, most of the WZO's monies were imported during and after the First World War). By way of rough approximation, he postulates that the last sum was at the disposal of the workers' movement, while the philanthropic funds, by and large, went to the farmers. The economic resources of the workers then made up around a sixth of the resources of the farmers. In the years 1921–39 the WZO's resources made up again about one sixth of the private resources at the disposal of the bourgeois groups.[41] A breakdown of capital investment in the leading economic branches: construction, citrus, plantations, field crops, industry, and mixed farming, reveals a similar picture: only in the last category did the workers' cooperative settlement have economic superiority, and even that began only in the 1930s. The political dominance of the workers in Israeli society is certainly puzzling as it is contrary to the imbalance between the economic resources of the labor movement and the bourgeois elements, and its sources are not strictly economic. The foundation of the workers' strength was their alliance with the WZO based on a common demographic interest, and their self-organization.

In general, Giladi points out, the difference between Jewish bourgeois and working strata in Palestine resulted from their different position toward the relationship of private and public, which derived from their dissimilar connection to public funds.

The economy of bourgeois circles was not dependent on public budgets, hence they did not place themselves as individuals or organizations at the disposal of the Zionist movement's leadership. It was precisely the dependence of the workers and their need of national financial support . . . that turned them into a "national army" that conquers targets set by commands from above.[42]

But in Giladi's view, this dependence was rooted in the workers' "personal choice and free decision made in a typically social manner" to be organized in a centralized fashion. When speaking of choice, and especially in such a laudatory way, it is usually worthwhile to present the alternatives between which the choice could have been made. In this case, given the necessity of making a living in an inhospitable labor market, the *ashkenazi* agricultural workers wishing to stay in Palestine hardly had a realistic alternative. They needed to bypass the labor market, hence they needed the WZO. The counter example of the planters clearly demonstrates this.

The reverse relationship between economic vigor and political organization, in this case the connection between labor market conditions and the need for organization, was just as clear in the case of the planters as it was for the workers. We may conclude this by looking into what they might have done to acquire their own political power basis. In 1914, in a conference devoted to the problem of "Hebrew Labor," planters and their supporters examined various policies, in consultation with representatives of the WZO.[43] Three alternatives were debated. Ruppin, trying to formulate a unifying platform, suggested the setting up of a joint employer–worker arbitration body. The majority planters' suggestion, put forward by Dizengoff, was to appoint a fact-finding commission with the aim of setting a realistic wage level. Dizengoff's view defined the conflict in economic terms, provided no venue for increasing the number of Jewish workers, and essentially vacated the political arena to the workers. There was, however, an alternative policy, raised by Mordechai Ben-Hillel Hacohen, the most class-conscious member of the planter group. Hacohen was well aware of the necessity of increased Jewish worker immigration, but wished to be in control of the new arrivals, by making them dependent on the economic resources of the planters. He suggested the establishment of a "Central Committee for Workers' Affairs," by which he meant that "our man would set foot on the ship and disembark the new worker. Whoever wishes to work will come to us – to our institutions." Shenkin, emboldened by Hacohen's ideas, went even further, suggesting the establishment of a planters' organization for "Hebrew Labor," with branches abroad to recruit "real workers." The Hacohen–Shenkin alternative could have served as the foundation for an effective control mechanism of employers over workers, as it did in other societies and even in Israel when employed by the Histadrut, and might have become the cornerstone of the planters' own political organization. It was not, however, seriously debated in the conference. Why?

Hacohen recognized that his proposal would require the cooperation of the WZO. Ruppin, however, chose to ignore his suggestion. The reason for his reluctance, I believe, was expounded by Glusskin, the Manager of the Vinegrowers' Cooperative. Glusskin pointed out that the planters had failed once in importing Yemenite Jewish workers whom they could not gainfully employ, and had no desire to repeat the same mistake. By 1914, Ruppin also knew better than to import low-paid Yemenite Jews, let alone Eastern European ones. But, ultimately, the planters themselves did not wish to take up the gauntlet thrown by Hacohen because they did not have to. They did not suffer from shortage of hands since they possessed an almost unlimited supply of low-paid Arab workers. The conference settled on Dizengoff's alternative.

After the First World War, the workers' parties began developing the tools of domination, an organization and paid cadre. The workers also expanded their influence through the development of the Jewish-owned economic sector during the Mandate but, as is obvious from Michael Shalev's and Abraham Cohen's work, the circumstances of the bourgeois elements did not require any political organization on their part during that period either. The development of an industrial sector was retarded by the virtual lack of comparative advantages in Palestine and the preference for speculative profits accruing to land speculators. Industrial firms produced mostly for the domestic market and hence were more open to pressures to employ Jewish workers, and remained isolated from the citrus growers, the major export branch and largest employer of Arab workers. Different bourgeois sectors had opposing labor market interests, and could not coalesce in a political body.[44] Labor market interests continued, even if not exclusively, to provide the rationale, and circumscribe the parameters, of political organization in the *Yishuv*.

Chapter Six

From "conquest of labor" to "conquest of land": the identity of soldier and settler, 1907–1914

In one area, the "conquest of guard duty," the workers of the Second *Aliya* achieved an exceptional, though temporary, success of the kind that eluded them in the labor market. The reason for this opening was the upsurge of Arab hostilities, unleashed after the Revolt of the Young Turks in July 1908, which revealed the vulnerability of Jewish settlement.

Though public safety had improved dramatically after the Ottoman reconquest of Palestine from Ibrahim Pasha, it still left a lot to be desired. In addition to the simmering and occasionally open Palestinian opposition to foreign settlement, Jews shared with everyone else the oppressive results of this low level of public safety in Ottoman Palestine. In consequence, privately purchased security was a necessity. While in the early years of the First *Aliya*, moshavot were occasionally protected by Jewish guards,[1] the rule, certainly by the end of the century, was the contracting of outside guards. In the plantation moshavot, the guarding pattern closely resembled the model of the economy: a combination of Jewish supervisors and Arab guards. In general, the moshavot submerged themselves in the prevailing local relations of force, and sought to use them for their own benefit by purchasing the services of the strongest local potentate. The latter usually came from among the Bedouins, or martial ethnic minorities, such as Circassians, Maghrebians, or Turkomans. But paying off one group of likely assailants and potential thieves always remained at best an incomplete solution because the moshava now exchanged vulnerability for dependence.

Under these conditions, the aim of the Jewish settlers became the minimization of damage. Major attention was paid to the protection of life and limb in the moshava itself. The houses and farm structures were joined by a protective wall, pierced with embrasures, and were guarded separately from behind the wall.[2] As far as the fields and plantations were concerned, the guards' contracts contained a clause which obligated them to repay losses and damages due to theft. It was not easy, however, to enforce this provision.[3]

This was the background to the establishment of the Bar-Giora group (named after the last leader of the Jewish Revolt against the Roman Empire) by Israel Shochat, with the assistance of Israel Giladi, Alexander Zeid, and others on September 29, 1907, and its extension into Hashomer (The Guard) on April 12, 1909. This initiative was closely linked with the rest of the Second *Aliya*'s aims: Hashomer continued to serve as a vanguard in the "conquest of labor," and its demand to moshava Boards to expand the number of Jewish workers became "an integral part of the conditions for assuming guarding."[4] At the same time, Jewish guard organizations had their autonomous origins, and ran their courses on separate, if parallel, tracks until 1920.

First of all, Bar-Giora and Hashomer, in contradistinction to the political parties and trade unions, were established as conspiratorial bodies. Hashomer members were carefully selected on the basis of personal traits after a year-long trial period and sworn in midnight ceremonies to secrecy and loyalty.[5] Incidentally, the strong emphasis on individual qualifications and suitability opened in Hashomer a crack to the entry of a small number of non-*ashkenazi* Jews: Yemenites, Sephardim, etc. Even women, who in general were expected by the men of the Second *Aliya* to adhere to traditional roles within the movement of national *renaissance*,[6] were accepted as full members, though mostly by virtue of being guards' spouses, and were not sent on guard duty.

Secondly, though almost all the members of Hashomer belonged to Poalei Zion, and Israel Shochat and Ben-Zvi were prominent leaders of both, the former was not officially overseen by the latter. What was the reason for this confounding organizational duality? In principle, as a Borochovian-Marxist body, Poalei Zion could hardly have countenanced the protection of private property and the replacement of Arabs by Jews in guard work. Both these tasks were justifiable only in strictly nationalist terms. At first sight, it might even seem odd that this organizational innovation did not emerge from within the ranks of Hapoel Hatzair. But Hapoel Hatzair, on account of the opposition of some of its prominent members to any form of militarism, was less well equipped to play the role of sponsor to Jewish military might.

Poalei Zion itself, as we have already had the opportunity to observe, was not made of one cloth. One of its pillars was the popular-romantic direction which, like part of the Bund and non-Zionist young Jewish socialists, was associated with self-defense groups during the 1903–4 pogroms in the Pale. In the townships of the Pale: in Homel, Yechezkel Henkin, in Grodno, Israel Shochat, and in other places additional future members of Hashomer, were among the organizers of Jewish self-defense.[7] Here was an experience and a strategy of action which could establish legitimate continuity, even if, ideologically it was not above suspicion. But first, like every other Palestinian Jew in search of funds to finance his "pet idea," Shochat turned to Ussishkin. Only after being rebuffed did he decide to approach Ben-Zvi, himself a past member of the Poltava self-defense group, with the expectation that he "would succeed in bridging socialist theory and the Eretz Israeli reality."[8] Indeed, Ben-Zvi assumed such a Kautskian role in both Hashomer and the party.[9] But as long as the Palestinian Poalei Zion was scrutinized, supported by, and still part of the international party, this organizational dualism allowed it to avoid the embarrassment of being held responsible for Hashomer's "conquest of labor and guard duty," while the latter provided the party with the leading role which had eluded it in other areas. Ironically, it was the leader of the party's right wing, David Ben-Gurion, who was left out of Hashomer, and who criticized its apparent independence.

Thirdly, while Hapoel Hatzair continued to encourage the "conquest of labor" strategy, and Poalei Zion spoke highly of the creation of a Jewish proletariat, Bar-Giora, from its inception, as Hashomer later, was keenly interested in settlement. In this they were a product of the Galilee, as it was here that the JCA settled a very small number of workers – the only such experience in the early years of the Second *Aliya*. Though Shochat spoke of the guards' intention of becoming "some kind of Bedouin farmers," that is farmers who are also guards and who migrate from one piece of Jewish-owned land to another,[10] their settlement aims were not based solely on local experience but were more thorough and visionary. In a typical memoir, Saadia Paz related that one of their aims was "to establish a moshava in a place remote from population, in the pattern of the Cossacks, the inhabitants of the Don region. The residents of this moshava will be instructed in herding, guarding, and every kind of agricultural work."[11] The young Russian Jewish immigrants were well aware that the Cossacks, who led a semi-nomadic equestrian life, served the Russian Tsars as an elite corps of border guards and, subsequently as advance troops for the extension of Russia into the northern Caucasus, which brought the whole of the Ukraine beyond the Dnieper under the rule of the Tsars.[12] Bar-Giora, and subsequently Hashomer, contemplated, if so, the importation of yet another foreign method of settlement: the Russian-Cossack pattern. The Jewish guards' preferred settlement area was the Houran mountain in Syria, where the Baron de Rothschild had already purchased a large domain which remained cultivated by Arab farmers. Hashomer's settlement, Kfar Giladi in the Upper Galilee, was established only during the First World War. By then a number of kibbutzim, whose structure wielded influence on all workers' settlements including on Kfar Giladi, had already been founded, and the model of Cossack border villages never became an autonomous version of Israeli settlement.

In spite of these differences, Bar-Giora responded to the same conditions as the rest of the Jewish workers. Bar-Giora was not born solely as a guard organization, but rather as a self-selected elite group in which "Hebrew Labor," settlement, and guarding all occupied pride of place. It is easy to find a parallel between the evolution of Bar-Giora and the Second *Aliya* in general, although varying with the basic differences between the southern coastal zone and the Galilee. Like the first immigrants to the southern coastal plantation colonies who sought wage equalization with the Arab worker, the members of Bar-Giora worked as *charats* in the JCA's Sedjra training farm's field crops, in 1908, under conditions identical to those of Arabs. They saw this period as a preparation for settlement on the Houran.[13] With the failure of downward equalization Hapoel Hatzair turned to "conquest of labor," while Bar-Giora, began gradually focusing its attention on guard duty. Shortly after arriving at Sedjra, Bar-Giora decided that it had "to take the guarding of the Hebrew moshava and the herding of the flocks out of alien hands."[14] Indeed they became the guards of the training farm and the adjacent moshava while continuing their agricultural labor. In 1909 Hashomer even established a militarized "Legion of Labor" after its own image, but, failing to branch out, the legion disintegrated.[15] Finally, Bar-Giora abandoned the work of the *charat* to focus its energies solely on the conquest of guard duty.

In making the turn toward guarding as its primary undertaking, Bar-Giora was responding to the escalation of Palestinian hostilities after the Young Turks' Revolt in July 1908 and, specifically, to the subsequent attempts of villagers and Bedouins in a number of locations in the Lower Galilee to reverse Jewish land purchases. It was against the background of these land conflicts that Bar-Giora decided upon the establishment of a specialized guard organization – Hashomer.[16] Already in August 1908, Bar-Giora had signed a guard contract with the Board of Mescha (Kfar Tavor),[17] and subsequently with the rest of the moshavot of the Lower Galilee. The real recognition of Hashomer's services by the *Yishuv* was signaled, in October 1910, by its invitation to guard the large plantation colony of Hadera, followed by Rechovot and Rishon Letzion.

"Bar-Giora and Hashomer were not satisfied only with guarding, the main object of their activity was the dynamic of conquest" as Israel Shochat attested.[18] A parallel, and more significant, task of Hashomer was its involvement in the work of the "conquest of land." The initiator of this course was Yehoshua Hankin, the most prominent land purchasing agent of the JCA, and later of the JNF, and an early supporter of the founding of a Jewish guard organization.[19] Without military conquest of Palestine, argues Kimmerling, Jewish presence through cultivation was the key to ownership, and ownership the foundation of future sovereignty.[20] But, in fact, military might sometimes already entered into confirming presence. It was Hankin who first convinced Shochat to use Hashomer to plow a contested terrain purchased by the JCA near Mescha and in this way to ensure its transfer into Jewish hands.[21] Landownership in Palestine, if so, could be ensured only through cultivation, not so much because of the Ottoman law of *mahlul* which threatened confiscation of land left fallow for over three years (of the enforcement of which against Jews I have not been able to find a single instance), but mostly because of the opposition of evicted Palestinian cultivators.

David Rubin, of the early Second *Aliya* workers in the Galilee, saw the goal of Jewish colonization in the formation of a "healthy and strong element for future settlement" through the "development of a farmer-soldier." "If in other colonies, these are separate roles – in Eretz Israel they need to be united," he concluded, since given its "lack of civilization," the "hour of pioneering" still lay ahead.[22] Hashomer signaled this emerging identity of the settler and the soldier.

Subsequently Hankin called Hashomer into the service of the Palestine Office.[23] Hashomer now evolved a new method of Jewish presence through "conquest groups" that initially settled and prepared newly purchased land until it was handed over to its permanent Jewish owners. The best known Hashomer land conquest was in the Jezreel valley (Marj Ibn Amar), where the village of Fulla was purchased to make room for Oppenheimer's *Siedlungsgenossenschaft* in Merchavia. Additional "conquest groups" were sent to Karkur, Tel Adash, etc.[24]

In 1912, Hashomer was at the zenith of its public importance. It moved from its base in the small Lower Galilean field crop moshavot into the large plantation moshavot of the southern coastal zone. With the exception of Petach Tikva, Zichron Yaacov, and Rosh Pina, that maintained mixed guarding, Hashomer assumed the protection of all important Jewish moshavot.[25] It enjoyed the support of Hovevei Zion, which posted surety against losses which occur while Hashomer members were guarding and paid its members' life insurance, and of the Palestine Office which financed a large part of its weapons purchases.[26] But within six months it was forced out of Hadera and Rechovot and had retreated to the poor and exposed moshavot of the Galilee.[27]

A number of reasons account for Hashomer's rout before the War. First, there was the familiar argument against "Hebrew Labor": Hashomer was much more expensive than Arab guards. A guard in

Sedjra in 1908 was paid 41 francs per month, but by 1913 /14 Hashomer charged 70 francs for a guard on foot, and 120 for a mounted guard.[28] In Hadera, the sum total of guard compensation rose from 4,000 francs paid to Arabs, to 10,000 – one third of the Board's expenses – to Hashomer. In Rechovot, costs rose from 11,000 to 18,000 francs.[29] The growing expenses were frequently viewed as excessive.

But it was not costs alone that fueled the opposition. Even after the termination of the contracts with Hashomer, the moshavot did not return to the employment of Arab guards but chose to engage relatively expensive Jewish guards not associated with Hashomer. The opposition to Hashomer towards the end of our period was not only of an economic character but came to assume a political nature. Well-armed and organized Jewish guards were seen as a potential class enemy by the planters. Vinegrowers from Rishon Letzion, for example, opposed the employment of Hashomer in fear that it would "strengthen the foreign element in the moshava," and "expel us from our vineyards, and in a year or two from the moshava."[30] And Hashomer's conspiratorial character was an added source of anxiety for the planters.

A third, and equally weighty cause of opposition was the dissatisfaction with the central role that devolved on Hashomer, in consequence of its guard duty, in shaping Jewish–Palestinian relations. There is a certain irony in this reproach as the new pattern of relations imposed by Hashomer was shot through with contradictory intentions. This topic merits close analysis.

So far, the moshavot, with the exception of the encounter in the various markets, were content to keep apart from the surrounding Arab environment. Arab guards, coming from the outside into the Jewish moshava, necessarily carried out an important role in mediating between the two societies. Hashomer's own *raison d'être* was the need to break the moshava's dependence on the Bedouin, Circassian, Maghrebian, or Turkoman guards so as, in its words, "to boost the respect of Jews in the neighbors' eyes."[31] For that aim, "it was necessary to demonstrate strength."[32] The potentially belligerent character of this enterprise must have been obvious to Bar-Giora and Hashomer members when they accepted Ben-Zvi's choice of slogan for their organizations: "in blood and fire Judea fell; in blood and fire shall Judea rise."[33]

At the same time, to carry out their role effectively, Hashomer members learned, nay, had to learn, the methods of the Arab guards. Even more, they had to understand Arabs, that is to comprehend their language, manners, sense of honor, and morality. In imitation of the Palestinian village, Hashomer established hospitality rooms (*madfia*), to entertain passers-by. Contemporary photographs invariably show Hashomer members in Arab clothing and *kafia*. Not only did they imitate the Bedouin outwardly, Hashomer also derived its idea of heroism from the Bedouin and the Circassian. In the Second *Aliya*, to be an upright Jew meant to be like a mounted Bedouin! In view of this, Hapoel Hatzair accused members of Hashomer of assimilation into the Palestinian environment.[34] But as Mania Shochat remarked: "experience taught them that if courage is required in the moment of a clash, much more important is the daily contact, which alone can create an atmosphere of good relations and security in the vicinity."[35] Such close contact ensured a relatively free flow of information on thieves and potential assaults.

There was one Arab custom, the blood feud, that made both sides especially cautious, and paradoxically cut down the number of casualties. The killing of a Palestinian villager, a Bedouin etc. demanded, according to this code, vengeance through the killing of a person from the assailer's kin group and, by extension, if the act was committed by a Jew then of anyone from his moshava. Both sides was equally circumspect, and Hashomer, which on rare occasions carried out retaliatory actions (and even decided, on two occasions, to revenge the death of its members by locating and killing the murderer himself and not one of his kin) never, in fact, carried out a blood revenge.[36]

Though Hashomer tried to walk a thin line in asserting Jewish presence and demonstrating strength, while avoiding provocation of local Palestinian strongmen, it was not very effective in doing so. Planters, and even Hashomer supporters, maintained that its members behaved aggressively and rashly in using firearms, especially in the Merchavia incident of May 1911, and the Rechovot episode of July/August 1913. In the latter case for example, Hashomer members were accused of endangering lives "for the sake of a bunch of grapes."[37] Why was Hashomer unable to strike the balance it sought?

The *Hagana Book*'s editors argue that the reason for this criticism was the general apprehension of the planters that armed Jews as such were the source of provocation.[38] This argument might have been plausible in 1908/9, but hardly in 1912/13, when Hashomer had already been invited into most moshavot. Ro'i takes us one step closer to the more concrete causes of these objections by his apt remark that the allegations against Hashomer were directed "not just at the hasty use of arms, but at the general opposition of Hashomer towards Arabs." This reproach "was part and parcel of the criticism aimed at the people of the Second *Aliya* and the conquerors of labor."[39] The conflict in Rechovot exploded when the planters refused to accept the separate demands of Hashomer and the Jewish workers to fire all Palestinian workers who came from Zarnuga, the village of the murderers of one of the Jewish guards, on pain of

Hashomer leaving the moshava.[40] Eisenberg, the director of Agudat Netaim, was one of the outspoken opponents of Hashomer in Rechovot.[41] There are other examples of such conflicts. The events that led up to the voluntary withdrawal of Hashomer from Hadera had to do with its refusal to acquiesce in the reintroduction of mixed guards. In Rishon Letzion, Hashomer demanded the fining and firing of all Palestinian workers who snatched the gun of one of its guards; the Board decided only to warn the workers and to pay them damages for loss of workdays and bodily harm sustained during the clash.[42] Ultimately, even if Hashomer had adopted a less contentious attitude toward the Bedouins and the outside Arab environment, it could not have accepted the presence of the Palestinian worker or co-guard in the moshava. It was not a professional guard organization, but was established to obtain and to ensure exclusive Jewish access to land and labor markets. Hashomer threw in its support, like the Second *Aliya*'s agricultural workers, for a colonization method based on exclusive Jewish employment.

Hashomer had its own reasons for seeking such exclusivity. There are many indications that the presence of Arabs in the moshava was a major source of Hashomer's unsuccessful guarding experiences. An early experimental employment in Zichron Yaacov of a few Jews mixed with Arab guards, made the latter apprehensive of competition and ended in the beating of the guard Zeid and the firing of the Jewish guards by the planters, disquieted by increased violence. The principled conclusion learned by future members of Hashomer from this and similar experiences of "mixed guarding" was that, "one should not guard together with Arab guards."[43] The same, noted by Itzhak Tabenkin, was true for mixed labor forces in general: "the bonds between the Arab guard and the Arab worker were much stronger than between the Jewish worker and the Arab worker. Moshavot which harbored Jewish guards and Arab labor were always liable to failures."[44] Consequently, Jewish guards considered the Palestinian agricultural workers a "fifth column" which was likely to reveal to outsiders the weak spots of the moshava's security,[45] and so instituted harsh measures to restrict their freedom of movement. In Rechovot and Hadera a curfew was instituted and Arab workers sleeping in the cowsheds were instructed to lock the gates behind them; in Metulla, the workers were forbidden to sleep on the trashing floor and were forcibly removed to adjacent huts.[46] Generally, it seems that Hashomer treated Palestinian workers harshly. Moshava Boards, for example, found it necessary to demand of Hashomer that Arabs, and the reference is obviously to workers, only be struck in self-defense.[47]

The adverse relations between Hashomer and Arab guards and workers found its counterpart in the Hashomer's desire to expand the number of Jewish workers in the moshava. Though Hashomer was resented by Jewish workers for its elitism and higher wages,[48] its functioning was contingent on the sustained backing of the agricultural workers of the Second *Aliya*. Between 1907 and 1920, Hashomer had no more than one hundred full members, reaching its peak at any given time of forty in May 1914. In the same period, it employed about 300 Jewish guards with the status of hired employees. During the harvest seasons the number of guards hired from among the workers and the Hashomer members about equalled one another.[49] But the support of the Jewish workers extended to other areas as well. The Jewish *charats* and workers, who were employed by the moshava at the behest of Hashomer served as its "reserve army": guardsmen taken ill were replaced by workers and during assaults the workers reinforced the guards.[50] Conversely, when Hashomer left a moshava, the number of Jewish workers dropped drastically.[51] In fact, the connection between "conquest of guarding" and "conquest of labor" was too close for the planters' comfort, who ultimately preferred to replace Hashomer with independent professional Jewish guards.

It was among the children of the planters – especially in Zichron Yaacov, the moshava which most exclusively employed Arab workers – that a self-conscious, potentially ideological opposition emerged to the Second *Aliya*. This had the makings of a plantation owners' ideology, and its major articulator was Aharon Aaronsohn.

Aaronsohn, though he never concluded his higher education, was a world-renowned botanist, the discoverer of wild-wheat – ancestor of all cultivated wheat. During a tour of the US in 1909, he was offered the famed Professor Hilgard's chair in agronomy at the University of California, Berkeley. But when his fundraising for an experimental station in Atlit, near Hadera, proved successful, he chose to return there.[52] During his tour he became close to Louis Brandeis, Felix Frankfurter, and other leaders of American Zionism, who were to clash after the war with Weizmann and the labor movement in their opposition to extensive public subsidies to Jewish settlement. Aaronsohn combined a paternalistic attitude to Arab society, justifying the employment of lower-paid Arab men, women, and children wherever possible, with the demand to utilize their ecologically sound traditional knowledge in agriculture. In Aaronsohn's view, the penetration of Jews into agricultural work would have to be the gradual result of technological and economic development, not of a political movement. He regarded "conquest of labor" harshly and condemned the "fanaticism, and lack of humanism and Jewishness, in the separatism of our workers" that, in his view, accompanied it.[53]

While Aharon Aaronsohn was the living spirit behind the self-articulation of the younger generation of the planter class, his brother Alexander, with Avshalom Feinberg from Hadera, in October 1913 organized the "Gideonites," a body of the native-born. Its members advocated the extension of voting rights in the moshava to all permanent male residents, and sought a variety of outlets for their activity, the most important being the supervision of the Arab guards of Zichron Yaacov, and the dispatching of a conquest group of Shuny, south of Zichron Yaacov – which, however, slowly disintegrated. Between the Second *Aliya* workers and the "Gideonites" there was no love lost: they quarreled and clashed on various occasions.[54]

This antagonism assumed more dramatic consequences during the war, when the Aaronsohn siblings recruited a spy organization named Nili from amongst the Gideonites and others, to support the British efforts to conquer Palestine from the Ottomans, who in the meantime were exploiting the hostilities to undermine Jewish settlement in Palestine. Though Nili's expectations of being armed by the British and participating in the conquest itself came to naught, Aharon Aaronsohn gained the confidence of General Allenby, the military conqueror of Palestine. Hashomer members, whose leaders were exiled and activities proscribed, were scattered and with limited influence until 1916. Being fearful of Ottoman retaliation, Hashomer, like the rest of the *Yishuv*, adopted a loyalist position. In spite of some openings from both directions, and a few individual crossovers, the two organizations treated one another with hostility, and jockeyed for increased influence in the *Yishuv* during the war.

Two different conceptions of military might and military operation collided here. Nili members expected to gain power and influence British policy by military audacity and by diplomatic activity alone; Hashomer foresaw the growth of Jewish influence in Palestine as a derivative of its socio-economic strengthening. Nili, lacking a strong public hinterland, put its store by a small activist group; Hashomer aspired, by and large, to the establishment of a defense force through the overlapping of guarding and laboring. Nili was more adventurous; Hashomer more cautious. Though at this stage the differences between the labor movement and the propertied groups, I listed, were embryonic, they were far from accidental and would come to full development in the struggle against the British Mandate in the 1940s, between the labor movement's Hagana on the one hand, and the Revisionists' Ezel and Stern's independent Lechi, on the other hand.

As Poalei Zion shed its Borochovism, and reconstituted itself as the core of the broader-based Achdut Haavoda Party, the semi-autonomy of

Hashomer lost its justification[55] and, in spite of the tepid opposition of some of Hashomer's veteran leaders, it was disbanded and absorbed in 1920 into the defense force of the Histadrut: the Hagana.[56] Subsequently, the military might of the labor movement (such as the Jewish Brigade and the Palmach), following the tradition laid down by Hashomer, was usually affiliated with the left wing of the movement. One might only speculate that the nationalism, inherent in the military orientation, put a damper both on the socialism of the organizations from which the military forces were recruited and ultimately on attempts at the full autonomy of the military wing. In the identity of settler-laborer and soldier, the former function always remained predominant. And the settlers, especially members of kibbutzim, always provided the paramilitary forces of the *Yishuv* with a disproportionate portion of its commanders and fighters.

Chapter Seven

The unintended means: cooperative settlement, 1910–1914

Given the present condition of the farmers and workers, there is no possibility whatsoever for the conquest of labor . . . but to our joy this is no tragedy, since now . . . starts the era of the Hebrew workers' self liberation.

Yaacov Rabinovitch, Presentation to the Fourth Congress of the Federation of the Agricultural Workers of Judea, 1913

No individual initiative of the rugged personality or "pioneer" type that opened up vast tracts of America, Australia, New Zealand and other countries . . . came into play here, but the concentrated force of a collective of settlers, in whose front rank stood the so-called *haluzim* (or worker-settlers, lit. pioneers). By creating an original form of mutal aid and self-employment suited to the immigrants and the country's condition at the time, excluding hired employment of any kind – which would have necessarily involved the exploitation of cheap non-Jewish labor – this force was able to create the conditions for a grandiose Jewish colonization effort. In these circumstances, the choice of the collective, the commune, the cooperative, was a necessary expression of the situation and the only way out, representing a synthesis of national and social aspirations and the claims of immigration and settlement such as they were then . . .

Walter Preuss, *Cooperation in Israel and the World*, 1967

The decisive organizational innovation which provided the infrastructure of effective Jewish colonization, that is, the method of Israeli state formation, and set the parameters of the core of the Israeli nation, was the kibbutz. Taking account of the kibbutz's importance, it is remarkable therefore that cooperative settlement never was envisioned by the workers' political parties and was even opposed by some of their leaders; in short, it was an unintended means and consequence of Jewish colonization.

Collective settlement resulted from the initially asymmetrical "alliance" forged between the organized Eastern European agricultural workers of the Second *Aliya* and the World Zionist Organization. The kibbutz, I will argue, was only in part, maybe only in small part, the child of the inchoate legacy the workers carried of Russian forms of cooperation, traditional and modern, and their penchant for cooperative forms of life. Theirs were only vague stirrings that required shaping by programs of agrarian reform, cooperation, and nationalist colonization promoted by the leadership of the WZO. Though both the workers and the WZO had reasons to seek out one another, close cooperation between them emerged only after a stormy period of accommodation and mutual transformation, in which each side had to abandon its illusions concerning the ethnic plantation type settlement.

In the first section of this chapter I will examine the colonization policy of the WZO and its Palestine Office, especially those features that favored cooperative settlement and an alliance with the agricultural workers. Then I will review the workers' initial opposition to the WZO and to settlement. In the second section, I will explore the circumstances under which Degania, the first kibbutz, came into being, and the influences that were fused in its making. In the final section, I will analyze the reasons for the predominance of the kibbutz in Jewish colonization in Palestine and in Israeli state formation.

The "pure settlement methodology" of the World Zionist Organization

The conviction that a significant portion of the Jewish population in Palestine had to be rural was already a central element of the program of Hovevei Zion, and later an article of consensus in the WZO. For Hovevei Zion the productivization drive was the cultural legacy of Jewish Enlightenment, and its agricultural bent an article of faith. The WZO initially also viewed agriculture not as a means for an aim, but as the aim itself,[1] since under Herzl's leadership its means was diplomatic: the gaining of a "charter" from the Ottoman Sultan, which would recognize the right of Jews to a home in Palestine. Upon its receipt, Herzl envisioned mostly a gigantic process of organization and transportation of the Jewish masses to their new location. Herzl not only failed to develop a "settlement theory" of active colonization but also objected to what he derogatorily described as the *Kleinkolonisation* of Hovevei Zion.

In 1903 Herzl received his only offer of a charter – one issued by His Britannic Majesty's government in *lieu* of the Sultan, and referring to the fertile upper plateau of Kenya, then a target of British colonization, instead of Palestine. This split the WZO between the Palestine-centrists, who represented the masses of the movement, and the territorialists. The struggle around the so-called "Uganda proposal" and the blow delivered to Herzl's diplomatic Zionism opened the road for "practical Zionism," that is, the active pursuit of land purchase and agricultural settlement in Palestine, and the rising influence of its adherents from both Eastern Europe and Germany in the WZO. The gradual realignment that took place in the WZO did not, however, simply imply a return to Hovevei Zion's *Kleinkolonisation* or to Rothschild's plantation-based settlement. Rather, between 1903 and 1909, borrowing a colonization method from central Europe, the WZO slowly and hesitantly evolved the elements of what I would like to call a rudimentary "pure settlement theory." Under the aegis of the WZO, rural settlement gradually became transformed from an ideal goal into the *sine qua non* condition for the success of the colonization project itself, and the WZO became the major Jewish colonizing society.

In general, I wish to point out that the formative forces of Zionism originated not only in the ideological influences carried by the immigrants from the Pale of Settlement but, perhaps even more importantly, in the West, whether from the Baron Edmund de Rothschild or the WZO, that financed the Zionist project. It seems to me necessary, therefore, to round out our understanding of the shaping of Israeli state formation by exploring this source of material and cultural influence.

The German and Austrian background

When, in response to economic displacement and waves of pogroms, 2.75 million Eastern European Jews began their migration to the New World between 1881 and 1914, Germany served as their temporary transfer station, and the German ports of Hamburg and Bremen as their gateways. For example, in the decade 1905–14 the number of East European Jews who passed through Germany is estimated at 700,000. The more assimilated and prosperous German Jewry was therefore the first to be affected by the tragedy of Eastern European Jewry. German Jews mobilized to assist their less fortunate co-religionists, but with the aim of redirecting them to yet another location, mostly in the US. German Jews were fearful "that the mass presence of destitute Jewish refugees would threaten the fragile fabric of local Jewish integration," and the coincidence of the mass migrations with the outset of organized political anti-Semitism in Germany and Austro-Hungary lent considerable force to their anxieties. In a true chain of historical paradoxes, Eastern European Jews who, once in Palestine, became Europeans and Westerners by virtue of their dependence on a European standard of living, were put down as Easterners by their Western European Jewish brethren, who, for their part, were not accepted by Western Europeans as

Westerners. The relief operation, then, served to emphasize and magnify the differences between the *West* and *Ostjuden*, and bore the marks of a patronizing Western attitude.[2]

Though German Zionists, in general, portrayed *Ostjuden* in more positive light than non-nationalist German Jews, they were also animated by concerns and fears similar to other German Jews. The reason was that the overwhelming majority of German Zionists neither planned to leave Germany nor expected Zionism to change their lives.[3] In fact, both leaders of Eastern European Hovevei Zion, such as Pinsker, and of German Zionism, typically Nordau, viewed Western Jews only as the economic and cultural benefactors and the leaders and organizers of the emigration of the "surplus population" of *Ostjuden*.[4]

Under the double impact of the stream of Eastern European immigration and rising anti-Semitism, the Zionistische Vereinigung für Deutschland (ZVfD – German Zionist Association), though always a tiny group, became the largest Western branch of the Zionist movement. In consequence, before the First World War, "Western Zionism was articulated essentially within the German-speaking cultural world," the offices of the WZO were located on Austrian and German soil between 1905 and 1920, and its central publication *Die Welt* was published in German. In short, "to a great extent the leadership of the German and the World Zionist Organization was identical."[5]

The formative impact of the German, and to a lesser extent, the Austrian, Zionist leadership on the practices of Israeli state and nation formation before the First World War, therefore, cannot be ignored.[6] These individuals, Bodenheimer, Warburg, Ruppin, Oppenheimer, Böhm, etc., and of course Herzl, were influenced by the historical conditions of Germany and Austro-Hungary, which served, therefore, as the context for the development of the foundations of Zionist "settlement theory" in the first decade of this century.

Two major facets of German life were central in this respect: the contemporary crisis of German agriculture, and the age-long ethnic conflict between the German-speaking countries and the Slavic peoples, especially Poles and Czechs (the latter was felt equally in Austro-Hungary).

The last quarter of the nineteenth century saw the crisis of European agriculture which was felt most profoundly in Germany. The extension of the area under cultivation in the US and in Russia, and the development of cheap international transportation exerted downward pressure on prices, and German agriculture, and especially its grain producers, were dealt a severe blow. Germany turned from a grain exporting into a grain importing country and the economic gap between its rapidly expanding industrial sector and more slowly modernizing agriculture broadened.[7] Agricultural crisis also exacerbated the social and regional imbalance in Germany, since grain for export was grown mostly on the large Junker estates east of the Elbe.[8] Small farmers and agricultural workers, however, were also adversely affected. One significant consequence of the decline of rural incomes relative to industrial and urban incomes was accelerated *Landflucht*: the flight of agricultural workers from the Prussian estates first abroad and later to the industrial cities. Their place was taken over, further augmenting the *Landflucht*, by Eastern European, mostly Polish, workers, especially in the province of Poznan (Posen) that accrued to Prussia as a result of Poland's partitions.

A significant part of German political life was taken up by the debate over the proper responses to the agricultural crisis. Curiously, the Social Democratic Party remained on the margins of this controversy. Even Kautsky's *Agrarian Question*, published in 1899, equivocated on the issue, and, hemmed in by Marxist orthodoxy, could not develop a viable agrarian policy. The intellectual responses to the crisis, therefore, came from the extensive liberal socialist circles that opposed both capitalist encroachment and socialist class struggle. Liberal socialists sought not piecemeal reforms, but evolved complete, if somewhat simplistic programs derived from their premises. One of their major intellectual inspirations was Henry George's *Progress and Poverty* of 1879. Henry George's major thesis was that the expansion of agriculture and urbanization benefits mostly idle landowners who receive excessive land rent and monopolize land. By taxing the rent away, argued Henry George, governments could generate immense revenues and do away with other taxes.[9]

The mass appeal of Henry George's single remedy was enormous, and it was taken up in 1888 in Germany by the Deutsche Bund für Bodenbesitzreform. Its major theorist was Michael Flürscheim,[10] who advocated radical measures such as the nationalization of land and compensation of its owners, the establishment of colonies on collectively owned land, etc. Flürscheim also tried to find support for his ideas of land reform and subsequently of monetary reform in the US and Australia, while other members of the organization made such attempts in Africa and Mexico.[11] In 1898, Adolf Damaschke established the more moderate Bund der Deutschen Bodenreformer, which dispensed with the aim of nationalization.[12] In Austria in 1890, Theodor Hertzka, a journalist at the *Neue Freie Presse*, published a "political romance" entitled *Freiland* in which he detailed an imaginary colonization project in Masailand in Kenya. In Freeland, cultivation and production would be conducted under the auspices of "self governing associations," and "every inhabitant of Freeland [would have] an equal and inalienable claim upon the whole of the land, and upon the means of production accumulated by the community."[13] Another response to capitalist intrusion and the agrarian crisis was the cooperative movement, created in Germany by Friedrich Wilhelm Raiffeisen and Hermann Schulze-Delitzsch, aiming at the comprehensive reorganization of social life through the establishment of various forms of cooperative bodies, such as consumer, producer, marketing cooperatives, etc. The movement's most tangible result was the spread of cooperative credit societies.[14]

One of the prominent liberal socialist figures was Franz Oppenheimer, a member of the Berlin *Freiland* organization, a follower of Henry George, a close friend of Damaschke but a critic of his moderation of George's views, and a supporter of the cooperative movement.[15] Oppenheimer attempted in his main thesis *Die Siedlungsgenossenschaft* (The Settlement Cooperative) from 1896, to synthesize land reforms with the cooperative movement.[16] A physician turned sociology professor, Oppenheimer's formative experiences occurred while working as a physician in a remote Eastern Prussian province from 1886 to 1896. Facing the poverty and ill health of many of his clients and under the influence of the views of Henry George and the German land reformers Flürscheim and Damaschke, he came to recognize the Junker class and the monopoly of its ownership of land as the cause of all "social ills."[17] In his analysis the "pure economy" of competition was corrupted by the "political economy" of monopolization. Oppenheimer worked out the "cure" – a theory of public ownership of land and cooperative settlement.

One line of influence on Zionist colonization, as has been recognized by such experts of the Israeli agricultural system as Alfred Bonné and Efraim Orni, led from Henry George, via Flürscheim and Damaschke of the German land reform movement, and the Austrian Hertzka, to Herzl, Bodenheimer, and Franz Oppenheimer.[18] Many of the founders and leaders of the WZO and the German and Austrian Zionist Associations were familiar with and influenced by these reformers. In *The Jewish State* Theodor Herzl worked out a settlement program for Palestine, drawing from hearsay on the work of Hertzka, his colleague at the journal. Only in a subsequent diary entry did he mention Henry George.[19] Bodenheimer corresponded with Flürscheim, but as a self-proclaimed bourgeois, he had the most mixed reactions to ideas of land nationalization.[20] Oppenheimer's influence on the Zionist movement was tremendous, and in 1903 Herzl, on the floor of the Sixth Congress, characterized his affiliation as one of the greatest conquests of Zionism.[21] Though Oppenheimer's program had been intended originally for eastern Germany, he offered it to Herzl and the WZO as a model for overseas colonization.

While the land reformers generated only lukewarm support in

Germany, the ruling circles of the Prussian state, after complex accommodations typical to the hybrid character of the regime, were able to put many of their own ideas into practice. In 1879, the Junkers received tariff protection for their products, with significant consequences for German history far beyond the scope of this study. More relevant for our purposes, in September 1885 the influential National-Liberal Party anxious at the influx of Polish workers into the Junkers' estates, demanded the "internal colonization" (*innere Kolonisation*) of the region by parcelling out large estates to small German peasants.[22] But Bismarck, who had already been interested in resuming the tradition of German colonization in the East, used their outcry to eliminate only the specter of "denationalization," which haunted many of Germany's leading intellectuals, among them the young Max Weber.[23] When at an auspicious moment in 1886, Bismarck had a resolution passed in the Prussian *Landtag* to set up a Colonization Commission (*Ansiedlungskommission*), with the purpose of buying up large estates, first Polish and later also German, and instituting on them a process of "internal colonization," its aim was not to reform land tenure but to alter demography, i.e. to ensure German majority and control of the Ostmark (the Eastern Marches).[24]

The Prussian government's *Ansiedlungskommission* in the Ostmark was focused on the Poznan and West Prussian provinces between 1886 and 1914. Polish provinces had been annexed to Prussia following the partitions of Poland at the end of the eighteenth century and incorporated into it in 1815. In these provinces, the aim of the 1886 Colonization Law of the Prussian Diet was to achieve "by means of an active, institutionalized policy . . . a German population majority by encouraging internal migration."[25]

The German Colonization Commission was a many-sided body involved in purchasing, leasing, developing, and parcelling land, and providing credit and guidance to its farmers. The Colonization Commission sought to buy up large Polish-owned estates, subdivide them and set up new villages for German farmers and laborers. Two types of colonies were set up. The first was a small farmer's colony, in which the average farm held 10–15 hectares. "The main principle underlying the choice of this size was that it would provide for the subsistence of one family without the help of hired labor. This was intended to prevent the employment of Polish labor in areas settled by Germans."[26] The second was a working people's colony, in which the small plots, intended only for growing vegetables, ranged from 0.5 to 1.5 hectares, as the inhabitants were to be employed in urban centers. Though the Commission was authorized to sell the land to German buyers, by and large it preferred to lease it to them on a long-term basis, charging rent below the market value and simultaneously provided the infrastructure, such as roads, irrigation, and public services.

The record of the colonization effort seemed at the time impressive, as far as the German side was concerned. One-tenth of the lands in the Poznan province were bought up, and hundreds of new villages were established, but the 16,000 families settled in the region failed to change the demographic balance of the Ostmark. One of the reasons was the energetic Polish opposition, which in 1890–1, during the more liberal Caprivi chancellorship, which ironically allowed Poles to participate in peasant colonization on parcelled estates, found an effective counter-measure in the institution of the Polish Land Bank (Bank Ziemski).[27] The Bank Ziemski adopted in part the method of the German Colonization Commission by buying up indebted estates, from both German and Polish owners, and selling them in small holdings to Polish farmers. But even more powerful than the Polish response in its negative impact on German colonization was the continuous *Landflucht* of peasants from the east to more developed western areas in Germany or overseas. By the outbreak of the First World War, the Colonization Commission failed to reach its demographic aims, and had, at most, compensated for the German exodus.[28]

The Austro-Hungarian Empire suffered from similar types of national conflicts between the manifold ethnic groups in its eastern regions, but it toyed with solutions that were not relevant at the time to Zionist colonization designs. Nevertheless, the helplessness of the Habsburgs in face of territorially based ethnic strife was not lost on Adolf Böhm, a leader of the Austrian Zionist Association. Shlomo Kaplansky and Nathan Gross, the earliest supporters of Oppenheimer's "settlement cooperative" from within Zionist workers' parties, also were members of the Austrian branch of Poalei Zion. While historians of the Jewish labor movement have pointed to the critical lobbying efforts of Poalei Zion on behalf of Oppenheimer's plan in the WZO, and the more meticulous historians singled out the Austrian wing of the party as its main champion, it is more correct to point to the significance of the support of Austrian (and German) Zionists of whatever social persuasion.[29] It was the central European, mostly the Austro-Hungarian, experience that Böhm, Gross, and Kaplansky invoked to justify their support for pure, i.e. demographic, settlement. This, they believed, could be achieved only by organizations such as Oppenheimer proposed. In 1907 Gross told the Eighth Zionist Congress, "every one hundred Jewish families attract six thousand Arabs; if things continue thus, we shall fall victim to the same fate as the Germans in certain Slavic lands."[30] Kaplansky was even more emphatic in asking:

do we have to point to Eastern Galicia where the Polish landowners are the ruling class, nevertheless there is no doubt that the future of the country belongs to those cultivating the land – the Ukrainians? Did Bohemia become a German country solely by virtue of its industrialists being German, while the workers are Czech?[31]

All three dwelt on the lessons connected with the rolling back of Austrian (and in one instance Polish) political power in regions where only a landowning or ruling class had been settled.

A *second* line of influence on Zionist colonization led from the national conflict that beset the Habsburg Empire and Germany east of the Elbe via the "internal colonization" favored by the Junkers to Warburg, Ruppin, Böhm, Kaplansky, and Gross. Oppenheimer shared the fears of the loss of Western Prussia, and saw in state intervention and land purchase a positive process, though one that did not go far enough.[32] The experience of Prussian internal colonization and the Polish counter-colonization were, as pointed out by Shalom Reichman and Shlomo Hasson in a pathbreaking study, an even more important and self-consciously chosen model for Otto Warburg and Arthur Ruppin.[33]

In sum, the WZO's "pure settlement theory" drew on liberal socialist, national liberal, and conservative attempts to deal with the "agrarian problem" of Germany and the experience of national conflict between the German-speaking and Slavic peoples on the historical frontiers of German expansion. Its basic principles were that the political questions would find their solution once most of the land in Palestine was in Jewish hands, most of the population was Jewish, the Jews dominated the economy, especially agriculture, and the Jewish residents demanded autonomy. Demography and agricultural work were interconnected in assuring control of land. These were the operative conclusions of Arthur Ruppin's 1907 plan, upon the submission of which he was appointed to head the Palestine Office, in 1908.[34]

The evolution of the WZO's "pure settlement methodology"

While the significance of agriculture and the formation of a class of agricultural cultivators as the tools of colonization came to occupy the status of a fundamental principle in the WZO's "pure settlement theory," the methodology of their implementation still suffered from a major contradiction in regard to its demographic imperative. Subsequent to the transfer of the First *Aliya* moshavot by Rothschild to the JCA, the concomitant abandonment of philanthropy in favor of capitalist coloniz-ation was accepted by all concerned, including the Jewish workers. Capitalist colonization, as Warburg's Palestine Department recognized only too well, required wealthy colonists. But the WZO expected to settle mostly the *Ostjuden* in Palestine amongst whom those willing "to make *aliya*" were mostly the poor. The latter could not make a living without some form of assistance, hopefully only temporary. To assist settlers without means, the WZO had to adopt a new philanthropic approach, though one legitimated on national grounds. Under these conditions, as Warburg, for example, already recognized in 1909, the WZO had to transform the agricultural workers into settlers. Little attention was paid to the fact that the workers themselves were intent at the time on the "conquest of labor" in the moshavot. Finding a correct solution to their plight, Warburg wrote, would mobilize support for the JNF among the Jewish working masses in Europe and the US, and increase the immigration of Eastern European Jewish youth to Palestine.[35] Zionism, then, was a colonization movement which simultaneously had to secure land for its settlers and settlers for its land.

The WZO evolved its "pure settlement method" hesitantly and discontinuously. We may divide the part of this process which took place before the First World War, usually in the form of establishing a string of colonizing bodies with ever differentiated functions, roughly into three, partially overlapping, sequences.

The *first sequence* saw the decision of the First Zionist Congress of 1897 to set up, in principle, a Jewish National Fund for the purpose of purchasing land. The fund came into existence in 1901 at the Fifth Congress. Its unique aim, as suggested by Professor Hermann Schapira, was the national ownership of land. Article 3 of its Memorandum of Association set clear limits on the allocation of land once acquired by stating that the object of the JNF was

to let any of the land or other immovable property of the Association to any Jews upon any terms: provided that no lessee shall be invested with the right of subletting or assigning (whether by way of sale, transfer, mortgage or charge) any interest in the soil of the prescribed region . . .[36]

These legal principles had far-reaching implications. Not only did they exclude non-Jews from control of land once acquired by the JNF, but at one fell swoop abolished private ownership of land and replaced it by hereditary land leasing. Land purchased by the JNF could not be resold, as it was held in trusteeship for the whole nation.[37] Nor could it be sublet in order to ensure that the usufruct would belong to the actual cultivator.[38]

We know that when Schapira first proposed the idea of a National Fund for land purchase to the Kattowitz Congress of Hovevei Zion in 1884, it did not contain the clause of national ownership, and other contemporaneous programs for the establishment of a national fund from Russia or Palestine did not envision it either.[39] In other words, nationalization of land was not inherent in Zionism; though Schapira rooted it in Biblical tradition, I tend to find its causes in circumstances that changed between 1884 and 1901. Significantly, the European land reform movement which advocated ideas so strikingly similar in some of their aspects to Schapira's evolved only in this interim period,[40] and Bodenheimer, in introducing Schapira's proposals at the First Zionist Congress at Basel, in 1897, specifically pointed to Flürscheim's and Hertzka's influence on them.[41] Soon after the Congress, Flürscheim himself published a call in the WZO's periodical for public land ownership in the New Zion.[42]

The experience of German–Slav ethnic conflict in central Europe also was seen as justifying the unique character of the JNF. Adolf Böhm, a Viennese practical Zionist and a member of the JNF's board, connected the nationalization of land by the JNF with the intention to combat "the abuses that arise out of private landownership." The abuses he cited were the displacement of the small peasantry by large estates, the *Landflucht* of badly paid laborers to the towns, and their replacement with foreign workers who leave their national mark on the land. The examples of this development were Prussia, Hungary, and Sicily, but he also cited the Czech, Polish East Galician, and Italian Dalmatia regions of the Habsburg Empire which gradually became Czechified, Ruthenified, and Slavified.[43]

Inalienable Jewish ownership of land purchased by the JNF, in sum, was inspired by solutions of governments and social reformers to the agrarian crisis and frontier conflicts in central Europe in which social and national questions were superimposed.

It has to be emphasized that only few in the WZO understood from the outset the full potentials of the JNF's charter, and furthermore that the WZO's majority did not want to eliminate private purchase of land by Jews in Palestine, nor could it even if it so desired. Even so, the nationalization of land by the JNF did not have general approval. Lilienblum, of Hovevei Zion, argued that the proscription of land sale by the JNF would slow down the circulation of its working capital, as it could not take advantage of the speculative rise of land prices.[44] But while public ownership created unique problems in the use of the JNF's lands, Ottoman law made traditional methods of colonial agricultural production impossible. Since corporations were not recognized as *personae iuris*, and therefore as legal owners of landed property, the WZO could not establish an effective bank for the purpose of extending agricultural credit to private landowners and accept land as collateral. Restriction of credit affected mostly private landowners, making public control of land even more sensible. This was the lesson learned by an uneasy JNF at the beginning of its operations.

When the JNF was authorized by the Sixth Congress to begin land purchase, it failed to produce viable results. A plot of 6,500 dunams, purchased in Daleika and Um Djunni (on the left and right banks of the Jordan respectively, at its outflow from Lake Tiberias), was leased, in obvious violation of the JNF's Memorandum of Association, to local Arab farmers. Under the criticism of the Eastern European leaders, the first annual meeting of the JNF's directorate decided in May 1907 not to use the authorization received to purchase land but, in its stead, to assist private and other public bodies in buying land and cultivating it.[45]

The problem faced by the JNF was that while land purchase was a relatively sound investment, land cultivation was not. Given the infeasibility of extending agricultural credit to private buyers, the dangers cited for leaving land fallow,[46] and constitutional restriction on land sale, the Zionist movement needed to supplant its land purchasing policy with a settlement method to make possible the land's agricultural exploitation. During the first four years of its activities, sums up Margalit Shilo, the JNF had not created any theoretical approaches to or practical methods of settlement.[47] By vacating the center stage, this task devolved on the WZO's plenum and the Palestine Office, both of which offered their respective, though in part overlapping, solutions, under the influence of the same forces we examined.

In a *second sequence*, a Palestine Commission of three members, Otto Warburg, Selig Soskin, and Franz Oppenheimer, was set up in 1903 to examine the possibilities of practical work in Palestine. In April 1904 the Greater Actions Committee of the WZO called for the foundation of the Oppenheimerian "settlement-cooperative," and the Eighth Congress resolved to found it on land belonging to the JNF.[48] Only the decision of the Ninth Congress of 1909 to set up a special fund, the Erez Israel Siedlungsgesellschaft, to carry out Franz Oppenheimer's "settlement-cooperative" plan, made the realization of this goal finally possible.

Oppenheimer's colonization project envisioned three stages. In the first, there would be an agricultural training farm under the management of an agronomist, who was to consult an advisory board chosen by the workers. The workers would cultivate the land collectively and were to be remunerated individually by wages and share in the profit relative to their effort. When the farm became profitable and began repaying the loans to its founding society, the manager would be removed and the second stage commence. The farm then would become a cooperative society, run by its members or by a manager they appointed. At a third stage the cooperative would open its doors to non-agricultural members.

The "settlement-cooperative" was to be built on publicly owned land, given to the members in life-time hereditary lease. It would be left to the workers to decide whether they wished to convert the estate into small separate holdings (and become a Producers' Cooperative Society) or cultivate the main portion collectively and allocate the members only smallholdings near their home (and become a "real" Workmen's Productive Cooperative Society). Additional areas for cooperation might include housing, consumer, and credit cooperatives.[49]

The *third sequence* comprised the resolution of the Eighth Congress in 1907 to turn the Palestine Commission into the Palästina-Ressort: a full-fledged department of the WZO for Palestinian affairs, under Otto Warburg, and the subsequent opening of a Palästina-Amt (Palestine Office) in Jaffa, under Arthur Ruppin. Upon his appointment, Ruppin demanded the simultaneous setting up of a Palestine Land Development Company.[50]

While the Oppenheimer plan was the official Zionist method of colonization, the Palestine Office experimented with another approach. The PLDC, just like the "settlement-cooperative," was created "to enable [the JNF] to carry out its very aim." The PLDC promised "to inaugurate a purposeful land policy (*einer zielbewussten Landpolitik*) in Palestine."[51] Its two goals were the purchase, development, and parcelling of land to be sold to private Jewish buyers, and the administration of agricultural training and the creation of opportunities for propertyless Jews to become smallholders.[52] The PLDC was planned as a profit-making joint stock company, in line with the experience of the JCA after 1900 in the moshavot of the First *Aliya*, though it failed to attract a significant number of shareholders.

The PLDC, however, was not just the coinage of Warburg's and Ruppin's brains. As demonstrated by Shalom Reichman and Shlomo Hasson, the PLDC was modelled after the Prussian government's Colonization Commission in the Ostmark.[53] Prussian "internal colonization" was well known, and frequently referred to by practical Zionists from among the leaders of Hovevei Zion and the labor movement, such as Tschlenov, Vilkansky, and Zeev Smilansky.[54] As "most German Zionists were born or educated in the 'Ostelbien,'"[55] their familiarity with this method of settlement may also be assumed. But the two figures who decided to adopt it for the WZO were Otto Warburg and Arthur Ruppin. Warburg's own interest in Zionism developed out of his involvement with the various European colonial ventures, and he continued to advocate, even while heading the Palestine Department of the WZO, additional territorial solutions for Jews.[56] Doukhan-Landau even argues that, as part of his interest in colonial ventures in general, Warburg was a member of the German Colonization Commission for Poznan.[57] Though his name is not listed among the members of the *Ansiedlungskommission*,[58] Warburg was well acquainted with its workings. In a letter to Ussishkin from 1908 Warburg noted that in launching the PLDC "we do not propose new ways, new experiments whose nature is unknown. We assume instead the Prussian colonization method as it has been practiced in the last ten years by the Colonization Commission."[59]

Ruppin himself was born in the province of Poznan and had experienced in his childhood and youth "the permanent struggle between the Polish majority living on the land and the dominant, mainly urban, German population." The Jewish inhabitants of the region "educated as they were in the German language and culture, usually supported the Germans in this national struggle." The Jews of the Ostmark nevertheless were and remained between a rock and a hard place: the Polish nationalist opposition to German settlement organized cooperatives that competed with Jewish tradesmen, while German nationalists persisted in their anti-Semitism towards Jews whom, despite their German loyalty, they viewed as an alien element.[60]

Ruppin viewed Prussian colonization in the Poznan province as a model to emulate and improve on. Warburg still believed in May 1908, that the PLDC could fill the gap due to the absence of an effective colonial bank,[61] but by October 1909, Ruppin assigned it different aims. Ruppin pointed out that first it was necessary to undertake the agricultural-technical preparation of smallholdings for potential buyers. It was at this point that the Prussian example was significant. In Ruppin's words "the method of settlement here proposed for Palestine is not an innovation; it is being used wherever latifundia, which were badly cultivated, are divided up and sold to small farmers. It is, in particular, the method used in disposing of Polish latifundia in the East Marches to German farmers."[62] The German Colonization Commission was attractive as a model, since it offered a method of practical work, in preparing land for European-type settlement and cultivation, even in the absence of a credit institution.

In December 1911, addressing directly the question of the Jewish agricultural workers, but examining the ways in which they might be turned into independent farmers, Ruppin asked how the worker, suffering from low wages, was to receive initial financial credit? The solution, he felt, was in making the worker qualify for credit by securing him the means and inventory for his first year of work. In this context, wrote Ruppin, "we are thinking of the credit given customarily in the colonization work of the Prussian government in its eastern regions."[63]

In regard to workers' settlement, Ruppin felt, though erroneously as he was to find out, the model of German colonization was pertinent even in solving the perennial problem of credit.

The reason that the Poznan model was potentially more applicable to Palestine than the Algerian colonial agriculture favored by Rothschild, or the absentee landownership of urban Californians in Maywood Colony which seems to have been a source of inspiration for Agudat Netaim, also had to do with the decline of the capitalist character of the work of colonization. This is well argued by Reichman and Hasson:

the adoption of the Posen model involved something much deeper than a transfer of a specific colonization technique. Essentially, it meant an acceptance of or agreement with a political philosophy that assigned a leading role to the national needs and thus was congruent with the goals of the Zionist movement.[64]

This explanation is supported by Ruppin's position in a debate with Hubert Auhagen, an agricultural expert who was involved in the setting up of German colonies, who also served as counsellor to the PLDC. Auhagen was invited by the WZO to tour Palestine in 1911 and wrote in his report that the German model was not appropriate for Palestine, since the Prussian *Ansiedlungskommission*'s aims were national rather than economic.[65] Reichman and Hasson marvel how Auhagen could have so misunderstood the aims of the PLDC,[66] but we have to remember that the PLDC was launched at first as a joint stock company, in line with the dominant view of the necessity of the capitalist path of colonization. The PLDC's initial preference for private initiative was also obvious from its lack of commitment to exclusive employment of Jewish workers. But Ruppin's rejection of Auhagen's criticism is already an indication that he was at the threshold of a new era. The PLDC, he answered, was not established to undertake economic ventures but to enhance national colonization.[67] And national colonization subjected all other goals of colonization to the transformation of the demographic character of the colony, i.e. it alone was guided by the "demographic interest" of pure settlement.

The agricultural workers' early opposition to settlement

The concentration of the Second *Aliya* workers' efforts in the labor market struggle drew criticism from public figures in Eretz Israel. The agricultural workers were accused of failing to recognize that no labor market conquest would be effective without "redemption of land," since it would not make room for the expansion of the Jewish population. But for the workers, the failure of the exclusionary labor market struggle demonstrated that "this necessary condition, the redemption of land, by no means makes necessary or entails the redemption of labor." In their view, the order had to be reversed: "not every purchase is worthy of being called redemption, and every land purchase that does not mean [Jewish] labor, will not last."[68] As long as the creation of employment by private enterprise was viewed as unavoidable, Jewish settlement and Jewish labor seemed antithetical, and the workers focused on the task of monopolizing the labor market.

The establishment of the PLDC generated alternative visions outside and on the margins of the workers' camp. In the first quarter of 1908, Dr. Hillel Jaffe, a physician and one-time head of the Hovevei Zion's Office in Jaffa, argued, on the pages of *Hapoel Hatzair*, for the necessity of settling the workers as a way of removing their predicament. The basic condition for the realization of such a plan was the foundation of a land leasing company to make land and basic services available to workers. The lease-holders, on their part, were to organize themselves into collective groups (*kvutzot*) which, on the basis of the "mutual guarantee" of their members, would sign the contract with the company. The settlers-to-be had to be workers with one to two years of work experience in Palestine, and the *kvutza* would filter, by means of a "natural selection," the most appropriate candidates among newcomers. Whether, ultimately, the land would be worked individually or collectively, only time would tell. This visionary article had its source, I believe, in addition to Jaffe's great insight into the life of the agricultural workers, in the opportunities offered by the foundation of the PLDC at the time, though in the article Jaffe made the rather doubtful claim that he conceived of his plan independently of the PLDC, and viewed the latter's simultaneous establishment as a proof that his ideas "were dear not to [him] alone."[69]

The most celebrated controversy of the Second *Aliya*, focusing on the dilemma of "conquest of land" versus "conquest of labor," took place in mid 1908, between Joseph Vitkin, a teacher and member of the Hapoel Hatzair Party, and Joseph Aharonowitz, the editor of the Party's paper. Vitkin pointed to the well-known disappointments of "conquest of labor" and suggested a new "historical mission" to Hapoel Hatzair.[70] Their public debate allows us to observe not only the Party's rigid official position, but also the contradictory impulses behind it, demonstrating that landless Jewish workers were not all that different from their counterparts on other frontiers.

While the urban proletarian was created through the loss of his private property, argued Vitkin, the agricultural worker, as the German *Landflucht* amply demonstrated, existed only as long as he retained access to a small plot of land. Nor was the situation different in Palestine, where workers persisted in agricultural labor mostly in the Galilee where they had hope of future settlement on JCA lands. Vitkin concluded that Hapoel Hatzair Party "had to approach conquest of labor in the moshavot through conquest and settlement of land."

In Vitkin's view, a "rational colonization method" was required, to be sought "mostly in those countries whose population is recent and small." These countries attracted working hands by ensuring, through public and government supplied land and agrarian credit in the form of installment payments and low interest loans, that "the worker passes *via* agricultural labor to settlement." Vitkin offered not only general guidelines for settling workers but envisioned the realization of his program by the relevant bodies of the WZO: for provision of land – the JNF; for credit, through the establishment of exclusive Jewish farms, where the workers could save money – the Jewish Colonial Trust. Vitkin rejected the PLDC only on the grounds that it did not espouse exclusive Jewish labor on its farms; simultaneously he rejected the "settlement cooperative" on the more fundamental grounds that it would stifle the powers of the individual.

Vitkin was criticized and ridiculed by Aharonowitz who represented the prevailing view of the almost insurmountable opposition between conquering land and labor. The worker's difficulties in "conquest of labor" were due not to objective factors, argued Aharonowitz, but to supposedly psychological ones. He subsumed his argument under the dichotomy of "idealist" versus "natural worker" that, as we already saw, was later used to distinguish the *ashkenazi* and Yemenite Jewish workers. The "idealist" workers, Aharonowitz argued, could have "been capable of sacrificing their private lives for our national ideal," but the standstill in the national movement threw these youngsters into crisis. Nevertheless, he expected two factors to help the "idealist workers." First, the growing confrontation between Jews and Arabs would bring about the replacement of the latter with the former by the farmers, and secondly, the developing capitalist character of the Jewish plantations would allow a further rise in the wages of the Jewish workers. When the worker's work "yielded national results on the one hand, and hope for private existence on the other hand," the crisis would end.

While upholding the value of conquest in the labor market, Aharonowitz's opposition to Vitkin's recommendation of conquering land was less than total. Aharonowitz's anxieties were practical: he did not expect the WZO to be able to collect enough money for the settlement of a significant number of workers, and believed that private initiative would be necessary to complement it. In addition, Aharonowitz conceded that if a member of the party found a way of becoming a farmer

"Hapoel Hatzair Party could only sympathize and offer its moral support," though he still believed that it should not waste energy on a task outside its direct course.[71]

Aharonowitz's practical mindedness reveals that underneath the official commitment of Hapoel Hatzair Party to "conquest of labor" lurked the unfulfilled desire to acquire cheap land and attain speedy mobility, which, as I have argued already, has been the vital motive force of settlers on all frontiers. The "standstill" in the Zionist movement, which betrayed the "idealist workers" was, therefore, nothing but the cessation of settlement activities. Zeev Smilansky expressed even more strongly than Aharonowitz the "permissive" attitude towards the aspiration to become a farmer. In his words: "it is obvious that none of us – even someone who is willing to remain a lifetime laborer – can demand of our workers that they object to becoming farmers (*shichlul karkai*)."[72] Finally, Berl Katznelson admitted in late 1912 that "the workers' aspiration for settlement and secure bonding with land (*amida al hakarka*) was born simultaneously with Hebrew labor, and never ceased, in spite of the fact that it was, and still is, considered in the dominant conception a sign of decline, of major heresy."[73]

Though, after the virtual freezing of the frontier in 1904, the workers abandoned the aim of settlement, individuals and bodies that were connected with such attempts during the First *Aliya* kept urging its resumption. Hovevei Zion, for example, undertook a number of experiments to equip the Jewish worker with an auxiliary farm (*meshek ezer*) and housing, in order to compensate him for the indirect subsidy of the traditional economy to Arab workers, and put the two groups on par at their point of entry into the market. The aim of the *workers' settlement* (moshav *poalim*), then, was "to entrench (*levatzer*) the worker and ensure his existence as [a worker]."[74] Four workers' settlements were set up: Beer Yaacov in 1907, Ein Ganim in 1908, Nachlat Yehuda in 1913, and Ein Hai (later Kfar Malal) in 1914. The former two, that preceded the work of the Palestine Office, will occupy us here.

No matter how small the plots alloted to the auxiliary farm were (50 dunams, i.e. 12.5 acres, at Beer Yaacov, and only 15 dunams at Ein Ganim), their owners viewed their land as a means of becoming small farmers or planters and thus independent of the labor market. But even the development of these plots, that needed irrigation for growing vegetables or oranges, required substantial investment, of which an agricultural worker, as one of them pointed out, could have saved up from his wages no more than 10 percent in ten years.[75] As a result, among the actual members of Beer Yaacov and Ein Ganim a process of social polarization evolved. "Some of the early settlers, those who really were workers living from their work, had to sell their plots to others who were richer." Only the latter possessed enough capital to introduce irrigation, turn their plots into small plantations, and wait years for the harvest. Many of the members became debt-ridden without any hope of repaying. Ein Ganim, in the middle of 1914, it was argued, was already in the hands of the third or fourth group of owners. Among the new members there were many foremen, employed in Petach Tikva or other moshavot in the supervision of Arab workers. Foremen and skilled workers sometimes employed wage workers on their plots in the moshav *poalim*. Furthermore, a contemporary observer of Beer Yaacov sounded the alarm: "a workers' settlement, meant to assist in the conquest of labor by Jews – employs alien hands!" In general, the smallholding worker-settlers, according to Vilkansky, "have gotten used too much to the idea of being independent, and will in no way be able to work permanently for others afterwards." The results of these experiments were very disquieting from the workers' viewpoint. Workers' settlements did not become instrumental in aiding the "conquest of labor" strategy, most contemporary writers agreed. In consequence the workers themselves either rejected the establishment of additional workers' settlements or demanded the reduction of the size of their plots, in one case to as much as half a dunam.[76]

Oppenheimer's plan, not surprisingly, did not give rise to any public debate in Hapoel Hatzair Party, officially committed as it was to "conquest of labor." Such a debate took place in the international congresses of Poalei Zion. The "settlement-cooperative" met with the total opposition of the party ideologue, Ber Borochov, who wanted no association with the bourgeois WZO, and expressed his concern that settlement would undermine the proletarian character of the workers.[77] The only whole-hearted support for the "settlement-cooperative" came from the Austrian wing of Poalei Zion, notably from Shlomo Kaplansky and Nathan Gross, who justified their support on the basis of the similarity they found between the experience of national conflict in Palestine and the Austro-Hungarian Empire.[78] In 1907, the Eretz Israeli delegation still took a middle path, not opposing settlement in principle but being skeptical about the potential of the WZO's plan on practical grounds. Ben-Gurion was concerned that the failure of Oppenheimer's "settlement-cooperatives" would deliver a blow to settlement in general, and Ben-Zvi was fearful that as a universal model it might not be directly applicable to Palestine.[79]

Private land was the nemesis of the workers of the Second *Aliya*. Aharonowitz of Hapoel Hatzair, and Ben-Gurion and Ben-Zvi of Poalei Zion were not averse to settlement but remained unsure of the WZO's potential to create a type of settlement appropriate for the penniless agricultural worker. Before the end of 1909, only leaders of Hovevei Zion and people on the margins of the labor movement saw nationally owned land as the solution to the antithesis of Jewish land and labor. In consequence of these limits, the agricultural workers' perspective was narrowly focused, in the years 1904–9, on the struggle for employment. They came to share with workers on other frontiers apprehension of additional immigrants, and the Fifth Congress of Hapoel Hatzair Party decided, in October 1909, that the "entrenchment" of workers already in Palestine was more vital than the growth of their numbers through immigration.[80] The aim of pure, or demographically significant, settlement which they wished to champion was undermined, and the significance of the Second *Aliya*'s agricultural workers for the national movement seemed to have become restricted. It seemed, therefore, very likely, on the eve of the entry of the WZO and its manifold colonizing agencies, that the agricultural workers of the Second *Aliya* had entered a *cul-de-sac* and would not leave their mark on history.

The origins of the kibbutz

Jewish agricultural proletarian life in Palestine was fertile ground for a variety of cooperative styles of life, most of which were of temporary duration. Jewish cooperation was rooted mostly in the immediate need to make up, indirectly, for the low wages that resulted from the downward pressure of competition from Palestinian Arab workers in the moshava. Though Jewish workers' initial *price of labor* did not change as a result of their mutual assistance, by pooling resources the workers were better able to survive on the same individual wage. Moreover, their *total labor cost*[81] for the planter went down, since the productivity of a group of workers of various skill levels was larger than that of the sum of its individual members, and as part of the contractual relationship the planter could dispense with supervision.[82] Similar background, the workers' youth, and the fact that their wages did not usually suffice to support a family, made sharing easier and more attractive. Most widespread were the *communes* – i.e. communal living and cooking arrangements, and frequently a common treasury – joining workers employed by different farmers at the same moshava.[83] There were also rural and urban contract groups established to undertake cooperatively various seasonal agricultural tasks, or even to lease land for cooperative cultivation.

It is likely that the communal organization of life in Palestine had been modelled on the "imported" model of the Russian *artel*. Originally a medieval cooperative practice of an elite of farmers, artisans or workers to carry out joint projects, with industrialization the *artel* came to be used by seasonal migrant workers as a tool of transition to the conditions of city life. As such *artels* were mostly temporary "cooperative living arrangements" of workers from a common place of origin, serving as a "surrogate 'family'" that "formed and disbanded according to the needs of the casual labor market."[84] Ussishkin, for example, who recommended in his 1904 essay "Our Program" that Jewish youth come to Palestine for a temporary three-year-long quasi-military labor service in the moshavot, viewed them as being organized in a "worldwide Jewish workers' *artel.*"[85] All these forms, in Russia as in Palestine, arose in response to the exigencies of the labor market, and were limited by its parameters. What is mostly relevant for us is that the *artel*, as pointed out by Jonathan Frankel, was the equivalent of "a temporary, *ad hoc* labor association," and not "a permanent cooperative or collective settlement."[86]

Two other cooperative organizations, "conquest groups," aimed at establishing Jewish presence on land newly purchased or transferred for the first time to Jewish cultivators, until the owners could take over, and the permanent collective settlement, to be named, after the First World War, kibbutz, were organized outside the labor market. Accordingly, new considerations and interests entered into their formation. Both, by and large, were connected with the Palestine Office and the JNF, and the former was a tool for dealing with the Jewish–Palestinian conflict in the land market. The "conquest group," however, was a temporary expedient, requiring no special elaboration. The kibbutz, a new type of settlement organization, was an altogether different kind of body, and in this section I will examine the balance of influences that shaped it. We should remember in what follows that, although all examples of cooperative organization were known at the time under the same name, *kvutza* (group), and there is therefore a temptation to treat them as subspecies of the same phenomenon, and even as step-by-step more complex forms of organizational evolution,[87] they were diverse phenomena.[88]

The less known facet of the period is that the cooperative tendency among the agricultural workers of the Second *Aliya* had to contend with a strong individualist current. This was expressed, for example, by Aharonowitz who argued that the pioneers were "developed" people who could not tolerate collective forms of economic organization in the long run, and would be expected to break them up into individual enterprises.[89] Similar views were held by such prominent figures as Vitkin, Yaacov Rabinovitch, and Vilkansky. In general, individualism was frequently a logical extension of the idea that only "idealist" workers stayed in Palestine. For some years, then, it was an open question whether the demands of cooperation would be manageable or too trying for the immigrants of a petty bourgeois background. In fact, during the Second *Aliya* the individualists were frequently more vocal, while the members of the *kvutzot* counselled caution. In Jonathan Frankel's succinct summary "undiscipline, individualism, and downright anarchy were the norm" of the Second *Aliya*.[90]

The most serious early experiment at communal living took place at the JCA's farm in Sedjra, by a group of eighteen men and women, known as "the collective." An examination of the Sedjra collective, which did not evolve into a permanent collective settlement, will serve me as a counter-example for weighing the different elements that went into the formation of Degania – the first kibbutz.

The initiative for the formation of the "Sedjra collective" was Mania Wilbushewitz-Shochat's, one of the few immigrants actively promoting not just communal living, but communal settlement. She read profusely about secular and religious collective utopias and visited some in Russia and the US. When she sought to mobilize support for establishing one in Palestine, she was rebuffed by the two political parties. She was, however, able to attain the consent of Eliyahu Krauze, the agronomist-manager of the Sedjra farm, to lease the field-crop lands of the farm, which had suffered from repeated losses, to a group of workers. Shochat organized the "collective," without realizing at the time that the majority of its members joined out of an ulterior motive. Most were simultaneously members of the secret para-military organization Bar-Giora (the forerunner of Hashomer), that Israel Shochat (her future husband) "wanted to concentrate in the Galilee . . . in order to prepare them for their roles in the order." Though this might not have been the only reason for their membership in the collective, only a few joined, she conceded subsequently, because they were "interested in the experiment of collective life and work itself."[91] The experiment lasted for one full agricultural season, in 1907/8, and for the first time field-crops were cultivated at Sedjra "without deficit."[92] The historical accounts and memoirs of the Sedjra experiment end abruptly at this point, merely by stating that upon successfully completing its task the collective broke up.

The most likely reason for the discontinuation of the Sedjra collective, it seems to me, is that the Sedjra experiment revealed to the workers the limits of their own initiative. The contract with Krauze gave the Sedjra collective the field-crop area "under the very same terms as to the *fellah*, when leasing land from an *effendi*, that is a one-year lease of land, traction animals, seeds, tools, an advance until harvest time in money or staples, and a place to live."[93] There is no mention of any intention on the part of the JCA to take the decisive step and offer the members of the collective land to settle on,[94] and lack of land and financial support made permanence unlikely. Sedjra therefore remained an inspirational event but not the foundation of a model. It was at Kinneret where Degania, the first kibbutz, was born. Moshe Ingberman, one of the members of the Kinneret work force, saw clearly the reasons for the potential of development unique to his place. He wrote in 1912:

the worker in Eretz Israel has a beautiful and shining perspective *via* the settlement *kvutzot* and associations. There already are a number of *kvutzot* in Eretz Israel, but the lands they are cultivating have been already intended for other aims. Only the land of one *kvutza* was not intended for any purpose. This is Degania, and this *kvutza* may indeed develop.[95]

Even under the best of circumstances the workers' penchant for communal life could not bridge the gap between "conquest of labor" and "conquest of land." The Sedjra collective had to be content by demonstrating that Jewish workers were capable of living collectively and performing heavy agricultural labor, without incurring losses. Even less potent were imported ideas of cooperation. Neither Mania Shochat nor Joseph Trumpeldor, almost alone in the Second *Aliya* inspired by imported ideologies of full-scale cooperation from Eastern Europe and the US, had much following or impact.[96] Nor was there much subsequent emulation of the collective's practice of full participation of women in the performance of the agricultural tasks, including plowing. This conclusion brings us from the examination of the internal characteristics of the *kvutza* to the more decisive external conditions and, therefore, to the WZO and its aims.

The training farm of Kinneret and the birth of Degania

Like so many of the experiments, organizations, and blueprints of the Ottoman era, the WZO's training farms also proved a passing experiment, and were abolished in early Mandatory times. Nevertheless, in the Ottoman period they superseded the plantation colonies as the central arena for the evolution of Zionism's state-building methods. The farms' long range impact was rooted in the *kvutza*, which though not born in the training farm, found there the resources and formative influences that transformed it from a temporary expedient into a lasting entity of colonization.

The PLDC's first project was the establishment of the Kinneret training farm at the southern tip of Lake Tiberias. At this initial stage of its work, the PLDC attempted to fuse the capitalist direction prevalent in

the colonization of Palestine with the nationalist and statist approach of
the Prussian *Ansiedlungskommission* in the Poznan and Western Prussian
provinces. The early years of Kinneret were characterized by this
duality. The farm was expected to combine the realization of two goals:
the improvement of land to be used for establishing new moshavot, and
the agricultural training of the workers in order to turn them eventually
into settlers.[97] In regard to the workers again two different objectives
existed: they were to be trained but also to use their share of the farm's
profits to become independent farmers. In sum, the farm was double-
headed: both farm and workers were to make money, while simultaneously the former be improved and the latter trained. However, as we
had ample opportunity to observe, the capitalist and nationalist objectives were contradictory in the Eretz Israeli context. They gave rise to
conflicting tendencies in the attitude of the workers to the farm.

Kinneret, and the additional farms established in Hulda and Ben
Shemen (Beit Arif) on the southern coastal zone, and the *achuzot*
established in imitation of them, had an immediate positive impact on the
employment situation of Eastern European Jewish agricultural workers.
A contemporary chronicler recorded that the workers' "living conditions
are not bad in comparison with the conditions prevailing in the country":
they were paid a daily wage of 2 francs for an eight-hour workday,
received housing and the possibility of setting up a communal kitchen
and, above all, had permanent employment.[98] In consequence of these
favorable conditions, a dramatic shift in employment patterns was
observed in September 1911 by Ben-Gurion, who reported the "typical
phenomenon of the emptying out of the moshavot of their Hebrew
workers and the concentration of the latter in the farms." The moshavot
of the Lower Galilee, which a few years earlier employed dozens of
Jewish workers were left, in consequence, with just a few, while Rishon
Letzion and Rechovot had no *ashkenazi* workers. Only two kinds of
Jewish workers remained behind: Yemenites in Rishon Letzion and
Rechovot, and small farmers and foremen in Petach Tikva (he probably
meant Ein Ganim).[99]

Though the farms were valued as enclaves of Jewish employment, they
were bitterly scorned for not becoming foolproof buffers of exclusive
Jewish work. In consequence, enmity between the workers and first
manager marred the early years of Hulda and Kinneret. The rift between
the profit motive and the national theme, as in the private moshavot,
periodically erupted into open conflict over the employment of Arab
workers. A famous incident took place in the Hulda farm during the
management of the agronomist Moshe Berman, when the JNF decided to
plant a forest in memory of Herzl in part of the farm. Berman employed

Arab workers to plant the Herzl forest, and on March 7, 1908 Jewish workers from a number of settlements and Jaffa met and decided to send a group of four Jewish workers to uproot the saplings and replant them in a symbolic gesture illustrating the demand for the employment of Jewish workers. In response, Berman offered to replace half of the Arab workers by Jews. When Zvi Yehuda, the head of the workers' deputation, insisted on exclusive Jewish employment, emphasizing the symbolic character of the forest to be named after the founder of the WZO, Berman gave in and promised to employ solely Jews.[100] Brisch, his successor, however, recommenced the employment of Arab workers.[101]

The same conflict was replayed between some of the same protagonists in Kinneret, when Zvi Yehuda and other participants of the Hulda incident were in the first group of workers accompanying Moshe Berman, who was appointed as the agronomist-manager. The ending of the clash, however, was in every respect different – more dramatic and historically potent. Degania's pre-history started on June 6, 1908, when the first group of eight workers arrived at Daleika – the site of the Kinneret training farm, to be joined a few days later by Sarah Malkhin to tend the kitchen. Hachoresh, the first organization of the workers of the Galilee, initially boycotted the farm, because of Berman's record of employment of Arab workers at Hulda. The relationships between the workers and Berman, however, proved to be satisfactory for the time being. Living conditions were harsh, sanitation poor, and they obviously were dependent on one another. In addition, the setting up of the Kinneret farm at Daleika was the very first new settlement act in Palestine since 1903/4 and the first time the WZO broke new ground, and these pioneering efforts infused the participants with a high measure of dedication and desire to unite forces around the common cause.

Nevertheless, the idyllic relations did not last long. Gradually the number of workers grew to about forty, and they became heavily stratified through differential working conditions and wages. The farm suffered from a big turnover in its labor force, and failed to generate "intensive cultural life."[102] Most of the workers suffered from bouts of malaria.[103] Feelings of dissatisfaction and disappointment became the order of the day. But a more important cause of despair than the hardships suffered by the workers was the heavy losses sustained by the farm.[104]

In the fall of 1909, Berman fell back on the strategy of the private farmers that, like him, needed to turn out profit, and decided to gain a freer hand by employing Arab workers. In fact, Arabs were already employed at Kinneret as construction workers and shepherds,[105] but Berman sought to introduce them into seasonal agricultural work as well.

The background to his demand was the fact that the crop was placed in jeopardy by the shortage of Jewish workers at harvest time. Berman tried to get his way by treading gingerly. He offered the workers a new contract, in which he would be given the right to employ Arab workers, but only if the Jewish workers could not supply additional Jewish workers within ten days.[106] The extent of displacement, it seems, would have been minimal, but in a market with a seemingly unlimited supply of cheap local labor – just like in the case of the South African Rand Rebellion of 1922 – almost any measure of displacement was threatening and provoked an eruption. There is some lack of clarity as to the immediate trigger of the conflict. According to some of the workers' memoirs, Berman had already hired the Arab workers,[107] while Berman argued that the workers had agreed to the conditions of the contract.[108] Be that as it may, there is no disagreement that the cause of the conflict was an attempt at displacing Jewish by Arab workers. The Jewish workers of the farm went on a four-day strike between October 11 and 15, 1909, and, even though Berman again yielded to their demands, the eight founding members of Kinneret left the farm for Hadera where they organized themselves into a commune.

The crisis was not over. Hachoresh stepped in and demanded the firing of Berman by Ruppin.[109] Ruppin already had reasons at the time to doubt Berman's suitability for his task. Berman had failed him by raising ardent hopes of making Kinneret profitable already in its first year. Moreover, Berman kept no reliable accounts, making it necessary to appoint a full-time bookkeeper for the farm.[110] Nevertheless, Ruppin refused to comply with the demands of Hachoresh. Instead, he decided to leave the training farm in Kinneret (spreading on the left bank of the Jordan in Daleika) under Berman's management, but offer 1,500 dunams of Um Djunni's lands (on the right bank, which until then was a separate unit and relatively hard of access), for cultivation by an independent group of workers. This *kvutza* of six workers and a woman cook, chosen by Hachoresh, was directed by two of its members, that were chosen by the *kvutza*. On December 1, 1909, a contract was signed between Ruppin and the six workers, who subsequently renamed the place Degania. Degania's first group ended the agricultural season with a net profit of 4,000 francs, seeming to prove the financial viability of the *kvutza*. Subsequent *kvutzot* were less successful in economic terms, and though the Sedjra collective and the first Degania *kvutza* offered new hope, the economic rationale of the autonomous *kvutza* was debated for years to come. In one year's time the Hadera commune, i.e. Kinneret's founders with some additional members, returned to Degania (marking 1910 as the founding year of the first kibbutz) and in 1912 decided to make it into a permanent home. In 1913, Kinneret also became a permanent cooperative settlement. In the difficult last years of the First World War, when most of the Jewish community suffered and contracted, three more kibbutzim: Kfar Giladi, Tel Hai, and Ayelet Hashachar were formed. At the end of the war the number of *kvutzot*, including both temporary and potential settlement ones, was thirty, and they boasted a membership of 446 workers.[111] After the war, the kibbutz would be viewed as a fundamental and typical form of colonization in Palestine by all concerned.

Genesis of Degania: the workers

The lack of clarity as to the kindling of the first *kvutza* at the Kinneret farm is reminiscent of that surrounding the initiation of the Yavnieli mission. Some view kibbutzim as the original creation of the agricultural workers, who designed it *ab ovo* on the basis of socialist ideals.[112] Others point vaguely to influences issuing from the WZO or personally from Ruppin, who is supposed to have been unique among Western European Zionists in understanding the Eastern European workers' psychological needs. Alex Bein, the foremost historian of Zionist settlement, for example, wrote that Hachoresh used the opportunity of the conflict between the workers and Berman "and, with Ruppin's participation, organized from among the best workers of the Galilee a small *kvutza* that was ready to undertake the daring experiment."[113] In Kolatt's view:

the characteristic settlement aspect of the Eretz Israeli labor movement was not determined by an immanent development only. Without some crystallization of settlement theory in the Zionist movement, a crystallization that only in part was influenced by the parallel development in the labor movement, the history told here would not have been possible.[114]

Jonathan Frankel, whose work combines the broadest vision with the greatest attention to detail, states that

from the moment of Ruppin's arrival in the country, a dynamic process of interaction had developed between the settlement oriented wing of the WZO and sections of the labor movement in Palestine. Therefore, it is not always possible to ascertain who first influenced whom in specific cases such as this.[115]

This emphasis on "interaction," while not entirely incorrect, is misleadingly vague; we would be better served by moving one step further and attempting to establish what each side brought to the interaction in order to understand its end result and the implications of that result.

I will start out by examining the view which links the establishment of the kibbutz with ideological designs on the workers' part. In assessing this influence we come across a paradox, since the founders of Degania deny any ideological basis to their action. A typical view was expressed by Joseph Baratz in 1923: "the *kvutza* is not the fruit of the international cooperative idea. We did not learn from it, and in the beginning of our path we paid no attention to it . . . Its origin is in the Eretz Israeli reality."[116] The five major works on the history of the Israeli labor movement by Landhurst, Braslavsky, Even-Shoshan, Darin-Drabkin, and finally Kolatt, have all denied the significance of ideological considerations in creating the kibbutz.[117] The attribution of the kibbutz to imported socialist ideas, then, is less widespread than one would expect on the basis of the popular hold of this interpretation.

It was only in 1968, that the thesis affirming the kibbutz's ideological origins and demanding the re-examination of the dominant view, was raised by Yehuda Slutsky. His call was first heeded in 1975 and more spiritedly in the early 1980s, when debates, mostly on the pages of *Cathedra*, the foremost Israeli historical periodical, pitted the "ideologists" Shmuel Gadon, Raphael Frankel, and Henry Near against the "pragmatist" Baruch Ben-Avram. It seems to me, therefore, that the search for ideal causes of the kibbutz is contemporary: the farther we move away from the historical period under study, and the further the differences between the kibbutz and ordinary Israeli society lessen, the more Slutsky's request to find the ideological roots in the actions of the kibbutz's founders becomes pressing. This biased beginning, however, does not yet free us from an examination of the substantive arguments in Gadon's, Raphael Frankel's, and Near's essays.

The most important new arguments are: (1) the connection established by Gadon between three founders of Degania – Israel Bloch, Tanchum Tanfilov, and Joseph Elkin, immigrants from Romny, a small Ukrainian town – and the Techiya (Renaissance) Zionist organization centered in Pinsk, and (2) the influence of the Russian *artel* on Joseph Bussel, Degania's ideologue and leader, in Raphael Frankel's view.[118]

(1) In Techiya's program, adopted in its 1906 Congress, we read: "broad-based settlement of Jews in Eretz Israel, which will be directed by the General [should be, World] Zionist Federation, must be based on cooperative (communist) principles." Members of Techiya believed that basing the Jewish settlement on "the principles of socialism" was a realistic prospect, since Palestine lacked a well-formed Jewish socio-economic system or landowning class.[119] Techiya's program, however,

wavered between "cooperation," "communism," and "socialism," as did its members who migrated to Palestine. While the Romny group ended up being instrumental in creating the kibbutz, which is an organization based on "full cooperation in all spheres of life,"[120] Eliezer Yaffe, also of Techiya, was the ideologue of the moshav ovdim (Laborers' Moshav), which is only a consumer, marketing and mutual-aid cooperative,[121] and, furthermore, was viewed by its members as an alternative to the kibbutz.[122] Finally, Bloch's reference to Techiya, cited by Gadon, connected Techiya's program not with the formation of the kibbutz but with the setting up of the commune (a consumer cooperative) by the three Romny expatriates upon boarding the ship to Palestine.[123] If full and partial cooperation, as well as consumer and producer cooperation, may equally be derived from the same program then its determining impact on any one of them is probably overrated.

(2) Raphael Frankel points out that the expression "Romny group" "so frequently used in history books, appeared neither in the letters describing Kinneret in its early years, nor in the memoirs of the founders written in close proximity to the events."[124] Another idiom – the "Hadera commune" – was commonly used at the time. The reason, in R. Frankel's view, is that the commune's nine members (three of the Romny group, and six others, of whom three or four also came from Kinneret), "had united around a common goal, and with time have crystallized a common ideology: the establishment of an independent collective farm."[125] In Raphael Frankel's opinion the group's leader: the 18-year-old Joseph Bussel, single-handedly and single-mindedly formulated the ideology around which the Hadera commune coalesced, out of his opposition to capitalism and exploitation. According to Moshe Smilansky's recollection "the Russian *artel* was probably at the root of [Bussel's] thinking and influenced him a great deal."[126]

The *artel*, as we already had opportunity to observe, was an old form of Russian cooperation, that with industrialization became mostly a common living arrangement in the slowly expanding Russian cities. Victoria Bonnell's recent study of workers' organizations in St. Petersburg and Moscow between 1900 and 1914 reveals an interesting change in the *artels'* character. During the Stolypin era, which saw the repression of labor between mid 1907 and 1912, some workers, subscribing to the legalist and gradualist position contemporaries called "liquidationism," turned to the establishment of *artels*, together with other legal opportunities for collective organization, such as clubs, educational and cultural societies, consumers' and producers' cooperatives. These bodies "frequently attracted young and idealistic workers," and seemed to promise "independence, self-reliance, and self-help," and allowed the workers to "bypass the contractor by substituting collectively owned contracting organizations,"[127] in short merged with the modern cooperative movement.

Nevertheless, "cooperation in Russia," according to Kolatt, both as program and practice, was not necessarily connected with a clear social perspectIve. The Russian *artel* was a many-sided phenomenon, and the amorphous ideological character of cooperativism is also well known elsewhere. "Though it was propagated by the narodniks, and the Social Revolutionaries adopted it into their worldview, not all cooperation was connected with the Social Revolutionary Party."[128] The *artel*, then, provided an example and ideology as vague as Techiya's program. Nor could Joseph Bussel, who in the year 1907 was learning agricultural work in the little village of Novapoltavka in the Kharson region of the Ukraine, and who reached Palestine in February or March of 1908, have experienced the new winds of the Stolypin era and the workers' responses to them. Furthermore, his wife, who had known him already before his immigration to Palestine, connected his yearning for communal living with his ambition to break away from the oppression of wage labor.[129] Finally, Bussel himself, in presenting his credo to his fellow workers at the Second Congress of the Federation of the Agricultural Workers of the Galilee, justified the transition from the failed strategy of "conquest of labor" to settlement, without as much as mentioning communal living.[130]

If the formation of the Um Djunni *kvutza* cannot be led back directly to the influence of either Techiya's program or the new form of the *artel*, was it at least initiated by the workers? Sarah Malkhin, a member of the first group of workers, related in her memoirs, that when the relations between the workers and Berman began cooling off

an idea was born, namely that we, the first workers, and two others that arrived later, would join together into a *kvutza* that would not disassociate anymore, and we would undertake the work at Um Djunni, without Berman's management. We told Berman, and he liked the idea. We thought to carry out our idea at the beginning of the new year.[131]

Malkhin's recollection places the innovative thrust squarely in the camp of the workers. This version *prima facie* is highly plausible since communal living arrangements were familiar to the workers and the impact of the Sedjra collective's economic success was still fresh. But in a contemporary letter Warburg reported that the workers sought to lease the land for cooperative cultivation for a couple of years,[132] while

Malkhin described, probably with hindsight, a permanent settlement endeavor.

In fact, the workers' offer to lease 1,500 dunams of Um Djunni was just one of the responses to the attempt, first by the JNF and subsequently by Berman on behalf of the PLDC, to find private leaseholders for the lands of Um Djunni. Earlier, the JNF directorate rejected the proposal of a group of sixty Jewish families from Kharson in the Caucasus to lease the land of Daleika, since it doubted whether the leaseholders, after planting and building on the JNF's land, would be willing to return it, and decided against the leasing of JNF land to individuals.[133] Berman tried to interest his friend, the agronomist Aharon Aaronshon in Um Djunni but was rebuffed. In the meantime the preparatory work at Um Djunni was financed from the budget of Kinneret, even though one reason for setting Um Djunni up as a separate entity was to cut back on the expenses of the training farm.[134] It was against this background that, according to the contemporary account of an anonymous worker from Degania,

already in the first year it was announced to the workers then at Kinneret, by Berman in Dr. Ruppin's name, that the latter wish (*yes beretzonam*) to give the work at Um Djunni to a group of workers (*kvutzat poalim*). The conditions he offered were these: the workers take the work on their own responsibility, and only the supreme supervision be given to the manager.[135]

The genesis of Degania: the WZO

The "Ruppin Plan," as termed by Margalit Shilo, was really a series of offers, with fewer and fewer strings attached, made by Ruppin to the workers of Kinneret. The revisions of this plan showed a decreasing attachment to principles of good capitalist economic sense and a growing readiness to take risks dictated by the national aim of Zionist land settlement.

Initially Ruppin sought to lend 1,500 dunams of the Um Djunni land from the PLDC to from ten to twenty workers, who would buy the inventory from their own funds, and cultivate the land until such time (he estimated that to be between six and ten years) when they would be able to purchase their own land, and establish a new settlement. Ruppin's plan, conceived in February 1909, was significant in two respects. First, it indicated a shift, as Shilo emphasized, from letting Um Djunni to a "leasing group" to letting it to a "group of workers." Secondly, Ruppin called his plan a "bridge to settlement," a telling proof of the long-range goal, under the influence of the Prussian model of national settlement, that he had in mind.[136]

It soon became obvious that substituting workers for private leaseholders would require other changes as well in the plan. Simply, no workers were found with sufficient funds to purchase their own inventory, and consequently Ruppin suggested easier terms, namely that 12,000 francs be loaned by the cooperative fund of the JNF to the workers. Both Warburg and Bodenheimer registered their support, and in mid October 1909 the sum was made available with the stipulation that it not be extended to individuals, even if they acted as mutual guarantors, but "solely to cooperatives."[137] By then, however, the planting season was about to begin and it was dubious whether the plan could be executed the same year. In addition, the members of the *kvutza*-to-be from among the founders of Kinneret had already decided, in September, to postpone the execution of the plan. The reason the group's members gave was that they wanted to prepare themselves for the task.[138] Another reason was probably even weightier. The terms of the loan: 12,000 francs to be returned in three to four years with 4 percent interest seemed forbidding, and according to a contemporary report the workers preferred not to take the offer for various reasons, among them "fear of responsibility," probably meaning financial responsibility.[139]

If so, the October 1909 strike only acted as a catalyst to bring to a head ongoing processes. The eight members of the group that originally arrived with Berman, but were yet unwilling to undertake the experiment, left the farm for Hadera over the employment of Arab workers at harvest time. In response to the Hachoresh's demand to fire Berman, Ruppin suggested the realization of his earlier plan, i.e. the leasing of part of Um Djunni's land by a *kvutza* of six workers. This *kvutza* was to be the recipient of the loan of 12,000 francs, to be administered by the PLDC and paid out to its members as monthly wages. Ruppin added now one final concession: the workers would be responsible only for carrying out the work but the PLDC would be liable for potential losses incurred. It was Ruppin then, who provided the land, ensured the loan on ridiculously easy, i.e. hardly business, terms and viewed the project as a corridor to permanent settlement, while the directorate of the JNF insisted that the leasers be a cooperative society. Finally, a year later, it was Ruppin who called on the members of the Hadera commune "to settle permanently on Um Djunni's land."[140] At each stage, in sum, the initiative belonged with the WZO and Ruppin.

What were the reasons behind Ruppin's (and the WZO's) enthusiastic, for no other word fits better, support for the *kvutza*? Obviously, Ruppin did not want to lose the pending agricultural season or forfeit the possibility of settlement he saw in Um Djunni. Furthermore, the dearth of resources and trained farmers made it impossible for the WZO to emulate Rothschild or the JCA in the establishment of settlements of private farms.[141] But much more than that was involved in his initiative. Ruppin in his memoirs assumed responsibility for Degania. In his words:

when I established [!] the *kvutza* at Degania, I thought that in this fashion the idea of the *Siedlungsgenossenschaft*, which was advocated by Franz Oppenheimer in the 1903 Congress, was realized, though Degania might have diverged from Oppenheimer's rules in a few particulars. For me, the cooperative side of this settlement was the essential aspect, the rest was incidental.[142]

Ruppin's contemporary letters in which he explained to the WZO his reason for setting up the Um Djunni *kvutza* support his memory of the events. In his first report, written less than a week after the signing of the agreement with the six members of the *kvutza*, Ruppin wrote to the JNF the following: "we succeeded in bringing about the foundation of the settlement-cooperative (*Siedlungsgenossenschaft*)," in obvious reference to Oppenheimer's plan. In a letter written four days later to the PLDC, Ruppin referred even more directly to the successful establishment of "the *planned* settlement-cooperative." The centrality of Oppenheimer's plan in Zionist settlement at the time made Ruppin write:

The expressed wish of the workers and ourselves is that this first experiment of the establishment of the *Siedlungsgenossenschaft* in Eretz Israel not be revealed immediately in public, since its publication would bring about a long series of debates in the papers, in which this modest experiment might be interpreted as an epoch making event.[143]

It was not the establishment of the Degania *kvutza* then that was epoch-making, notwithstanding such interpretation by historians,[144] but the setting up of Oppenheimer's settlement-cooperative. Both the workers and Ruppin were united in this interpretation. In fact, in his subsequent letter Ruppin attributed the request for secrecy in the implementation of the settlement-cooperative to the workers alone.[145]

The most likely reason for subsequent historical slighting – rather, ignoring – of the close connection between the *Siedlungsgenossenschaft* and the *kvutza* at Um Djunni was that almost simultaneously with Ruppin's founding of the Um Djunni *kvutza* on December 1, 1909, the Ninth Zionist Congress that opened on December 26, 1909 in Hamburg, decided on its own to collect and commit funds for the realization of the Oppenheimer plan. But the association between the *kvutza* at Degania and the *Siedlungsgenossenschaft* preceded the establishment of the *kvutza* at Um Djunni and even when the two projects came to exist side by side continued in various ways.

Warburg initially supported the granting of a loan to the proposed *kvutza* since, being in the Oppenheimerian spirit, it would provide the beginnings for the realization of this program, and furthermore, would allow the Jewish workers of Palestine to move out of the working stratum by being transformed into independent farmers.[146] Already the first 12,000 francs allocated for the *kvutza* were explicitly derived from the cooperative fund.[147] Even after the Ninth Congress, Bodenheimer was not opposed to the Degania experiment but wanted it to be distinguished from the "real thing" and, in fact, expected that with the decision taken in the meantime "it would not be surprising if public interest in the small leasing *kvutza* would diminish."[148] This condescending view should not surprise us, since the budget envisioned for the Erez Israel Siedlungsgesellschaft was to be 100,000 francs, that is, close to ten times the sum of the initial loan to the Um Djunni group. Oppenheimer also was interested in seeing both the "settlement-cooperative" set up in 1910 at Merchavia and the *kvutza* at Degania through to be able to compare them. As far as the workers were concerned, most members of the first *kvutza* left Um Djunni after their one-year contract was up to become, on November 1, 1910, the "conquest group" of Merchavia.[149] Some members of the "Hadera commune," that eventually returned to Um Djunni, also vacillated at the same time between going to Merchavia and Um Djunni.[150] The following year, Degania was transferred from the control of the PLDC to the financial trusteeship of the Erez Israel Siedlungsgesellschaft Fund, in spite of the financial difficulties of the latter.[151] Oppenheimer continued to express his willingness to have the Degania group financed by a loan from the fund of the Merchavia cooperative.[152]

Only towards the end of 1911 did the paths of Merchavia and Degania begin publicly to diverge. This happened when the *kvutza* discussed and rejected the Erez Israel Siedlungsgesellschaft's suggestion to transfer the settlement-cooperative of Merchavia to Kinneret and unite it with Degania.[153] Though the heads of the Siedlungsgesellschaft were angry at the *kvutza* at Degania they reiterated that they attached "the greatest importance" to "cooperative experiments," and therefore expressed their readiness "to make sacrifices" to render them successful.[154] The reasons given by the members of the *kvutza* against the merger were that they preferred Degania's self-employment and equal wage system over the management of an agronomist and unequal wages that were fundamental to Oppenheimer's plan.[155]

Neither of the two reasons, however, were matters of principle, and even as partial considerations had limited direct bearing on the Degania *kvutza*'s refusal to merge with Merchavia and the *Siedlungsgenossenschaft*. During the Second *Aliya*, *kvutzot* employed their own wage laborers, paying them the lower rates of Jewish workers on the open market, and the decision of both the Judean and Galilean Federations of Agricultural Workers demanding the equalization of the members of the *kvutza* and its wage workers indicate the magnitude of the problem.[156]

Much more important was the second objection, though more for what it hid than for what it revealed. Though the Second *Aliya* has been described as being opposed in principle to management, it is good to remember that among the agronomist-managers of the period of the Second *Aliya*, Berman became the only villain in the labor movement's annals. Two other agronomist-managers, Vilkansky and Krauze, were among its heroes, and some others, such as Dyk of Merchavia and Golde remained uncharacterized. The workers' opposition to the agronomist-manager was not direct, but occasioned by the sword of displacement by Arab workers that managers held over the workers' heads. Margalit Shilo expressed the identity between the two in a simple and powerful way:

> The presence of an agronomist in a farm constituted something like a "time bomb" for the workers. A farm managed by an administrator was more complex, it became the site of experiment in various branches of agriculture, and the expenses, due not only to wages paid to management, piled up. The easiest outlet, for economizing was always "Hebrew labor" and, in consequence, deep-seated discord developed between the manager and the workers. In Merchavia, as in Kinneret, the central differences of opinion were manifested in regard to Hebrew labor. Without the protection of this principle the workers refused to shoulder the burden.[157]

But Shilo's view requires further refinement, since not all agronomists behaved the same.

Her attempt to relate the differences between Berman's and Vilkansky's standing in the workers' eyes to their different personal attitudes to the workers is hardly plausible.[158] Vilkansky was also embroiled in conflict with his workers, while Berman had a honeymoon with the workers of Kinneret. Furthermore Berman's approach to "Hebrew Labor" was not characterized by the principled opposition typical of Aaronsohn, as he did not complain of its added expense, but of shortage of Jewish workers. It seems that Berman's antagonistic approach was due in part to the objective constraints under which he labored, which were not shared by Vilkansky. Vilkansky was employed at Hulda by the Olive Tree Fund, the most popular fund-raising effort of the WZO, and his farm was strictly aimed at providing workers with agricultural training and consequently was never expected to turn out profit.[159] Berman, on the other hand, was employed by Ruppin and the PLDC, which was a joint stock company, and promised them that the farm in Kinneret would be making a profit of 11 percent its very first year, and therefore was under pressure at the very least to minimize the farm's deficit. Berman and Vilkansky, then, represented not just two individual preferences or even world-views, but two positions connected with the different resources and aims of the PLDC and the Olive Tree Fund of the

WZO and, ultimately, the conflicting perspectives of capitalist and national colonization.

The opposition of the Degania *kvutza* to merger with Merchavia, in short, was because in the former the threat of national conflict had already been eliminated, while in the latter not. In fact, the fear of displacement was well justified, as Merchavia's agronomist-manager, Dyk, under pressure of the WZO to cut Merchavia's very big losses, demanded in 1914 the employment of lower-paid Arab workers in the harvesting, weeding, and hoeing of summer crops. But the results were similar to the ones in Kinneret: "the differences of opinion became finally so aggravated that Dyk had to leave Merchavia,"[160] and the management of the cooperative devolved on its members, thus bringing on the second stage of Oppenheimer's plan, but earlier than he intended and for obviously different reasons. It was in protecting its national, not social character, that the Degania *kvutza* set a decisive precedent. Here, for the first time, the threat of displacement by lower-paid Palestinian Arab workers – which was the immediate trigger of the separation of Um Djunni from Kinneret and through the setting up of its *kvutza* the corridor leading to the establishment of Degania itself – was eliminated and genuine national colonization began.

The predominance of the kibbutz in Israeli state formation

In the founding of the *kvutza* at Um Djunni, cooperation from above met with cooperation from below. Both sides brought practical consider-ations and foreign models to the new creation, but these were hardly equal in potency and clarity.

The workers learned to live together and share, to lower their *total labor cost* and enhance their competitiveness in a market characterized by low wages paid to Palestinian Arab workers that undercut them. In undertaking communal forms of living arrangements and organizations, Zionist bodies such as the Techiya were very likely influenced by traditional and modern Russian cooperative practices, such as the example of the Russian *artel* that penetrated into Zionist socialism in the Pale of Settlement. But Kolatt, who so often is the most penetrating scholar of the era, put these influences in the correct perspective by pointing out that:

in arguing that the *kvutza* grew "out of reality" one is not saying that it was not preceded by ideals concerning communal life as a form of exemplary life and method for "renewal" of social life and men. It is, however, hard to demonstrate any direct influence and it is impossible to prove that the founders of the *kvutza* a priori saw in their lives some sort of exemplary social life, and established the *kvutzot* for its realization.[161]

Most significant in this respect is the fact that, since their basic orientation called for employment in the market economy, neither Poalei Zion nor Hapoel Hatzair, the respective organs of whatever ideological orientation existed among the workers, were willing to go as far as to contemplate workers' settlements in 1908/9, let alone "to propose the establishment of *kvutzot* characterized by collective living and working."[162] The permanent collective settlement, as the failure of the Sedjra collective demonstrated, could hardly have emerged as the extension of communal life. The *artel* in Russia was set up with the combined resources of its participants; the members of the "Hadera commune" had to borrow the resources with which to cultivate Um Djunni. The gap between the commune and the permanent collective agricultural settlement was immense in terms both of the resources, above all the land, required, and of the theoretical framework justifying and orienting the latter's implementation. And the WZO's "theory of pure settlement" preceded the evolution of the workers' own.

Since the poorer WZO found it impossible to emulate Rothschild or the JCA in the establishment of settlements of private farms, Ruppin concluded, the *kvutza* provided the "only possibility" for the WZO "to start something new in the sphere of agricultural settlement."[163] In so doing, Ruppin's contemporary letters and explanations demonstrate that he was carrying out the intention of the WZO to set up cooperative settlements. The long string of concessions he made to the workers, coming to a head with his suggestion that Hachoresh set up the *kvutza* at Um Djunni without any financial risks, chronicles Ruppin's evolving disillusionment with the possibility of finding reliable private investors, and his subsequent abandonment of the linkage of the settlement project with capitalist schemes. The cooperative practices of the workers, many-sided but experimental, and limited in their potential, accorded well with the WZO's approach, especially when the gap between the two was reduced by the elimination of the requirement of any economic investment or risk-taking on the workers' part. But more fundamentally, Ruppin's division of Um Djunni from Kinneret was the first symbolic step in the formation of an exclusive Jewish employment sector of the economy, and was accepted by the workers because of the elimination of the national conflict in the labor market. In joining Oppenheimer's vision of publicly owned land and cooperative principles with nationally inspired and state-sponsored Prussian "internal colonization," Ruppin evolved the elements necessary for an alliance with the only group of available settlers: the agricultural workers. Through the agency of the *kvutza* the WZO found the settlers for Palestine while "cooperative organization" became for the WZO and the workers the accepted formula for national colonization.

"Degania," Kolatt assures us, "began to assume ideological significance only slowly and belatedly. Insofar as Degania assumed such
significance, it was depicted initially more as a place of 'autonomous
labor' [I prefer this expression to the literal but atrocious English
translation of *avoda atzmit* as "self labor"] than as a collective group."[164]
Furthermore, Kolatt adds "the kibbutz movement in Eretz Israel is not
just the history of the unfolding and realization of the nucleus of Degania,
but the addition of new motives, forms and tasks."[165] Two such revisions
are evident: the first concerned the aim of demographic, or pure,
colonization, the second, the socialism of the kibbutz.

The cooperation favored by members of the Second *Aliya* was of a
restricted type, probably best described as a half-way solution between
the communal orientation and the strong individualist tendency that
characterized so many of the immigrants before the First World War.
This compromise found its expression in the preference for the small and
intimate group of about a dozen families, which was ultimately to
appropriate for itself the term *kvutza*. This organizational framework
arose out of the experience of a wave of immigration that saw the
overwhelming majority of its members leave the country and, therefore,
identified those remaining as "idealists," i.e. as an elite. After the First
World War, with the onset of the Third *Aliya* in 1918, it became obvious
that the *kvutza* was not fit to be the tool of mass colonization, and as such
was savagely criticized by Shlomo Lavie of the Second *Aliya* and by the
new immigrants of the Third *Aliya*. Lavie pointed out that the small and
closed *kvutzot* "do not have the potential to generate a movement." The
abandonment of the comprehensive perspective, i.e. what was called in
this study the goal of pure settlement, was seen by Lavie as the failure of
the Second *Aliya*, presenting, I might add, an obvious analogy between it
and the First *Aliya*. He wrote that if

We want to become a movement . . . we cannot be satisfied by remaining a
handful of self-congratulatory idealists. This was not our desire. Our intention
was one of becoming a movement, a human movement encompassing everybody,
a movement that does not allow the distinction between the dull and the
dexterous, and the sentencing of the one to hunger and the other to affluence.[166]

When the *kvutza* at Kinneret decided in 1919 to admit as members new
immigrants that were only sent to live there while drying a marsh, the
intimate *kvutza* was for the first time replaced by the inclusive kibbutz.
The first large kibbutz was established at Ein Harod in 1922.

The transition from the *kvutza* to the kibbutz signaled another major
revision: the equalization of living and working conditions in *lieu* of
intimacy and sharing. In the kibbutz, in contradistinction to the *kvutza*,
solidarity derived not from personal bonds but from the common project.

This change underlay the theory and legitimation of the kibbutz. Only the Third *Aliya*, arriving between 1918–23, having freshly experienced the Russian Revolution of 1917, painted the kibbutz in its subsequent ideological armor, viewing it as the Eretz Israeli path to socialism. Some sought to realize in the kibbutz the socialist-anarchist ideas of Gustav Landauer, others the ideas of Martin Buber, etc., while the leaders of Ein Harod, and the Labor Legion which evolved there, attempted to interpret the meaning of collective forms of life in Eretz Israel in Marxist terms, notwithstanding the fact that most immigrants of the Second *Aliya* sought to dissociate themselves from communism.[167] "Without the arrival of the youth of the Third *Aliya*, and their many-sided socialists ideals," argues Ben-Avram, "it is doubtful whether the idea of the *kvutza*, as it was formulated during the Second *Aliya*, would have coalesced into a social conception of general significance and a pattern of full cooperation in all spheres of life."[168] It was then that inchoate cooperativism was reinterpreted as ideologically grounded collectivism. Ironically, the communist aspirations of some immigrants of the Third *Aliya*, expressed most powerfully in the establishment of the shared expense account of the Labor Legion, were defeated through the bureaucratic centralism of the Histadrut. But the socialist character of the kibbutz remained an article of faith among its members.

Nevertheless, as we have seen, the national character of the kibbutz was its foundation and first *raison d'être* and determined its composition, and in part its structure. The kibbutz became the most homogenous body of Israeli society: it included almost exclusively Eastern European Jews, since it was unwilling to embrace Middle Eastern and North African Jews,[169] and was constructed on the exclusion of Palestinian Arabs. I tried in this study to give these two groups their due place in the kibbutz's prehistory, since the former, having been allowed only the most limited access to the JNF's land, and the latter, no access at all, are missing from the kibbutz's history. The kibbutz was built on such land and hence became the real nucleus of Israeli state formation, despite the fact that kibbutz members always constituted a distinct minority of the Jews in Palestine.

Examining the changing character of the *kvutza* subsequent to the Second *Aliya* a new question arises: why was the kibbutz capable of shouldering the tasks of mass colonization and also becoming the focus of intense social experimentation, while remaining a viable and attractive institution throughout the Mandatory period? The reason, in my mind, should be sought in the firm economic infrastructure of the kibbutz, which had bypassed with unequalled success the threat of competition by Palestinian Arab workers – that is, in its national character. Protection from the market provided the kibbutz with a guaranteed, even if low, European standard of living. In addition, the self selection of the members ensured a high level of solidarity, the commonly owned resources promoted economic rationalism and efficiency under conditions of a relatively undeveloped economy, the settlement on nationalized land encouraged dedication to the national cause, and the new body's frequent origin in a "conquest group" disciplined the members. The Third *Aliya* already took for granted this grand success of the Second *Aliya* in the elimination of Arab competition; what caught their imagination was the elimination of the employer and the cooperative forms of life that made it possible. The latter then served as the basis of the Third *Aliya*'s experimentation with and increase of its impressive and world-renowned, though exclusively Jewish, collectivist socialist potential.

National ownership of land was even more important than exclusive Jewish employment in accounting for the significance of the kibbutz for Israeli state formation, as the comparison with Jewish towns demonstrates. Since urban land was more expensive and therefore easily given to speculation, the WZO could not overturn the market principle in the town. As a result, the Palestinian Jewish town, which frequently also developed in partial or complete separation from the Palestinian Arab population, but mostly on private land, never was mobilized as thoroughly for national causes as was the kibbutz. Thus, the significance of the kibbutz in the formation of the Israeli state and nation was much greater than its share of the *Yishuv*'s population would indicate. Finally, "quality" did outweigh "quantity."

The transition to independence also bears out the argument which views the kibbutz as the major state-forming tool. After 1948, when the independent State of Israel undertook the regulation of Jewish–Arab relations and a "*caste* system" was substituted for *exclusionary* labor market practices, and the size of the remaining Arab population was relatively small, the significance of the kibbutz for Israeli society dwindled, its share of Israeli population remained stationary and subsequently decreased, and it came to be characterized by waves of desertion. We may also observe the historically contingent character of the kibbutz by pointing out that even when Jewish frontier settlement was restarted in the Jordan Rift after the Six Day War of 1967 by the labor movement, the kibbutz occupied a small and ever declining share of it.

Collective and utopian organizations, among which it is customary to include the kibbutz, have almost invariably failed throughout the world, and certainly never flourished in a similar fashion. Why has the kibbutz enjoyed such a different fate from the others? The answer to this question lies, it seems to me, in the fact that most forms of self-governing cooperatives were established to reform the existing social and economic order by offering an alternative social organization, and therefore invoked the wrath of the powers-that-be. By contrast, the kibbutz was not set up in opposition to the "state," but with the active support of the quasi-state of the WZO to which it attached itself. Indeed the kibbutz was established as the foundation of the Israeli state-to-be.

Chapter Eight

Conclusion: Israeli nationalism and the Israeli–Palestinian conflict

The past is never dead, it is not even past.

William Faulkner

A generation that denigrates the preceding generation and fails to see its greatness and necessary significance, cannot but be narrow-minded and without faith in itself, even if it assumes a gladiator-like pose and a frenzy for greatness.

Antonio Gramsci, *Prison Notebooks*, 1927/37

The shaping of the Israeli state and nation

The course of Jewish state and nation formation in Palestine before the First World War was checkered and hesitant. In the span of thirty odd years it went through many experiments and reversals. And yet, organizational experiments that were begun during the Second *Aliya* proved formative for later periods and point to an unbroken historical continuity from Ottoman times to independent Israel, though, obviously, subsequent processes had to nourish these early buds to maturity.

In all, I distinguished six essential stages of Jewish activity in the land and labor markets. The arrival of the first members of Hovevei Zion in 1882 opened the *earliest stage*, which endeavored to create a smallholding farmer stratum, though one combining field-crop and plantation agriculture, and only in part self-reliant in labor. Within less than a year in Rishon Letzion and Zichron Yaacov, and somewhat later in most other moshavot of the First *Aliya*, the tutelary Rothschild administration was deployed. This *second stage* witnessed the intensification of the typical pattern of colonial plantation agriculture and the reliance on employment of a large, unskilled, seasonal Palestinian Arab labor force, mixed with a small Jewish labor force. It also was a period of large-scale territorial acquisition. In a *third phase*, set off by the abrupt termination of the financially non-viable Rothschild system in 1900, the plantation system was ruthlessly rationalized under the aegis of the JCA, and its Jewish labor force well-nigh eliminated.

A new wave of experimentation began with the onset of the Second *Aliya*, at the end of 1903. In a brief and frustrated *fourth phase*, propertyless immigrant Jews entered the labor market again, attempting to lower their standard of living to the level of the Palestinian Arab workers. Thus, the first stages in the lives of the First and Second *Aliyot* were based on embracing, respectively, Arab agricultural methods and Arab standards of living. These attempts were abandoned, in both cases, within months. While the inadequacy of the First *Aliya*'s original design enhanced the transition toward a capitalist plantation system that was aimed at the international market, the frustration of the Second *Aliya*'s initial strategy intensified the nationalist dimension of its aims. These experiences reveal that the evolving strategies of the first two *Aliyot* represent, to an important extent, different responses to the same crucial problem: the dire necessity to find a type or mix of crops or employment, along with a corresponding form of social and economic organization, that could assure their members a quasi-European standard of living or wages. This fundamental constraint was a constant – and remained so for subsequent *Aliyot* – even if the choices they made in response, dependent as they were on the social circumstances of the members of the two waves and on the nature of their major outside supporters, were different. The creative efforts of the two early *Aliyot*, so different yet so similar, demonstrate the extent to which the very possibility of Jewish settlement in Palestine was determined by definite economic considerations, and how little the forms it took represent the simple unfolding of Zionist ideological goals.

The critical step in Israeli state building and nation formation took place with the inauguration of the *fifth stage* in 1905 when the productivization drive of the Eastern European Jewish Enlightenment (*Haskala*) was transformed, in Palestine, into "conquest of labor" – an aspiration to monopolize at first all manual labor, subsequently at least skilled jobs, by Jewish workers. Already in the "conquest of labor" phase the boundaries of the Israeli nation were determined. Yemenite, as well as other *mizrachi* Jews, were incorporated into Israeli society but placed in an inferior position in the labor market and social structure, while Palestinian Arabs were definitively excluded even as a labor force. This strategy, though not effective before the First World War, and even later yielding only modest results, left the legacy of *Jewish exclusivism*.

After 1909, a *sixth phase* opened up in the settlement of Palestine. It was characterized by "autonomous labor," the conceptualization of settlement in its cooperative phase. The advent of this expression corresponded to an important terminological metamorphosis which took place in the self-description of our protagonists: they gradually stopped referring to themselves as "workers" (*poalim*) and began viewing themselves as "laborers" (*ovdim*). As long as they fought for employment in the labor market, the term "worker" was appropriate; the new term signaled renewed access to settlement on the JNF's land. Instead of a "working class" the new self-image became "laboring settlement" (*yishuv oved*, and later *hityashvut ovedet*). The following was Yaacov Rabinowitz's summary of this new phase, which he delivered at the Fourth Congress of the Federation of the Agricultural Workers of Judea, in December 1913:

The laboring settlement will not produce workers *per se*, but laborers . . . The laborer of the future will be a blending of the worker and the farmer. And instead of having, as we do now, workers without work and without land, and farmers without work whose land is dropping out from under their feet, we will have in the future a laborer who will be a worker-farmer, in possession of both labor and land.[1]

Kolatt points out that "one of the distinguishing characteristics of the Eretz Israeli labor movement is its being a settlement movement,"[2] but it is doubtful whether one can call a settlement movement a labor movement at the same time. Rather, in the second decade of this century, the former was transformed into the latter and the laborer became for all practical purposes a settler. Consequently, the Jewish exclusivism of "conquest of labor" was gradually complemented with and superseded by the dominant method of Israeli state and nation formation, still exclusionary in its focus on "autonomous labor" but implemented outside the domain of the market economy. We should remember, though, that the establishment of the kibbutzim did not put an end to the "conquest of labor" drive, since the JNF could not immediately provide land for all new arrivals, and consequently until 1948 unskilled Jewish agricultural workers suffered from considerable unemployment.[3] At the same time, employment in the labor market was intended to be temporary and ceased being the dead end it used to be for Second *Aliya* workers.

Initially, the workers of the Second *Aliya* were hostile to settlement, since it seemed only to increase the employment opportunities of Arab workers and consequently to exacerbate their own plight,[4] while the WZO, under Herzl's leadership, expected to attain Palestine through diplomatic means rather than through actual colonization. The first decade of this century witnessed the gradual forging of an "alliance" between the two, an "alliance" in which the WZO, for many years and without doubt during the Ottoman period, played the leading role. It was the WZO which first evolved a "pure settlement theory," while the workers were called on to implement it. While the WZO finessed its "method" of settlement in the years before and after the First World War, the workers evolved their own "pure settlement theory," which in many ways dovetailed with, even if in specifics it revised, the WZO's own "theory."

The agricultural workers of the Second *Aliya* began changing their attitude to settlement when it was linked with a solution to the "problem of the worker" – that is, when the WZO's initiative of cooperative settlement ended up eliminating wage labor and *eo ipso* the worker. This method, synthesizing the land reform, cooperative settlement, and internal – i.e. national – colonization methods of the JNF, PLDC, and the Palestine Office, with the cooperative practices of the organized *ashkenazi* agricultural workers, became the basis of the alliance between the two. "The respect for the Berlin school of German Zionism," asserts Jonathan Frankel, "rose in direct proportion to the decline in the prestige of the Russian Hovevei Zion."[5] On the eve of the First World War, Shprintzak recognized that the WZO had taken over the role of Rothschild and the JCA, since it was accepted as "the only body able to create national settlement shaped by autonomous labor, nationalization of land, and Jewish culture – a settlement that carries in it the seeds of real renaissance." Walking "the path of simultaneous land and labor redemption," as in the case of Degania and Merchavia, the Palestine Office gained "trust, recognition, and respect."[6] But to cement an alliance with the WZO, the workers first had to evolve, on top of their "pure settlement methodology," also their own "pure settlement theory" – their understanding of the necessary conditions for working-class, and after the First World War, socialist colonization.

The clearest and earliest version of a "settlement theory" for the propertyless was already offered, beginning in 1907, by Shlomo Kaplansky, a leader of the Austrian wing of Poalei Zion, an early supporter of the Oppenheimer plan, and leader of the opposition within Poalei Zion to Ber Borochov. Though many others contributed to the intellectual metamorphosis, the overcoming of the opposition to settlement and the transition from "conquest of labor" to "autonomous labor," was essentially legitimated in the work of two ideologues: in Hapoel Hatzair, A. D. Gordon, and in Poalei Zion, Nachman Syrkin.[7]

Gordon's articles, which he began publishing in *Hapoel Hatzair* in 1909, removed the discussion from the insufferable external conditions of the "conquest of labor" to the internal potentials of the worker, and ultimately pointed in the unlikely direction of spiritual liberation. In want of real power to meet the demands of the day, he invoked "an intangible power – the very ideal of labor." A. D. Gordon demanded that labor be viewed not as a way of improving one's life conditions by earning wages, but as an end in itself which, especially when connected with agricultural cultivation, tied the worker to nature, and like a religious calling inspired him spiritually. This abstract and romantic *tour de force* was tied in some of his articles with timely matters. To be "assimilated" with labor and devoted to it as a means of self-transformation, the worker needed to be free, to possess a spiritual tie with like-minded workers, and to be in possession of the tools of work and of land. These Gordon demanded that the JNF provide for the worker.[8] It is hard to convey the tremendous moral and social impact of the new teaching. Gordon's "religion of labor," as his contemporary Rabbi Benjamin called his ideas, constituted a powerful tradition for the kibbutz movement, though his actual writings lost the interest they held and the readership they commanded soon after his death in 1922.

Poalei Zion, for their part, rediscovered in 1912 the writings of an equally unlikely ideologue: Nachman Syrkin, a territorialist, who rejoined the WZO. Syrkin shared with Borochov the quest for a synthesis of working-class nationalism with a universal historical process. This he found in the cooperative movement, and his theoretical formulation signals the beginnings of the appropriation of the kibbutz for socialist ideology – linking it, however, not with Marxism but with, of all things, "utopian socialism." The cooperative enterprise, according to Syrkin, became an important branch of socialism. Robert Owen's cooperative colonization had failed, according to Syrkin, due to the inappropriate mixture of communist and cooperative elements. The linking of cooperation and colonization – "socialist settlement" – he expected to be successful.[9]

The workers' "pure settlement theory" that evolved on the heels of settlement practices of "autonomous labor" may best be described as being founded on four major elements. The *first* one called for the rejection of the capitalist path. Zerubavel posed the question rhetorically on the pages of *Haachdut* in 1911:

Which has the advantage? Private property or public property? Experience has now shown us the road to be taken . . . Only public property, that sets before itself historical ideals and goals and is not pursuing momentary victories, is capable of experiments, trials, and dangers. Only [public property] and no other, therefore, is appropriate for the economic conditions of Eretz Israel, and [capable of] preparing the ground for the activities of the masses of Jewish workers – the true carriers of our ideals . . .[10]

Though Vilkansky already expressed his doubts about the capitalist path of colonization in *Hapoel Hatzair* towards the end of 1909,[11] the shift and its language in Zerubavel were more remarkable. After all, Zerubavel was a prominent leader of Poalei Zion, and a member of its weekly's editorial board. Not only had Zerubavel thrown overboard the theme of capitalist development but he also justified association with "public property" in terms of the idealism the WZO and the workers shared!

The *second* element in the transition from labor to the land was accompanied by the demand to nationalize land. In Vilkansky's words: "the nationalization of land is a necessary condition for the creation of a laboring settlement."[12] The Israeli labor movement in Palestine, under the formative influence of the Jewish–Palestinian labor market conflict, and in contradistinction to early socialist movements, demanded the nationalization of only one means of production, land, and was by and large oblivious to others. The reason was that it sought employment opportunities and not improved working conditions, and the former turned on nationalization of land and not on socialization of the means of production in general: it was the principle of exclusive Jewish land-ownership that could be extended into a guarantee of exclusive Jewish employment. It was recognized that the basic principles of the JNF's Memorandum of Association – public ownership of land, hereditary lease to tenants, proscription of subleasing, etc. – were the best guarantees of workers' colonization if the WZO was willing to put them systematically into practice.

Thirdly, the organization best suited to take advantage of public property in the form of national land was the *kvutza*. The appropriateness of the *kvutza* for its role in the workers' "settlement theory" was overdetermined by many reasons. Kaplansky for example listed the following ones:

the worker has to free himself from being dependent on the private moshava's labor market; he has to learn all the tasks of agricultural work; he has to be credit worthy; finally this settlement method haas to be sophisticated in all technical-agricultural aspects in order to raise the profits of Eretz Israeli agriculture and make possible the employment of Jewish workers. The agricultural collective fulfills all these requirements.

The fact that the lands of the kibbutz were cultivated by its members ensured that the competition of Arab and Jewish workers would not recur in the cooperative settlement. To attain this aim, a great deal of attention was paid to the necessity of tailoring the size of the kibbutz's land to the size of its membership. Arabs, therefore, could not work or live in a kibbutz, and the *ashkenazi* workers also preferred by and large to exclude Yemenite Jews from membership in their settlements. In consequence, the kibbutz became an exclusively Eastern European Jewish form of settlement.

But the major interest served by the cooperative form of life was demographic. In Kaplansky's words, since most immigrants to Palestine were propertyless, "they come with their labor power, and therefore they examine every settlement method from one angle only: whether it is able to supply work and living to the broad stratum of the people." The *kvutza* was the solution to this problem "and it is clear to us now that the development of the *Yishuv* demands of us the widest use of the agricultural cooperatives."[13]

A *fourth* element in the agricultural laborers' "settlement theory," which was to gain in significance with time, was their quest for increased influence within the WZO. Aharonowitz demanded the exclusive concentration of the WZO on the "creation of a laboring settlement (*yishuv oved*)."[14] But it was Berl Katznelson who transformed the "self-liberation" of the laborers from the labor market and their settlement, and the unfolding "alliance" with the WZO, into the moral foundation and conviction of a hegemonic group. He asked rhetorically:

what are we to the *yishuv* and what is the *yishuv* to us? Are we just workers, laborers, machines – in which case we carry no responsibility for general projects . . . or are we participants in the creation who want to become something, some power, and who then carry the moral responsibility for all the projects which we are part of?[15]

Jonathan Frankel locates at this juncture the foundation of the labor movement's "struggle for hegemony."[16] This struggle was to rest on the broad shoulders of the Israeli-state-in-the-making: the Histadrut.

The Histadrut was established in response to two kinds of pressures. Internally, it served the leaders of the Second *Aliya* as the tool for the cooptation of the third wave (1918–23) of immigrants who, soon after their arrival in Palestine, began organizing themselves in autonomous and potentially competing bodies to the parties of the Second *Aliya*. The concern of the "oldtimers" was that the Third *Aliya* which, under the influence of the Russian Revolution, increased its socialist convictions, would not follow the path of "constructivism" they laid down.[17] Externally, as Yonathan Shapiro so keenly demonstrated, the organizational unity of the workers was the only barrier to the potentially unsympathetic use of the WZO's resources and ensured the standing of the agricultural laborers within the continued "alliance" of the two bodies.[18]

When the Histadrut was established at the end of 1920 the interconnection of the Second *Aliya*'s three principal, but autonomous, organizational attempts to bypass the inhospitable labor market – in the political sphere by the establishment of Hapoel Hatzair Party and the reinterpretation of Poalei Zion's doctrines; in the military sphere by the setting up of the Hashomer guard organization; and in the economic and social sphere by bringing into existence the organizations of cooperative "autonomous labor" and above all the kibbutzim – was revealed. The Histadrut came to be based, though not without dissension, on this tripod. The economic goals of the cooperative organizations of the workers in agriculture and other spheres of life were transferred *tout court* to the Histadrut, and the kibbutzim were affiliated with the Histadrut through its "Agricultural Center" (Merkaz Hachaklai). When Hapoel Hatzair opposed the inclusion of the military organization Hagana in the Histadrut it was overruled by Achdut Haavoda with the help of the new immigrants.[19] Only in the political and bureaucratic area did the Third *Aliya* leave its distinct organizational mark on the Histadrut. When Achdut Haavoda wished to transfer political tasks to the new body while the new immigrants of the Third *Aliya*, under the influence of the Leninist perspective, insisted on maintaining separate party organizations, a compromise emerged. Though the Histadrut became mostly an economic body, the elections to it were conducted on the basis of proportional representation of the existing parties. Parties, if so, existed and competed both inside and outside the Histadrut, while in most other societies trade unions usually are either non-partisan or are affiliated with only one political party. The subjugation of trade-union and market interests to political control also created, as Shapiro observed, the primacy of bureaucratic politics over electoral politics,[20] favoring cooptation above democratic practices within the Jewish community.

As we have had the opportunity to observe, in all three areas – politics, security, and settlement – the national goals of pure settlement became predominant during the period of the Second *Aliya*. The workers' trade-union interests, usually represented by the Histadrut's urban wing, subsequently remained, though not without periodic opposition, subjugated to this national goal.[21] The Histadrut's charter, displaying a near-absence of socialist objectives, accurately reflected its national character, and conveyed the radical nationalist legacy of the Second *Aliya*.

In general, the Second *Aliya*'s organizations, and their successors, proved formative for the Jewish community in Mandatory Palestine and for independent Israel, and predominated in the emerging Israeli society – and, in many areas, still do. The kibbutz became during the First World War and increasingly during Mandatory times the cornerstone of a comprehensive cooperative economy that included: an agricultural marketing company – Tnuva; a general marketing organization – Hamashbir Hamerkhazi; a road building and construction company – Solel Bone; a workers' bank – Bank Hapoalim; an insurance company – Hashne; a sick fund – Kupat Holim; an industrial concern – Koor; a public bus company – Eged; – and many more, most of them giants of the Israeli economy today. All these cooperative and financial bodies are administered and owned by Hevrat Haovdim (the Workers' Society) of the Histadrut that was created in 1924. These cooperative bodies, like the kibbutz itself, were protected from outside competition and enjoyed the advantage of shared resources and an internal market. Being a-state-in-the-making, the Histadrut developed employment opportunities, and set up its own economic enterprises, required for absorption of new immigrants.

This direct continuity, however, cannot be asserted with equal vigor in regard to Israeli *nation formation*, i.e. to intra-ethnic Jewish relations, since between the First World War and Israel's establishment there was no sustained *mizrachi* immigration to Israel. Nevertheless, when *mizrachi* immigrants arrived in massive numbers after 1948, the same structural relationship between *ashkenazim* and *mizrachim* found in the Yavnieli wave reasserted itself. With the forcible scattering of the Palestinian Arab population during the War of Independence, the new *mizrachi* immigrants came in effect to occupy many of the lower rungs of the occupational ladder and also served as the labor force of the government-propelled Israeli drive for industrialization in the 1950s and 1960s.[22]

The predominance of the Second *Aliya*'s method of state and nation formation was not due to the non-national or the particularly unimaginative nature of the First. We encountered in this study attempts undertaken by some of the prominent planters to claim the prerogative as the real founders of the Jewish settlement in Palestine, and examples of their resourcefulness in attaining the support of the various colonizing bodies, above all the WZO, for some aspects of their method. Eisenberg established Agudat Netaim as a tool of capitalist colonization and received the financial backing of the WZO for the catalysis of Yemenite Jewish immigration: a potentially "ideal" solution of the demographic question within the framework of the ethnic plantation settlement. Aaronsohn emphasized agricultural and technological innovation in economic development and diplomatic and military initiative in the political arena. The WZO, and especially its bank, the APAC, indeed almost never backed "conquest of labor." Aaronsohn also enjoyed the support of the leadership of American Zionism in the economic realm, and for a brief period during the First World War his association with

General Allenby overshadowed the rest of the First *Aliya*'s less adventurous leaders. Finally, Mordechai Ben-Hillel Hacohen sought to invoke, though without success, the assistance of the WZO in establishing effective economic, and potentially political, control of the planters over propertyless immigrants. In all spheres – economic, demographic, military, and political – the planters sought to maintain and expand their version of Zionist colonization.

But the WZO's *raison d'être* was to direct a massive share of the Eastern European Jewish refugees to Palestine. Hence the WZO sought "pure Jewish settlement," and the First *Aliya*'s commitment to ethnic plantation type settlement, being based on the labor of the Palestinian inhabitants of the land, could not find favor with it. Even so, the evolution of cooperation between the WZO and the agricultural workers of the Second *Aliya* had to wait until *both* disabused themselves of the feasibility of massive plantation based colonization.

The workers evolved their "pure settlement method" first, and their "pure settlement theory" only later, towards the eve of the war. The WZO, which was the first to possess the "pure settlement theory," had prepared itself for its pending alliance with the labor movement between the closing period of the First World War and the July 1920 Zionist interim Conference in London by putting the final touches on its "method." Freed of the illusions of generating mass Jewish colonization in Palestine through the capitalist method of ethnic colonization, the various organs of the WZO, and especially the JNF, sought to develop a full-scale method of nationalist colonization. This process was particularly tortuous since, as a result of the war, German Jewry lost its prominent position at the head of the WZO, the JNF's head office was transferred to the Hague, the political leadership surrounding Chaim Weizmann concentrated in London, and the American branch emerged as a full-scale participant and competitor for the mantle of leadership. Even so, ultimately the new leadership around Weizmann ended up by and large reaffirming and expanding, that is reappropriating for itself, the lessons of the "German period."

The initial steps were taken by the JNF which, under Nechemia de Lieme's lead, published a series of position papers in 1917/18, trying to recapture for the JNF that central stage in the WZO[23] which was usurped in the preceding years by Ruppin, the PLDC, and the Palestine Office. These pamphlets by de Lieme, Oppenheimer, Böhm, and especially the WZO's rising new agronomist Jacob Oettinger, extolled the practical benefits of the JNF's hereditary lease of land for facilitating what I termed pure settlement, and they called national colonization. The hereditary lease could expedite the immigration of masses who would not need to sink their meager resources into land purchase. It could become the tool for ensuring the employment of Jewish workers, attaching the farmer to the land, and preventing the denationalization threatening privately owned land. Finally, it limited the rise of land values due to speculation.[24] On the basis of these advantages de Lieme demanded that the JNF be recognized as "the sole organ of Jewish land policy in Palestine."[25]

The July 1920 interim Zionist Conference debated and set guidelines for land policy.[26] Though the representatives of the Eretz Israeli workers' parties failed to gain approval for their motion that the JNF alone be permitted to purchase land in Palestine (a demand which had little chance of gaining the support of the British Mandate authorities anyway), the Conference resolved that the aims of its policy, to be carried out by the JNF were:

> to use the voluntary contributions received from the Jewish people as a means for making the land of Palestine the common property of the Jewish people; to give out the land exclusively on hereditary leasehold and on hereditary building-right; to assist the settlement on their own farms of Jewish agricultural workers; to see that the ground is worked, and to combat speculation; to safeguard Jewish labor.[27]

Although the Conference, being concerned with the paucity of its resources, refused to close the door to private colonization, it restricted its assistance to those private settlers who "cultivate the land themselves." Finally, the WZO decided "to cooperate with the workers' institutions in the fields of the provision of employment, cooperation, education, medical aid, mutual credit, and the organization of the immigration of active workers."[28] Still the new colonizing body – the Keren Hayesod (Foundation Fund) – established by the Conference as a handmaiden to the JNF, in order to fund mostly "permanent national institutions or economic undertakings" – was expected to be a dividend-paying body, though, like so many times before, this never happened.[29] Although the workers' leaders – who, burdened by a decade of negative experience sought ironclad assurances for national protection of Jewish labor and full support for settlement – left the Conference in the throes of despair, not even being fully backed by Ruppin,[30] in fact, the alliance was now operative at the highest level. This misreading of the writing on the wall is the final confirmation of the dominance of the WZO at the early stages of the two groups' relations. Though the path of capitalist colonization – indirectly advocated by the American delegation headed by Justice Brandeis, and beaten back in 1920 – came back to haunt the WZO's deliberations on a number of occasions, the reversals suffered by the cause of the workers were always temporary as the makeup of the potential settlers rarely changed for long.

Palestine, however deeply it was embedded in the Jewish psyche, was a less desirable European settlement society than many of the alternatives available to Jewish immigrants. As long as other shores were open only a small percentage of *ashkenazi* Jews chose Palestine. They came only twice in massive numbers and then only as refugees, first from Nazism, before and after the Second World War, and later, following the War of Independence, were joined by *mizrachim* fleeing Arab hostility in North Africa and the Middle East. To attract voluntary Jewish immigrants and attain the critical demographic mass necessary to establish a claim to parts of Palestine, a popular social program remained essential. Though the land area of Palestine purchased by all Jewish organizations and individuals before 1948 – 7 percent of its total, and about 12 to 15 of its cultivable area – was limited, the continued provision of "free land" by the JNF was indispensable in this respect.

The Histadrut and the JNF, operating in the labor and land markets respectively, were the two pillars of the separatist method of Jewish state formation around which the practice of Israeli nationalism evolved. Their respective aims were the closing of the labor and land markets (though the JNF's success required the initial openness of the land market while Jewish purchases were effected and its subsequent closing to retain Jewish ownership).[31] In the "alliance" between the organized sectors of the Eastern European agricultural laborers and the WZO, the former were transformed from workers into settlers, while the WZO became a truly popular movement. This close relationship between the various branches of the WZO and the Histadrut that was "heavily subsidized" by them[32] focused on the facilitation of immigration, absorption, and settlement, and in Michael Shalev's telling formulation, represented "a practical alliance between a settlement movement without settlers and a workers' movement without work."[33]

The evolution of the Israeli–Palestinian conflict

Having surveyed in this study the paramount effect of the Palestinian–Jewish conflict on the shaping of Israeli state and society, I would like in the balance of this chapter to focus on the character of the conflict itself, and to examine its impact on the Palestinian Arabs. In this section I will examine this topic in two stages: the escalation of the conflict from its "hidden" beginnings to its open confrontations. Finally, in the last section, I will present the impact of the particular method of Jewish state building and nation formation in Palestine on Jewish–Arab relations.

The opening of the frontier and the "hidden question"

In their comparative study of *The Frontier in History*, Lamar and Thompson chart a chronological sequence from the opening of the frontier "when the first representatives of the intrusive society arrive" to its potential closure "when a single political authority has established hegemony."[34] The extended frontier encounter, for example between white settlers and native Americans, roughly followed a

> succession of initial contact which offers friendly welcome to the white invaders and mutual exchange; then a period of competition, conflict, and conquest; followed by a time of adjustment and accommodation by the tribes to their altered situation, which often includes removal or reduction.[35]

Examining in Palestine not the gamut of a frontier conflict, but the much shorter period of initial intrusion, I detect great internal variation even in this phase. One of the reasons seems to be that on a frontier characterized by nationalist opposition, the early cycles of cooperation are less clearly articulated and hostility is apparent much earlier. It seems, on the basis of the historical record, that in the case of the Israeli–Palestinian conflict we may observe a number of phases, all of which had witnessed escalation between the contending parties, but were interrupted by the intervention of outside powers and events (such as the First World War, and the British repression of the 1936–9 Revolt) forcing the conflict to retire to a lower level, only to resume the process of escalation and bring it to a higher pitch in the next round. Cyclical escalation, then, would be an appropriate term to describe these relations.

The first cycle of this trajectory leads from an initial *modus vivendi* of coexistence and minor clashes from the outset of the First *Aliya*, to an open, though still not consequential, level of hostility by 1914.

Without the cooperation of Palestinian Arab villagers the earliest Jewish settlers would have been in dire straits. Early immigrants in Hadera, Mishmar Hayarden, Metulla, Machanayim, etc. received part of their agricultural training from their Arab neighbors or laborers, and frequently they also learned how to perform semi-agricultural and non-agricultural tasks from experienced Palestinians. In the Galilee they used the traditional Arab nail-plow drawn by oxen; in many places they took to raising crops that were successfully grown in adjacent Arab villages.[36] The Jewish settlers of Sedjra, Hadera, Kinneret dwelled initially in Arab caravansarais or large houses (*han*).[37] Since the moshavot soon came to be based on monoculture, vegetables, milk, and eggs were regularly purchased from surrounding Palestinian villages, and some of the produce, including oranges, was typically sold to Arab merchants, who could advance cash to the planters.[38] In many odd ways Jewish settlers relied on Arab work or assistance: Palestinian water-drawer women carried water in jugs on their heads to Metulla; in Hadera, Jews and Palestinians jointly planted watermelons; in many places they purchased manure heaps as organic fertilizers from Palestinian villagers.[39] The guards of almost all Jewish settlements until 1908, but frequently even after, were Bedouins, Maghrebis, or Circassians. And, of course, the overwhelming majority of the *charats* in field-crop settlements of the Galilee and the labor force of the Judean plantation moshavot was Palestinian.

But probably the most important factor in accommodating Palestinians to Jewish settlers was that the latter, whether in Rechovot, Hadera, Rosh Pina, Kastina, etc., were incapable of cultivating all their new land at once and continued re-leasing part of it to previous cultivators. The eviction of past cultivators was only partial and many of these were not fully proletarianized. This situation minimized for a time the break between old and new ownerships. In most places, however, the leasing of land was ended even before the arrival of Second *Aliya*.[40]

Kalvarisky's description, in Brit Shalom's magazine, that "in general, the relations between Jews and Arabs in the old moshavot were fairly good," was based on this kind of evidence.[41] But such accommodation was only one part of the total picture, and the settlers of the First *Aliya* also found themselves to be objects of hostility and attack from the beginning.

The foremost bone of contention between Jewish settlers and Palestinian Arab peasants was land, but the particular forms land conflicts took varied. Mandel and Beeri emphasize that some of the confrontations were connected with the backwardness of Ottoman land registration, others with "mistakes" – Jews being "ignorant of Arabic and Arab ways; inadvertently . . . flouted local custom."[42] Finally, additional conflicts were rooted in dispossession, real or intended.

All these factors, in their multifarious entanglement, were present in the first mass attack on a Jewish moshava, directed by the Arab villagers of Yahudiya, in March 1886, against Petach Tikva. The 14,200 dunams of this colony were purchased from Anton Bishara Tayan and Salim Kaser, two Christian Orthodox merchants and moneylenders from Jaffa, who acquired the land, and retained its owners – the villagers of Umlabess and Yahudiya – as tenant farmers, when their land was sequestered by the authorities for being in arrears in the payment of taxes. Given the crude character of the *tapu*, the Ottoman land register, parts of the purchase were disputed: the Arab tenant farmers very likely were legally entitled to the possession of 2,600 dunams, though Tayan claimed to have sold the whole area to its new owners. But even the rest of the area could not be registered in the *tapu* because of the opposition of Rauf Pasha, the Mutasarrif of Jerusalem, who conscientiously enforced Ottoman restrictions on Jewish settlement. As long as the Jewish settlers cultivated only part of the land themselves and subleased other parts to its previous cultivators these animosities did not break into the open. This situation lasted for a number of years, since the early settlers of Petach Tikva, who came from the traditional Old *Yishuv* in Jerusalem, abandoned the colony and its settlement was renewed only upon the joining of a group of First *Aliya* immigrants from Bialystok.

The new settlers, however, demanded in 1886 that the Arab tenant farmers of Yahudiya vacate some of the fields to which they claimed ownership. The latter invoked the traditional right of having already completed the first part of the two-year crop rotation and expected to be allowed to plant the fields with the economically more valuable winter crop. To secure the claim they plowed these fields, and when one of the settlers on his way home rode across their field, they seized his horse. The Jewish settlers reciprocated by impounding nine Arab-owned donkeys which, again following traditional usage, were sent to graze freely on fields already harvested. Next day, when most Jewish colonists were absent, a few hundred Arab villagers attacked Petach Tikva with stones and sticks, broke doors and windows, robbed some houses, retrieved the donkeys and took possession of a Jewish herd, and wounded five people. Following the intervention of the Austrian, German, American, and Spanish consuls, thirty-one villagers from Yahudiya were arrested, but eventually the two sides compromised and no trial was held. The authoritative Jewish report emphasized that the attack was not motivated by national hatred, and therefore should not be construed as a pogrom.[43]

Similar assaults were directed in 1888 by villagers of Katara on Gedera, and in 1892 and 1893 by villagers of Zarnuga and Sateria on Rechovot. The pretexts of these acts were similar – conflicts over boundaries, grazing rights etc. – and they all ended in compromise in *lieu* of trial. While Mandel and Beeri attach great significance to the disagreement over customs and lack of clear boundaries, it seems to me that defense of traditional rights and roundabout methods of harassment to which the Palestinian Arab peasants resorted were seen by them as more legitimate and potentially more successful methods of struggle than the addressing of legal questions of outright ownership. The former pitted them against the weaker Jewish settlers; the latter would have set them against the powerful landowners and the government.

The conflicts over customary rights were only the upper layer of a decisive historical encounter between two theories and legal bases of ownership: the absolute right of private ownership on which European capitalism rested and which already was indirectly introduced into the Ottoman Empire by the Land Code of the Tanzimat, and the more diffuse, but not less extensive, rights of usage in practice in many pre-capitalist societies. The capitalist concept of private property could not concede the preemption of exchange value by inextinguishable rights attached to use value. In addition, as Edward Said pointed out, the justification for European exploitation of land in Asia, Africa, and the Americas, was derived from the settlers' conviction that they possessed the ability to cultivate it in an efficient way as compared with the "uncivilized people" who either farmed land badly, or left it to rot.[44] Ultimately, even disregard for local custom was not just a matter of ignorance, but the unavoidable opposition of two types of property systems, and at stake was the very legitimacy of European overseas settlement.

During this period, however, most clashes – with the exception of Metulla in 1895, where the conflict was over outright ownership rights and therefore was more violent – were of a limited character. But it was in response to the repeated attacks of the ejected Druz of Metulla that Itzhak Epstein's noted article raised for the first time seriously the "hidden question" of Jewish–Arab land conflict.[45] But until over fifteen years later, the hostility of the Ottoman authorities and the opposition of the tenant farmers, as we saw for example in the case of Petach Tikva, took place on separate planes and hence did not take the form of a generalized and politicized movement. This demarcation was briefly overcome in the last years of the period under study (and again in 1936).

The Young Turks Revolt and open conflict

It used to be commonly assumed that the Israeli–Arab conflict could be traced back to its political form, generated by a political act – the Balfour Declaration of 1917.[46] The reasoning behind this dating is that Palestinian Arab nationalism is assumed to have emerged only as a result of British intrusion and the crushing of Arab hopes of independence, and therefore that "all was well between Arab and Jew in Palestine before the First World War."[47] In the last two decades, however, there has been a growing number of studies, the most important ones being by Neville Mandel, Yaakov Ro'i, Rashid Khalidi, A. W. Kayyali, and Eliezer Beeri, which demonstrate that not the Balfour Declaration but the Revolt of the Young Turks in July 1908 is to be viewed as the beginning of open Jewish–Arab conflict as well as the cradle of the Arab national movement, which emerged in opposition to the centralizing tendencies in the dominant wing of the new Turkish rulers. Most, but not all, of these studies also indicate that the Israeli–Palestinian conflict emerged not as a full-blown political phenomenon, but as the stirring of popular opposition to early Jewish settlement in Palestine.[48]

The sudden increase in the level of hostility between Jewish settlers and Palestinians after the Young Turks Revolution is a clear indication of a smoldering popular opposition that the Revolt was crucial in fanning into life. In the twenty-seven years between 1882 and 1908, thirteen Jews were killed by Arabs under varying circumstances. Only two of them, one in Metulla by displaced Druz tenant peasants, the other in Bat Shlomo by a discharged guard, were murdered against the background of the national conflict. In other cases they fell victim to criminal acts, not necessarily directed at Jews, or to accidents.[49] But in 1909 alone, four Jews were killed for nationalist motives, and between 1909 and 1913 twelve Jewish guards lost their lives.[50] The "hidden question" produced an open conflict.

While before the Revolt most Jewish observers were at pains to emphasize that the attacks on Jewish settlements were not motivated by "national hatred,"[51] in the years just before the First World War the local Jewish community and even the leadership of the WZO attested to a radical change, that spelled real danger, in the attitude of the Palestinian population toward Zionist aims. They viewed this change as resulting from the broadening of the initial hostility of Christian merchants, afraid of urban competition, into a general Palestinian opposition that included the peasantry, and a transition from localized conflicts to the beginnings of "national hatred and jealousy."[52] The various responses to this escalating threat included, for example, the establishment of Federations of the Moshavot of the Galilee and of Judea, the opening of a bureau in the Palestine Office for the translation of Arab language newspapers,[53] and a more active role given to the representatives of the WZO in Istanbul.

Typical of these trends is the "continuous sobering" in Ruppin's and Thon's views of the causes of Arab opposition, as is revealed from their official correspondence. Their outlooks evolved from attributing the sources of opposition to jealousy of Christian merchants and quarrels between neighboring communities in 1908, to concluding that both Arab and Turkish sides used Jews as a cover for their conflicts in 1911, to viewing the Muslims as the major opponents in 1912, to speaking of an "Arab movement" in 1913, and evaluating the relations with the Arabs as the central problem of Zionist politics just before the outbreak of the war.[54] Ben-Gurion went through similar stages: in his early years in Palestine he attributed Arab attacks to local custom, banditry, or blood feud, but by 1910/11 he recognized the reality of Arab "hatred," and between 1914 and 1916 "he openly spoke and wrote about the 'hatred' of the Arabs for the Jews in Palestine." Curiously, between 1917 and 1936 he resumed his earlier position and denied the existence of the conflict. But even then, according to his biographer "this was [only] his public position. In his diary, and behind the closed doors of party forums, he showed himself alert to the problem of Arab rejection." His public denial was a delaying tactic "born of pragmatism rather than profundity of conviction."[55]

We may, therefore, lay to rest the myth of Jewish ignorance of the overwhelming presence of Palestinian Arabs in their *Altneuland,* even during the Ottoman period. In an important historical symposium at the Zalman Shazar Center in Jerusalem, the editor concluded that

all the lecturers refuted the widespread assumption that the Zionist movement – with the exception of small and marginal groups – supposedly, closed its eye to the Arabs living in Eretz-Israel and to the "Arab question," thus precluding the possibility of mutual understanding between the two national movements. At the same time, there is no doubt that all the Zionist executives and almost all the currents in the Zionist movement underestimated the strength of Arab nationalism and the weight of its opposition to Zionist aspirations.[56]

It seems, then, more correct to say that Jews were not ignorant of the Palestinian Arabs, but in their assessment of the balance of forces estimated that the Palestinian Arab population could put obstacles in the way of Jewish rebirth in Eretz Israel but ultimately was not capable of arresting the process.

The two spheres in which Palestinian nationalism was articulated and developed were the local newspapers and the Parliament in Istanbul, both the fruits of abolishing Abdul Hamid's autocratic rule. The first Palestinian paper to set the struggle against Zionism as its main aim was Najib Nassar's *al-Karmil,* published almost continuously from 1909 until the Second World War in Haifa. In 1914 its circulation reached 700 to 1,000 copies. Nassar, a Protestant, was employed for a number of years as a land purchasing agent of the JCA, and presumably apprehensive of its aims took to journalism "to write against the Jewish newcomers in Palestine so that the Arabs would not continue selling land to the Jews."[57] While *al-Karmil* opposed Zionism mostly on grounds of Ottoman patriotism, *Falastin,* a paper published from January 1911 twice a week in Jaffa by the Greek Orthodox brothers Isa and Yusuf al-Isa, graduates of the American University of Beirut, was Palestinian proper. Initially, its position on Zionism was not very clear, but by 1914 *Falastin* probably had surpassed *al-Karmil* in its hostility to Zionism. Though the anti-Zionist press in Palestine was in Christian hands, Nassar also succeeded in enlisting the support of larger Muslim-owned dailies, *al-Ray al-Am, al-Mufid*, and *al-Haqiqa* in Beirut, and *al-Muqtabas* in Damascus, to the anti-Zionist cause.[58] Given the Ottoman administrative division of Palestine, which grouped its northern regions with Lebanese and Syrian areas, and the existence of Palestinian student bodies in Cairo, Beirut, and Istanbul, the knowledge of the emerging conflict began spilling over into the Arab world.[59]

The second focus of opposition to Jewish aspirations in Palestine was the Ottoman Parliament. Between the Revolt and the First World War three electoral campaigns were held. In the *Mutasarriflik* of Jerusalem three MPs, and in the *Sanjaks* of Nablus and Acre one each, were elected to the 275-member Parliament. During the first campaign in 1908, members of the Jewish community and the Palestine Office hoped to field a Jewish candidate or at least to support an Arab candidate acceptable to Jews. In fact, no such coalition worked out, and all five MPs elected were Muslims unfavorable to Zionism. The dominant ones among them were the representatives of Jerusalem: Ruhi al-Khalidi and Said al-Husayni, both of whom studied in the Alliance Israélite Universelle in Jerusalem; the latter was fluent in Hebrew. Both of them, as well as other representatives from the Palestinian *Sanjaks*, expressed mounting opposition to Jewish immigration and land purchase. In doing so, they basically repeated the official policy of the government which contested the concentration of Jewish immigration in Palestine, but at the same time expressed Palestinian criticism of the laxity of the central government's response.[60]

By 1914, Mandel and Kayyali also report the emergence of small anti-Zionist, mostly student, societies, in Jerusalem, Haifa, Nablus, Jaffa, Cairo, Istanbul, and Beirut.

The major confrontation of the Second *Aliya*'s period, taking place in 1910 over the lands of the village Fulla in the Jezreel valley (Marj Ibn Amir), revealed not only a new level of intensity but also a new lineup of parties, who chose to define the conflict between themselves in terms of opposing principles. A major valley in the north, this was to be the site of the first major settlement plan of the WZO – Oppenheimer's *Siedlungsgenossenschaft* – Merchavia. Though the valley provided the connecting diagonal of Ruppin's "N" shaped settlement map, the timing of the purchase depended really on the readiness of Elias Sursuq, an Orthodox Lebanese banker who successfully exploited the 1858 Land Code to acquire thousands of dunams in the *Sanjak* of Acre, to sell 9,515 dunams to the WZO and the PLDC.

In May 1910, when the news of the purchase leaked out, the Palestinian political and religious elite tried to intervene by sending two telegrams, one from Haifa, inspired by Najib Nassar, the other from

Nazareth, signed by the religious representatives of all the communities, in ccondemnation of the sale, to the government in Istanbul. The former, according to Mandel, justified its opposition mostly by claiming to defend the Ottoman state, the latter, as protecting the local population. The latter wrote: "all the press is unanimous in recognizing that the Zionists nourish the intention of expropriating our properties. For us these intentions are a question of life and death."[61] Ruppin, and Hankin his land agent, also viewed this purchase as a "test case, with implications for all their work in Palestine."[62] The Ottoman government reiterated its previous restrictions on sale of land to foreign nationals, but this made little difference since the land of Fulla, like others in the past, was to be registered in the name of a Jewish Ottoman subject.

According to the memorandum signed between the seller and the purchasers' representatives, it was to be the responsibility of the former "to remove (*faire déguerpir*) all the peasants from the purchased terrains, houses, and mills."[63] At this point, the new *Kaimakam* of Nazareth, the Damascene Druz Shukri al-Assali, set out to hold up and possibly block the registration of the transfer of ownership in the *tapu* to a "straw man," and forbade the peasants from leaving. Throughout the confrontation *al-Karmil* served as al-Assali's mouthpiece.[64] The Ministry of the Interior, however, ruled that Sursuq was legally entitled to sell the land to any Ottoman subject, and the *Kaimakam* was instructed by the *Vali* of Beirut to allow the transfer to take place, and in December 1910 the peasants left. Al-Assali tried to stop the settlement of Jews on the spot by pointing to the vicinity of Merchavia to the connecting railroad between Haifa and the Hijazi pilgrim line. In mid January he vacated his post to conduct a successful campaign for the post of an MP from Damascus, finally removing the last obstacle from the members of Hashomer from occupying the place, but providing an outspoken leader for the parliamentary opponents of Zionism.[65] The relationships between Merchavia and adjacent Arab villages remained tense, and during the harvest of 1911 the guard Yigal Mordechai killed an Arab of a group that ambushed him. In a few hours the villagers of Sulam attacked Merchavia and the authorities had to intervene to remove the siege.[66]

While in both our examples of major confrontations, that in Petach Tikva in 1886, and Merchavia in 1910, government officials, Rauf Pasha and Shukri al-Assali respectively, were opposed to Jewish settlement, the difference in their rationales reveals the extent to which Jewish–Arab relations were transformed in the meantime. Rauf Pasha was carrying out Ottoman regulations; al-Assali, though doing the same, was a member of a secret Arab nationalist organization opposed to the Ottoman government, and only used, even overstepping at a risk to himself, the Ottoman regulations to advance the Palestinian cause. After the Young Turks

Revolt, as demonstrated by Yehoshua Porath, on the basis of his examination of Palestinian newspapers and political life both within the country and in exile, pro-Ottoman and nationalist Palestinians were equally opposed to Zionist settlement.[67] Hence, by the end of the Ottoman period, not external, i.e. Arab–Ottoman, but internal, i.e. Jewish–Palestinian relations were the key to the evolving Arab attitude to Zionism.

Mandel's conclusion of his study was that "the political elite among the Arabs in Palestine and the surrounding areas" had already evolved its hostility to Zionism before the First World War.[68] What is more significant, however, is that after the revolt of the Young Turks, popular opposition and political opposition were united and generated a distinctly anti-Zionist form of Palestinian nationalism. Because of the hybrid character of his study – prior to 1908 examining popular hostility, and after that date elite opposition – Mandel could not piece together these two social levels. But this amalgamated opposition was the reason for the growing strength of Palestinian nationalism before the First World War.

We should, however, beware of two errors in analyzing Palestinian resistance to Jewish settlement. First, we should remember that it was precisely the inability of Palestinian Arabs to combine in the long run these two levels of opposition to Zionism that undermined effective Palestinian efforts.

The Israeli–Arab conflict evolved within the broader context of growing dissatisfaction in the Middle East with the economic dependence of the region, the continual shrinkage of the Ottoman Empire's borders, and the autocratic methods of Abdul Hamid – who used European investment and tools of domination to prop up his despotic rule, while the European powers, the ultimate authority behind the Empire, stood by complacently. These factors "produced the beginnings of a 'national' reaction among certain sections of the local elites."[69] This opposition was slow in coming and developing, and even slower in linking the elites to a popular base. Even when this linkage occurred in Palestine, mostly on the basis of opposition to land sale to Jewish organizations and individuals during the Mandate, it was of a temporary and unstable nature, since the landowners frequently had a solid economic incentive to sell parts of their land regardless of the purchaser's identity.

Another potential weakness of the Palestinian cause – the need for coordination between the all-Arab and Palestinian interest – is also already apparent at this time. Alleged support for Zionism was one of the important justifications behind the organization of parliamentary opposition to the centralizing, or rather Turkeyfying, tendencies of the dominant party of the Revolt, the Committee of Union and Progress, in 1910/11. The main motive behind the opposition, according to Rashid Khalidi, "was by no means a sincere interest in the threatened rights of the Palestinian peasants," but "an opportunistic political manoeuvre" which, in fact, wished to weaken the CUP. When this aim was achieved, these attacks immediately were stopped.[70] The Palestinian–Zionist conflict was a focus of Arab unity when it coincided with pan-Arab and particular Arab interests, but not when the latter took precedence over Palestinian interests proper.

A second error to avoid is the overestimation of the impact of the Palestinian national movement at this time. Though "the foci of hostility already existed in the years before the First World War, and especially in the period between the Revolt of the Young Turks, in 1908, and the outbreak of the War, in 1914,"[71] during the period 1882 to 1914, the confrontation was yet of a localized and limited character. But Ro'i was mistaken in concluding that the two sides lacked yet "the theoretical framework for the legitimation of the acts of hostility between them."[72]

In fact, the newspapers, parliamentary representatives, and organizations mentioned, elaborated in the years 1908–14, "the essentials of the Arab 'case' against Zionism, as the world came to know it in the 1920s and 1930s."[73] Among these Mandel and Khalidi list the arguments that Jewish settlers preferred independent institutions of self-government and defense over integration into the local population, that they were flag-bearers of the Great Powers and instead of adopting Ottoman citizenship retained their foreign nationality, etc. But above all "the basic Arab demands were an end to Jewish immigration into Palestine and an end to land purchase by them," the second probably the more central one. After the Young Turks Revolt these demands were "pressed vigorously."[74] The clear awareness and opposition of the Palestinian Arab elite to the aims of Zionism by 1914, rounds out, and in a complementary way validates, the argument of this study to the effect that Jewish positions toward "the Arab question" were also established before the First World War.

Finally, I would like to ponder what made the Jewish settlers of the Second *Aliya* ready – and some of them even willing – to put up with the growing hostility towards them among the Palestinian Arab inhabitants, and to insist on the continuation and enhancement of Zionist immigration and settlement. This readiness, as I have already argued, was not the result of turning a blind eye to the presence and, perhaps, even the aspirations, of the Palestinian Arabs. In fact, the opposite was true. The "hidden question," in the form raised by Epstein, had according to Moshe Smilansky no practical solution, because it is one of two: if Eretz Israel belongs – in the national sense – to those Arabs who settled here lately then there is no room for us here and we have to admit openly: our ancestral land is lost to us. And if Eretz Israel belongs to us, to the people of Israel, then our national interests take precedence for us over everything. There is no room for compromise in that case.[75]

But it was precisely the acknowledgment of the conflict of real interests that led the Jewish immigrants to transform their position as combatants in a clash of forces into one of champions of a socially, psychologically, and ultimately a morally coherent and legitimating vision.

The *first* level of justification was rooted in a level of comparative social reckoning: the Jewish–Arab conflict in Palestine did not stand for the Jewish settlers by itself, it was always assessed against the alternative of Jewish life in the diaspora. For Zionists, and for that matter for the majority of Jews, life outside of Eretz Israel was also one of confrontation. The *Jewish Chronicle*, referring to the expected Eastern Jewish immigration to Eretz Israel, wrote in 1882 that "our fate there cannot be worse than here." Arab hostility seemed, to the Kattowitz chapter of Hovevei Zion in 1884, to dwarf in comparison with the wickedness and unculturedness of Russian peasants.[76]

The *second* measure of legitimacy, built on the first one, promised psychological liberation. Jews, it was argued, suffered not only from being *hated* everywhere they lived, but because of their weakness and humility their host societies also heaped *contempt* on them. While there was repeated concern among the Jewish immigrants of the awakening of Arab hatred, they saw no contempt aimed at the Zionist enterprise. Life free of contempt and shame was an ideal that the more militant among the workers, especially the members of Hashomer, felt was well worth fighting for. When Yehezkel Nissanov, a member of Hashomer, was killed in 1911 refusing to surrender his mules to attacking Palestinians, Israel Giladi, one of Hashomer's leaders, wrote:

When [Arabs] stole the animals from some farmer Nissanov would reproach him bitterly: "How is it that you are still alive and your animals are gone? Shame on you!" And now he has shown that he was as good as his word. "I have shown," Nissanov would say, "that a Jewish worker will not permit himself to be put to *shame*, even if it costs him his life, for on this [attitude] depends the honor and future of his nation.[77]

Zionist state and nation formation provided a sensation of liberation from the "deep insult of diaspora life."[78] Jewish immigrants felt that even in migrating to Palestine they were still potentially moving within tragically narrow parameters, and only ridding themselves of the contempt of generations allowed some, by no means all, to be unconcerned with the hatred they experienced.

While the form of psychological liberation I have presented was the preserve of a minority among the workers, the *third*, the moral level, of legitimation was almost universal among all walks of immigrant-settlers and Zionist leaders. The quest for a moral dimension to their colonization demanded justice for both the Jewish and Arab sides. A customary justification of Jewish colonization was that it would not replace the Arab population of Palestine, since the intensification of agriculture would create more than enough room for both indigenous and immigrant farmers. This self-vindication was common enough among European settlers in North America, New Zealand, etc., and Eretz Israel was not different in this respect.

But an original, and by far more arresting, promise the Jewish settlers made to the Palestinian Arabs and to themselves, was rooted in particular Jewish circumstances, and could be termed "the morality of the weak." Indeed, it used the experience of weakness to set new and high standards of morality. Moshe Smilansky lectured Epstein on this question:

Giving the weak into the hands of the mighty and hoping for his fairness is not a moral deed. Moral is the deed that gives the weak the ability to resemble the mighty. We do not want to remain weak and demand mercy and fairness from our opponents. We will become mighty like them, more than them, and then we will meet in the market place, and reach a compromise and will make peace as equals.[79]

Ben-Zvi's minimum and maximum programs for the Jewish proletariat are an example of this extension of the beneficial effects of colonization. Until such time that Jewish workers "become a force, that others, willingly or unwillingly, have to take into account" it would be too soon to work for international working-class solidarity. But, in the short run, Jewish workers had to struggle to create higher forms of economic life, in order to help in the future both themselves and the opponents they were fighting against at the time.[80]

It is remarkable that even Jabotinsky's most militant articles on "The Iron Wall," from 1923, repeated this theme, though in a blunt and provocative fashion. Though he was viewed as an enemy of the Arabs, wrote Jabotinsky, he did not support their removal. He sought justice, meaning that everyone would receive what he was entitled to; especially the one who had nothing would at least receive something. Morality could only be anchored in mutuality, and between Jews and Arabs this did not yet exist. Once the Palestinian Arabs lost all hope of ridding themselves of Jews, the moderates among them would seek a platform of mutual concessions "guaranteeing against removal, equal rights, or national self-determination; and I believe and hope that then we will be able to give them such guarantees."[81]

This promise of equality – whether to be achieved within Israel or between the Israeli state and a Palestinian state – is still an unfulfilled, but not forgotten, moral vow.

The impact of Israeli state formation on Palestinian society

Having familiarized ourselves with the emergence of the particular method of Israeli state and nation formation in Palestine, and the growing Palestinian opposition to Jewish penetration, we should conclude this study by asking: what did, not just Jewish colonization in general, but the predominant *exclusive Jewish employment* approach, aimed at the formation of a pure Jewish settlement, mean for the future of Palestinians in Palestine?

While most Israeli sociologists and historians, as I pointed out in the Introduction to this study, credit intra-Jewish social processes and ideal interests with shaping their society, and concomitantly ignore the massive formative impact of the conflict on Israeli society, their Palestinian and pro-Palestinian counterparts are only too aware of the effect of Zionism on Palestinian society. It is therefore with the examination of the major theoretical frameworks offered by some of the latter for explaining this impact that such analysis must begin. Though these theoretical approaches, like the Israeli ones, were worked out in regard to the Mandate period, with some modifications they are applicable to the Ottoman era as well.

The orthodox pro-Palestinian theoretical perspective views Palestine as a "typical European colony with a typical European settler minority."[82] Maxime Rodinson, for example, writes that

the creation of the State of Israel on Palestinian soil is the culmination of a process that fits perfectly into the great European–American movement of expansion in the nineteenth and twentieth centuries whose aim was to settle new inhabitants among other peoples or to dominate them economically and politically.[83]

Furthermore:

The advancement and then the success of the Zionist movement . . . definitely occurred within the framework of European expansion into the countries belonging to what later came to be called the Third World. Given the initial aims of the movement, it could not have been otherwise. Once the premises were laid down, the inexorable logic of history determined the consequences. Wanting to create a purely Jewish, or predominantly Jewish, state in Arab Palestine in the twentieth century could not help but lead to a colonial type situation . . .[84]

Rodinson's simplistic catch-all characterization, however, fails to heed the multifaceted character of the European overseas expansion drive and distinguish between its contradictory impulses, and to address the ones specifically relevant to Zionism. Moreover, his focus on "initial aims" removes the actual events from history, replacing them with an "inexorable logic," which recognizes only a direct path of evolution leading from presuppositions to the aims of Zionist history.

By lumping together the terms colonial (or colonialism) and settler (or colonization), Rodinson obscured the differences between the interests of Great Britain, the colonial power, and the Jewish immigrant-settler population, and the conflicts within the different strata of settlers. Under Great Britain's military and administrative rule, but without its direct control of land or labor, Palestine did become an "occupation" colony in the Fieldhouse–Frederickson typology, but at the same time it was approached as a settlement colony by Jewish immigrants. The latter's aims, initially, were facilitated by the British Mandate, but gradually Britain also began distancing itself from the explicit aims of the Balfour Declaration.[85] The central conflict of the Ottoman period between Jewish planters and workers, over the question of the place of Arabs in the Jewish economy, also has no place in Rodinson's work. Neither does the very fact that the state and nation forming method of the Second *Aliya* evolved in response to the moderate method of the First *Aliya* which would have considerably slowed down Jewish immigration and would thereby have considerably changed the history of Israeli–Palestinian relations. The six different phases of organizing the Jewish economy, and concomitantly the methods of state and nation formation, before the First World War were rooted in economic realities and interests, and hardly point to an "inexorable logic" derived from unchanging "premises." Many other examples may be added: for example, the impact of the Palestinian economic boycott on the Jewish community, during the Revolt of 1936–9 and later, ironically contributed to the strengthening of the Jewish sector of the economy. But this has no place in Rodinson's approach. Really, the success of the Jewish side in establishing its state and winning its military victory against the Arab world in 1948 was much more doubtful and contorted at many junctures than Rodinson's determinism would lead us to believe.

An analogous, but notably more subtle, position is Edward Said's emphasis that the "negation" of the Palestinians "is the most consistent thread running through Zionism." No doubt, without underestimating the Palestinians and their aspirations the Zionist enterprise could not have been embarked upon. But while Said asserts that he takes into account "the whole dialectic between theory and day-to-day effectiveness" in Zionism, he also tends to overemphasize the actual influence of the voluntary dimension of ideas in creating outcomes and, therefore, the force this conviction carried against objective obstacles. Such is the case when he argues that "all the constitutive energies of Zionism were premised on the excluded presence, that is, the functional absence of 'native people' in Palestine."[86] But in the labor market, this exclusion was not the cause but the result of the Jewish workers' struggle to defend their livelihoods. And the partial willingness to accede to the partition of Palestine in 1936, its acceptance in 1948, and the limitation of the original Allon Plan to the relatively sparsely settled Jordan Rift of the West Bank in 1967, certainly diminishes the case made by Said.

Fredrickson criticizes the kind of ahistorical bias found in Rodinson's and Said's views eloquently but forcefully in regard to the historiography of the first two white settler societies, the United States and South Africa:

the process of stripping the indigenes of their patrimony and reducing them to subservience and marginality was, from the historian's perspective, a complex and uneven one that cannot be fully appreciated in teleological terms, or merely looking at the final outcome as the predetermined result of white attitudes, motivations, and advantages. Not only did the indigenous peoples put up a stiff resistance that at times seemed capable of stalling the white advance indefinitely, but the lack of firm consensus of interests and attitudes within the invading community, or between the actual settlers and the agents of a metropole or mother country, could lead to internal disagreements concerning the character and pace of expansion and even on whether it should continue at all.[87]

This certainly is true, probably even more clearly, in regard to our case, where the frontier was so much less attractive, the support of the metropole lackluster, and Palestinian opposition stronger, and where a bifurcated economy evolved in response to the inhospitability of the labor market itself. In sum, the "colonial-settler perspective," Roger Owen has observed, "if pushed too far, produce[s its] own systematic distortion of the picture as a whole," as do a number of other paradigmatic approaches.[88]

It is indeed remarkable just how Eisenstadt, Lissak and Horowitz, Kolatt, and Gorny, who focus mostly on the supposedly unchanging intentions of the immigrant-settlers, meet Rodinson and Said, who believe that Zionism was so powerful it could do whatever it wished, halfway along this teleological emphasis. But the approaches of Rodinson and Said, neither of whom delved into the details of the history they interpret, suffer from the same one-sidedness that results from the value consensus viewpoint: they all study Israeli society apart from Palestinian society, rather than, as Ehrlich demanded, viewing them "as forming and reshaping each other through the historical process of the conflict."[89]

Elia T. Zureik's theoretical perspective, based on thorough and penetrating research into the history and structure of Palestinian Arabs in Israeli society, already disclaimed the "orthodox" Palestinian position "which postulates that the Palestinians in pre-1948 were colonized by either the British or the Zionist settlers, or both, in the classical sense of colonialism." He argues that the socio-political structure of the Jewish community in Palestine was different from that of settler societies in Africa.[90] Zureik is being precise in pointing to the difference between the colonialisms of what were called in this study, the "occupation" and the straightforward "pure settlement" kind, and the case of Zionist settlement in Palestine. As we have seen, the uniqueness of Jewish settlement was in the combination of its inability to create a pure settlement in the whole area of Palestine according to the Australian or North American model, and refusal to accept an ethnic plantation colony of the North African type.

What was the special relevance of the labor movement's dominant method of state formation for the Jewish–Palestinian conflict? I believe that its major significance was rooted in the fact that, precisely because it was militant in its demand for *exclusive* Jewish employment, the labor movement could eventually bear to be more *modest* in its demand for territorial expansion. In Anita Shapira's astute observation,

The ideology of Hebrew labor . . . brought about the reduction of the settlement area in Eretz Israel. In the long run, the establishment of separate Jewish areas of settlement entailed the relinquishment of those areas that did not possess a Jewish majority. This decision was the first step on the way toward Eretz Israel's partition.[91]

While the First *Aliya*'s aim of incorporating the Palestinians as a lower caste was not opposed to the aspiration, shared by virtually all Jews before the First World War, for the control of the whole of Palestine, the termination of the hazards of Palestinian competition by means of economic bifurcation slowly became the basis of the emergence of a new perspective on possession of land for the Second *Aliya*. The attractiveness of the coastal zone and the inland valleys for contiguous Jewish settlement, which already drew Ruppin's attention, was reinforced by the strategy of "put[ting] islands of purely Jewish settlement on the map of the country."[92] Gradually, as the labor movement's assets expanded and its cooperative institutions became able to safeguard the interests of the propertyless Jewish immigrants, the militant nationalism of the workers, typical of the years of the Second *Aliya* itself, expressed itself in a territorially moderate form in the later Mandate years, when the question of sovereignty emerged for the first time in a significant way. It opted for partition.

Though the labor movement did not originate this approach, it was better equipped to support *de jure* partition, having created the context of economic bifurcation and consequently being less dependent on Palestinians than any other Jewish group. It was from its mainstream that the majority of the supporters of the various partition plans – the 1937 Peel Plan, the 1947 UN plan, and the 1967 Allon Plan, spanning thirty years – emerged. If in "1936 Palestine, partition was firmly grounded in reality,"[93] this was in large measure due to the labor movement's strategy of state formation. The mainstream of the labor movement, in short, modified and moderated its "demographic interest." Connecting effective control with cultivation and settlement, the labor movement came to the conclusion that in order to increase the ratio of population to land, the latter had to be narrowed so the density of the former would grow. The priority of demography over territory was the natural interest of the labour movement which, on the basis of its formative experience in the labor market, always retained the best sense within Zionism for the need for effective demographic presence to attain permanence and safety in Palestine, for the emerging Israeli society. *The radical nationalism of exclusive Jewish employment (and economic bifurcation) could be ensured only through the territorial moderation of separatism, to be achieved through partition.* The aim of the labor movement became the realization of a pure, i.e. Jewish, settlement society, in *part* of Palestine. This was its alternative both to maximalist exclusivism *and* to Jewish supremacy; the Palestinian Arabs had to be military confronted, but ideally there would be no need to oppress them.

Beneath this moderation, however, the vigilant protection of the exclusive Jewish employment sector never wavered. In general, noted Dan Giladi, "this issue left its imprint on all social relations in the *Yishuv*, and excited the passions more than any other single question."[94] In consequence of this struggle, the labor movement "won a most important propaganda, moral, and political victory, which it knew how to exploit to the last drop (*ad tom*), both politically and educationally." At the same time, the moral damage to the cause of the farmers, and indirectly to the right wing, was immeasurable.[95] For example, when the rise in the political strength of the Revisionists and the citrus growers in the years 1932–36 threatened the control of the Histadrut over the workers, the latter conducted, in spite of economic prosperity and the decline in unemployment, "a demonstrative and often violent 'principled' struggle . . . against the employment of Arab labor by Jewish employers." This struggle served to brand the Histadrut's opponents as anti-Zionist "and cement the popular identification of the labor movement as the vanguard of the Jewish national struggle."[96]

When, in 1931, Jewish and Arab drivers struck jointly against hardships imposed by the Mandatory authorities, the Histadrut discouraged further Jewish–Arab collaboration and recommended the setting up of a separate cooperative of Jewish drivers.[97] At the outset of the Arab Revolt, a group of five Jewish businessmen and civic leaders – Judah Magnes, President of the Hebrew University, Gad Frumkin, Justice of the Palestine Supreme Court, Moshe Smilansky, Head of the Citrus Growers Association, Novomejsky, Director of the Palestine Potash Co., and Pinchas Rutenberg, Director of the Palestine Electrical Co. – worked out a set of proposals, in consultation with Musa Alami, an advisor of the Mufti, for a third, joint Jewish–Arab sector of the economy, as well as numerical restrictions on Jewish immigration and much vaguer limitation of land purchase. Such goals were unacceptable to the leaders of the labor movement, such as Moshe Sharett who, using his position in the Jewish Agency, sought to discredit the Jewish negotiators.[98]

The synthesis of moderation in territorial expansion and militancy in creating a pure Jewish society within that territory, I wish to argue, was also the basis of the influence of the organized Jewish labor movement within the *Yishuv*. The authority commanded by the Histadrut and the labor movement was rooted in their realistic assessment of the initial weakness of the Jewish side in the balance of forces with the Palestinian Arab population and their willingness, nevertheless, to engage in the painstaking practice of separatist settlement to create the speediest and least reversible *faits accomplis*. Not less important was the consistently militant nationalism of the labor movement within its sector for making it as exclusively Jewish as possible. For example, the kibbutz became the champion of "mixed farming," an idea raised as far back as 1900, but slow in being realized. The development of dairy farming and vegetable gardening, in addition to and in mutual dependence with the field crops, freed the collective settlement from dependence on the Arab market, and allowed it to counter the competition of cheaper Arab-produced agricultural products, as "mixed farming" made the supply of the surplus to the Jewish urban population possible. Jewish dependence on the Palestinian economy was further reduced. It was, in sum, the specific combination of territorial moderation and militancy in regard to employment that served as the basis of the labor movement's realism and self-confidence.

In comparison, the militant military and diplomatic aims of the Revisionist movement that ignored the demographic reality and sought maximum territorial expansion were seen as wild and unfounded. Hence, not the Revisionists but the planter stratum was "the strongest opponent of the labor movement on its way towards hegemony in the *Yishuv*."[99] But the planters' strategy, seeking abundant land but being ready to incorporate part of the Palestinian population into the economy as a lower caste, in pursuit of its particularistic interests, was also seen as contradictory in that it threatened to undermine the potential of Jewish demographic superiority. The planters' moderation, hence, was regarded as misplaced, and the Revisionists' militancy as counterproductive, while the nationalism of the labor movement, with its peculiar synthesis of militancy and moderation, was accepted by the majority of the *Yishuv*, especially after the Arab Revolt of 1936, as the dominant method of state formation. The term usually used to describe this strategy is "separatism," which, in Gorny's presentation, was

an economic outlook which served as the basis of a political view, according to which the balance between the Jewish and Arab societies, and consequently peaceful and good neighborly relations between them, may be accomplished not through mutual integration, but only through separation. The purpose of separatism was the creation of the foundation of [Jewish] economic–political strength, without which a Jewish community could not survive and have a chance of normalization with the Arab community.[100]

Gorny's formulation admirably expresses the strengths, and the optimistic aspirations, of the separatist strategy; it is also important not to lose sight of its ambiguities and limitations. The "separatism" the labor movement encouraged was, at least potentially, a relatively moderate form of Israeli nationalism. But it did not, in fact, represent a fully separate path of development, nor could it ensure moderation in the long run.

One reason these points are obscured is that the term "separatism" (or its frequent synonym, "dualism") is too often used in simplistic or misleading ways. Horowitz and Lissak – to take a characteristic example – use the terms "dual society" and "dual economy," or speak of "separate centers," as if these referred to parallel systems developing in mutual isolation.[101] They are certainly correct in so far as they point to structural differences between the two unevenly developed economies and societies, but they fail to see that as long as Jewish society was expanding it could not be self-contained and had a direct impact on its Palestinian counterpart, e.g. through the purchase of part of its land. Further they downplay the fact that the Jewish economy itself had two parts: the pure settlement sector of the labor movement which was separatist, and the mixed sector of the ethnic plantation. Hence they ignore the economic reality of continued interconnection between the two societies. Israeli economic historians, for example Metzer and Kaplan,[102] rectify this exaggerated picture of separatism by pointing to such interconnections as intersectoral sales making up in 1935 a quarter of Palestinian, and 8 percent of Jewish net national product[103] but, on their part, ignore the relative political weight and significance of the labor movement's "separatism."

Zureik's attempts to dispel those views which deny the impact of

Jewish colonization on Palestinian society (as he did earlier in regard to the Palestinian view of Israel as an undifferentiated European colonial venture), but he overstates in the opposite direction. In his use, the term "dual society" implies an interconnected but asymmetrical relationship, in which Palestinian society and economy were rendered dependent on their Jewish counterparts. Metzer and Kaplan's data indeed indicate that three-quarters of Jewish sales to the Palestinians were manufacturing products, while 14 percent of their purchases were of labor services, 23 percent of agricultural produce and building materials, and a staggering 43 percent of land.[104] These numbers lend some weight to Zureik's perspective, according to which the economic and social structure of the Palestinian population were transformed in "the context of superimposing a capitalist economy upon a traditional peasant social order," and the uneven character of modernization in a "dual economy" distorted and weakened its class structure.[105] In the context of the "dual economy" Zionist settlers benefited from the sponsorship of imperial powers and the *de facto* support of large Arab landowners, at the expense of rural Palestinian society.[106] Zureik, however, underrates the larger force of capitalism, which affected *both* Jews and Palestinians. The peripherization of the Palestinian economy began with European penetration into the Ottoman Empire, and continued under the British Mandate, which exposed both Palestinian and Jewish economies to outside competition through a low rate of import duties. (Their exports were similar: 11.4 percent of Palestinian and 13.9 percent of Jewish NNP, in both cases citrus making up more than 80 percent.)[107] Furthermore, Zionism, even in its "pure settlement" phase, as we had ample opportunity to observe, did not have the dynamic force of capitalism on its side. In spite of the concentration of resources on land purchase, even when Jews made up about 35 percent of the population, the Palestinians, as they like to remind everyone, continued owning over 90 percent of the land. It can hardly be the case that in the other areas of the economy Jews were more influential, and the economic data gives an indication not only of Jewish impact but also of its limits. Hence, it seems to me better to speak of the two economies as undergoing a turbulent process of *bifurcation* within a clearly interconnected framework. We need to avoid the misleading implications of "separatism" as enunciated by Gorny, and of the term "dual society," taken in either Zureik's sense or that of Horowitz and Lissak. "Separatism" is most usefully conceived of as a strategy – and, we must not forget, the militant strategy of an embattled national movement. Economic bifurcation was a goal for which the Jewish labor movement struggled in Palestine, and whose implications it could not really control.

As the experience of Algeria showed, the imposition of an ethnic plantation colony, even combined with sizable immigration, is a recipe for catastrophic conflict. Bifurcated development, calling for the creation of a Jewish majority in Palestine, offered, perhaps, a less grim alternative; but it certainly could not have avoided confrontation with the Palestinians who, themselves evolving a radical nationalism, were not willing to give up any part of Palestine. Separatism is a strategy for managing conflict, but not for eliminating it. Here lies the historical dilemma of Israeli nationalism, which we now confront again in a new form. By following a strategy of exclusive Jewish employment, the labor movement steered the emerging Israeli society towards the territorial separation of Jews from Palestinians, and thus was able to bring about a small Jewish state. But, by bowing not to Palestinian national aspirations but only to the compelling facts of Palestinian demography, the labor movement perpetuated the Israeli–Palestinian conflict and left the door open to Israeli territorial maximalism. Separation, by itself, not only maintained but widened the gap between the two communities. In the long run, without mutual recognition, and most likely also some form of reintegration and power sharing, it is unlikely that antagonism between them can be overcome. But, for all its limitations, today, separatism – i.e. territorial partition – is again the most viable strategy for moderating the antagonism of two rival nationalisms, and opening up a breathing space within which a more long-term solution can be pursued.

Under the force of restricting circumstances, first in the land and later in the labor market, exclusivity in the labor market, through "autonomous labor" performed in the cooperative settlement, was combined with the potential willingness for partition of land to form the *separatist* pure settlement nationalism of the Israeli labor movement. The militancy of this method within its more restricted parameters made possible the creation of an Israeli state in the relatively short period of two generations, but even so too late for the majority of the Jewish people in Europe. This labor market based nationalism planted the seeds of deep suspicion between *ashkenazim* and *mizrachim*; and though it overwhelmed the Palestinian population in the areas of its sparse settlement in the coastal zone and the valleys without making inroads into its densely populated centers in the mountains of Palestine, it could not avoid the Israeli–Arab conflict. The victories of the War of Independence and the forcible scattering of large parts of the Palestinian population have eliminated the nexus between Israeli nationalism and the labor market, and the conquests of the Six Day War connected nationalism with territorial and demographic interest, demanding the redefinition of Israeli nationalism. The hegemony of the parties of labor in Israeli society was gradually weakened and the intensification of both Israeli–Arab and *ashkenazi–mizrachi* conflicts undermined, by 1977, their political preeminence as well. The linking of the internal and external conflicts, a phenomenon foreshadowed in a number of areas, is in the process of bringing about the rise of a new type of Israeli nationalism. Not being restricted by the need to purchase land for settlement, and in the possession of military and state power, it is militantly *maximalist* in its territorial aspirations. This approach is clearly seductive to many Israelis, but its foreseeable consequences can only be morally and politically catastrophic. It is essential to re-learn, in altered circumstances, the hard lessons drawn by the labor movement from the early phase of the Israeli–Palestinian conflict: the necessity to combine militancy on the fundamental issues with realism and moderation.

Notes

1 Introduction

1 S. N. Eisenstadt, 1967, pp. 1–4, 17–19; Horowitz & Lissak, 1978, similarly argue that "at this early stage, Zionism was still an ideological and cultural movement rather than a political one" (p. 3).

2 Shapiro, 1976, p. 4 and Shapiro, 1980, *passim*.

3 S. N. Eisenstadt, 1967, pp. 17–19.

4 *Ibid.*, p. 286.

5 Kolatt, 1964a, *passim*; Gorny, 1973, p. 3.

6 Shapiro, 1976, pp. 25, 29, 78.

7 Jonathan Frankel, 1981, p. 367.

8 Gramsci, 1971, pp. 180–182.

9 Shapiro, 1976, *passim*; Giladi, 1972, p. 58.

10 Deutsch, 1985, pp. 3–4.

11 Ehrlich, 1987, p. 129.

12 *Ibid.*, p. 130.

13 See mostly Kimmerling, 1983. For a balance of the strengths and the shortcomings see my review in *Contemporary Sociology*, Vol. 13, No. 3, May 1984.

14 Ehrlich, 1987, p. 122.

15 Seton-Watson, 1977, p. 383.

16 See 1986, p. 5.

17 In Hungary, for example, assimilation was a powerful trend among Jews, even without conversion. See Barany, 1974, p. 39.

18 The analysis of these solutions cannot be part of this study, but they have received many an excellent treatment. See, for example, Jonathan Frankel, 1981, and the most recent work by Yoav Peled.

19 Brass, 1980, concluded that "Jewish religious distinctiveness [cannot] explain Jewish ethnic separatism that culminated in Zionism, for Jews chose often enough to assimilate in Eastern Europe when conditions were favorable" (p. 13).

20 In attempting to reconcile the uniformly central place accorded to Eretz Israel in the classical Judaic sources with the experience of diaspora life, there emerged one very important trend within classical rabbinical lore, subscribed to even by Maimonides, in which, "until very recently, when external and internal pressures made themselves felt, the doctrine of The

Land tended to be ignored or spiritualized. It was an embarrassment"
(Davies, 1982, pp. 104–105).
21 Gellner, 1983, p. 1.
22 Wallerstein, 1974, pp. 145–146.
23 Elements of this method are presented in Nairn, 1977, pp. 334–348.
24 Portugal's empire also consisted of trading depots. Fieldhouse, 1965,
   pp. 11–22, 372; Fredrickson, 1988. Cf. also See, 1986, pp. 19–21.
25 Fredrickson, 1988, pp. 218–221.
26 Hancock, 1940, pp. 16–18; maxwell, 1923, p. 270; Fredrickson, 1981, p. 59;
   Willard, 1968, pp. 6–16.
27 Lamar & Thompson, 1981, p. 7.
28 De Silva, 1982, pp. 66–72; see also Fredrickson, 1988, p. 221.
29 De Silva, 1982, pp. 53–60, 194; Emmanuel, 1972, p. 156.
30 Lustick, 1985, pp. 1–16.
31 Fredrickson, 1981, p. xv.
32 *Ibid.*, pp. xxi–xxiv.
33 *Ibid.*, pp. 4, 54.
34 Billington & Ridge, 1982, pp. 49–52, 57–58, 80–83.
35 Christopher, 1972, pp. 208–225; Davenport, 1978, p. 22.
36 Heathcote, 1972, pp. 232–239.
37 Turner, 1956.
38 Good, 1976, p. 605.
39 Mosley, 1983, p. 236.
40 Broude, 1959, pp. 11–25.
41 Turner, 1956, pp. 24–25.
42 Butlin, 1959, pp. 26–27.
43 Aitken, 1959, p. 80.
44 This three-tiered control system by settlers is suggested by Kimmerling,
   1983, pp. 20–25.
45 Fredrickson, 1981, pp. 65–67; Davenport, 1978, pp. 20–21.
46 Willard, 1968, pp. 4–5.
47 *Ibid.*, pp. 119–134.
48 Parkin, 1979, pp. 44–88.
49 Murphy, 1984, p. 555.
50 Bonacich, 1972, pp. 547–559 and 1979, pp. 17–64.
51 For the development of this theme see Peled & Shafir, 1987, pp. 1435–1460.
52 Parkin, 1979, pp. 95–97.
53 Heathcote, 1972, pp. 227–229; Simmons, 1981, p. 11; Wa-Githumo, 1981,
   pp. 178–180; von Albertini, 1983, p. 266.
54 Fredrickson, 1988, p. 221.

2 Dependent development in the Ottoman Empire

1 McNeill, 1983, p. 9.
2 Salmon, 1981, pp. 121–122. Opposition to Jewish immigration, however,

originated about thirty years earlier, and was directed at the *ashkenazi* Jews who preferred to be registered as the protégés of Austrian, British, Prussian, etc. consulates to taking Ottoman citizenship. See Friedman, 1983, pp. 47, 62.

3 Heathcote, 1972, pp. 227–229.
4 Simmons, 1981, p. 11.
5 Billington & Ridge, 1982, p. 213.
6 See structure of its rule in Davenport, 1978, p. 18.
7 Wa-Githumo, 1981, pp. 178–180.
8 In the United States, the reservation system was, at first, intended by the federal government to give native Americans individual non-alienable land rights, as a way of integrating them into white society. But it faltered at the opposition of the states. See Sheehan, 1974, p. 272. These ideas were raised in southern Africa in 1774, see Davenport, 1978, p. 98; in Rhodesia, in the 1890s, see Riddel, 1978, pp. 6–11; in Queensland, only in 1897, see Markus, 1979, p. xiii; in Kenya see Wa-Githumo, 1981, pp. 224, 242.
9 Denoon includes in his comparative study of southern "settler capitalist" societies Australia, South Africa, New Zealand, Chile, Argentina, and Uruguay.
10 "Almost the first act of European administrative penetration in the settler economies was to restrict, indeed to outlaw, the market as the means by which land should be transferred into the hands of the incoming European colonists" (Mosley, 1983, p. 13).
11 Swedenburg, 1980, p. 3.
12 Issawi, 1982, p. 29.
13 Kark, 1984, pp. 357–362; Giladi & Naor, 1982, p. 19; Hershlag, 1964, pp. 29–39; Issawi, 1982, p. 106.
14 Owen, 1981, p. 292.
15 A classical statement of dependency theory is in Frank, 1972, pp. 3–17; a more complex version is presented by Wallerstein, 1974.
16 Issawi, 1970, p. 409.
17 Issawi, 1982, pp. 20, 29.
18 Significantly, this impressive list of assets was not always acquired through aggressive risk-taking in an undeveloped area, because risks, for example in railway construction and operation, were sometimes eliminated by government guarantees of income levels. Hershlag, 1964, pp. 47, 49.
19 *Ibid.*, p. 47.
20 Eliav, 1982, pp. 117–118.
21 Issawi, 1982, pp. 80–83.
22 The connection, direct and indirect, between Jewish immigrants and the European powers that were involved in the Middle East always remained a double-edged sword. For example, Lawrence Oliphant pointed to the annexation of Egypt by Britain as one of the reasons for the refusal of the Ottoman authorities to negotiate with the representatives of the Bilu group over their planned settlement in Eretz Israel. See Friedman, 1983, pp. 56–57.

23 Davison, 1973, p. 6.
24 Holt, 1966, p. 167.
25 Migdal, 1980, p. 12.
26 Gilbar, 1951, p. 188.
27 Baer, 1975, pp. 495–498.
28 Schölch, 1982, p. 55.
29 Gross, 1981, p. 42; Gad Gilbar, 1986, p. 205.
30 Schölch, 1982, p. 12.
31 *Ibid.*, p. 19.
32 Gad Gilbar, 1986, pp. 195–198.
33 Elazari-Volcani, 1930, pp. 21, 29–38; Avitsur, 1965, p. 56; Ilan, 1974, p. 25.
    According to Elazari-Volcani's calculation the investment in a typical farm
    was between £55 and £60 (Elazari-Volcani, 1930, p. 48). According to
    Ruppin's calculations, that were revised by Gross, 1981 (pp. 30–31) national
    income per capita in Syria and Palestine, on the eve of the First World War,
    amounted to 235 French francs per year.
34 As measured during the years 1921–8 by the Mandatory official in charge of
    agriculture. See Pinner, 1930, pp. 4, 67; Issawi, 1982, pp. 118–119.
35 Pinner, 1930, p. 7; Gross, 1981, p. 42.
36 Though some kinds of wheat were imported even earlier. Pinner, 1930,
    pp. 7–11.
37 Ben-Artzi, 1984, pp. 153–154.
38 Gross, 1981, p. 46.
39 Calculated from Table 1.4 in Schlöch, 1982, p. 59; Gad Gilbar, 1986,
    p. 191.
40 Gad Gilbar, 1986, p. 193.
41 Gross, 1981, p. 45; Ilan, 1974, pp. 43–45.
42 Firestone, 1975, *passim*.
43 Issawi, 1982, p. 132.
44 Schölch, 1982, p. 17.
45 Issawi, 1982, p. 3; for the enormous expansion in Syria and Transjordan see
    Lewis, 1955, pp. 48, 58.
46 Schölch, 1982, p. 21; see also Issawi, 1982, p. 138.
47 Issawi, 1982, pp. 134–137. For a detailed survey of this thorny topic see the
    first chapter of Granott, 1952, pp. 13–33.
48 Karpat, 1968, pp. 75–76 and 1977, pp. 90–91.
49 Issawi, 1982, pp. 135–136; Karpat, 1968, p. 75 and 1977, p. 90.
50 Shaw & Shaw, 1977, p. 114; Karpat, 1968, pp. 86–87.
51 Shaw & Shaw, 1977, pp. 86, 96; Stanford J. Shaw, 1975, p. 422.
52 There is wide agreement on this point. Porath, 1974, pp. 9–13; Ma'oz, 1968,
    p. 87; Hourani, 1968, p. 62; for Syria see Khoury, 1983, p. 94 and Roded,
    1984, p. 342.
53 Shaw & Shaw, 1977, p. 87.
54 *Ibid.*, p. 114.
55 Hourani, 1968, pp. 45, 48, 52.
56 This is Roded's assessment of the Syrian urban notables, which seems to fit

comfortably the Palestinian notables as well. See Roded, 1984, pp. 34–35; Hourani, 1968, pp. 48–49.
57 Karpat, 1968, p. 77 and 1977, p. 92; Hourani, 1968, pp. 49, 53.
58 Karpat, 1968, p. 86.
59 The full text is reproduced in Fisher, 1919, pp. 1–42.
60 Davison, 1973, p. 99.
61 Warriner, 1966, p. 73.
62 Karpat, 1977, pp. 97–98; Davison, 1973, p. 256.
63 Karpat, 1968, p. 86.
64 *Ibid.*, p. 87, my emphasis.
65 Karpat, 1977, p. 99.
66 Davison, 1973, p. 99. S. Bergheim observed in 1894 that: "The Turkish laws . . . are changing . . . [the] ancient laws and customs, much against the will and wish of the people. The lands are divided by an Imperial Commissioner into various portions and are given to individual villagers. They receive title deeds of individual ownership, and each one is at liberty to sell his portion to whoever he pleases, either to a member of the village or to a stranger" ("Land Tenure in Palestine," in *Palestine Exploration Fund Quarterly Statement*, 1894, p. 195).
67 Karpat, 1968, p. 88.
68 Kark, 1984, p. 373.
69 Shaw & Shaw, 1977, pp. 114–115.
70 Hourani, 1968, p. 78.
71 Shaw & Shaw, 1977, p. 115.
72 Ma'oz, 1968, pp. 163–165; Shaw & Shaw, 1977, p. 115.
73 Shaw & Shaw, 1977, p. 115.
74 Batatu, 1978, p. 11; Khoury, 1983, p. 4.
75 Khoury, 1983, p. 3.
76 *Ibid.*, pp. 5, 94.
77 Wallerstein, 1974, pp. 29–31.
78 Issawi, 1982, p. 136.
79 Owen, 1981, p. 292.
80 Davison, 1973, p. 259; see also note 7.
81 Issawi, 1982, pp. 17–18, 89.
82 Though discussing an earlier period, an analysis that is also relevant to the nineteenth century is Islamoğlu-Inan & Keyder, 1977, pp. 40–53; and Islamoğlu-Inan, forthcoming.
83 Hütteroth & Abdulfattah, 1977, p. 8.
84 Tax registers and censuses count only households. There is disagreement as to the average size of the Middle Eastern household, and therefore, of the total population. While once the size of the household was estimated to be very large, the tendency today is to put it at five people.
85 Hütteroth & Abdulfattah, 1977, pp. 45–47.
86 *Ibid.*, pp. 56, 78–79. Of course, the transition from tax yields to size of cultivated area is somewhat problematic.
87 *Ibid.*, p. 50.

88 *Ibid.*, p. 56.
89 *Ibid.*, p. 61.
90 Reilly, 1981, p. 82.
91 There is no agreement whether we are speaking of relatively small but permanent swamps, or larger, and seasonal marshes. See debate in Ben-Gal & Shamai, 1983, pp. 163–174. Responses by Hillel Birger, Menachem Zentner, Gideon Bieger and Amnon Kartin in *Cathedra*, No. 30, December 1983, pp. 161–182, and Ben-Gal's answer, pp. 185–195 (Hebrew).
92 For example, Jazzar Pasa, who is known for having defended Acre against Napoleon in 1799, successfully curtailed the power of the local Bedouin tribes, but as the tax collector of his regions he imposed such an unbearable burden that 20–33 percent of tax revenue, in spite of the efficiency of collection, had to be written off. From this, Cohen concludes that large areas, maybe as much as a quarter of cultivated land in Palestine, was abandoned by the end of the century. Amnon Cohen, 1973, pp. 197–203, 314–316, 324–327.
93 Amiran, 1953, p. 69; Amnon Cohen, 1973, pp. 158–172; Reilly, 1981, pp. 82–83.
94 Schölch, 1985, p. 503.
95 Karpat, 1978, pp. 262, 271.
96 McCarthy, 1981, pp. 25–28.
97 Owen, 1981, p. 287.
98 Shimoni, 1947, p. 106; Avneri, 1984, pp. 12–15.
99 Schölch, 1982, p. 48; Shaw & Shaw, 1977, pp. 115–118; Ever-Hadeni, 1955, p. 37.
100 Owen, 1981, p. 26.
101 For Syria see Lewis, 1955, p. 58.
102 Owen, 1981, pp. 174–175.
103 His most recent study is Grossman, 1986.
104 Grossman, 1983, p. 100.
105 Grossman & Safari, 1980, pp. 446, 455.
106 Swedenburg, 1980, pp. 163–170. In the light of Grossman's work, Swedenburg's additional thesis that cultivation on the plains continued through satellite villages has to be restricted by and large to the areas adjacent to the hills and does not hold for the plains in general.
107 Ben-Arieh, 1981, p. 88.
108 Owen, 1981, p. 264.
109 Ro'i, 1981, p. 258, my emphasis.
110 Karpat, 1977, p. 99.
111 Khalidi, unpublished manuscript.
112 Granott, 1952, Table 32, p. 227. Data for whole period, from CZA sources, in Stein, 1984, pp. 226–227.
113 See partial list of Palestinian Arab politicians and notables involved in land transfer to Jews in Appendix 3 to Stein, 1984, pp. 228–239.
114 Kimmerling, 1983, p. 11.

115 Porath, 1978, p. 514.
116 Ussishkin, "Our Program," in *Ussishkin Book*, p. 105.
117 *Ibid.*, p. 105.
118 *Ibid.*, p. 106.
119 Kimmerling, 1983, pp. 106, 145–146.
120 Arthur Ruppin, "Memorandum to the Executive of the World Zionist Organization," in Reichman, 1979, pp. 139–141.

3 "Conquest of labor"

1 Buber, "Regeneration in a People's Life," in Buber, 1983 (1942), pp. 206–209 and "An Experiment that Did Not Fail," in Buber, 1958 (1945), pp. 142–145.
2 S. N. Eisenstadt, 1948, pp. 7–9, and "*Aliya* and Immigration," in S. N. Eisenstadt *et al.* (eds.), 1969, pp. 269–276 and 1952, pp. 21–22 and 1954, pp. 35–45, 92–97.
3 Kellner, 1978, pp. 29–35.
4 Aaronsohn, 1979, pp. 123–130.
5 Giladi, 1975, pp. 176–183; Issawi, 1982, p. 143.
6 Schama, 1978, pp. 63, 68, 79–80.
7 Giladi & Naor, 1982, pp. 38–39.
8 Moore, 1966, p. 48.
9 Freiman, 1907, lists in the appendix land holdings, true for July 1905, pp. i–vi. For Petach Tikva, listing is for 1887, in Druyanov, 1925, Vol. 2, table on pp. 47–50 (Hebrew). I deleted from the lists a few smallholders that obviously did not make their living from agricultural work, and all publicly owned land. All calculations are based on Turkish dunams, that hold 919.3 m^2, and are equal to 0.227 acres.
10 Laskov, 1981, p. 166; Giladi, 1981, p. 204.
11 Kolatt, 1981, p. 342.
12 Letter of Jehuda Grazowsky to Yehoshua Barzilai (Eisenstadt) in Druyanov, 1932, Vol. 3, pp. 66–67.
13 "Mémoire présenté à Monsieur le Baron Edmond de Rothschild et à la Jewish Colonization Association par la Délégation nommée à l'Assemblée générale extraordinaire de la Société pour l'Assistance des Colons et Ouvriers en Syrie et en Palestine qui a eu lieu le 13 Fevrier 1901," CZA – A32:17.
14 Z. S. [Zeev Smilansky,] "The History of the Workers in the Eretz Israeli Moshavot," *Haolam*, May 4, 11, 18, 24, 1909; Kolatt, 1964a, p. 39.
15 Moshe Smilansky, 1959, Vol. 2, p. 67; Lewin-Epstein, 1932, p. 158; Giladi & Naor, 1982, p. 41.
16 Moshe Smilansky, 1959, Vol. 2, p. 67.
17 Yaffe, 1971, p. 146.
18 Giladi & Naor, 1982, p. 94.
19 Komarov, 1901, p. 375; Yaffe, 1971, p. 146.
20 Komarov, 1901, p. 372.

21 Hirschberg, 1979, pp. 107–108.
22 "From the Beginning of the Year to its End: A Review of the Events of the Year 5661 [1901 /2]," *Achiassaf: Measef Safruti*, Vol. 9, 1901 /2, p. 385.
23 The delegates of the workers from the moshavot of Judea and the Galilee, "An Essay about the Jewish Workers that are Working in the Moshavot of Judea and the Galilee," (handwritten), January 29, 1901, CZA – A24:15(1) No. 20; Braslavsky, 1942, p. 177.
24 Letter of the General Board of the Jewish Workers in Eretz Israel to the members of the General Board of the Peasants of Eretz Israel, Vadi Hanin, March 31, 1901, CZA – A32:47; Achad Haam, "The Envoys of a Poor People," in Achad Haam, 1947, pp. 305–308.
25 Freiman, 1907, p. 58; Giladi, 1974, p. 68.
26 Vitkin, 1908; Levine, 1912.
27 Bonacich, 1972, p. 549.
28 Smilansky, 1959, Vol. 2, p. 21.
29 Levine, August 9, 1912.
30 Vitkin, 1908.
31 "The ideology of Hebrew labor was directed against the Jewish employer, but in fact it affected the Arab worker . . ." Anita Shapira, 1977, p. 23.
32 Yona Hurwitz, "From Conquest of Labor to Settlement," in Habas, 1957, p. 202.
33 Eliyahu Even-Tov, "In Petach Tikva During the Boycott," in Habas, 1957, p. 182; Sarah Malkhin, "From Conquest of Labor in the Moshavot to Self-Settlement," in Yaari, 1947, p. 785.
34 Ussishkin, "Our Program," in *Ussishkin Book*, p. 118.
35 Anita Shapira, 1977, pp. 21, 26.
36 Jonathan Frankel, 1981, pp. 374, 385; Levine, August 9, 1912.
37 Such attempts were reported, for example, by Neta Harpaz, "Pangs of Conquest," in Habas, 1957, pp. 225–226.
38 Joseph Shapira, 1967, p. 19.
39 See for example Braslavsky, 1942, p. 85.
40 Belkind, 1983, pp. 49, 53, 148.
41 Beit-Halevi, July 5, 1894. There are additional examples from Yessod Hamaala (Komarov, 1901, p. 375), Rishon Letzion and Zichron Yaacov (Letter of Members and Directors of the Central Board of the Workers [Association] to the Society for the Assistance of Jewish Farmers and Craftsmen in Syria and the Holy Land, Vadi Hanin, October 11, 1901, CZA – A25:48). Indeed, we know from various sources that the workers complained of lack of motivation as they were not remunerated individually for their efforts, the reason being that the administrators treated their wages as charity.
42 Beit-Halevi, July 5, 1984.
43 Aharonowitz, November 26, 1909.
44 Aharonowitz, June /July 1908.
45 Bonacich, 1972, p. 549, my emphasis.

46 See speeches by Glusskin and Eisenberg, Kolatt, 1964b.
47 Giladi, 1970, p. 69 and Smilansky, 1959, Vol. 3, pp. 123–125.
48 See speeches of Lubman and Shenkin, Kolatt, 1964b.
49 "Report from the Central Committee," *HH*, Vol. 2, No. 1, September/October 1908.
50 Board Meeting of the Moshava Rechovot, No. 2, on December 21, 1890, MAR – Protocol Book No. 1, p. 4.
51 General Assembly Meetings of the Moshava Rechovot, Nos. 25 and 51, on December 16, 1899 and December 21, 1902, MAR – Protocol Book No. 2, pp. 182, 270.
52 Letters of Aharon Eisenberg to Zeev Glusskin, November 8, and December 12, 1903. CZA – A208:4 (Nos. 256, 291).
53 "Concerning the Draft Regulations of the Association of 'Order Keepers'" from June 13, 1905, originally in MAH.
54 Komarov, 1901, pp. 368–369; Yehoshua Barzilai composed three tables that outline the agricultural tasks in the moshavot. The most comprehensive one is "Work Schedule in the Judean Plain," CZA – A:25/40.
55 Yehoshua Barzilai, "Table of All Working Days according to Months and Branches in the Plantations of the Judean Plain," CZA – A:25/40.
56 Kaplansky, "The Agricultural Worker and the *Kvutza*," in Kaplansky, 1950, p. 418.
57 Aharonowitz, August/September 1908.
58 "The Fourth General Congress," *HH*, Vol. 2, No. 1, September/October 1908; Kolatt, 1964a, p. 107.
59 Hirschberg, 1979, pp. 107–108; Komarov, 1901, p. 371.
60 Aharonowitz, November 29, 1909.
61 Frader, 1981, pp. 187–188; Warner, 1975, pp. 3–5.
62 Poncet, 1962, p. 479.
63 Isnard, 1954, pp. 211–223.
64 Frader, 1981, pp. 188–189.
65 *Ibid.*, pp. 187, 205 note 5.
66 Poncet, 1962, pp. 155, 164; Isnard, 1954, p. 223.
67 See note 13 above. Mémoire, February 13, 1901.
68 Beit-Halevi, January 8 and February 7, 1894.
69 Z.S. [Zeev Smilansky], "The History of the Workers in the Eretz Israeli Moshavot: Part III," *Haolam*, May 18, 1909.
70 Aharonowitz, November 26, 1909.
71 In August 1914 the Central Board of the Federation of the Agricultural Laborers of Judea conducted a census of the Jewish laborers of Petach Tikva, Kfar Saba, Ein Hai, Rishon Letzion, Nachalat Yehuda, Kalandia/Dilab, Beer Yaacov, Ben Shemen, Hulda, Kfar Uria, Gedera, Beer Tuvia, Ruchama, Ness Ziona, Karkur, Ein Ganim, and Machane Yehuda. Census takers of the Federation recorded the answers of 803 respondents to twenty questions. This is the first time the census, found in CZA – L2:75/II, is being analyzed.
72 Beit-Halevi, May 7, 1894.

73 Levine, August 16, 1912.
74 Ilan, 1984, pp. 49–50.
75 Ronald Kimmelman, Chief of the Training Section for Vineyards in the Plantation Department of the Ministry of Agriculture, assured me that grafting and pruning are still considered skilled jobs in the vineyard, though certain types of pruning are being gradually mechanized. At the same time, these are skills which may be acquired in one agricultural season.
76 Aharonowitz, November 29, 1909.
77 Beit-Halevi, March 9, 1894; Komarov, 1901, p. 371; Hirschberg, 1979, pp. 107–108; Katzenelson, 1961, p. 567; Levine, August 16, 1912.
78 Freiman, 1907, pp. 186–193.
79 "Work Schedule in the Judean Plain," CZA – A25:40.
80 Komarov, 1901, p. 368.
81 From letter he sent from Petach Tikva to his family on October 11, 1906, see Ben-Gurion, 1971, p. 26. Frequently this became the plight of Jewish women immigrants, whose own aspiration to become agricultural workers were denied and they were redirected to the kitchen.
82 Levine, August 9, 1912.
83 Hirschberg, 1979, p. 107; Katzenelson, 1949 [1928], p. 26.
84 Nawratzki, 1914, p. 262.
85 Trietsch, 1910, p. 146.
86 J. Even-Moshe, "Rechovot," *HH*, Vol. 2, No. 14, May 21, 1909.
87 Arthur Ruppin, "The Problem of the Agricultural Laborers in Eretz Israel," *HH*, Vol. 5, No. 5, December 16, 1911.
88 Israel Cohen, 1911, p. 182.
89 Kaplansky, "The Agricultural Worker and the *Kvutza*," in Kaplansky, 1950, p. 418.
90 Kolatt, 1964a, p. 254.
91 Sussman, 1974, p. 50.
92 N.A., "In the Party," *HH*, Vol. 1, No. 12, August/September 1908.
93 Man from Sedjra, "Sedjra," *HH*, Vol. 3, No. 7, January 15, 1911.
94 A., "Letters to a Friend," *HH* [Vol. 1], No. 1, 1907.
95 Z.S. [Zeev Smilansky], "The History of the Workers in the Eretz Israeli Moshavot: Part II", *Haolam*, May 1909, pp. 3, 6.
96 Vitkin, 1908.
97 Aharonowitz, November 4, 1909.
98 Gurewitch, Gertz and Bacchi, 1944, pp. 20–21.
99 Gorny, 1970, pp. 205–206.
100 Though we should remember that our census does not include the agricultural workers of the Galilee, which developed into an important center of employment towards the end of the period.
101 Gorny, 1970, pp. 205–206.
102 Habas, 1957, pp. 17–18.
103 Poncet, 1962, pp. 164–234.
104 Estourelles de Constant, 1943, p. 404.
105 Poncet, 1962, p. 154.

106 Isnard, 1954, pp. 211–212.
107 *Ibid.*, pp. 212–222.
108 *Ibid.*, p. 220.
109 Paul Perrenoud, "La situation de l'ouvrier agricole en Algérie," *Bulletin de la Société d'Agriculture de Constantine*, No. 7, 15 Avril 1894, quoted in Isnard, 1954, pp. 216–217.
110 Isnard, 1954, p. 481.
111 *Ibid.*, p. 216.
112 *Ibid.*, pp. 480–500.
113 Kolatt, 1964b.
114 Dromi [Meir Dizengoff], "The Workers' Question," *Hatzvi*, September 21/22, 1909.
115 Issawi, 1982, p. 82.
116 Kolatt, 1964b.
117 *Ibid.*
118 Dromi [Meir Dizengoff], "The Workers' Question," *Hatzvi*, September 21/22, 1909.
119 A. Aaronsohn, "Die französische Kolonisation in Nordafrika," *Palästina*, Vol. 8, Nos. 1/2, January 1911.
120 Moshe Smilansky, 1959, Vol. 3, p. 127; Esco Foundation, 1947, p. 561; Kalvarisky, 1931, pp. 52–53.
121 See for example Gorny, 1985, p. 12; Kolatt, 1964a, pp. 97, 261.
122 Gorny, 1985, p. 12; or see slightly different English version, pp. 2–3.
123 Gorny, 1973, p. 3, my emphasis.
124 Kimmerling, 1983, p. 101.
125 Anita Shapira, 1977, p. 26 versus p. 348.
126 Preuss, 1965, pp. 22–23.
127 Quoted in Johnstone, 1976, p. 180.
128 Letter of Itzhak Ben-Zvi in Istanbul to the members of the Central Committee of Poalei Zion, [between January and June] 1914, *Ashuphot*, No. 7, March 1961, p. 70. The only notable exception was Zeev Smilansky, who argued that, among other reasons, Arab workers also ought to be displaced by Jewish workers, since "the youth of the moshava, in spite of themselves, learn the ugly habits, strange grimaces, and hideous vices and gesticulations of the semi-savage Arabs, and get used to the deceptions, false oaths, cheating, stubbornness and savage egoism, that are a mark of many of the lower-class Arabs" Z.S. [Zeev Smilansky], "Hebrew or Arab Laborers?" *Hashiloah*, Vol. 19, 1908/9, p. 262.
129 Though its early struggles were not labor but land related. Gollan, 1960, pp. 8, 33–49.
130 *Ibid.*, p. 77.
131 *Ibid.*, p. 196.
132 Clark, 1906, p. ix.
133 Gollan, 1960, p. 193.
134 *Ibid.*, p. 162.
135 Willard, 1968, pp. 119–120.

136 Norris, 1975, p. 78.
137 *Ibid.*, pp. 82–83; Gollan, 1960, pp. 165–166.
138 Ndabezitha & Sanderson, 1987.
139 Yaacov Rabinovitch, "Protection of National Labor," *HH*, Vol. 6, No. 15, January 10, 1913.
140 A. Hederati, "The Demand of the Farmers," and M. Zagorevsky, "Labor Legions," *Haezrach*, 1919, pp. 234, 302.
141 Zerubavel, "The Two Methods," *Haachdut*, Vol. 22, No. 36, July 14, 1911.
142 Avner [Itzhak Ben-Zvi], "National Protection and Proletarian Perspective: Parts I & II," *Haachdut*, Vol. 4, Nos. 16 and 17, January 31 and February 7, 1913. He builds here on Borochovian themes.
143 Political Protocols of the Sixth Conference of the Central Committee of the Poalei Zion Party, April 3/4, 1910, LA – 4031IV:27.
144 Aharonowitz, August/September, 1908.
145 Gorny, 1968b, pp. 69, 72.
146 Ro'i, 1964, Vol. 2, pp. 226–227; Copy of letter from A. Eisenberg to David Wolfshon, October 6, 1908, LA 104IV:41; Letter of Kalvarisky to Ussishkin, Metulla, May 28, 1913, CZA – A24:68/25.
147 Kolatt, 1964a, p. 108.
148 Letter of Lichtheim to Ruppin, April 24, 1914, CZA – Z3:65, quoted in Ro'i, 1964, Vol. 2, p. 227.
149 Ro'i, 1968, p. 223.
150 Anita Shapira, 1977, p. 347.
151 *Ibid.*, p. 23.
152 Member of the Central [Committee], "To Our Fifth Congress," *HH*, Vol. 2, Nos. 23/24, September 14, 1909; "From the Resoltions of the Fifth General Congress," *HH*, Vol. 3, No. 1, October 22, 1909.
153 Kolatt, 1964b.

4 "Natural Workers" from Yemen

1 David Ben-Gurion, "A Single Constitution," *Haachdut*, Vol. 3, Nos. 25/26, April 1, 1912.
2 Letter of Arthur Ruppin, the Palestine Office, Jaffa, to the JNF, Cologne, February 23, 1909, CZA – Z2:633.
3 Nini, 1982, pp. 179–182; Tuby, in Seri, 1983, pp. 35–40.
4 Kolatt, in Eliav, 1981, pp. 348–349 and 1964a, pp. 9–10.
5 Y. Ratzchabi, "Concerning the History of the Yemenite Laborers' Association Peulat Sachir," *Sheivat Zion*, Nos. 2/3, 1953, p. 456; copy of letter of "Peulat Sachir," Jaffa, to the Board of Rishon Letzion, May 1, 1903, LA – 107IV:6a.
6 Copies of Aharon Eisenberg's letters to the Members of the Central Committee of the Eretz Israeli Assembly (Knessiya) and Zeev Glusskin, November 8, 1903, LA – 104IV (Aharon Eisenberg): 39a; see also Ever-Hadeni, 1947, pp. 73–74.

7 Joseph Shapira, 1968, p. 40; "Protocol of the Delegates' Congress in Shavuot of 1908: Part II," *HH*, Vol. 1, No. 10, June/July 1908.
8 "Events and Deeds: Rechovot," *HH*, Vol. 2, No. 7, December 1908/January 1909; "Events and Deeds: Rishon Letzion," *HH*, Vol. 2, No. 10, February/March 1909; Hapoel Hatzair Pary sent messengers to the colonies' boards calling on them to employ the recent Jewish Yemenite arrivals. See MARL – Procotol of the Meeting of the Board No. 307, Protocol Book No. 14, September 26, 1909; Avraham Tabib, "Concerning The History of One Settlement," in Yeshayahu & Zadok, 1944, pp. 59–60.
9 Protocol of the Meeting of Rechovot's Board, January 7, 1909, quoted in Kapara, 1978, p. 56.
10 Nini, 1982, p. 230; Kushnir, 1972, p. 59; A. Yaari, "The Immigration of Yemenite Jews to Eretz Israel," in Yeshayahu & Zadok, 1944, p. 31; Even-Shoshan, 1963, Vol. 1, p. 221; Braslavsky, 1942, p. 96; Gorny, 1974, p. 60.
11 Shmuel Yavnieli, "The Work of Renewal and Eastern Jews: Parts I & II," *HH*, Vol. 3, Nos. 16 and 17, June 7 and 22, 1910. Obviously, these articles could not have induced Aharonowitz to change his negative opinion concerning the undesirability of a Yemenite Jewish labor force, as claimed in Kushnir, 1972, p. 63, and Nini, 1982, p. 230.
12 Ruppin, 1947, Vol. 2, p. 103; Tabib in Yaari, 1947, p. 880; Israel Yeshayahu, "The Jews of Yemen in Eretz Israel," in Yeshayahu & Gridi, 1938, p. 35.
13 Ofrat, 1981, pp. 129–130.
14 Glusska, 1974, p. 100; See also Druyan: "The Yemenites who knew of Yavnieli's journey – were reticent," (p. 118); Ofrat, 1981, p. 130. A contract was also signed, on November 8, 1910, between Thon and Meir Haim Nadaph, sending the latter on this errand. Yavnieli was not mentioned in this document. See CZA – L2:163.
15 Rabbi Benjamin [Yeshaya Redler-Feldman], "Shmuel Yavnieli's Mission to Yemen," in Yaari, 1947, pp. 884, 887, 893.
16 Palestine Office, *Settlement Conditions in Eretz Israel for Agriculturalists* (pamphlet), Jaffa, A. Atin, 1913, pp. 3–4 (Hebrew).
17 Druyan, 1981, p. 118.
18 Yavnieli, 1952, p. 8.
19 Copies of letters from Aharon Eisenberg to Zeev Glusskin, January 19, February 12, 1902 and July 7, 1904, LA – 104IV (Aharon Eisenberg): 43.
20 Though the percentage of Jewish workers in the labor force varied it never did so as sharply as in privately owned plantations. Lewin-Epstein, 1932, p. 160.
21 Copies of letters from Aharon Eisenberg to Zeev Glusskin, from December 24, 1903, January 6, and July 10, 1904, LA – 104IV (Aharon Eisenberg): 43.
22 [Prospectus] *Agudat Netaim: Its Establishment and Development*, [1917/18], CZA – A199:24/1. I introduced a few stylistic changes into the English language prospectus on the basis of the Hebrew original, from 1914, in CZA – A208:12.
23 The Jüdische Orient-Colonisations-Gesellschaft which was established by Davis Trietsch, with the participation of Oppenheimer, Louis Brisch and

others, also boasted in its prospectus that "the main objective of the Society is the employment of a method of settlement that has already yielded superlative results in many cases, particularly in California." See Bein, 1971, p. 99.

24 Katz cites a number of articles from Zionist newspapers of the period: Ben-David, "Eine californische Colonisations Methode," *Die Welt*, Vol. 3, No. 25, 1899, pp. 4–5; reprinted in *Palästina*; E. Lasson, "Kalifornische Kolonisation: Maywood-Colony," *Palästina*, 1903, pp. 92–98; and D. Trietsch, "The Progress of the Jewish Settlement in Eretz Israel," *Haolam*, Vol. 1, No. 44, October 31, 1907, pp. 529–530, which described repeatedly, and in great detail, the California model. The last of these articles, by Trietsch, already referred to the colonization method used in California and the Eretz Israel methods of Agudat Netaim as being identical. Though Katz found no direct reference in Eisenberg's letters to the California scheme, he thinks it obvious that Eisenberg knew of it. Katz, 1983, pp. 242–243.

25 Foster & Woodson, *Maywood Colony, California: The Place of Opportunity: Health in the Atmosphere: Wealth in Olive Culture: Comfort in the Climate*, Boston, 1898 and *When You Purchase a Piece of the Earth for a Home: It is not so Much what You Pay as what You Get: The Best is None too Good: In Maywood Colony, California You Get the Best*, Corning, 1900. These pamphlets and some issues of the Maywood Colony Advocate are to be found at the Bancroft Library of the University of California, Berkeley.

26 Katz, 1983, pp. 235–346.

27 Letters from Aharon Eisenberg to Itzhak Har-Zahav, July 30, 1906, CZA – A208 /5; to Weiner, November 29, 1906, and to Gad Frumkin, July 5, 1907, CZA – A208 /1; Also English prospectus, CZA – A199 /24 /1 quoted in Katz, 1983, p. 236. In a French prospectus, probably from 1919, facilitating the absorption of new Jewish working elements, is indicated as one of the major aims of Agudat Netaim. LA – 104IV (Aharon Eisenberg): 32.

28 Katz, 1983, pp. 253–254.

29 *Ibid.*, p. 294.

30 When Eisenberg planned to extend Agudat Netaim's work to Istanbul's environs, Ussishkin fired off an angry letter, telling Eisenberg that one quarter of the company's shareholders came from the Odessa area: "and it is obvious to me that they bought the company's shares not in pursuit of good business and out of their desire to be paid dividends no matter what, but because they are interested, some more some less, in the Jewish *yishuv* in Eretz Israel," Letter to M. Ussishkin, Odessa, to Aharon Eisenberg, Rechovot, September 25, 1912, CZA – A208:16.

31 Though the company cultivated close to 800 acres in 1909 and had yearly orders of 300,000 French francs (by 1914 the corresponding figures were over 4,100 acres and 1.3 million francs) it was deeply in debt, and after the First World War went into receivership. See Katz, 1983, pp. 267–308 (Hebrew).

32 Katz, 1983, p. 264.

33 See note 8 above.

34 Letter of Aharon Eisenberg, Agudat Netaim, to M. M. Ussishkin, Odessa, March 21, 1909, CZA – A24:63 /15 /1. Copy of this letter is in A208:7.
35 Copy of letter from Aharon Eisenberg to [Isaac]Turoff [of the Esra], Berlin, December 10, 1908, CZA – A208:7, and copy of letter from D. L. Landau, Esra Central Committee, Berlin, to Z. D. Levontin, APAC, Jaffa, January 11, 1909. It should be noted that Esra's letter suggests that some of the workers to be settled would be Yemenite Jews. This part of the initiative, however, has to be put down to sheer coincidence, since the meeting of Esra's Central Committee, in which the housing scheme was discussed took place on December 20, 1908 (invitation of M. Dorn to meeting of Esra's Central Committee, December 14, 1908, CZA – A12:21; from this meeting no documentation seems to have survived) while the first group of spontaneous Yemenite Jewish immigrants reached Jaffa on December 25, 1908 (Yeshayahu, in Yeshayahu & Gridi, 1938, p. 70), and the first public report of their arrival was a brief item in the Ben-Yehuda's paper, *Hazvi*, from January 1, 1909. The decision of Rechovot's Board to employ them was taken on January 7, 1909 (Kapara, 1978, p. 56), and even on January 10, 1909, the Jaffa correspondent of *Hazvi* reported them as looking for work. Their employment by Agudat Netaim could not have been known to Esra before Landau's letter to Levontin was dispatched. We should also remember in this context that *mizrachim* from the old *Yishuv* were occasionally employed by the moshavot.
   That Eisenberg himself referred to Yemenite Jews, when writing of "families content with little" is clear from the great similarity between his and Levontin's letter, which spelled out the identity of those needing housing assistance, written a day later to Esra.
36 Letter of Aharon Eisenberg, Agudat Netaim, to M. M. Ussishkin, Odessa, March 21, 1909, CZA – A24:63 /15 /1. Copy of this letter is in CZA – A208:7.
37 Letter of M. Ussishkin, Odessa (no. 728) to Eisenberg, April 14, 1909, CZA – A208:16.
38 Letter from Arthur Ruppin, Palestine Office, Jaffa, to the JNF, Cologne, February 23, 1909, CZA – Z2:633. Copy of letter by Z. D. Levontin, APAC. Jaffa, to Dorn, Central Committee of Esra, Berlin, February 15, 1909, CZA – Z2:1638.
39 Letter to Ruppin, Palestine Office, Jaffa, to President of Zionist Executive, Cologne, November 9, 1910, CZA – Z2:635.
40 Copy of letter from Aharon Eisenberg to Itzhak [Peckler], February 29, 1912. Copybook no. 6. Quoted in Ro'i, 1964, Vol. 2, p. 194 note 70.
41 Copy of letter from Aharon Eisenberg to [Isaac] Turoff, Esra, Berlin, August 13, 1911, CZA – A208:6.
42 Memoirs of Saadia Masswari in Druyan, 1982, p. 105.
43 Oral histories of Jephet Masswari & Zecharyah Redai (taken on July 4, 1977), Institute for Contemporary Jewry, Oral History Division, Jerusalem.
44 For Rechovot see: B.I., "Letter from Rechovot," *HH*, Vol. 4, Nos. 5 /6, December 23, 1910; One of the Company, "Sisyphean Labor," *HH*, Vol. 5, No. 5, December 16, 1912; Left and Returned, "Letter from Rechovot,"

HH, Vol. 5, Nos. 19/20, July 12, 1912; "Letter from Rechovot," *HH*, Vol. 7, No. 35, June 19, 1914; letter of Zeev Smilansky to Y. Feldman, the Palestine Office, CZA – L2/165; *Die Welt*, No. 10, 1914. For Hadera: Yeshayahu in Yeshayahu & Gridi, 1938, p. 85, "Chronicle," *Haaachdut*, Vol. 5, No. 36, July 3, 1914; Parzel, "Hadera," *HH*, Vol. 6, No. 37, July 4, 1913; Letter of Nathan Hofshi, the Board of Hadera's Workers to Palestine Office, June 21, 1913, CZA – L2:165.

45 Druyan, 1981, p. 93.

46 "Chronicle," *HH*, Vol. 3, No. 1, October 22, 1909; B-A, "Rishon Letzion," *HH*, Vol. 3, No. 3, November 12, 1909; Yeshayahu & Gridi, 1938, pp. 80–81; MARL – Sheivat-Zion, Aharon and Bat-Zion Eraqi, "The Sheivat-Zion Quarter;" Tabib in Yeshayahu & Zadok, 1944, p. 60.

47 Resident of Zichron, "Zichron Yaakov," *HH*, Vol. 5, No. 21, August 1, 1912; "This Week," *HH*, Vol. 6, No. 10, November 29, 1913; "This Week," *HH*, Vol. 7, No. 26, April 10, 1914.

48 "Chronicle," *Haachdut*, Vol. 3, Nos. 45/46, September 5, 1912.

49 —any, "Letter from Kinneret – The Yemenites in the Galilee," *HH*, Vol. 5, No. 13, June 5, 1912; Z., "This Week," *HH*, Vol. 6, No. 40, July 25, 1913.

50 Druyan, 1981, p. 100.

51 Glusska, 1974, p. 103; "Chronicle," *Haachdut*, Vol. 3, No. 5, November 17, 1911.

52 Shmuel Yavnieli found that "in Hadera, Petach Tikva and Rechovot the Yemenites conquered the hoe." "After the Immigration," *HH*, Vol. 6, No. 23, March 14, 1913; Shmuel Yavnieli, "Concerning the Improvement of the Yemenites' Situation," *Haadama*, No. 1, September/November 1919, p. 91; see also Resident of Rechovot, "Rechovot," *HH*, Vol. 2, No. 9, January/February, 1909.

53 Left and Returned, "Letter from Rechovot," *HH*, Vol. 5, Nos. 19/20, July 12, 1912; [Itzhak Ben-Zvi], "Letter from Petach Tikva," *Haachdut*, Vol. 4, Nos. 14/15, January 24, 1912; Letter of Nathan Hofshi on behalf of the Board of Workers in Hadera to the Palestine Office, January 7, 1913, CZA – L2:164.

54 Letter of David Madar-Halevi, from the Yemenite Board of Shaarayim by Rechovot, to the Palestine Office, October 1917, quoted in Tuby, 1982, p. 88.

55 Resident of Rechovot, "Rechovot," *HH*, Vol. 2, No. 9, January/February, 1909 who reports that Yemenite Jews receive a quarter *medjidie* which is the going rate for unskilled Arab workers, for pruning. A list, from the spring of 1913, which obviously includes skilled Yemenite Jewish workers from three colonies and their wages, gives higher wages, but most are still lower than those paid for the same work to *ashkenazim*, CZA – A237:3/3/d.

56 B-T, "Letter from Rechovot," *HH*, Vol. 7, No. 35, June 19, 1914.

57 See for example Even-Shoshan, 1963, p. 222; *History Book of the Hagana*, 1954, Vol. 1, p. 145.

58 Meir, 1983, p. 95; Druyan, 1981, pp. 137–138.

59 Joseph Shprintzak, "Among the Yemenites, Part II," *HH*, Vol. 5, No. 12,

March 19, 1912; [Itzhak Ben-Zvi], "Letters from Petach Tikva," *Haachdut*, Vol. 4, Nos. 14/15, January 24, 1913; Shmuel Yavnieli, "After the Immigration, Part II," *HH*, Vol. 6, No. 24, March 21, 1913; Letter of David Madar-Halevi, Yemenites' Board of Shaarayim nearby Rechovot, to the Palestine Office, October 1917, quoted in Tuby, 1982, p. 89.

60 Shprintzak, 1968, p. 187.

61 Tabib in Yaari, 1947, p. 877.

62 Shmuel Yavnieli, "After the Immigration, Part III," *HH*, Vol. 6, No. 25, April 4, 1913.

63 Druyan, 1981, pp. 102–103.

64 *Ibid.*, pp. 127–129, 131; see also Meeting of Committee for Yemenite's Affairs [adjoining the Palestine Office], August 21, 1913, CZA – L2:166.

65 Druyan, 1981, pp. 130–132.

66 Shmuel Yavnieli, "Concerning the Improvement of the Yemenites' Situation," *Haadama*, No. 1, September/November, 1919, pp. 81–82; "Resident of Petach Tikva," *HH*, Vol. 6, No. 31, May 23, 1913.

67 Druyan, 1981, p. 107.

68 "Illusory Victory," *Haachdut*, Vol. 4, No. 1, October 14, 1912.

69 Druyan, 1981, p. 134.

70 Aharonowitz, November 26, 1909.

71 J. Even-Moshe, "Letter from Rechovot," *HH*, Vol. 3, No. 3, November 12, 1909.

72 B.I., "Letter from Rechovot," *HH*, Vol. 4, Nos. 5/6, December 23, 1910; J. Even-Moshe, "Rechovot," *HH*, Vol. 3, Nos. 20/21, November 12, 1909.

73 J.R., "Notes," *HH*, Vol. 4, No. 19, July 11, 1911; B-A., "Rishon Letzion," *HH*, Vol. 3, No. 3, November 12, 1909.

74 "Chronicle," *Haachdut*, Vol. 3, No. 5, November 13, 1911.

75 A. M. Koller, "From Inside the Camp: Part I," *HH*, Vol. 6, No. 40, July 25, 1913; Footnote to Joseph Aharonowitz, November 26, 1909.

76 "The Resolutions of the Fourth Congress of the Workers of Judea," *HH*, Vol. 7, No. 12, December 26, 1913.

77 Zerubavel, "The Congress of the Judean Workers: Part I," *Haachdut*, Vol. 5, No. 14, January 23, 1914.

78 Druyan, 1981, p. 93.

79 Ben-David, "Letter from Gedera," *HH*, Vol. 2, No. 14, May 21, 1909.

80 Letter and appended wage list of Z. Abramowitz to the Board of Rishon Letzion, December 9, 1902, MARL – File of Incoming Letters (September 1902–January 1903).

81 Zeev Smilansky, "Clarification," *HH*, Vol. 3, No. 12, April 12, 1910.

82 J.R., "Notes," *HH*, Vol. 4, No. 17, July 11, 1911; See also Shprintzak, "in the cultural sense [the Yemenite Jews] will not be able to do anything" in "Summary of the Debate on Working Conditions in our General Assembly," *HH*, Vol. 4, Nos. 1/2, November 11, 1910.

83 "Report of [Poalei Zion] Party's Council, in Jaffa, on October 18/20," *Haachdut*, Vol. 2, Nos. 2/3, November 11, 1910.

84 Editorial footnote to M. Shenkin, "Concerning the Workers' Question," *HH*, Vol. 2, No. 8, January/February 1909.

85 "Resolutions Adopted at the Eleventh Congress of Hapoel Hatzair in Passover," *HH*, Vol. 5, Nos. 14/15, May 2, 1912. Another method for down playing, not the implications, but the motivations in fighting the danger of displacement, is through the idealization of the conflict, as is evident from the following statement made at the Twelfth Congress: "is it desirable in our present situation that the Yemenite Jew take the place of the *ashkenazi* youngster? . . . It is self-evident that this is not a question of competition for making a living (*parnassa*), but mostly a question of principles," "A Summary of the Debates in our Annual Assembly," *HH*, Vol. 6, No. 10, November 29, 1912.

86 Kolatt, 1964a, pp. 109, 126.

87 Copy of letter by Z. D. Levontin, APAC, Jaffa, to Dorn, Central Committee of Esra, Berlin, February 15, 1909 in CZA – z2/1638; and letter of Arthur Ruppin, Palestine Office, Jaffa, to the JNF, Cologne, February 23, 1909 in CZA – z2:633.

88 Letter of B. Katznelson, Board of [Federation of] Judean Workers, to Palestine Office, March 19, 1914, CZA – L2:66/II. The opposing attitude of the leadership and the rank and file may also be discerned from the fact that in the February meeting of the "Committee for Yemenite Affairs" of the Palestine Office, in which a representative of the Ein Hai settlers participated, the project of joint settlement was stalled, while in the June meeting, in which only the national leaders were present, there was anger expressed at the JNF's decision to cancel the construction of housing for Yemenite Jews. It is also revealed that since the future settlers of Ein Hai could not reach agreement with the Yemenite representative over the choice of the settlers, these negotiations were taken over by the Federation of the Judean Workers. Memorandum [of Committee for Yemenite Affairs] "Concerning the Setting Up of the Workers' Moshava at Ein Hai", February 5, 1914, CZA – L2:66/II and Meeting of the Committee for Yemenite Affairs, June 7, 1914, CZA – KKL3:142.

89 Letter of the Palestine Office to Shifris, the Board of the Federation of the Agricultural Workers of Judea, June 22, 1914. CZA – L2:66/II.

90 "Meeting of the Agricultural Workers in the Galilee," *Haachdut*, Vol. 3, Nos. 16 and 17, January 26 and February 2, 1912.

91 Blubstein, 1943, pp. 31–38.

92 "B[erman] brought *sephardim* but, after the [*ashkenazi*] workers explained to them that it is forbidden to work here, the *sephardim* demonstrated their feelings of solidarity, and returned to Tiberias saying that even if they were paid ten *bishliks* a day [about two and half times the daily rate] they would not work here," Worker, "Letter from Kinneret," *Haachdut*, Vol. 2, Nos. 20/21, March 15, 1911.

93 Moshe Smilansky, 1953, p. 40.

94 There is an attempt to contradict Smilansky's version by Ben-Zion Israeli, a member of the Second *Aliya* who was one of the workers at Kinneret. Israeli,

however, was not present in February–May 1912, and he confused the group discussed above with another group of Yemenite Jewish wage laborers who lived in the adjacent moshava of the Jewish Colonization Association carrying the same name. This was the first group of Yemenite Jews to be settled in Kfar Marmorek, its own moshava, in 1930. Ben-Zion [Israeli], "Concerning the 'Yemenite' Affair in Kinneret," *Alon Kinneret*, 1953, in Archive of Kinneret, file 41.

95 "Council of the Agricultural Workers of the Galilee," *Haachdut*, Vol. 3, No. 27 and No. 28, April 23 and 29, 1912.

96 "Bau von Yemeniter-Häusern 1914" and Protocol of the Committee for Yemenite Affairs, June 7, 1914, CZA – L2:163.

97 *Course of Degania*, 1961, pp. 56–57: in English in Viteles, 1967, Vol. 2, p. 35.

98 Kolatt, 1964, p. 109.

99 "Chronicle," *Haachdut*, Vol. 4, Nos. 24/25, April 6, 1913.

100 Letter of David Madar-Halevi, from the Yemenite Board of Shaarayim by Rechovot to the Palestine Office, October 1917, quoted in Tuby, 1982, p. 89.

101 [Itzhak Ben-Zvi], "Letters from Petach Tikva," *Haachdut*, Vol. 4, Nos. 14/15, January 24, 1913.

102 M. Harizman, "Concerning the Situation of the Yemenite Immigrants," *HH*, Vol. 6, Nos. 3 and 4, October 13 and 22, 1913; Giladi, 1974, p. 76.

103 Ben-Zvi, 1936, Vol. 5, p. 67.

104 Druyan, 1981, p. 107.

105 *Ibid.*, p. 109.

106 *Ibid.*, p. 108. Jewish women were not regularly taught Hebrew in Yemen.

107 The currency referred to, in the document, is still the French franc, the foreign currency of the Ottoman era, which was replaced with the Palestinian and British pound in the British Mandate.

108 "Meeting of all the Agricultural Yemenites from all the Moshavot of Judea," LA – 402IV:3

109 Letter of Arthur Ruppin, the Palestine Office, Jaffa, to the JNF, Cologne, February 23, 1909, CZA – Z2:633.

110 "Mourning Scroll of the Yemenite Community of Jerusalem," originally published in *Havzelet*, No. 29, 1891, and reproduced in Druyan, 1982, pp. 58–62; Herzog, 1981, pp. 33–34; Eli-Podiel, 1982, pp. 120–124.

111 [Itzhak Ben-Zvi], "Letters from Peach Tikva," *Haachdut*, Vol. 4, Nos. 14/15, January 24, 1913.

112 In Druyan's view, "the beginning of ethnic organization in agriculture . . . was intended to improve the working conditions of the Yemenites." The regulations of the Boards she referred to in this context, however, addressed only questions of internal organization, religious observance, administration of justice, and so on (Druyan, 1981, p. 109). In fact, early Yemenite Jewish organization took place outside the labor market, and was aided by the concern of the *ashkenazi* workers for the Yemenite Jewish organization took place outside the labor market, and was aided by the concern of the *ashkenazi* workers for the Yemenite Jewish immigrants' living conditions.

113 Left and Returned, "Letter from Rechovot," *HH*, Vol. 5, Nos. 19/20, July 12, 1912.

114 Ofrat, 1981, p. 144.
115 Ever-Hadeni, 1951, p. 246.
116 See, for example, letter of the Palestine Office to Z. Shapira, their representative for the Yemenites Affairs in Zichron Yaacov, November 25, 1913, CZA – L2:166.
117 For example, in Hadera the Yemenite Board was too weak even to collect the fines that were due to the moshava from their community. Letter from Jephet Ben-Yaakov, Shlomo Cohen, Naphtali Ben-Aharon, of the Yemenites' Board and from Zecharya Ben-Saadya and [?] of the "Peace Committee" to the Board of Hadera, September 5, 1917, MAH – file of incoming letters.
118 "Chronicle," *Haachdut*, Vol. 4, No. 22, March 14, 1913.
119 "Report of the [Poalei Zion] Party's Council in Sukkhot, in Jaffa," *Haachdut*, Vol. 2, Nos. 2/3, November 17, 1910.
120 A. M. Koller, "From the Camp: Part II," *HH*, Vol. 6, No. 42, August 8, 1913.
121 Worker, "Rechovot," *HH*, Vol. 6, No. 22, March 7, 1913; Shprintzak, 1952, p. 283; Druyan, 1981, pp. 111–112.

5 Between trade unions and political parties

1 Shapiro, 1976, pp. 189–190.
2 Etzioni, 1959, p. 204.
3 Kolatt, 1964a, p. 87.
4 Laskov, 1986, pp. 68, 128.
5 Tsemach, 1965, p. 154.
6 Laskov, 1986, p. 57. Ussishkin's call, in the Minsk Congress of Russian Zionists in September 1902, however, is different from "Our Program" and calls for propaganda work in the diaspora and not for national service in Palestine, see *Hatzfira*, Vol. 29, No. 201, September 17, 1902.
7 Joseph Shapira, 1967, p. 470.
8 Sochobolsky, "The Beginnings of Hapoel Hatzair," in Habas, 1957, pp. 616–617.
9 Kolatt, 1964a, pp. 89, 93, 132–133. Its major source of influence was its journal, *Hapoel Hatzair*, that was published under the editorship of Joseph Aharonowitz, as a monthly in 1907, a bi-weekly in 1908, and when it came to be a weekly in 1912, it sold 1,140 issues, 470 in Eretz Israel and 640 abroad.
10 Ben-Netz, "Construction and Contradiction," *HH*, Vol. 1, No. 2, October/November, 1907.
11 Joseph Shapira, 1967, p. 470.
12 Peled & Shafir, 1987, pp. 1440–1447.
13 Kolatt, 1964a, pp. 147–153.
14 *Ibid.*, p. 171.
15 Jonathan Frankel, 1981, pp. 370–371.
16 Joseph Shapira, 1967, p. 28.
17 Sochobolsky in Habas, 1957, pp. 614–615.

18 Kolatt, 1964a, p. 148; Jonathan Frankel, 1981, pp. 385–386, argues that "internationalism" was the major factor.
19 "The Ramla Platform," in Slutsky, 1978, p. 18.
20 Ben-Gurion, 1971, pp. 23–25; Teveth, 1977, p. 98.
21 Anita Shapira, 1977, p. 29.
22 [Editorial], *HH* [multilith edition], [Vol. 1], No. 2, 1907.
23 Letter of Joseph Aharonowitz, Hapoel Hatzair, and Itzhak Goldberg, Poalei Zion, to Ruppin, Palestine Office, received May 8, 1910, CZA – L2:572.
24 Ben-Zvi, 1950, p. 9.
25 Frankel, unpublished, p. 4.
26 Ben-Gurion, 1971, p. 35; Teveth, 1977, p. 168.
27 Kolatt, 1964a, pp. 194, 199.
28 *Ibid.*, p. 195.
29 *Ibid.*, pp. 153–168.
30 But while Gorny, who examines accumulative changes, emphasizes the early reflection of these changes in Poalei Zion's program, Kolatt, who pinpoints the complete transformation, sees them only in 1913. Gorny, 1974a, pp. 96–108; Kolatt, 1964a, p. 178.
31 Protocol of the Third Congress of Poalei Zion, Jaffa, September 1908, LA – 403:4 Ben-Zvi Files, quoted in Gorny, 1974b, p. 98.
32 Quoted in Gorny, 1974b, pp. 103–104.
33 *Ibid.*, p. 108; Slutsky, 1978, pp. 29–31.
34 This happened during the long sojourn of the two in the US during the war.
35 Thus the debate recurred in 1913. Gorny, 1974b, p. 104.
36 *Ibid.*, p. 97.
37 Protocol of the Sixth Congress of *Poalei Zion*, Jaffa, April 23/24, 1910, LA – 403:3 Poalei Zion, quoted in Gorny, 1974b, p. 103.
38 Kolatt, 1964a, p. 180.
39 Gorny, 1974b, p. 104.
40 Giladi, 1969, pp. 86–98.
41 See also Metzer & Kaplan, 1985, p. 336.
42 Giladi, 1969, p. 97. The political organization of industrialists was not likely to yield any similar economic advantages from the British Mandate authorities.
43 Kolatt, 1964b.
44 Shalev in Pempel, forthcoming; Abraham Cohen, 1969, pp. 262–264.

6 Soldier and settler

1 Gera, 1985, pp. 12–13.
2 Allon, 1969, p. 241.
3 Typical contract in MARL – File of Outgoing Mail, 1900/1902, No. 90.
4 Israel Shochat, 1957, p. 19; *History Book of the Hagana* (hereafter, *Hagana*), p. 211.
5 For example, see, Tsalel, "Memoirs," *Hashomer Collection*, 1937, p. 200.
6 Bernstein, 1987, p. 19; Izraeli, 1981, p. 92.

7 Gera, 1985, p. 8.

8 Israel Shochat, 1957, p. 14.

9 Ben-Zvi's most important attempt at reconciliation: "Proletarian Perspective and National Defense," was written in conjunction with Hashomer's May 1913 Congress. Israel Shochat, 1957, p. 33.

10 Letter of Israel Shochat, Sedjra, to Ussishkin, June 7, 1907, CZA – A24:60/20.

11 Saadia Paz & Mendel Portugali, "A Bundle of Letters," in *Hashomer Collection*, 1937, pp. 199, 33.

12 *Hagana*, p. 199.

13 *Ibid.*, p. 244.

14 Kayla Giladi, "From Sedjra to Kfar Giladi," *Hashomer Collection*, 1937, p. 136.

15 *Hagana*, pp. 221–223.

16 *Ibid.*, pp. 212, 219.

17 Israel Shochat, 1957, p. 19.

18 *Ibid.*, p. 21.

19 Zeid in Gazit, 1966, p. 49; *Hagana*, p. 224; Israel Shochat, p. 28.

20 Kimmerling, 1983, pp. 21–25.

21 *Hagana*, pp. 219–221.

22 Letter of David Rubin, Sedjra, to M. Ussishkin, December 10, 1907, CZA – A24:60/16.

23 *Hagana*, p. 303.

24 *Ibid.*, pp. 245, 248.

25 Israel Shochat, 1957, p. 32; *Hagana*, pp. 233–234.

26 Elsberg, 1956, p. 170.

27 *Hagana*, p. 252.

28 Letter of Israel Shochat, Board of Hashomer, Haifa, to M. Ussishkin, July 20, 1914, CZA – A24:60/20; Israel Shochat, 1957, p. 38.

29 *Hagana*, pp. 229, 231.

30 X, "Rishon Letzion," *HH*, Vol. 6, No. 4, October 22, 1912; *Hagana*, pp. 238–239.

31 Kayla Giladi, "From Sedjra to Kfar Giladi," *Hashomer Collection*, 1937, p. 136.

32 Moshe Ilyowitch, "Efforts at Becoming Good Neighbors," *Hashomer Book*, 1957, p. 369.

33 From a poem of the famed Hebrew poet Yaakov Cohen. See, Alexander Zeid, "Life Chapter," *Hashomer Book*, 1957, p. 86.

34 Pinchas Shneursohn, "Behind the Wall," and Nachum Horowitz, "We and Our Neighbors," *Hashomer Book*, 1957, pp. 87, 375–376.

35 Mania Shochat-Wilbushevitz, "Guarding in Eretz Israel," *Hashomer Book*, 1957, pp. 75–76.

36 *Hagana*, pp. 226, 230.

37 Ro'i, 1964, p. 89; Ben-Gorni, "Letter from Rechovot," *HH*, Vol. 5, No. 1, October 22, 1911.

38 *Hagana*, p. 237.

39 Ro'i, 1964, p. 87.

40 Israel Shochat, 1957, p. 32; *Hagana*, pp. 241–242.
41 Ro'i, 1964, p. 88.
42 MARL – Protocol Book No. 15, Board Meeting, January 5, 1913.
43 Israel Shochat, 1957, pp. 10–11; *Hagana*, pp. 198–199, 217.
44 Tabenkin, 1979, p. 12.
45 Itzhak Ben-Zvi, "With Hashomer," *Hashomer Collection*, 1937, p. 69; Ben-Porath [Yosef Weitz],"Hebrew Guards and Foreign Workers," *HH*, Vol. 4. Nos. 9/10, February 2, 1911.
46 Zeev Assushkin, "From Hadera to Hamra," and Yigal, "Days of Conquest," *Hasomer Collection*, 1937, pp. 96, 176; Ever-Hadeni, 1951, pp. 220, 259–260; *Hagana*, p. 229.
47 Ro'i, 1964, p. 82 and 1970, pp. 159, 195–196. In a letter of Zvi Bitkovsky to the Board of Hadera, February 7, 1912, we read that one of [Hashomer's] guards entered the cowshed and vigorously beat up all the workers with no apparent reason. MAH – File of Incoming Mail.
48 Yosef Weitz, "A Year in Hadera," in *Working Hadera*, p. 70.
49 *Hagana*, p. 254.
50 *Hagana*, p. 211; Itzhak Ben-Zvi, "With Hashomer," *Hashomer Collection*, 1937, p. 69.
51 Ever-Hadeni, 1951, p. 244.
52 Livne, 1969, pp. 98–99, 130–131.
53 *Ibid.*, pp. 162–168; Yosef Klausner, "World in Formation: Part III," *Hashiloach*, Vol. 29, 1913/14, p. 63.
54 *Hagana*, pp. 281–286; Livne, 1969, pp. 173–75.
55 Shachaf, 1984.
56 Shapiro, 1976, p. 32.

7 Cooperative Settlement

1 "Die jüdische Nationalfonds," *Die Welt*, No. 29, 1905 describes land purchase and settling of farmers as "the purest and holiest goal."
2 "At times . . . conflicts sprang from the demands of New York [Jewish leaders] that as few emigrants as possible be sent, and on the other hand, from the quiet efforts of some of the European [Jewish Refugee Assistance] Committees to ship as many emigrants as possible to America in their endeavors to prevent these emigrants from otherwise remaining in Western and Central Europe," Szajkowski, 1951, p. 131; Aschheim, 1982, pp. 32–37.
3 Reinharz, 1975, p. 130. Only around 1910 did the ZVfD begin undergoing radicalization with the entry of a younger generation which raised the demand for personal emigration to Palestine. See Reinharz, 1975, pp. 144–170.
4 Pinsker wrote: "The fact that, as it seems, we can mix with the nations only in the smallest proportions, presents a further obstacle to the establishment of amicable relations. Therefore, we must see to it that the *surplus* of Jews, the inassimilable residue, is removed and provided for elsewhere. This duty can be incumbent upon no one but ourselves," Leo Pinsker, "Auto-Emancipation," in Hertzberg, 1959, p. 193. And Nordau wrote, in an

otherwise sympathetic presentation of the *Ostjuden*, that: "the contempt created by the impudent, crawling beggar in dirty caftan . . . falls back on all of us," quoted in Aschheim, 1982, p. 88.

5 Reinharz, 1975, p. 104; Aschheim, 1982, p. 81.

6 Too late to be of direct use, an outstanding dissertation by Derek Jonathan Penslar, "Engineering Utopia: The WZO and the Settlement of Palestine, 1897–1914," University of California, Berkeley, 1987, came to my attention. His central thesis is that: "while the German-centrism of pre-World War One Zionism on both the institutional and cultural levels has long been recognized, the effect of this orientation on Zionist policy has not" (p. 46). Penslar seeks to rectify this lacuna by presenting, one by one, the host of German Zionists, who together made up the "settlement engineers" of the movement and advocated concrete policies copied and adopted from German experience. Obviously Penslar's and my work evolved, on this issue, on strikingly similar lines and I see the two studies as mutually confirming. But in contradistinction to this study, Penslar remains satisfied with presenting the formative influences on German Zionist colonization, without trying to examine the relative weights of German Zionism and the labor movement with its Eastern European influences in the formation of Zionist colonization at the period. Furthermore I disagree with his view that the Zionist settlement methods used were "neutral," and therefore it seems to me that the "settlement technicians" may be seen with equal justice as settlement politicians and as such are not devoid of responsibility for the results.

7 Hussain & Tribe, 1981, pp. 20–24.

8 *Ibid.*, p. 25.

9 See Barker, 1955.

10 His major work was Flürscheim, 1884. For George's influence on Flürscheim see Barker, 1955, p. 531.

11 Bauer-Mengelberg, 1931, pp. 144–146; Gutzeit, 1907, pp. 72–93; J. H. Epstein, 1912, pp. 254–265.

12 Damaschke, 1903. For a brief history of the German land reform movement see Fricke *et al.*, 1983, pp. 282–288.

13 Hertzka, 1891, pp. 1, 137.

14 Wygodzinski & Müller, 1929, pp. 22–31.

15 Oppenheimer, 1931, pp. 138, 151–158.

16 Oppenheimer, 1913.

17 See the well-known connection between Oppenheimer and other land reformers' ideas in Böhm, 1910, pp. 32–33; and A. Tsiyoni [Itzhak Vilkansky], "The Oppenheimer Settlement Method: Part I," *HH*, Vol. 3, No. 17, June 22, 1910.

18 Bonné, 1956, p. 112; Orni, 1972, pp. 13–18; see also Metzer, 1979, p. 49.

19 Elon, 1975, p. 199; Patai, 1960, p. 282; Herzl was also instrumental in the publication of Oppenheimer's long essay on "Henry George und sein Werk," in the *Neue Freie Presse*, August 15, 22, 28.

20 Bodenheimer, 1965, p. 165.

21 Kressel in Agmon, 1951, p. 46.
22 Hagen, 1980, p. 134.
23 Weber, 1968, pp. 172–205. Weber, by the way, was also opposed to the tariffs that favored the Junkers.
24 Bruchhold-Wahl, 1980, in the most detailed history of German "internal colonization," highlights this shift, pp. 98, 180. A brief summary of the issues may be found in Jakobczyk, 1972, pp. 3–13. See also Blanke, 1981, who emphasizes Bismarck's role in initiating the Settlement Law of 1886, but also mentions that purchase by the Settlement Commission "was a factor causing land prices to rise rapidly" (p. 73).
25 Reichman & Hasson, 1984, p. 57.
26 *Ibid.*, pp. 63–64.
27 Hagen, 1980, p. 171; Bruchold-Wahl, 1980, does not see a radical change during the Caprivi era, pp. 260–264.
28 Reichman & Hasson, 1984, pp. 58–60.
29 This becomes clear from Singer, 1971, pp. 150, 152, 156, 159. Furthermore, the Russian Poalei Zion boycotted the 1909 Congress which finally adopted the practical tools for setting up the 'settlement-cooperative." See Gorny, 1974b, p. 104.
30 Quoted in J. Frankel, 1981, p. 400.
31 Kaplansky, 1950, p. 30. This essay is from 1907.
32 Oppenheimer, 1913, pp. 249–288.
33 Reichman & Hasson, 1984.
34 Ruppin put this in the following way: "the existence of a class of Jewish farmers in Eretz Israel is considered to be a necessary condition for the domination of its economy," Arthur Ruppin, Blueprint for the Palestine Land Development Co., December 14, 1907, CZA – A107:663. Adolf Böhm also pointed out that in all colonizing countries, such as Canada, South America, Asia Minor, Australia, and Palestine (with the exception of the US) agriculture was the primary branch of the economy and commerce and industry were only secondary branches, Böhm, 1910, p. 21.
35 "Vorschlag des Palästina-Ressorts an das Direktorium des Jüdischen Nationalfonds," [1907], CZA – z2:639 and Letter of Otto Warburg to Bodenheimer, June 10, 1909, CZA – LI:29.
36 Memorandum of Association of Jüdische Nationalfonds, Incorporated April 8, 1907, London, Lewis & Yglesias, CZA – z2:608.
37 The proposal submitted to the Sixth Congress in 1903 included the right to resell land purchased by the JNF, supposedly to allow exchange of plots. This clause was voted down, cf. Kressel, in Agmon, 1951, pp. 45–46.
38 *Ibid.*, p. 45.
39 Doukhan-Landau, 1979, p. 55. The issue debated by the Kattowitz Congress was not whether land purchased by the National Fund could be resold or not, but whether, as Schapira proposed, the National Fund would be used exclusively for purchase of land or, as Lilienblum suggested, the Fund could be used for a variety of purposes. N. M. Gilbar, in Agmon, 1951, pp. 167–168.

40 The German land reformers justified their aims, *inter alia*, by referring to the superiority of traditional German communal land ownership over the Roman legal concept of private property. The land nationalization of the JNF was also justified in reference to the overturning of the Roman legal system in land ownership, and with the inspiration of Henry George. See Josef Michaelsen, "Ein Wort zur russischen Landes-Konferenz in Minsk," *Die Welt*, Vol. 6, No. 43, 1902.

41 Bodenheimer's speech is reproduced in Bodenheimer, 1978, p. 179.

42 Michael Flürscheim, "*Sozialreformen für Neu-Zion*: Teil I," *Die Welt*, Vol. 1, No. 26, November 26, 1897.

43 Böhm, [1917], pp. 23–25.

44 Moshe Leib Lilienblum, "The Mission of the National Fund," *Hashiloach*, Vol. 19, 1908/9, p. 54. This restriction was, however, circumvented by various legal fictions when the more lucrative urban lands were concerned. See Doukhan-Landau, 1979, p. 81.

45 Doukhan-Landau, 1979, pp. 30–31.

46 The JNF directorate obviously felt that it could not leave the land uncultivated given the Ottoman statute which turned *miri* land left fallow for three years into *makhlul*, which reverted to state ownership. It is intriguing to note in this context, that in spite of the repeated allusion to this statute (for example, see Weintraub *et al.*, 1969, p. 10), there are no known examples of its application. Land purchased from Arab owners, however, could not be left fallow since the previous tenants continued trespassing on it and cultivating it. This was especially the case when it was purchased before the winter season after the land already had been prepared by the summer crops of the biannual crop-rotation system.

47 Shilo, 1985, pp. 61–63.

48 J. Frankel, 1981, pp. 398, 401.

49 For the features of Oppenheimer's plan see, for example, "The First Steps of Cooperative Settlement in Eretz Israel," *Haachdut*, Vol. 2, No. 14, January 27, 1911; Kaplansky, "The Argicultural Worker and the *Kvutza*," in Kaplansky, 1950, pp. 432–434; Vilkansky, "The Oppenheimer Settlement Method: Part I," *HH*, Vol. 3, No. 17, June 22, 1910; and Oppenheimer, 1917, p. 17.

50 Ruppin, 1947, pp. 39–40.

51 "Vorschlag des Palästina-Ressorts an das Direktorium des Jüdischen Nationalfonds," [1907], CZA – Z2:639.

52 Prospectus of the PLDC, April 15, 1908, CZA – A12:69.

53 Reichman & Hasson, 1984.

54 Each, however, learned from them somewhat different and, by and large, self-serving lessons. Vilkansky, the agronomist at Hulda, emphasized the antithesis between national and capitalist colonization on other continents (A. Tsiyoni [Itzhak Vilkansky], "In Expectation of Capitalism: Part II," *HH*, Vol. 6, No. 35, June 20, 1913). Tschlenov, a leader of Hovevei Zion, saw in "the experiments and methods of the Germans in the Posen region the justification . . . of the establishment of workers' settlements [such as Ein

Ganim] alongside the big moshavot" (see review of Tschlenov's book in Haim Grünberg, "Five Years of Work in Eretz Israel," *Haolam*, Vol. 7, No. 22, June 24, 1913).

Zeev Smilansky, an important figure among the workers, provided the readers of *Hapoel Hatzair* with a massive amount of information, including history and statistics, on German colonization and Polish countermeasures, making clear that he followed the German case with considerable interest. He emphasized, in his article, mainly the remarkable success of the Poles in withstanding the German pressure, that was backed with large quantities of money and political might. While this could have served as an ominous sign for Jewish colonization, Smilansky pointed to the German settlers' practice of employing lower-paid Polish workers, and the preference of the German workers to move to industrial cities inside Germany, as the reasons for the strengthening of the Polish population by the very actions of the Germans themselves. Equally important was the recognition of the importance of cooperative bodies and agricultural credit organizations that assisted poor Poles to remain on their land or acquire smaller lots of large estates purchased by Polish organizations (Z.S. [Zeev Smilansky], "The Decisive Factor," *HH*, Vol. 7, Nos. 1 /2, October 15, 1913).

55 Doron, 1982, p. 15.
56 *The Warburg Book*, pp. 16–17; Shilo, 1985, pp. 14–15.
57 Doukhain-Landau, 1979, p. 145 note 95.
58 See list, for the years 1886–1907, in Bruchhold-Wahl, 1980, p. 432.
59 "Briefwechsel zwischen dem Odessäer Palästinakommittee und Herrn Prof. Dr. Warburg," *Die Welt*, May 29, 1908.
60 Bein, 1972, p. 118.
61 Copy of letter from Warburg to Ussishkin, August 17, 1908, CZA – L1:38. See also Ruppin's blueprint for PLDC from December 14, 1907, CZA–A107:663.
62 Ruppin, "Credits for Colonists," 1975, p. 23.
63 Arthur Ruppin, "Concerning the Problem of Agricultural Workers in Eretz Israel, Part II," *HH*, Vol. 5, No. 6, December 27, 1911, reprinted in Ruppin, 1975, p. 31. Because of the low Palestinian wages Ruppin thought that such initial resources could be acquired via participation in the farm's profit in addition to wages.
64 Reichman & Hasson, 1984, p. 65.
65 "Bericht des Herrn Directors Hubert Auhagen an das Direktorium des Jüdischen Nationalfonds," January 1912, CZA – Z3:1349.
66 Reichman & Hasson, 1984, p. 64.
67 Letter from A. Ruppin to the JNF, Cologne, February 19, 1912, CZA – L1:103. Doukhan-Landau completely misses the context of the Auhagen–Ruppin exchange. According to her, Auhagen suggested that the PLDC should not emulate the example of the *Ansiedlungskommission*, a proposal Ruppin rejected since he favored national colonization (p. 145). The Prussian model, however, was chosen by Warburg and Ruppin precisely because it advocated national colonization and, therefore, there

was no contradiction between the German aims at Posen and the Zionist aims in Eretz Israel.

68 [Editorial], "On the Agenda," *Haachdut*, Vol. 3, No. 13, January 9, 1912.

69 Dr. Hillel Jaffe, "Jewish Agricultural Work in Eretz Israel," *HH*, Vol. 1, [No. 6], January/March 1908.

70 Vitkin, June/July 1908.

71 Aharonowitz, August/September 1908.

72 *Shichlul* was the contemporary expression signifying that a person became a farmer by acquiring stock and land. Z.S. [Zeev Smilansky], "New Step," *HH*, Vol. 2, No. 13, May 2, 1909.

73 Berl Katznelson, "Concerning Workers' Moshavot," *HH*, Vol. 6, Nos. 12/13, December 19, 1912. He probably raised these ideas even earlier, Anita Shapira, 1984, p. 39.

74 David Ben-Gurion, "Concerning the Arrangement of the Workers of the Moshavot," *Haachdut*, Vol. 2, Nos. 28/29, May 26, 1911.

75 P. Ben-Eliyahu, "Workers' Settlements," *Haachdut*, Vol. 3, No. 18, February 9, 1912.

76 Tishby, "Concerning the Workers' Settlements," *HH*, Vol. 6, Nos. 33/34, June 13, 1913 and A. Tsiyoni [Itzhak Vilkansky], "Workers' Settlements: Part III," *HH*, Vol. 7, Nos. 28/29, May 8, 1914.

77 Kolatt, 1964a, pp. 167–169; Gorny, 1968a, p. 72.

78 See J. Frankel, 1981, p. 400 and Kaplansky, 1950 [1907], p. 30.

79 See their arguments in Gorny, 1968a, pp. 73–74.

80 Member of the Central [Committee], "To Our Fifth Congress," *HH*, Vol. 2, Nos. 23/24, September 14, 1909; "From the Resolutions of the Fifth General Congress," *HH*, Vol. 3, No. 1, October 22, 1909.

81 See arguments for substituting the more inclusive concept of "total labor cost" for Bonacich's "price of labor" in Buraway, 1981, pp. 286–287; Peled & Shafir, 1987, p. 1448.

82 Richlin calculated that the cost of the Jewish supervisor in the private farm made up the difference between the wages paid to Arab and Jewish workers. Sometimes his wages were as high as the total cost of labor itself. Under these conditions, he concluded, the supervisor effectively displaced the Jewish worker (J. Richlin, "Contract Groups," *Haachdut*, Vol. 5, Nos. 32/33, June 12, 1914). A similar calculation for the farm at Kinneret, in 1912, demonstrated that it was twice as costly as the *kvutza* at Degania, hence the costs of management were viewed as being responsible for the losses incurred by the farm (Pro-Collective, "Concerning a Calculation," *Haachdut*, Vol. 3, No. 24, March 22, 1912). To remedy this situation, Richlin wrote: "It is necessary to alter substantially the working conditions and get rid of the supervisor, the middleman, and receive the work directly from the owners, at the workers' own responsibility. This can be made feasible through the formation of contract *kvutzot*."

83 Probably the earliest example during the Second *Aliya* was the Petach Tikva commune of Eliezer Shochat, A. D. Gordon, Avraham Krinitzi, and a few others. In Mania Shochat's evaluation "it had no connection with ideals

(*erech raayoni*). They had a joint treasury and shared expenses, since there was no other way of making ends meet. Some suffered from malaria and were able to hold out only because of the shared treasury," Mania Shochat, "Letter to Shmuel Gadon, July 22, 1956," *Niv Hakvutza*, Vol. 10, No. 1, 1961, p. 84.

84 Bonnell, 1983, pp. 43, 69; Bradley, 1985, pp. 27, 225–228.
85 Ussishkin, p. 118. For correct translation see J. Frankel, 1981, p. 337.
86 J. Frankel, 1981, p. 434.
87 This was attempted by past members of Hashomer, and leaders of Hakibbutz Hameuchad movement. See Near, 1983, pp. 65, 73.
88 This was recognized by Avner [Itzhak Ben-Zvi], "The Problems of Cooperative Settlement: Part II," *Haachdut*, Vol. 2, No. 36, July 14, 1911.
89 Joseph Aharonowitz, "Deeds and Preconditions for Deeds," *HH*, Vol. 7, No. 3, October 31, 1913; Itzhak Vilkansky, "Settlement Collectives: Part II," *HH*, Vol. 7, No. 14, January 16, 1914; Vitkin, June/July 1908; Yaakov Rabinowitz, "Concerning Hebrew Labor: Part III," *HH*, Vol. 7, No. 13, January 9, 1914. Kfar Giladi's Articles of Association, as late as 1918, said: "the present form of life is communal, we cannot be sure that we will always live in this way." *Hagana*, Vol. 2, p. 853 (quoted in Slutsky, 1968, note 4.
90 J. Frankel, 1981, p. 367.
91 Mania Shochat, 1958, pp. 52–53.
92 *Ibid.*, p. 53. Time makes the past even more golden. Ben-Gurion, in 1971, already wrote that "instead of loss . . . the first experiment of workers' organization and management ended with more than a small profit," p. 324.
93 Farmer [Moshe Smilansky], "The Galilean Worker: Part I," *HH*, Vol. 1, Nos. 7/8, April/May 1908.
94 Krauze even had to hide the innovation involved in the employment of a collective group from his superiors in Paris, Mania Shochat, 1958, p. 52.
95 Moshe Ingberman, "Notes Concerning the Worker's Question," *Haachdut*, No. 19, February 16, 1912. It was Ingberman's death by yellow malaria that occasioned the second strike at Kinneret which brought about Berman's dismissal.
96 Ben-Avram, April 1982a, p. 188. Raphael Frankel wrote "the Trumpeldor group did not have much influence on the members of Degania," 1975, p. 45 note 4.
97 Prospectus of the PLDC, CZA – LI:70.
98 Permanent, "Timely Matters," *HH*, Vol. 3, No. 22, September 4, 1910.
99 David Ben-Gurion, "The Past Year in the Workers' Life," *Haachdut*, Vol. 2, Nos. 47/48, September 22, 1911.
100 The agricultural workers were backed, in addition to the Hapoel Hatzair Party, by a public meeting that took place in Jaffa, and by Dr. Haim Hissin, the head of Hovevei Zion's Jaffa Office. J. Shapira, 1961, p. 76.
101 Shilo, 1977, p. 191.
102 *Ibid.*, pp. 71, 79.

103 Rabbi Benjamin, "About Kinneret," *HH*, Vol. 1, No. 5, November/December 1908.

104 Shilo, 1977, p. 114.

105 Permanent, "Timely Matters," *HH*, Vol. 3, Nos. 13/14, March 10, 1910; and Mamashi, "The Strike in Kinneret," *HH*, Vol. 4, No. 12, March 31, 1911.

106 Insider, "Inside the Country," *HH*, Vol. 3, No. 2, November 4, 1909. See also Shilo, 1977, pp. 109, 133.

107 Joseph Bloch, "From the Beginnings of Kinneret and Degania," in Habas, 1957, pp. 403–411.

108 Letter from Berman to Ruppin, December 1, 1909, CZA – A12:57.

109 Permanent, "Timely Matters," *HH*, Vol. 3, No. 22, September 4, 1910.

110 Letter from J. Thon, Jaffa, to O. Warburg, Berlin, October 4, 1909, CZA – Z2:634. See also Ruppin's dissatisfaction with Berman in Ruppin, 1971, pp. 101–102.

111 Ben-Avram, 1982b, p. 39.

112 See, for example, Weintraub, 1969, pp. 8–9.

113 Bein, 1954, p. 49.

114 Kolatt, 1964a, p. 260.

115 J. Frankel, 1981, p. 433.

116 Joseph Baratz, in the meeting of the *kvutzot* at Degania in 1923, and Tanchum Tanfilov, "Road Signs," *Niv Hakvutza*, October/November 1945, p. 6, quoted in Slutsky, 1968, p. 145, notes 46 and 47.

117 For example Darin-Drabkin, 1961, p. 47, writes: "[the *kvutza*] emerged out of the exigencies of Jewish settlement in [Palestine]. In establishing the *kvutzot*, their founders intended above all to address the practical aspects of the . . . problems of settlement, and did not necessarily intend a social experiment, that is, the paving of the road to a perfect human society. It is self evident, that one should not ignore the social aspirations of the founders, who were enthusiastic idealists, social justice being their ideal. These aspirations exerted their influence on the concrete development of the elements of cooperation. But, on the basis of their real intention and outlined action plan, the founders of the *kvutzot* addressed the shaping of the practical and efficient ways to Jewish settlement in Eretz Israel." Slutsky, 1968, p. 137.

118 There is one more, and indeed the strangest, argument in proof of the kibbutz's ideological roots. "Why was the social-collectivist aspect of [the kibbutz] so meagerly expressed at the period?" asks Near with the hidden assumption that it was extant. The reason Near gives was that the members of the Hapoel Hatzair Party, in their opposition to the Marxism of the Poalei Zion Party refused to employ a rigid ideological framework and preferred, as they were fond of saying, "to learn from experience (*min hachaim*)." This approach Near calls an "anti-ideological ideology." In a cavalier fashion, Near eschews the question whether an anti-ideology is still an ideology. The readiness to learn from experience, or in the contemporary idiom "from

reality," or "from life," was not only typical of members of Hapoel Hatzair, we find it equally in Ben-Gurion's, Zerubavel's, and Ben-Zvi's articles in Poalei Zion's weekly *Haachdut* and speeches in party congresses. But in a final ironic twist, Near argues that "from life" did not mean a pragmatic approach in the era of the Second *Aliya*, but rather it was seen as a source of renewal, of creative life (Near, 1982, p. 191). In fact, the term "from life" was used not in itself, but in contrast to its opposite "ideology" and it was creative precisely insofar as it negated imported ideologies!

119 Quoted in Gadon, 1980, p. 41, and in S. Eisenstadt, [1974], Vol. 2, p. 108.
120 Ben-Avram, 1982a, p. 187.
121 Jaffe lived in the US for a number of years and established an organization named Techiya which served as the nucleus of the local Halutz organization and adopted a similarly worded passage.
122 Ben-Avram, 1982a, p. 188; Eliezer Yaffe, "The Young Farmer," in Habas, 1957, p. 157.
123 Israel Bloch, "Immigrants of Romny," in Habas, 1957, p. 155. Bloch's memoirs were written in 1945. (See Near, 1981, p. 125, note 3.)
124 Raphael Frankel, 1975, p. 58. A replica of his views is presented in the symposium, R. Frankel, 1981, pp. 112–117.
125 Raphael Frankel, 1975, p. 59. Even if we discount Bussel's imported ideals as the source of his views on the permanent collective settlement, we still have to address R. Frankel's other argument which sees the sojourn in Hadera of the commune as the decisive period of its ideological crystallization. This, he argues, may be observed in the speeches of its members, on their way from Hadera to Kinneret, in the Sixth Congress of the Hapoel Hatzair Party in October 1910. While the other members of the party were in the throes of despair because of the hopeless struggle for "conquest of labor," Baratz, Tanfilov, Yehuda, Bloch, and above all Bussel were "a ray of confidence and optimism" and laid out, in Frankel's assessment, the alternative vision of settlement. In fact, Baratz and Tanfilov were optimistic not about collective settlement, but entertained hope about the possibility of making a living as agricultural workers, that is, of "conquering labor." The other three indeed advocated a sympathetic approach to settlement. But even here Zvi Yehuda described it as a "possibility," Bussel spoke of the "experiments (*nisyonot*) undertaken now in the Galilee" of which it is incumbent on the workers "to select (*levarer*) the most correct method," and Bloch, the only one of the group to spend two years in Degania, referred to "the new experiment in Um-Djunni . . . by which maybe we will find the right method for the entrenchment and numerical increase of the workers in Eretz Israel" ("Summary of the Debates in our [Sixth] Annual Congress," *HH*, Vol. 4, Nos. 1/2, November 11, 1910). It is gross exaggeration, therefore, to speak of a "clear ideological crystallization," as R. Frankel does (R. Frankel, 1975, p. 62).
126 Moshe Smilansky, 1938, p. 215.
127 Bonnell, 1983, pp. 321, 328, 337–338, 349, 440.
128 Kolatt, 1964a, pp. 161–162.

129 Bussel, Hayuta, "Life Chronicle," in *Bussel Book*, p. 292.
130 "Meeting of the Agricultural Workers in the Galilee: Part I," *Haachdut*, Vol. 3, No. 16, January 26, 1912.
131 Sarah Malkhin, "At the Farm in Kinneret," in Gadon, 1958, p. 73.
132 Letter of Warburg to Bodenheimer, JNF, Cologne, June 10, 1909, CZA – LI:29.
133 Copy of letter of Warburg to Ussishkin, July 3, 1908 and Report of JNF from end of 1908, CZA – Z2:617 quoted in Shilo, who unearthed this whole episode. Shilo, 1985, p. 221. This is a repeated misgiving among members of the JNF directorate, see letter of Ruppin to JNF, Cologne, March 28, 1910, CZA – Z3:1478.
134 Shilo, 1977, p. 134.
135 Worker, "Degania," *HH*, Vol. 5, No. 7, January 9, 1911.
136 Letter of Ruppin to Levontin, February 18, 1909, CZA – LI:97 quoted in Shilo, 1985, p. 222; and letter of Warburg to the JNF, June 10, 1909, CZA – KKL2:51.
137 Protocol of JNF, October 14, 1909, CZA – KKLI:657.
138 Letter from Thon, Palestine Office, Jaffa, to Warburg, PLDC, September 12, 1909, quoted in J. Frankel, 1981, p. 433.
139 Worker, "Degania," *HH*, Vol. 5, No. 7, January 7, 1912.
140 Miriam Baratz, "From Petach Tikva to Um-Djunni," *Niv Hakvutza*, August 1957, pp. 638–639 and May 1958, pp. 356–358. Selections are reproduced in English in Viteles, 1967, Vol. 2, p. 27.
141 Ruppin, "The *Kvutza*," in Ruppin, 1975, p. 132.
142 Ruppin, 1947, pp. 84–85, my exclamation mark.
143 My emphasis in second letter. Letter from Ruppin to the JNF, Cologne, December 6, 1909 and to PLDC, Berlin, December 10, 1909, reprinted in Ruppin, 1947, Vol. 2, pp. 81–83. Partial English version is in Ruppin, 1971, p. 103.
144 E.g. Bein, 1954, p. 49.
145 Letter from Ruppin, Jaffa, to the PLDC, Berlin, December 10, 1909, reprinted in Ruppin, 1971, p. 103.
146 Copy of Warburg's letter to Bodenheimer, JNF, Cologne, June 10, 1909, CZA – LI:29.
147 Protocol of the JNF, October 14, 1909, CZA – KKLI:657.
148 Letter from the JNF to Ruppin, January 6, 1910, reprinted in Ruppin, 1947, p. 85.
149 Worker, "Degania," *HH*, Vol. 5, No. 7, January 9, 1911.
150 Miriam Baratz in Viteles, 1967, p. 27.
151 Ruppin's original request was submitted on May 22, 1911. Letter from Hoffein & Gross of the Eretz Israel Siedlungsgesellschaft to Ruppin, Jaffa, October 12, 1911, CZA – Z3:1371.
152 Letter of Oppenheimer, June 9, 1911 to Ruppin, reprinted in Ruppin, 1947, p. 86.
153 Letter of Erez Israel Siedlungsgesellschaft, to Ruppin, Jaffa, January 29, 1912, CZA –Z3:1371.

154 *Ibid.*
155 Protocol of the *kvutza*'s debate, December 26, 1911, CZA – KKL2:8.
156 Kaplansky, "The Agricultural Worker and the *Kvutza*," Kaplansky, 1950, p. 428, and Kolatt, 1964a, p. 208.
157 Shilo, 1985, p. 243.
158 Shilo, 1977, pp. 88, 212. In general, Shilo's work suffers from lack of coherence due, in part, to her vacillation as to the impact of structural constraints and attempts to remedy the imbalances of analysis that ensue by reference to personality factors in a *deus ex machina* fashion.
159 Shilo, 1977, p. 191.
160 L. I. Oppenheimer, "The Significance of Merchavia in the History of Settlement in Israel," pp. 53–54 and Gershon Gefner, "My Road to Merchavia," both in Lubriani, 1961, p. 106.
161 Kolatt, 1964a, pp. 162–163.
162 *Ibid.*, p. 206.
163 Ruppin, "The *Kvutza*," in Ruppin, 1975, p. 121. This article appeared originally in *Die Welt* in 1924.
164 Kolatt, 1964a, p. 207. The same holds true for the moshav, Anita Shapira, 1977, pp. 27–28.
165 Kolatt, 1964a, p. 163.
166 Ben-Avram, 1984, p. 46.
167 Ben-Avram, 1982a, p. 189 and 1982b, p. 54.
168 Ben-Avram, 1984, p. 50.
169 Ultimately the kibbutz came to be known as the institution whose members are "content with little," the term applied earlier to Yemenite Jews. See Garber-Talmon, 1972.

8 Conclusion: nationalism and conflict

1 Yaacov Rabinovitch, "Concerning Hebrew Labor: Part II," *HH*, Vol. 7, No. 13, January 9, 1914.
2 Kolatt, 1964a, p. 260.
3 Sussman, 1974, p. 50.
4 The workers, however, were not adverse to seeking the support of the WZO for strengthening them in the "conquest of labor" even at the early stage of the WZO's activities in Palestine. Zeev Smilansky demanded in May 1909 that if the WZO established an agrarian credit institution then the latter should reduce the interest paid by farmers who employ Jewish workers. Eliyahu Munchik, another leader of Hapoel Hatzair, demanded even more bluntly that the APAC refuse to loan money to Jewish farmers or artisans employing foreign workers. While in Zeev Smilansky's view this method was similar to the labelling of cigarette boxes produced by unionized white American factory workers, who suffered from lowered wages in consequence of Chinese immigration, to arrest the Chinese "tide," Munchik found his justification in the tariffs imposed on agricultural products in Germany in

order to protect the agricultural class (*maamad karkai*). Z.S. [Zeev Smilansky], "A New Step," *HH*, Vol. 2, No. 13, May 2, 1909; Ben-Ephraim [Eliyahu Munchik], "Public and Private Accounts," *HH*, Vol. 3, No. 24, October 3, 1910. The APAC, under Levontin, of course was a bastion of opposition to "Hebrew labor," and Munchik's demand was a cry in the wilderness.

5 Jonathan Frankel, 1981, p. 441.

6 Joseph Shprintzak, "The Transitory Period in the Work of the Palestine Office: Parts I & II," *HH*, Vol. 7, Nos. 39/40 and 41, July 31 and August 7, 1914. See a similarly positive attitude in Eliezer L. Jaffe, "Workers' moshavot," *HH*, Vol. 7, No. 26, April 24, 1914.

7 Kaplansky, "Problems of Zionism," in Kaplansky, 1950, pp. 24–32.

8 See, for example, the Introduction by Yehuda Aiges to *The A. D. Gordon Book – His Philosophy and Teachings*, Tel-Aviv, Haoved Hatsiyoni, 1943, pp. 37–44; Shlomo Tsemach, "Introduction to the Writings of A. D. Gordon," in Yehuda Aiges, ed., *The Aharon David Gordon Collection*, Jerusalem, The Zionist Federation, 1948; and Kolatt, who wrote: "though [Gordon's publicistic work] sometimes seems to us not from this world, its historical influence was great and in certain matters decisive," Kolatt, 1964a, p. 119.

9 Nachman Syrkin, "*Achva*," *Haachdut*, Vol. 4, No. 33, June 13, 1913 and "The Jewish Question and the Jewish Socialist State," in Syrkin, 1939, pp. 53–59.

   The rise of Poalei Zion to power in the Histadrut may be attributed to the Marxist and Borochovian emphasis on effecting social change through political and organizational channels. Directing its energies inward, as Hapoel Hatzair endeavored, by sublimating the notion of the "idealist worker" into individual regeneration and to the development of a new work ethos while retaining its elitest bent, was by far less effective in the twentieth century than organizational mobilization. A "religion of labor," as an *ersatz* "Protestant Ethic," carried on the collective frontier less weight than the "organizational weapon" of the late modernizers.

10 Zerubavel, "Who is Departing?: Part II," *Haachdut*, Vol. 2, Nos. 41/42, August 13, 1911. In what may be seen as an intermediary stage in this transition, Ben-Zvi demanded that the facilitation of capitalist development be undertaken by the Zionist bodies. Avner [Itzhak Ben-Zvi], "The Immigration and Our Task," *Haachdut*, Vol. 1, No. 2, September/October 1910.

11 A. Tsiyoni [Itzhak Vilkansky], "Waiting for Capitalism," *Hapoel Hatzair*, Vol. 3, No. 1, October 22, 1909.

12 A. Tsiyoni [Itzhak Vilkansky], "Workers' moshavot: Part IV," *HH*, Vol. 7, No. 30, May 15, 1914.

13 Shlomo Kaplansky, "The Problem of the Agricultural Workers and the Collective: Part I," *Haachdut*, Vol. 6, Nos. 1/2, October 4, 1914.

14 Aharonowitz, November 26, 1909.

15 Berl Katznelson, "The Problem of Labor and Settlement: Part II" (Lecture delivered at Fourth Congress of Federation of the Agricultural Workers of Judea), *Haachdut*, Vol. 5, No. 14, June 16, 1914.
16 Jonathan Frankel, 1981, p. 444.
17 Tzahor, 1979, pp. 42–44, 45–46, 51, 54, 78–79; Shapiro, 1976, p. 24.
18 Shapiro, 1976, *passim*.
19 *Ibid.*, pp. 41–43; Tzahor, 1979, pp. 90–99.
20 Shapiro, 1976, pp. 260–262.
21 Kolatt, 1971, pp. 95–99.
22 Bernstein & Swirski, 1982, pp. 67–69.
23 Böhm, 1937, p. 128.
24 De Lieme, "Concerning Construction in Eretz Israel," in Bistritsky, 1950, pp. 175–180; Oettinger, [1917a], pp. 12–13, 26 and [1917b], p. 24; Oppenheimer, [1917], p. 12. Moreover, land was habitually leased at rates below the market value, thus further subsidizing immigrants, see Metzer, 1979, p. 46.
25 De Lieme, "Concerning Construction in Eretz Israel," p. 164 and "Conclusions and Propositions," in Bistritsky, 1950, p. 201.
26 "The WZO's Interim Conference," *Haolam*, Vol. 9, Nos. 38, 39, 40, July 9, 16, 23, 1920; Böhm, 1937, pp. 122–132.
27 Reprinted in the *Reports of the Executive of the Zionist Organisation*, p. 95.
28 *Ibid.*, p. 96.
29 *Ibid.*, p. 101.
30 Berl Katznelson, "The London Conference," *Haadama*, No. 2, March 1920/March 1923, pp. 463–467. Ruppin, 1919, had proposed earlier a colonization program which would benefit both the private and cooperative sectors. See also Metzer, 1979, pp. 69–76.
31 Kimmerling, 1983, p. 14.
32 Shapiro, 1976, p. 72.
33 Shalev in Pempel, forthcoming.
34 Lamar and Thompson, 1981, pp. 7–9.
35 Robert F. Berkhofer Jr., "The North American Frontier as Process and Context," in Lamar & Thompson, 1981, p. 67.
36 Avitsur, 1965; Gvati, 1981, pp. 54, 55, 58, 65, 132.
37 Gvati, 1981, pp. 53, 78, 123.
38 *Ibid.*, pp. 58, 131.
39 *Ibid.*, pp. 55, 64, 142.
40 For example in Rechovot, MAR – Protocol Book No. 3, General Assembly No. 65, September 6, 1903; Ro'i, 1964, p. 50.
41 Kalvarisky, 1931, p. 53.
42 Mandel, 1976, p. 35.
43 Letter of S. Hirsch, Mikve Israel, to Pinsker, April 4, 1886, in Druyanov, 1932, Vol. 1, pp. 746–754; Mandel, 1976, pp. 34–37; Beeri, 1985, pp. 57–64.
44 Said, 1979, pp. 75–76.
45 Itzhak Epstein, 1907/8, pp. 196–198.

46 Beeri, 1985, pp. 12–13 and Mandel, 1976, pp. xvii–xix.
47 Mandel, 1976, p. xvii.
48 *Ibid.*, p. 231; Kayyali, [1978?].
49 *Hagana*, pp. 85, 97, 107, 108, 655, 687, 704, 804, quoted in Beeri, 1985, p. 65.
50 Beeri, 1985, pp. 150, 154.
51 Ro'i, 1964, pp. 70, 118; Assaf, 1970, p. 19.
52 Ro'i, 1964, pp. 70, 93, 95, 119.
53 *Ibid.*, 1964, pp. 110, 122. Protocol of the Founding Session of the Federation of the Moshavot of Judea, September 18, 1913, CZA – A32:55.
54 Shilo, 1985, pp. 187, 95–103.
55 Teveth, 1985, pp. 17, 18, 198–199.
56 Shmuel Ettinger, "Introduction," in *Zionism and the Arab Question*, p. 7.
57 Nissim Malul, "The Arab Press," *Hashiloach*, No. 31, 1914, p. 446, quoted in Mandel, 1976, p. 85.
58 Mandel, 1976, p. 87.
59 *Ibid.*, pp. 224, 231.
60 Beeri, 1985, pp. 146–147.
61 Mandel, 1976, pp. 103–104.
62 Letter from Ruppin, Jaffa, to JNF, Cologne, October 23, 1910, CZA – L1:102, quoted in Mandel, 1976, p. 106.
63 Memorandum between Mohammed Affifi and Elias Blumenfeld, Haifa, April 21, 1910, CZA – L18:2 /1. On other occasions and at various periods of Jewish settlement, Palestinian tenants who were being evicted were also offered monetary compensation in addition to the purchase price paid to the landowner. This practice, however, was irregular, mostly due to the Jewish settlement organizations' chronic shortage of money. An even more important obstacle to the spread of this practice was the preference of the evicted tenants for alternative land instead of money. The settlement bodies could not accede to this demand because most other land available for purchase was also targeted by them for Jewish settlement.
64 Beeri, 1985, p. 156. Summary of Merchavia events in *Hagana*, pp. 224–227; Assaf, 1970, pp. 62–65; Doukhan-Landau, 1979, pp. 36–42; Avneri, 1984, pp. 92–93.
65 Khalidi, 1980, pp. 223–228, 231.
66 Beeri, 1985, pp. 154–156.
67 "It . . . emerges that outside Palestine there was an obvious connection between the awakening of Arab nationalism and opposition to Zionism, while in Palestine itself opposition to Zionism was common to the two political trends which fought for dominance over the Arab public: the Arab nationalist and the Ottoman Unity movements" (Porath, 1974, p. 30).
68 Mandel, 1976, pp. xviii–xix.
69 Owen, 1981, p. 293.
70 Khalidi, 1980, pp. 226–7.
71 Ro'i, 1981, p. 245.
72 *Ibid.*, p. 246.
73 Mandel, 1976, p. 228.

74 *Ibid.*, pp. 228–229; Khalidi, 1982, p. 120.
75 Moshe Smilansky, "Concerning the *Yishuv*: Part II," *HH*, Vol. 1, No. 5, January/March 1908.
76 Beeri, 1985, pp. 38–41.
77 Israel Giladi, "Memoirs," in *Yizkor: Memorial to the Slain Jewish Workers in Eretz-Israel*, edited by A. Z. Rabinovitch, Jaffa, 1911, p. 16, quoted in J. Frankel, forthcoming, p. 14, my emphasis.
78 Zerubavel, "The Two Methods," *Haachdut*, Vol. 2, No. 36, July 14, 1911.
79 Moshe Smilansky, "Concerning the *Yishuv*: Part II," *HH*, Vol. 1, No. 5, January/March 1908.
80 Avner [Itzhak Ben-Zvi], "National Defence and Proletarian Perspective: Part II," *Haachdut*, Vol. 4, No. 17, February 7, 1913.
81 Jabotinsky, "On The Iron Wall," and "The Morality of the Iron Wall," in Jabotinsky, 1946, pp. 6–16.
82 Owen, 1982, p. 4.
83 Rodinson, 1973, p. 91.
84 *Ibid.*, p. 77.
85 Fieldhouse, 1966, p. 4; Owen, 1982, pp. 4–5.
86 Said, 1979, pp. 56–57, 82, 84.
87 Fredrickson, 1981, p. 5.
88 Owen 1982, p. 4.
89 Ehrlich, 1987, p. 134.
90 Zureik, 1979, p. 195.
91 Anita Shapira, 1977, p. 26. "Hebrew Labor," in her view, "originated in the aspiration for integral Zionism," and not in the threat of displacement. This position I do not accept.
92 Kimmerling, 1983, p. 104.
93 Kleiman, 1980, p. 287.
94 Giladi, 1969, p. 95.
95 *Ibid.*, p. 98.
96 Shalev in Pempel, forthcoming; Anita Shapira, 1977, pp. 252–7.
97 Grinberg, 1986.
98 Flapan, 1979, pp. 226–230.
99 Anita Shapira, 1977, p. 31.
100 Gorny, 1968b, pp. 77–78.
101 Horowitz & Lissak, 1978, pp. 16–17.
102 Metzer & Kaplan, 1985, p. 328.
103 *Ibid.*, Table 2, p. 332.
104 *Ibid.*, Table 6, p. 340.
105 Zureik, 1979, pp. 28–29, 196.
106 *Ibid.*, pp. 29–30, 195.
107 Metzer & Kaplan, 1985, p. 334.

Glossary

Achdut Haavoda Party (United Labor): the dominant Jewish workers' party in Palestine in the 1920s, formed in 1920 by amalgamation of Poalei Zion, unaffiliated workers, and immigrants from the Third *Aliya*.

achuza: private farm of initially absentee colonists. First one est. in Poriya in 1912 by shareholders from St Louis.

Agudat Netaim (Planters' Society): private enterprise company for agricultural colonization, established in 1905 by Aharon Eisenberg, in Palestine.

aliya: immigration, literally ascent, to Palestine.

Alliance Israélite Universelle: French Jewish philanthropic organization, founded in 1860 with aim of defending Jewish civil and religious liberties and providing education to Jews in less developed countries.

Anglo-Palestine Co. (APAC): a subsidiary bank of the WZO's Jewish Colonial Trust, incorporated in London in 1902 to undertake operations in Palestine. Its first director was Zalman Levontin.

Ansiedlungskommission: settlement commission, implementing the Prussian government's policy of "internal colonization" by German agricultural settlers in the Poznan and Western Prussian provinces, in which the Polish population constituted the majority.

artel: traditional form of Rusian cooperative organization, evolved during industrialization in new directions.

ashkenazi: Jew descending from Europe, or the West in general.

Bar-Giora: guard organization, founded in 1907. Forerunner of Hashomer.

Bund (General Jewish Workers' Union of Lithuania, Poland, and Russia): Jewish socialist party, founded in 1897. Initially demanded civil rights and political liberty, subsequently Jewish national cultural autonomy in Eastern Europe, and opposed the aims of Zionism.

charat: live-in landless agricultural worker, employed on yearly basis and paid one-fifth of the product. A method of agricultural employment customary in parts of the Middle East.

Esra: German Jewish philanthropic organization, founded in 1884 with the aim of supporting Jewish settlement in Palestine.

fellah: peasant in Arabic.

First *Aliya*: the first wave of an estimated 25,000, in part Zionist, immigrants, who arrived in Palestine between 1882 and 1903.

General Board of the Hebrew Laborers in Eretz Israel: organization of the First *Aliya*'s agricultural workers.
Hachoresh (The Plougher): the first organization of the Jewish agricultural workers in the Galilee, 1907.
Hagana (Defense): est. in 1920, on the foundations of Hashomer, as the Histadrut's military organization for Jewish self-defense in Palestine, and later broadened to become a people's militia under public control.
Hapoel Hatzair Party (The Young Worker): Jewish party in Palestine, founded in 1905 with the aim of supporting the "conquest of labor" in the Jewish owned plantations by Jewish workers. Also periodical by same name. In 1929 merged with Achdut Haavoda to form Mapai.
Hashomer (The Watchman): guard organization, founded by members of the Second *Aliya* in 1909, with the aim of defending Jewish settlements and newly purchased and contested land. Absorbed in 1920 into the Hagana.
Histadrut (The General Federation of Jewish Workers in Eretz Israel): the general Jewish trade union and cooperative organization established at Haifa in 1920.
Hovevei Zion: the first popular based, though pre-political, Zionist movement. Founded in 1882 in Russia and later established chapters in other Jewish centers as well with the aim of encouraging Jewish immigration to and settlement in Palestine. Recognized by the Russian government, under the name Society for the Support of Jewish Farmers and Artisans in Syria and Palestine, only in 1890.
Jewish Colonial Trust (JCT) – the WZO's bank, est. in 1899.
Jewish Colonization Association (JCA) – Paris-centered philanthropic body, founded by the Baron Maurice de Hirsch in 1891, for the resettlement and productivization of Eastern European Jews in various countries, such as Argentina, the US, etc. and only gradually drawn into activity in Palestine.
Jewish National Fund: land-purchasing and developing body of the WZO, est. in 1901, its first director was Max Bodenheimer.
Keren Hayesod (Foundation Fund): chief financial instrument of the WZO after 1920.
Keren Kayemet: see Jewish National Fund.
kibbutz: settlement based on full cooperation in most spheres of life. First kibbutz est. in Degania in 1910.
kolel: close-knit community of Old *Yishuv*, who share in charitable funds (*haluka*) sent from their country of origin.
kvutza: a fairly broad term describing a variety of cooperative ventures, such as communes, contract groups, land conquest groups for initial settlement.
Menucha Venachala (Rest and Estate): the founding company of Rechovot.
Mifleget Poalei Eretz Israel (Mapai) (Party of Eretz Israeli Workers): the largest mainstream party of laborers, est. 1930, through unification of Achdut Haavoda and Hapoel Hatzair.
mizrachi: Jew hailing from North Africa or the Middle East.
moshava: the type of settlement or colony typical of the First *Aliya*. Based on private ownership of land and wage labor.
moshav *ovdim* (laborers' settlement): smallholders' consumer, marketing, and

mutual aid cooperative form of settlement, split from the kibbutz in 1920 with the foundation of Nahalal in the Yezreel Valley.

moshav *poalim*: workers' settlement, founded with the aim of providing Jewish agricultural laborers with small auxiliary farms. First one, Beer Yaacov, was est. in 1907.

Nili: Jewish spy organization aimed at assisting the British forces against the Ottomans in Palestine during the First World War, recruited mostly from among the second generation of the First *Aliya*'s moshavot.

Old *Yishuv*: the Jewish religious community of Palestine, residing mostly in Jerusalem, Safed, Hebron, and Tiberias.

Palästina Ressort: the WZO's department for Palestinian Affairs, est. in 1907 through the upgrading of the Palestine Commission, under Otto Warburg.

Pale of Settlement: a western area of the Russia Empire, comprised of the territories captured from Poland since 1772 with some additions, to which Jews were residentially restricted.

Palestine Land Development Company (PLDC): colonizatory body of the WZO, initially set up as joint stock company in 1908, under the directorship of Otto Warburg and Arthur Ruppin.

Palestine Office (Palestine Amt): the representative agency of the WZO in Jaffa. Est. in 1908 under the direction of Arthur Ruppin.

Poalei Zion Party (Workers of Zion): Zionist socialist party, initially consisted of local and regional groups in Russia, and later in Austria, US and elsewhere. Its Palestine chapter was established in 1905, and a World Union of Poalei Zion was formed in 1907.

Second *Aliya*: the second wave of an estimated 35,000 Jewish immigrants who arrived in Palestine between 1903 and 1914.

sephardi: descendant of Jews living in the Iberian peninsula before 1492; used often, though erroneously, as synonymous with the term *mizrachi*.

Siedlungsgenossenschaft: settlement-cooperative, a form of settlement devised by Franz Oppenheimer and adopted by the WZO which est. Merchavia at the Yezreel Valley along its lines, but dissolved it after the First World War.

Tanzimat: period of intensive Ottoman reforms between 1839 and 1878.

Third *Aliya*: the third wave of an estimated 35,000 immigrants who arrived in Palestine between 1918 and 1923.

training farm: settlement specializing in training agricultural workers-to-be. The first settlement of this type was set up by JCA in Sedjra in 1899 and additional ones were established by the JNF in Kinneret, Ben-Shemen and Hulda in 1908/9.

Turkish dunam: land measure unit of 919.3 m², and is equal to 0.227 acres. The modern dunam comprises 1,000 m².

World Zionist Organization (WZO): the major organization of political Zionism, founded by Theodor Herzl in Basel in 1897. Held yearly, later bi-yearly, congresses. Its seat was in Vienna (1897–1905), Cologne (1905–11), Berlin (1911–20), London (1920–46), and later in Jerusalem. Its early presidents were Theodor Herzl, David Wolffsohn and Otto Warburg.

(New) *Yishuv*: the modern Jewish community (literally settlement) of Palestine.

Bibliography

Only works mentioned in the text, and only some of the most frequently mentioned articles from the contemporary press, are included here.

All Hebrew titles have been translated into English for the benefit of the non-Hebrew-speaking reader, and their original language is indicated in parenthesis following the reference. The following periodicals and scholarly journals are in Hebrew:

Achiassaf: Meassef Safruti	*Alon Kinneret*
Asuphot	*Baderech*
Cathedra	*Haachdut*
Haadama	*Haezrach*
Haolam	*Hapoel Hatzair* (abbreviated as *HH*)
Hashiloach	*Hatsiyonut*
Hatzfira	*Hatzvi*
Havazelet	*Kardom*
Keshet	*Kivunim*
Meassef	*Niv Hakvutza*
Sefar Hashana: Meassef Safruti	*Sheifotenu*
Sheivat Tsiyon	*Shorashim*

The following archives have been consulted:

Central Zionist Archives, Jerusalem	CZA
Labor Archives, Tel Aviv	LA
Municipal Archives of Rishon Letzion	MARL
Municipal Archives of Rechovot	MAR
Municipal Archives of Hadera	MAH

(The notebooks of the Board and General Assembly meetings of Hadera prior to 1913 were lost, but copies are to be found in the possession of Mr. Emanuel Kochavi in Hadera.)

Aaronsohn, Ran 1979. "The Establishment and the Beginnings of Zikhron Yaacov and Rishon Letzion as Agricultural Colonies, 1882–1883," unpublished MA thesis, Hebrew University (Hebrew).

1981. "Stages in the Development of the Settlements of the First *Aliya*," in Eliav, 1981.

Bibliography

Achad Haam 1947. "The Envoys of a Poor People," in *The Collected Writings of Achad Haam*. Tel Aviv: Dvir (Hebrew).

Agmon, Nathan, ed. 1951. *The Scroll of Land*, Vol. 1: *History*, by G. Kressel. Jerusalem: JNF (Hebrew).

Aharonowitz, Joseph 1908. "Conquest of Land or Conquest of Labor: Parts I & II,' *HH*, Vol. 1, Nos. 10 & 12, June/July & August/September.

  1909. "For the Clarification of the Situation: Parts I & II," *HH*, Vol. 3, Nos. 2 & 4, November 4 & 26.

Aitken, Hugh G. J. 1959a. "Defensive Expansionism: The State and Economic Growth in Canada," in Aitken, 1959b.

  ed. 1959b. *The State and Economic Growth*. NY: Social Science Research Council.

Allon, Yigal 1969. *Curtain of Sand*. Tel Aviv: Hakibbutz Hameuchad (Hebrew).

Amiran, D. K. H. 1953. "The Pattern of Settlement in Palestine," *Israel Exploration Journal*, Vol. 3.

Aschheim, Steven E. 1982. *Brothers and Strangers: The East European Jew in German and German Jewish Consciousness, 1800–1923*. Madison: University of Wisconsin Press.

Assaf, Michael 1970. *The Relations Between Arabs and Jews in Eretz-Israel: 1860–1948*. Tel Aviv: Educational and Cultural Enterprises (Hebrew).

Avitsur, Shmuel 1965. *The Native Plough of Eretz-Israel: Its History and Development*. Tel Aviv: Sifriat Hassade (Hebrew).

Avneri, Arieh L. 1984. *The Claim of Dispossession: Jewish Land Settlement and the Arabs 1878–1948*. New Brunswick: Transaction Books.

Baer, Gabriel 1975. "The Impact of Economic Change on Traditional Society in Nineteenth Century Palestine," in Ma'oz, 1975.

Barany, George 1974. "'Magyar Jew or Jewish Magyar?' (To the Question of Jewish Assimilation in Hungary)," *Canadian–American Slavic Studies*, Vol. 8, No. 1 (Spring).

Barker, Charles A. 1955. *Henry George*. NY: Oxford University Press.

Batatu, Hanna 1978. *The Old Social Classes and the Revolutionary Movements of Iraq*. Princeton: Princeton University Press.

Bauer Mengelberg, Käthe 1931. *Agrarpolitik*. Leipzig: B. G. Teubner.

Beeri, Eliezer 1985. *The Beginning of the Israeli–Arab Conflict, 1882–1911*. Tel Aviv: Sifriat Poalim (Hebrew).

Bein, Alex 1954. *The History of Zionist Settlement*, 3rd revised edn. Tel Aviv: Massada (Hebrew).

  1971. "Franz Oppenheimer and Theodor Herzl," *Herzl Year Book*, No. 7.

  1972. "Arthur Ruppin: The Man and his Work," *Leo Baeck Institute Year Book*, No. 17.

Beit-Halevi [pseudonym of Yehoshua Barzilai] *Letters from Eretz Israel* [published irregularly; n.p., n.d.].

Belkind, Israel 1983. *In the Path of the Biluyim*. Israel Ministry of Defense [written in 1926–8] (Hebrew).

Ben-Arieh, Yehoshua 1981. "Geographic Aspects of the Development of the First Jewish Settlements in Palestine," in Eliav, 1981.

Ben-Artzi, Yossi 1984. "Planning and Development of the Physical Pattern of the Jewih Moshavot in Palestine, 1882–1914," unpublished Ph.D. Dissertation, The Hebrew University of Jerusalem (Hebrew).

Ben-Avram, Baruch 1981. "The Emergence of the *Kvutza* from the Aspiration of the Pioneers of the Second *Aliya* for Autonomous Labor," *Cathedra*, No. 18, January.

    1982a. "The *Kvutza* and Indigenous Zionist Palestinian Collectivism," *Cathedra*, No. 23, April.

    1982b and 1984. "The Crystallization of the *Kvutza*'s Ideology," *Shorashim*, Nos. 2 & 3.

Ben-Gal, Yoram & Shmuel Shamai 1983. "The Swamps of the Jezreel Valley – Myth and Reality," *Cathedra*, No. 28, March.

Ben-Gurion, David 1971. *Memoirs*, Vol. 1. Tel Aviv: Am Oved (Hebrew).

Ben-Zvi, Itzhak 1936. *Writings*. Tel-Aviv: Mitzpe (Hebrew).

    1950. *Poalei Zion in the Second Aliya*. Tel Aviv: Mapai (Hebrew).

Bernstein, Deborah 1987. *The Struggle for Equality: Urban Women Workers in Prestate Israeli Society*. NY: Praeger.

Bernstein, Deborah & Shlomo Swirski 1982. "The Rapid Economic Development of Israel and the Emergence of the Ethnic Division of Labour," *British Journal of Sociology*, Vol. 33, No. 1, March.

Billington, Ray Allen & Martin Ridge 1982. *Westward Expansion: A History of the American Frontier*, 5th edn. NY: Macmillan.

Bistritsky, Nathan ed. 1950. *In Individual Paths: To the Memory of Nechemia de Lieme*. Jerusalem: JNF (Hebrew).

Blanke, Richard 1981. *Prussian Poland in the German Empire (1871–1900)*. Boulder: East European Monographs, Columbia University Press.

Blubstein, Shoshana 1943. *Pages of Yemen*. Tel Aviv: Yavne (Hebrew).

Bodenheimer, Henriette 1965. "The Statutes of the *Keren Kayemet*: A Study of their Origins. Based on the Known as well as Hitherto Unpublished Sources," *Herzl Yearbook*, No. 4.

    ed. 1978. *Der Durchbuch des politischen Zionismus in Köln 1890–1900*. Cologne: Bund.

Böhm, Adolf 1910. *Der Jüdische Nationalfonds: Ein Instrument zur Abhilfe der Judennot*. Cologne: Jüdischer Verlag.

    [1917]. *The Jewish National Fund*. The Hague: Head Office of the Jewish National Fund.

    1937. *Die Zionistiche Bewegung 1918 bis 1925*, Band 2. Jerusalem: Hotzaa Ivrat.

Bonacich, Edna 1972. "A Theory of Ethnic Antagonism: The Split Labor Market," *American Sociological Review*, Vol. 37.

    1979. "The Past, Present, and Future of Split Labor Market Theory," *Research in Race and Ethnic Relations*, Vol. 1.

Bonné, Alfred 1956. "Major Aspects of Land Tenure and Rural Social Structure in Israel," in Kenneth H. Parsons *et al.*, eds., *Land Tenure*, Madison, University of Wisconsin Press.

Bonnell, Victoria E. 1983. *Roots of Rebellion: Workers' Politics and Organizations in St. Petersburg and Moscow, 1900–1914.* Berkeley: University of California Press.

Bradley, Joseph 1985. *Muzhik and Muscovite: Urbanization in Late Imperial Russia.* Berkeley: University of California Press.

Braslavsky, Moshe 1942. *The Eretz-Israeli Workers Movement,* Vol. 1. Ein-Harod: Hakibbutz Hameuchad (Hebrew).

Brass, Paul R. 1980. "Ethnic Groups and Nationalities: The Formation, Persistence, and Transformation of Ethnic Identities," in Peter F. Sugar, ed., *Ethnic Diversity and Conflict in Eastern Europe.* Santa Barbara: ABC-Clio.

Broude, Henry W. 1959. "The Role of the State in American Economic Development, 1820–1890," in Aitken, 1959b.

Bruchhold-Wahl, Hannelore 1980. "Die Krise des Grossgrundbesitzes und die Güterankäufe der Ansiedlungskommission in der Provinz Posen, in den Jahren 1886–1898," unpublished Ph.D. dissertation, Westfälischen Wilhelms University.

Buber, Martin 1983. *Paths in Utopia,* Tel Aviv: Am Oved (Hebrew), selections translated into English as *Paths in Utopia.* Boston: Beacon, 1958.

Burawoy, Michael 1981. "The Capitalist State in South Africa: Marxist and Sociological Perspectives," *Political Power and Social Theory,* No. 2.

Bussel Book, Y. Shalom ed. Tel Aviv: Tarbut Vechinach, 1960 (Hebrew).

Butlin, Noel G. 1959. "Colonial Socialism in Australia, 1860–1900," in Aitken, 1959b.

Christopher, A. J. 1972. "Government Land Policies in Southern Africa," in Ironside, 1972.

Clark, V. S. 1906. *The Labor Movement in Australia.* New York: Holt.

Cohen, Abraham 1969. *The Emergence of the Public Sector of the Israeli Economy.* Givat Haviva: Hashomer Hatzair Publication Center.

Cohen, Amnon 1973. *Palestine in the 18th Century: Patterns of Government and Administration.* Jerusalem: Magnes Press.

Cohen, Israel, ed. 1911. *Zionist Work in Palestine.* London: Fisher.

Course of Degania: Story of Fifty Years of the Kvutza. Tel Aviv: Davar, 1961 (Hebrew).

Damaschke, Adolf 1903. *Die Bodenreform,* 3rd rev. edn. Berlin: Verlag von Johannes Räde.

Darin-Drabkin, Haim 1961. *The Other Society.* Merchavia: Hakibbutz Hameuchad (Hebrew).

Davenport, T. R. H. 1978. *South Africa: A Modern History,* 2nd edn. Toronto: University of Toronto Press.

Davies, W. D. 1982. *The Territorial Dimension of Judaism.* Berkeley: University of California Press.

Davison, Roderic H. 1973. *Reform in the Ottoman Empire: 1856–1876.* NY: Gordian Press.

De Silva, S. B. D. 1982. *The Political Economy of Underdevelopment.* London: RKP.

Denoon, Donald 1983. *Settler Capitalism: The Dynamics of Dependent Development in the Southern Hemisphere*. Oxford: Clarendon.

Deutsch, Karl 1985. "Preface," in Ernest Krausz, ed., *Politics and Society in Israel*. New Brunswick: Transaction Books.

Doron, Joachim 1982. "Social Concepts Prevalent in German Zionism: 1883–1914," *Studies in Zionism*, No. 5, April.

Doukhan-Landau, Leah 1979. *The Zionist Companies for Land Purchase in Palestine*. Jerusalem: Yad Itzhak Ben-Zvi (Hebrew).

Drori, Yigal 1975. "The View of the Eretz-Israeli Press and Intelligentsia toward the Labor Movement in the Years 1904–1914," *Meassef*, No. 7, May.

Druyan, Nitza 1981. *Without a Magic Carpet: Yemenite Settlement in Eretz Israel (1881–1914)*. Jerusalem: Ben-Zvi Institute (Hebrew).

ed. 1982. *The Pioneers of Immigration from Yemen, 1882–1914*. Jerusalem: Shazar Center (Hebrew).

Druyanov, A., ed. 1932. *Documents Concerning the History of Hibbat-Zion and the Settlement of Eretz Israel*. Tel Aviv: The Odessa Committee for the Settlement of Eretz Israel (Hebrew).

Ehrlich, Avishai 1987. "Israel: Conflict, War, and Social Change," in Colin Creighton & Martin Shaw, eds., *The Sociology of War and Peace*. London: Macmillan.

Eisenstadt, S. [1974]. *Chapters in the History of the Jewish Labor Movement*, Vol. 2. Tel Aviv: Likud (Hebrew).

Eisenstadt, S. N. 1948. *Introduction to the Research of the Sociological Structure of Oriental Jews*. Jerusalem: The Szold Institute (Hebrew).

1952. *The Absorption of Immigrants*. Jerusalem: The Jewish Agency for Eretz Israel and the Hebrew University of Jerusalem (Hebrew).

1954. *The Absorption of Immigrants: A Comparative Study Based Mainly on the Jewish Community in Palestine and the State of Israel*. London: RKP.

1967. *Israeli Society*. London: Weidenfeld & Nicolson.

Eisenstadt, S. N. *et al.*, eds. 1969. *The Social Structure of Israel*. Jerusalem: Academon (Hebrew).

Elazari-Volcani, I. 1930. *The Fellah's Farm*. Tel Aviv: Agricultural Experimentation Station.

Eli-Podiel, Malka 1982. *In Yemen's Tempests*. Jerusalem: Moreshet (Hebrew).

Eliav, Mordechai 1982. "Diplomatic Intervention Concerning Restrictions on Jewish Immigration and Purchase of Land at the End of the Nineteenth Century," *Cathedra*, No. 26, December.

ed. 1981. *The First Aliya Book*, Vol. 1. Jerusalem: Yad Izhak Ben-Zvi (Hebrew).

Elon, Amos 1975. *Herzl*. NY: Holt, Rinehart & Winston.

Elsberg, P. F. 1956. "The Arab Question in the Policy of the Zionist Executive Before the First World War," *Shivat Tsiyon*, No. 4.

Emmanuel, Arghiri 1972. *Unequal Exchange*. NY: Monthly Review.

Epstein, Itzhak 1907/8. "The Hidden Question," *Hashiloah*, Vol. 17.

Epstein, J. H. 1912. "Michael Flürscheim und die Bodenreform," *Jahrbuch des Freien Deutschen Hochstifts*.

Bibliography

Esco Foundation 1947. *Palestine: A Study of Jewish, Arab, and British Policies.*
New Haven: Yale University Press.
Estourelles de Constant, P. H. X. 1943. *La Politique en Tunisie.* Paris: Plon.
Etzioni, Amitai 1959. "Alternative Ways to Democracy: The Example of Israel,"
Political Science Quarterly, Vol. 74, No. 2, June.
Even-Shoshan, Zvi 1963. *History of the Workers' Movement in Eretz Israel.* Tel-
Aviv: Am Oved (Hebrew).
Ever-Hadeni [Aharon Feldman] 1947. *Aharon Eisenberg: His Life, Writings and
Epoch of Settlement.* Tel-Aviv: Massada (Hebrew).
    1951. *Hadera: 1891–1951, Sixty Years of History.* Ramat Gan: Massada
    (Hebrew).
    1955. *Fifty Years of Settlement in the Lower Galilee.* Ramat-Gan: Massada
    (Hebrew).
Fieldhouse, D. K. 1966. *The Colonial Empires from the Eighteenth Century.* NY:
Weidenfeld & Nicolson.
    1981. *Colonialism 1870–1945: An Introduction.* London: Weidenfeld &
    Nicolson.
Firestone, Ya'akov 1975. "Production and Trade in Islamic Context: *Sharika*
Contracts in the Transitional Economy of Northern Samaria, 1853–1943,"
International Journal of Middle East Studies, Vol. 6, Nos. 2 & 3, April & July.
Fisher, Stanley 1919. *Ottoman Land Laws.* Oxford: Oxford University Press.
Flapan, Simha 1979. *Zionism and the Palestinians.* London: Croom Helm.
Flürscheim, Michael 1892. *Auf friedlichem Wege,* 1884, translated into English as
Wages, Rent, and Interest. London: Reeves.
Frader, Laura L. 1981. "Grapes of Wrath: Vineyard Workers, Labor Unions,
and Strike Activity in the Aude, 1860–1913," in Louise Tilly & Charles
Tilly, eds., *Class Conflict and Collective Action.* Beverly Hills: Sage.
Frank, André Gunder 1972. "The Development of Underdevelopment," in
James D. Cockcroft *et al.,* eds., *Dependence and Underdevelopment.* Garden
City, NY: Doubleday.
Frankel, Jonathan 1981. *Prophecy and Politics: Socialism, Nationalism, and the
Russian Jews, 1862–1917.* Cambridge: Cambridge University Press.
    "The *Yizkor* book of 1911 – A Note on National Myths in the Second *Aliya,*"
    unpublished manuscript.
Frankel, Raphael 1975. "Joseph Bussel, The Hadera Commune, and the
Formation of the *Kvutza,*" *Hatsiyonut,* No. 4.
    1981. "Ideological Motives in the Formation of the *Kvutza* During the Period
    of the Second *Aliya,*" *Cathedra,* No. 18, January.
Fredrickson, George 1981. *White Supremacy: A Comparative Study of American
and South African History.* Oxford: Oxford University Press.
    1988. "Colonialism and Racism: The United States and South Africa in
    Comparative Perspective," in his *The Arrogance of Race,* Middetown,
    Wesleyan University Press.
Freiman, Aharon M. 1907. *The Jubilee Book of Rishon Letzion,* Vol. 1. Jerusalem
(Hebrew).
Fricke, Dieter *et al.* 1983. *Lexikon zur Parteiengeschichte: Die bürgerlichen und*

kleinbürgerlichen Parteien und Verbände in Deutschland (1789–1945), Band 1. Leipzig: Veb Bibliographisches Institut.

Friedman, Isaiah 1983. "The Effect of the System of Capitulations on the Attitude of the Turkish Government Towards the Jewish Settlement in Palestine: 1856–1897," *Cathedra*, No. 28, June.

Gadon, Shmuel 1958. *The Course of the Kvutza and the Kibbutz*, Vol. 1. Tel Aviv: Am Oved (Hebrew).

1980. "Aspiration toward Communal Life and Its Initial Realization During the Second *Aliya*," *Cathedra*, No. 16, July.

Garber-Talmon, Yonina 1972. *Family and Community in the Kibbutz*. Cambridge, MA: Harvard University Press.

Gazit, Dov 1966. *History of Agricultural Settlement in Eretz Israel*. Tel Aviv: Hamerkaz Hachaklai (Hebrew).

Gellner, Ernest 1983. *Nations and Nationalism*. Ithaca: Cornell University Press.

Gera, Gershon 1985. *Hashomer*. Tel Aviv: Ministry of Defense (Hebrew).

Gerschenkron, Alexander 1962. *Economic Backwardness in Historical Perspective*. Cambridge: Belknap Press.

Giladi, Dan 1969. "Private Initiative, National Capital, and the Political Crystallization of the Right-Wing" in S. N. Eisenstadt, 1969.

1970. "The Farmers' Position Towards Jewish Labor in the Second Aliya," *Baderech*, Vol. 3, December.

1972. "The Precedence of the 'Laboring Settlement' – Since When?," *Revaon lemechkar hevrati*, No. 2.

1974. "Jewish Workers and Hebrew Labor in Rishon Letzion," *Meassaf*, No. 6, March.

1975. "The Agronomic Development of the Old Colonies in Palestine (1882–1914)," in Ma'oz, 1975.

1981. "Baron Rothschild and the Patronage System of his Administration," in Eliav, 1981.

Giladi, Dan & Mordechai Naor 1982. *Rothschild: "Founder of the Yishuv" His Activities in Eretz Israel*. Jerusalem: Keter (Hebrew).

Gilbar, Gad 1986. "The Growing Economic Involvement of Palestine with the West, 1865–1914," in David Kushner, ed., *Palestine in the Late Ottoman Period: Political, Social and Economic Transformation*. Jerusalem: Yad Izhak Ben-Zvi.

Gilbar, N. M. 1951. "The Metamorphoses of the Idea of a National Fund," in Agmon, 1951.

Glusska, Zecharya 1974. *Book on Behalf of the Jews of Yemen*. Jerusalem: Yaakov Ben-David Glusska (Hebrew).

Gollan, Robin 1960. *Radical and Working Class Politics: A Study of Eastern Australia, 1850–1910*. Melbourne: Melbourne University Press.

Good, Kenneth 1976. "Settler Colonialism: Economic Development and Class Formation," *The Journal of Modern African Studies*, Vol. 14, No. 4.

The A. D. Gordon Book – His Philosophy and Teachings. 1943. Tel Aviv: Haoved Hatsiyoni (Hebrew).

Gorny, Yosef, 1968a. "Pangs of Transition: Concerning the Development of the

Idea of Laboring Settlement," *Baderech*, No. 2, April.

1986b. "The Ideology of the 'Conquest of Labor'," *Keshet*, No. 38, Winter.

1970. "Changes in the Social and Political Structure of the Second *Aliya* in the Years 1904–1914," *Hatsiyonut*, No. 1.

1973. "The Idea of 'Hebrew Labor' and Its Metamorphoses in Poalei Zion of the Second *Aliya*," *Asuphot*, No. 17, July.

1974a. "The Paradox of the Idea of National Unity in the Workers' Movement of the Second *Aliya*," *Meassef*, No. 6, March.

1974b. "Continuity and Transformation," *The Raphael Mahler Book*. Merchavia: Sifriat Hapoalim (Hebrew).

1987. *The Arab Question and the Jewish Problem*. Tel Aviv: Am Oved, 1985 (Hebrew), translated into English as *Zionism and the Arabs, 1882–1948: A Study of Ideology*. Oxford: Clarendon.

Gramsci, Antonio 1971. *Selections from the Prison Notebooks*. NY: International Publishers.

Granott, A. 1952. *The Land System in Palestine*. London: Eyre & Spottiswoode.

Grinberg, Lev Luis 1986. "The Jewish–Arab Drivers' Association Strike in 1931," unpublished seminar paper, Tel Aviv University.

Gross, Nachum *et al.* 1981. *Banker to an Emerging Nation: The History of Bank Leumi*. Ramat-Gan: Massada, (Hebrew).

Grossman, David & Zeev Safrai 1980. "Satellite Settlements in Western Samaria," *The Geographic Review*, Vol. 70, No. 4, October.

Grossman, David 1983. "The Development of Rural Settlement between the Yarkon and the Ayalon from the Sixteenth to the Twentieth Century," in David Grossman, ed., *Between Yarkon and Ayalon*. Ramat Gan: Bar-Ilan University Press (Hebrew).

1986. "Distribution of Settlements and Population in the Southern Coastal Plain," paper presented at the Congress on Palestine 1840–1948: Population and Immigration, June 1986, Haifa.

Gurewitch, David, Aharon Gertz & Roberto Bacchi 1944. *Settlement and the Demographic Changes of the Eretz Israeli Population*. Jerusalem: The Statistical Department of the Jewish Agency for Eretz Israel.

Gutzeit, Paula 1907. *Die Bodenreform*. Leipzig: Duncker & Humboldt.

Gvati, Haim 1981. *A Hundred Years of Settlement*, Vol. 1. Tel Aviv: Hakibbutz Hameuchad (Hebrew).

Habas, Bracha, ed. 1957. *The Book of the Second Aliya*. Tel Aviv: Am Oved (Hebrew).

Hagen, William W. 1980. *Germans, Poles, and Jews: The Nationality Conflict in the Prussian East, 1772–1914*. Chicago: University of Chicago Press.

Hancock, W. K. 1940. *Survey of British Commonwealth Affairs*, Vol. 2. London: Oxford University Press.

Hashomer Book 1957. Tel Aviv: Ministry of Defense (Hebrew).

Hashomer Collection 1937. Tel Aviv: Labor Archive (Hebrew).

Heathcote, R. L. 1972. "The Evolution of Australian Pastoral Land Tenures: An Example of Challenge and Response in Resource Development," in Ironside, 1972.

Hershlag, Z. Y. 1964. *Introduction to the Modern Economic History of the Middle East*. Leiden: E. J. Brill.

Hertzberg, Arthur, ed. 1959. *The Zionist Idea*. Garden City, NY: Doubleday.

Hertzka, Theodor 1891. *Freeland: A Social Anticipation*. NY: D. Appleton.

Herzog, Hanna 1981. "The Ethnic Lists to the Delegates Assembly and the Knesset (1920–1977): Ethnic Political Identity?," unpublished Ph.D. Dissertation, Tel Aviv University (Hebrew).

Hirschberg, Avraham Shmuel 1979. *The Course of the New Yishuv in Eretz Israel*. (Reprint of the 1901 Edition.) Jerusalem: Yad Izhak Ben-Zvi (Hebrew).

History Book of the Hagana, general editor Ben-Zion Dinur, vols. 1 (parts 1 and 2) and 2. Jerusalem: Zionist Library, 1954, 1956, 1959 (Hebrew).

Holt, P. M. 1966. *Egypt and the Fertile Crescent, 1516–1922: A Political History*. Ithaca: Cornell University Press.

Horowitz, Dalia 1977. "The Views of Non-Worker Groups in the *Yishuv* on Hebrew Labor in the Period of the Second *Aliya*, 1904–1914", unpublished MA Thesis, Tel Aviv University.

Horowitz, Dan & Moshe Lissak 1978. *The Origins of the Israeli Polity: Palestine Under the Mandate*. Chicago: University of Chicago Press.

Hourani, Albert 1968. "Ottoman Reform and the Politics of Notables," in Polk & Chambers, 1968.

Hussain, Athar & Keith Tribe 1981. *Marxism and the Agrarian Question, Vol. 1: German Social Democracy and the Peasantry, 1890–1907*. Atlantic Heights: Humanities Press.

Hütteroth, Wolf-Dieter & Kamal Abdulfattah 1977. *Historical Geography of Palestine, Transjordan and Southern Syria in the Late 16th Century*. Erlangen: Frankischen Geographischen Gesellschaft.

Ilan, Shlomo 1974. "Traditional Arab Agriculture: Its Methods and Attitude toward Eretz-Israeli Landscape at the End of the Ottoman Period," unpublished MA Thesis, Hebrew University of Jerusalem, (Hebrew).

1984. "The Traditional Arab Agriculture," *Kardom*, No. 34, September.

Ironside, R. G. *et al.*, eds. 1972. *Frontier Settlement*, Papers from the International Geographical Symposium in Edmonton and Saskaton, August.

Islamoğlu-Inan, Huri, "Introduction: 'Oriental Despotism' in World System Perspective," in her (ed.), *The Ottoman Empire and the World Economy*. Cambridge: Cambridge University Press, forthcoming.

Islamoğlu-Inan, Huri & Çağlar Keyder 1977. "Agenda for Ottoman History," *Review*, Vol. 1, No. 1, Summer.

Isnard, H. 1954. *La vigne en Algérie: Étude géographique*, Tome 2. Ophrys-Gap.

Issawi, Charles 1982. *An Economic History of the Middle East and North Africa*. NY: Columbia University Press.

1970. "Middle East Economic Development, 1815–1914: The General and the Specific," in M. A. Cook, ed., *Studies in the Economic History of the Middle East*. London: Oxford University Press.

Izraeli, Dafna N. 1981. "The Zionist Women's Movement in Palestine, 1911–1927: A Sociological Analysis," *Signs*, Vol. 7, No. 1.

Jabotinsky, Zeev 1946. *Selected Writings*, Vol. 3. Jerusalem: Massada (Hebrew).
Jakobczyk, Witold 1972. "The First Decade of the Prussian Settlement Commission's Activities (1886–1897)," *Polish Review*, Vol. 17, No. 1, Winter.
Johnstone, F. 1976. *Class, Race, and Gold*. London: RKP.
Kalvarisky, H. M. 1931. "The Relations Between Jews and Arabs Before the War," *Sheifotenu*, Vol. 2, No. 2 (March/April).
Kapara, Pinchas 1978. *From Yemen and in Shaarayim*. Rechovot: Published by the author (Hebrew).
Kaplansky, Shlomo 1950. *Vision and Fulfillment*. Merchavia: Hakibbutz Haartzi (Hebrew).
Kark, Ruth 1984. "Changing Patterns of Landownership in Nineteenth-Century Palestine: The European Influence," *Journal of Historical Geography*, Vol. 10, No. 4.
Karpat, Kemal H. 1968. "The Land Regime, Social Structure, and Modernization in the Ottoman Empire," in Polk & Chambers, 1968.
    1977. "Some Historical and Methodological Considerations Concerning Social Stratification in the Middle East," in C. A. O. Van Nieuwenhuijze, ed., *Commoners, Climbers and Notables: A Sampler of Studies on Social Ranking in the Middle East*. Leiden: E. J. Brill.
    1978. "Ottoman Population Records and the Census of 1881/82–1893," *International Journal of Middle Eastern Studies*, Vol. 9, No. 2, May.
Katz, Joseph 1983. "The Colonization Activity in Palestine of the Zionist Private Companies and Associations between the Years 1900–1914," unpublished Ph.D. Dissertation, The Hebrew University of Jerusalem (Hebrew).
Katznelson, Berl 1949. *Chapters in the History of the Workers' Movements*, 3rd edn. Tel Aviv: Habachrut Hasocialistit Haivrit Beeretz Israel (Hebrew).
    1961. *Letters, Vol. 1: 1900–1914*, ed. by Yehuda Sharet. Tel Aviv: Am Oved (Hebrew).
Kayyali, A. W. [1978?]. *Palestine: A Modern History*. London: Croom Helm.
Kellner, Yaacov 1978. "The Early Aliyot – Myth and Reality: Two Examples," *Kivunim*, No. 1, November.
Khalidi, Rashid I. 1980. *British Policy towards Syria and Palestine: 1906–1914*. London: Ithaca Press.
    1982. "The Role of the Press in the Early Arab Reaction to Zionism," *Mediterranean Peoples*, No. 20, July/September.
    "Palestinian Peasant Resistance to Zionism Before World War I," unpublished manuscript.
Khoury, Philip S. 1983. *Urban Notables and Arab Nationalism: The Politics of Damascus 1860–1920*. Cambridge: Cambridge University Press.
Kimmerling, Baruch 1983. *Zionism and Territory*. Berkeley: Institute of International Studies.
Kimmerling, Baruch, in collaboration with Irit Backer 1985. *The Interrupted System: Israeli Civilians in War and Routine Times*. New Brunswick: Transaction Books.

Kleiman, Aaron S. 1980. "The Resolution of Conflicts through Territorial Partition: The Palestine Experience," *Comparative Studies in Society and History*, Vol. 22, No. 2, April.

Kolatt, Israel 1964a. "Ideology and the Impact of Realities Upon the Jewish Labor Movement in Palestine, 1905–1919," unpublished Ph.D. dissertation, The Hebrew University of Jerusalem (Hebrew).

ed. 1964b. "Joint Session of the Executive of the Association of Judean Moshavot and the Board of the Agricultural Workers' Association at Rishon Letzion, March 2, 1914" and "Joint Session of the Executive of the Association of Judean Moshavot and the Representatives of the Institutions and Communal Leaders in Rishon Letzion, March 17, 1914," Jerusalem: Hebrew University (Hebrew).

1971. "The Idea of the Histadrut – Foundation and Modification: 1920–1948," *Measef*, No. 2, December.

1981. "Jewish Laborers of the First *Aliyah*," in Eliav, 1981.

Komarov, Ephraim 1901. "The Balance Sheet of the Year: A Review of the Situation of the Workers in Eretz Israel and Impressions from My Tour of the Galilee," *Sefer Hashana: Measef Safruti*, Vol. 2.

Kushnir, Shimon 1972. *He Who Sees Afar: Scenes from Shmuel Yavnieli's Life*. Tel-Aviv: Am Oved (Hebrew).

Lamar, Howard & Leonard Thompson 1981. *The Frontier in History: North America and Southern Africa Compared*. New Haven: Yale University Press.

Laskov, Shulamit 1981. "Hovevei Zion in Russia: Supporters of the *Yishuv* in Eretz Israel," in Eliav, 1981.

1986. *A Call from Zion: The Life and Time of Yosef Vitkin*. Tel Aviv: Papyrus (Hebrew).

Levine, Yaacov 1912. "The Workers' Problem in Eretz Israel," *Haachdut*, Vol. 3, Nos. 40/41, 42, 45/56, August 9, 16 & September 5.

Lewin-Epstein, Eliyahu 1932. *My Memoirs*. Tel Aviv: Lewin-Epstein (Hebrew).

Lewis, Norman N. 1955. "The Frontier of Settlement in Syria, 1800–1950," *International Affairs*, Vol. 31, No. 1, January.

Livne, Eliezer 1969. *Aharon Aaronsohn: The Man and His Times*. Jerusalem: Bialik Institute (Hebrew).

Lubriani, Eliezer, ed. 1961. *The Book of Merchavia: The Cooperative*. Tel Aviv: The Veterans of the Cooperative (Hebrew).

Lustick, Ian 1985. *State-Building Failure in British Ireland and French Algeria*. Berkeley: Institute of International Studies.

McCarthy, Justin 1981. "The Population of Ottoman Syria and Iraq," *Asian and African Studies*, Vol. 15, No. 1, March.

McNeill, William H. 1983. *The Great Frontier: Freedom and Hierarchy in Modern Times*. Princeton: Princeton University Press.

Mandel, Neville J. 1976. *The Arabs and Zionism before World War I*. Berkeley: University of California Press.

Ma'oz, Moshe 1968. *Ottoman Reform in Syria and Palestine 1840–1861*. Oxford: Clarendon.

ed. 1975. *Studies on Palestine during the Ottoman Period.* Jerusalem: Magnes Press.

Markus, Andrew 1979. *Fear and Hatred: Purifying Australia and California, 1850–1901.* Sydney: Hale & Iremonger.

Maxwell, Constantia, ed. 1923. *Irish History from Contemporary Sources: 1509–1610.* London: Allen & Unwin.

Meir, Joseph 1983. *The Zionist Movement and the Jews of Yemen.* Tel Aviv: Afikim (Hebrew).

Metzer, Jacob 1979. *National Capital for a National Home.* Jerusalem: Yad Itzhak Ben-Zvi (Hebrew).

Metzer, Jacob & Oded Kaplan 1985. "Jointly but Severally: Arab–Jewish Dualism and Economic Growth in Mandatory Palestine," *Journal of Economic History,* Vol. 65, No. 2, March.

Migdal, Joel 1980. *Palestinian Society and Politics.* Princeton: Princeton University Press.

Moore Jr., Barrington 1966. *Social Origins of Dictatorship and Democracy.* Boston: Beacon.

Mosley, Paul 1983. *The Settler Economies: Studies in the Economic History of Kenya and Southern Rhodesia 1900–1963.* Cambridge: Cambridge University Press.

Murphy, Raymond 1984. "The Structure of Closure: A Critique and Development of the Theories of Weber, Collins, and Parkin," *The British Journal of Sociology,* Vol. 35.

Nairn, Tom 1977. *The Break-Up of Britain.* London: NLB.

Newratzki, Kurt 1914. *Die Jüdische Kolonisation Palästinas.* München: Ernst Reinhardt.

Ndabezitha, Siyabonga W. & Stephen K. Sanderson 1987. "Racial Antagonism and the Origins of Apartheid in the South African Gold Mining Industry, 1886–1924: A Split Labor Market Analysis," paper presented at the 82nd meeting of the American Sociological Association, Chicago, August.

Near, Henry 1981. "Ideology and Anti-Ideology," *Cathedra,* No. 18, January.
    1982. "Was The *Kvutza* Shaped by 'Life?'" *Cathedra,* No. 23, April.
    1983. "Each Person and His Degania," *Cathedra,* No. 29, September.

Nini, Yehuda 1982. *Yemen and Zion: The Political, Social and Spiritual Background of the Early Aliyot from Yemen, 1800–1914.* Jerusalem: Zionist Library (Hebrew).

Norris, R. 1975. *The Emergent Commonwealth: Australian Federation: Expectations and Fulfilment, 1889–1910.* Melbourne: Melbourne University Press.

Oettinger, Jacob [1917a]. *Jewish Colonization in Palestine: Methods, Plans and Capital.* [The Hague]: Head Office of the JNF.

    [1917b]. *The Practical Advantages of Hereditary Lease.* [The Hague]: Head Office of the JNF.

Ofrat, Gideon 1981. "The 'Bezalel' Colony in Ben-Shemen, 1910–1913," *Cathedra,* No. 20, July.

Oppenheimer, Franz 1913. *Die Siedlungsgenossenschaft,* 11th edn. Jena: Gustav Fischer.

[1917]. *Collective Ownership and Private Ownership of Land.* [The Hague]: The Head Office of the JNF.

1931. *Erlebtes, Erstrebtes, Erreichtes.* Berlin: Welt.

Orni, Efraim 1972. *Agrarian Reform and Social Progress in Israel.* Jerusalem: JNF.

Owen, Roger 1981. *The Middle East in the World Economy.* London: Methuen.

ed. 1982. *Studies in the Economic and Social History of Palestine in the Nineteenth and Twentieth Centuries.* Carbondale: Southern Illinois University Press.

Parkin, Frank 1979. *Marxism and Class Theory.* NY: Columbia University Press.

Patai, Raphael 1960. *The Complete Diaries of Theodor Herzl,* Vol. 1. NY: Herzl Press.

Peled, Yoav, *Class and Ethnicity in the Pale: The Political Economy of Jewish Workers' Nationalism in Late Imperial Russia.* London: Macmillan, forthcoming.

Peled, Yoav and Gershon Shafir 1987. "Split Labor Market and the State: The Effect of Modernization on Jewish Industrial Workers in Tsarist Russia," *American Journal of Sociology,* Vol. 92, No. 6, May.

Pinner, Ludwig 1930. "Wheat Culture in Palestine," *Bulletin of the Palestine Economic Society,* Vol. 5, No. 2, August.

Polk, William W. & Richard L. Chambers, eds. 1968. *Beginnings of Modernization in the Middle East.* Chicago: University of Chicago Press.

Poncet, Jean 1962. *La colonisation et l'agriculture européenes en Tunisie depuis 1881.* Paris: Mouton.

Porath, Yehoshua 1974. *The Emergence of the Palestinian-Arab National Movement, 1818–1929.* London: Frank Cass.

1978. "The Land Problem as a Factor in Relations Among Arabs, Jews and the Mandatory Government," in Gabriel Ben-Dor, ed., *The Palestinian and the Middle East Conflict.* Ramat Gan: Turtledove.

Preuss, Walter 1965. *The Labor Movement in Israel,* 3rd edn. Jerusalem: Rubin Mass.

Reichman, Shalom 1979. *From Foothold to Settled Territory.* Jerusalem: Yad Izhak Ben-Zvi (Hebrew).

Reichman, Shalom & Shlomo Hasson 1984. "A Cross-Cultural Diffusion of Colonization: From Posen to Palestine," *Annals of the Association of American Geographers,* Vol. 74, No. 1.

Reilly, James 1981. "The Peasantry of Late Ottoman Palestine," in *Journal of Palestine Studies,* Vol. 10, No. 4, Summer.

Reinharz, Jehuda 1975. *Fatherland or Promised Land: The Dilemma of the German Jew, 1893–1914.* Ann Arbor: University of Michigan Press.

Reports of the Executive of the Zionist Organisation to the XII Zionist Congress, Part III: Organisation Report. London: National Labour Press, 1921.

Riddel, Roger C. 1978. *The Land Problem in Rhodesia.* Gwelo: Mambo Press.

Roded, Ruth Michal 1984. "Tradition and Change in Syria During the Last Decades of Ottoman Rule: The Urban Elite of Damascus, Aleppo, Homs and Hama, 1876–1918," unpublished Ph.D. Dissertation, University of Denver.

Rodinson, Maxime 1973. *Israel – A Colonial-Settler State?* NY: Monad.

Ro'i, Yaakov 1964. "The Attitude of the Yishuv towards the Arabs, 1822–1914," unpublished MA Thesis, Hebrew University (Hebrew).

1968. "The Zionist Attitude to the Arabs 1908–1914," *Middle Eastern Studies*, April, Vol. 4, No. 3.

1981. "Jewish–Arab Relations in the First Aliya Settlements," in Eliav, 1981.

Ruppin, Arthur 1919. *Der Aufbau des Landes Israel*. Berlin: Jüdischer Verlag.

1926. *The Agricultural Colonisation of the Zionist Organisation in Palestine.* London: Martin Hopkinson.

1971. *Chapters of My Life*, Vol. 2. Tel-Aviv: Am Oved, 1947 (Hebrew), selections translated into English as *Memoirs, Diaries, Letters*. London: Weidenfeld & Nicolson.

1975. *Three Decades of Palestine*. Westport: Greenwood.

Said, Edward 1979. *The Question of Palestine*. NY: Vintage.

Salmon, Joseph 1981. "The *Bilu* Movement," in Eliav, 1981.

Schama, Shimon 1978. *Two Rothschilds and the Land of Israel*. London: Collins.

Schölch, Alexander 1982. "European Penetration and the Economic Development of Palestine, 1856–1882," in Owen, 1982.

1985. "The Demographic Development of Palestine, 1850–1882," *International Journal of Middle East Studies*, Vol. 17, No. 4, November.

See, Katherine O'Sullivan 1986. *First World Nationalisms: Class and Ethnic Politics in Northern Ireland and Quebec*. Chicago: University of Chicago Press.

Seri, Shalom, ed. 1983. *Sei Yona: Yemenite-Jews in Israel*. Tel Aviv: Am Oved (Hebrew).

Seton-Watson, Hugh 1977. *Nations and States*. London: Methuen.

Shachaf, Mira 1984. "Hashomer – A Non-Partisan Vanguard?" unpublished seminar paper, Tel Aviv University.

Shalev, Michael, "The Political Economy of Labor Party Dominance and Decline in Israel," in T. J. Pempel, Cornell University Press, forthcoming.

"Jewish Organized Labor and the Palestinians: A Study of State/Society Relations in Israel," in Baruch Kimmerling, ed., *The Israeli State: Boundaries and Frontiers*. NY: State University of New York Press, forthcoming.

Labor and the Political Economy in Israel. Oxford: Oxford University Press, forthcoming.

Shapira, Anita 1977. *Futile Struggle: The Jewish Labor Controversy, 1929–1939*. Tel Aviv: Hakibbutz Hameuchad (Hebrew).

1985. *Berl: The Biography of a Socialist Zionist, Berl Katznelson, 1887–1944*. Cambridge: Cambridge University Press.

Shapira, Joseph 1961. *Labor and Land*. Tel Aviv: Ayanot (Hebrew).

1967. *Hapoel Hatzair: The Idea and the Deed*. Tel Aviv: Ayanot (Hebrew).

Shapiro, Yonathan 1976. *The Formative Years of the Israeli Labour Party: The Organization of Power, 1919–1930*. London: Sage.

1980. "Generational Units and Inter-Generational Relations in Israeli

Politics," in Asher Arian, ed., *Israel: A Developing Society*. Assen: Van Gurcum.

Shaw, Stanford J. 1975. "The Nineteenth-Century Ottoman Tax Reforms and Revenue System," *International Journal of Middle Eastern Studies*, Vol. 6.

Shaw, Stanford J. & Ezel Kural Shaw 1977. *History of the Ottoman Empire and Modern Turkey*, Vol. 2. Cambridge: Cambridge University Press.

Sheehan, Bernard W. 1974. *Seeds of Extinction: Jeffersonian Philanthropy and the American Indian*. NY: Norton.

Shilo, Margalit 1977. "The Training Farms of the Palestine Office, 1908–1914," unpublished MA Thesis, The Hebrew University of Jerusalem (Hebrew).

1985. "The Settlement Policy of the Palestine Office, 1908–1914," unpublished Ph.D. dissertation, Hebrew University of Jerusalem (Hebrew).

Shimoni, Yaakov 1947. *The Arabs of Palestine*. Tel-Aviv: Am Oved (Hebrew).

Shochat, Israel, 1957. "Mission and Course," in *Hashomer Book*.

Shochat, Mania 1958. "The Collective," in Gadon, 1958.

Shprintzak, Joseph 1952. *In Writing and Speaking*. Tel Aviv: Mapai Publishing House (Hebrew).

1968. *Tasks*. Tel-Aviv: Tarbut Vechinuch (Hebrew).

Simmons, R. C. 1981. *The American Colonies: From Settlement to Independence*. NY: Norton.

Singer, Mendel 1971. *Shlomo Kaplansky: His Life and Work*, Vol. 1. Jerusalem: Zionist Library (Hebrew).

Slutsky, Yehuda 1968. "The Role of the Orienting Idea in the Formation of the *Kvutza* in Eretz Israel," *Baderech*, No. 2, April.

1978. *Poalei Zion in Eretz Israel (1905–1919)*. Tel Aviv: Tel Aviv University (Hebrew).

Smilansky, Moshe 1938. *Writings*, Vol. 2. Tel Aviv: Hitachdut haikarim beeretz yisrael (Hebrew).

1953. *Resurrection and Holocaust*. Ramat Gan: Massada (Hebrew).

1959. *Chapters in the History of the Yishuv*. Tel Aviv: Dvir (Hebrew).

Stein, Kenneth W. 1984. *The Land Question in Palestine, 1917–1939*. Chapel Hill: University of North Carolina Press.

Sussman, Zvi 1974. *Wage Differentials and Equality within the Histadrut: The Impact of Egalitarian Ideology and Arab Labor on Jewish Wages in Palestine*. Ramat-Gan: Massada (Hebrew).

Swedenburg, Theodore Romain 1980. "The Development of Capitalism in Greater Syria, 1830–1914: An Historico-Geographical Approach," unpublished MA Thesis, University of Texas at Austin.

Syrkin, Nachman 1939. *Writings*, Vol. 1. Tel Aviv (Hebrew).

Szajkowski, Zosa 1951. "The European Attitude to East European Immigration (1881–1893)," *Publication of the American Jewish Historical Society*, Vol. 41, No. 2, December.

Tabenkin, Itzhak 1979. "Concerning Guarding and Hashomer in the Second Aliya," *Shorashim*, Vol. 1.

Teveth, Shabtai 1977. *David's Zeal: The Life of David Ben-Gurion*, Vol. 1. Jerusalem: Shocken (Hebrew).

1985. *Ben-Gurion and the Palestinian Arabs: From Peace to War*. Oxford: Oxford University Press.

Trietsch, Davis 1910. *Palästina Handbuch*, 2nd edn. Berlin: Orient Verlag.

Tsemach, Shlomo 1948. "Introduction to the Writings of A. D. Gordon," in Yehuda Aiges, ed., *The Aharon David Gordon Collection*. Jerusalem: The Zionist Federation (Hebrew).

1965. *First Year*. Tel Aviv: Am Oved (Hebrew).

Tuby, Joseph 1983. "Economic Changes in the Yemenite-Jewish Community During the Nineteenth Century," in Seri, 1983.

ed. 1982. *I Will Immigrate in the Year of the Date: Sources*. Jerusalem: Ben-Zvi Institute (Hebrew).

Turner, Frederick Jackson 1956. "The Significance of the Frontier in American History," in George R. Taylor, ed., *The Turner Thesis*, rev. edn. Boston: Heath.

Tzahor, Zeev 1979. "The Histadrut: The Formative Period," unpublished Ph.D. Dissertation, The Hebrew University; subsequently published as *On The Road To Yishuv Leadership*. Jerusalem: Yad Itzhak Ben-Zvi, 1981 (Hebrew).

Ussishkin Book. Jerusalem: Havaad Lehotzaat Hasefer, 1964 (Hebrew).

Viteles, Harry 1967. *A History of the Co-Operative Movement in Israel, Vol. 2: The Evolution of the Kibbutz Movement*. London: Vallentine.

Vitkin, Joseph 1908. "Conquest of Land and Conquest of Labor," *HH*, Vol. 1, No. 10, June/July.

Von Albertini, Rudolf 1983. *European Colonial Rule, 1880–1940*. Westport: Greenwood.

Wa-Githumo, Mwangi 1981. *Land and Nationalism: The Impact of Land Expropriation and Land Grievances upon the Rise and Development of Nationalist Movements in Kenya, 1885–1939*. Washington: University Press of America.

Wallerstein, Immanuel 1974. *The Modern World System*, Vol. 1. NY: Academic Press.

Warburg Book. Herzliya: Massada, 1948 (Hebrew).

Warner, Charles K. 1975. *The Winegrowers of France and the Government Since 1875*. Westport: Greenwood.

Warriner, Doreen 1966. "Land Tenure in the Fertile Crescent," in Charles Issawi, ed., *The Economic History of the Middle East, 1880–1914*. Chicago: University of Chicago Press.

Weber, Max 1968. "Developmental Tendencies in the Situation of East Elbian Rural Laborers," in his *Economy and Society*, Vol. 3. NY: Bedminster.

Weintraub, D., M. Lissak & Y. Atzmon 1969. *Moshava, Kibbutz, and Moshav*. Ithaca: Cornell University Press.

Willard, Myra 1968. *History of the White Australia Policy to 1920* (Reprints of Economic Classics). NY: Augustus M. Kelley.

Working Hadera: At Its Jubilee, 1891–1981. 1981. Tel Aviv: Histadrut (Hebrew).

Wygodzinski, W. & August Müller 1929. *Das Genossenschaftswesen in Deutschland*, 2nd edn. Leipzig: B. G. Teubner.

Yaari, Avraham 1944. "The Immigration of Yemenite Jews to Eretz-Israel," in Yeshayahu & Zadok, 1944.

ed. 1947. *Eretz-Israeli Memoirs*. Jerusalem: Youth Department of the Zionist Federation (Hebrew).

Yaffe, Hillel 1971. *The Generation of the Maapilim: Memoirs, Letters and Diary*. Jerusalem: The Zionist Library (Hebrew).

Yavnieli, Shmuel 1952. *Journey to Yemen*. Tel Aviv: Mapai (Hebrew).

Yeshayahu, Israel & Shimon Gridi, eds. 1938. *From Yemen to Zion*. Tel Aviv: Massada (Hebrew).

Yeshayahu, Israel & Aharon Zadok, eds. 1944. *Return from Yemen*. Tel Aviv: Meteyman Lezion (Hebrew).

Zionism and the Arab Question. Jerusalem: Zalman Shazar Centre, 1979 (Hebrew).

Zureik, Elia T. 1979. *The Palestinians in Israel: A Study in Internal Colonialism*. London: RKP.

Index

Gorny, Yosef, 3, 5, 75, 81, 87, 116, 131, 213, 217
Grat Britain /England
  colonialism, 17, 23, 27, 202, 212
  colonization, 8–10, 147
  Mandate in Palestine, 4, 18, 22–23, 38, 43, 47, 75, 89, 131, 194, 197, 207, 212, 218
Gross, Nachum 29
Gross, Nathan, 153, 154, 164
Grossman, David, 39–40
guarding, 135–145, 203

Haachdut, 62, 191
Habsburg Empire, 153–154, 156
Hachoresh, 170–171, 172, 177
Hacohen, Ben-Hillel Mordechai, 133–134, 196
Hadera, 38, 43, 51, 63, 96, 102, 103, 105, 120, 138, 139, 142, 199, 200
Hadera commune, 171, 174, 177, 179, 182
Hagana, 144, 145, 194
Haifa, 28, 37, 204, 205
Hankin, Yehoshua, 138, 139, 206
Hapoel Hatzair, 62, 71, 73, 88
  articles in, 94, 101, 110, 112, 122, 161, 190–191
Hapoel Hatzair Party, 87, 123, 124–126, 131–132, 163, 164, 194
  its congresses, 93, 111, 165
  and "conquest of labor," 59–61, 73–74, 125–128, 129, 130, 138, 161, 163
  its program, 125, 127, 182, 190–191
  and Yemenite Jews, 95, 111
Hashomer, 86, 123, 129, 136–143, 144–145, 194, 209
  and "conquest of labor," 136–138
  and Cossack colonization model, 10–11, 137–138
  and Jewish–Palestinian relations, 140–142
  and Nili, 144
  see also Bar-Giora, guarding
Hasson, Shlomo, 154, 158, 160
"Hebrew Labor" see "conquest of labor"
Hebron (Jabal al-Halil), 38, 40
hegemony, 4, 193, 219
Heine, Heinrich, 49
Henkin, Yechezkel, 136
Hertzka, Theodor, 150–151, 156
Herzl, Theodor, 147–148, 149, 151, 189
Hirsch, Baron Maurice de, 46
Hirschberg, Samuel, 54, 70
Hissin, Dr Haim, 100
Histadrut, 6, 20, 123, 132, 133, 184, 193–195, 198, 215, 216

Holt, P.M., 27
Homel, 97, 136
Horowitz, Dan, 2–5, 213, 217
Houran mountains, 24, 137, 138
Hourani, Albert, 32
Hovevei Zion, 46, 125, 126, 127, 139, 147, 149, 155, 187, 190, 209
  and Jewish workers, 55, 61, 101
  leaders of, 42, 49, 59, 100, 110, 156, 161
  and settlement, 50, 103, 112, 148, 163, 165
Hula Valley, 38
Hulda training farm, 63, 113, 129, 169–170, 180
al-Husayni, Said, 205
Hütteroth, Wolf-Dieter, 37

Ibrahim Pasha, 38, 40, 135
"idealistic workers" (and idealism), 46–50, 106–107, 109–110, 121, 128, 162, 183, 191–192; see also "natural workers"
Ingberman, Moshe, 168
internal colonization, see colonization
Iraq, 35
Ireland, 9, 10
al-Isa, Isa, 204
al-Isa, Yusuf, 204
Isnard, H., 66, 76–77
Israel, State of, 194, 195, 219
Issawi, Charles, 26, 30, 31, 79, 89
Istanbul, 32, 205, 206

Jabotinsky, Zeev, 210
Jaffa, 28, 29, 38, 39, 41, 43, 92, 124, 127, 170, 200, 205
Jaffe, Dr Hillel, 161
Jerusalem (and Mutasarriflik of), 37, 38, 92, 129, 205
Jewish Colonization Association (JCA), 127, 138, 154, 158, 188, 190, 204
  and capital imports, 132
  and Jewish workers, 54–55, 61, 103, 188
  and settlement, 46, 50, 52, 97, 137, 168
Jewish National Fund (JNF), 20, 102, 105, 112, 113, 116, 121, 138, 155–157, 170, 176, 177, 178, 184, 189, 190, 191, 192, 196–197, 198
Jezreel Valley (Marj ibn Amar), 38, 39, 43, 44, 139, 205
Jordan Rift, 38, 213
Judea, 24, 43, 86, 115, 200
Junkers, 150, 152, 154

Index

Kalvarisky H.M. 88, 200
Kaplan, Oded, 217–218
Kaplansky, Shlomo, 71, 153, 154, 164,
    190, 192, 193
Kark, Ruth, 34
Karkur, 139
al-Karmil, 204, 206
Karpat, Kemal H., 31, 33, 38
Kaser, Salim, 200
Katara, 201
Katz, Joseph, 97
Katznelson, Berl, 1, 71, 89, 113, 132,
    163, 193
Kayyali, A.W. 202, 205
Kellner, Yaakov, 48–49
Kenya, 13, 18, 23, 147, 150
Kfar Giladi, 137, 172
Kfar Marmorek, 121
Kfar Saba, 43, 112
Kfar Tvor (Mescha), 43, 124, 138, 139
Khalidi, Rashid, 41, 202, 208
al-Khalidi, Ruhi, 205
Khoury, Philip S., 35
kibbutz, 113, 115, 123, 137–138, 146–185,
    192, 194, 195, 216
  its origins, 165–181
  its predominance in Israeli state
    formation, 181–186
  see also kvutza, cooperative, commune,
    Siedlungsgenossenschaft
Kimmerling, Baruch, xii, 6, 82, 139
Kinneret, 172, 183, 199
Kinneret (Daleika) training farm, 113,
    114–115, 168, 169, 170–171, 174,
    176, 179, 180, 182
Kolatt, Israel, 3, 5, 53, 81, 111, 125, 130,
    131, 172, 173, 175, 181, 183, 189,
    213
kolel, 119
Koller, A.M., 122
Komarov, Ephraim, 54, 69, 76
Kook, Rabbi Abraham Itzhak, 95
Krauze, Iliyahu, 167, 180
kvutza, 161, 166, 168, 171, 173, 182, 192
  and kibbutz, 183–184
  see also kibbutz, cooperative, commune

labor
  autonomous, 183, 188, 190, 194, 219
  and caste system, 16
  and closure theory, 15–16
  and exclusionary movements, 16
  Jewish–Palestinian conflict over, 58,
    86–89, 123, 169–171, 185, 188, 215
  market, 198
  movement in Eretz Israel, 19, 188–189

wage, 18
  see also split labor market
labor force
  in Algeria, 66–68, 76–77
  in France, 66–68
  indentured, 14
  Jewish in Palestine, 52–58, 62–63, 72
  Palestinian Arab, 18, 52–58, 62–63, 72
  skilled, 65–69, 72, 76, 103, 109–111
  in Tunisia, 66–68, 75–76
  unskilled, 63–65, 72, 103, 109–111
Lamar, Howard, 199
land
  allocation of 12–13, 23
  appropriation of, 23
  availability of, 45–46
  "free land," 13
  Jewish–Palestinian conflict over, 80,
    200–202, 205–206
  market in Palestine, 19, 24, 198
  reform in Ottoman Empire, 32–36
  sales to Jews in Palestine, 41, 198, 218
  tenure in Middle East, 30–31, 34
Landauer, Gustav, 184
Landflucht, 150, 153, 156, 161
Lavie, Shlomo, 183
Lechi, 144
Levine, Yaakov, 57, 59, 67, 70
Levontin, Zalman David, 88, 101
libation wine, 55, 102–103
Lilienblum M.L., 49, 156
Lissak, Moshe, 2–5, 213, 217
Lukacs, Georg, 46

McCarthy, Justin, 38
Machane Yehuda, 105
Madar-Halevi, David, 103, 104, 116
Magnes, Judah, 216
mahlul, 33, 139
Malkhin, Sarah, 58, 170, 175–176
Mandel, Neville, 200, 201, 202, 205, 206,
    207, 208
Ma'oz, Moshe, 34
Mapai, 123, 124, 132
Maryland, 12
Masswari, Jephet, 102
Masswari, Saadia, 102
maximalism, *see* territorial maximalism
Meir, Golda, 1
Meir, Joseph, 104
Menucha Venachala, 69, 93, 96–97, 102,
    103, 107, 118
Merchavia, 139, 141, 179, 180, 181, 190,
    205–206
Metulla, 142, 199, 200, 202, 203

Index

Parkin, Frank, 15–16
partition, xi–xii, 21, 213, 215, 219; *see also* bifurcation, exclusivism, separatism, territorial maximalism
Paz, Saadia, 137
Peel Plan, 215
Petach Tikva, 43, 51, 52, 63, 70, 73, 93, 103, 105, 106, 113, 116, 118, 139, 164, 200–201, 202, 206
Peulat Sachir, 92–93, 99
philanthropy, 59, 74, 132
Pinsker, Leo, 149
plantation colony, 8–10, 14
Poalei Zion Party, 87, 111, 123, 124, 129, 131, 132, 153
  in Austria, 190
  its congresses, 128, 130, 131
  and Hashomer, 136
  its program, 126–131, 144, 164, 182, 190–191, 194
Poltava, 137
Poncet, Jean, 66–68, 76
Porath, Yeoshua, 31, 207
Poznan (Posen), 150, 152–153, 159, 160
Preuss, Walter, 82
Prussia
  agricultural labor force in, 150
  internal colonization in, 11, 152–153, 154
  lessons for Israeli colonization, 153–154, 158, 161
  see also Germany
pure settlement colony 8–10, 14, 22, 214
  in Australia, 83–84
  in Palestine, 11, 18–19, 97, 130, 148, 154, 217, 218, 219

Queensland, 15, 84

Rabbi Benjamin, *see* Redler-Feldman Yeshaya
Rabinovitch, Yaacov, 85, 166
Raiffeisen, Friedrich Wilhelm, 151
Ramla, 39
Rauf Pasha, 201, 206
Rechovot, 39, 51, 63, 69, 92–93, 96–97, 101, 102, 103, 105, 106, 107, 108, 118, 119, 138, 139, 141–142, 169, 200, 201
Redler-Feldman, Yeshaya (pseud. Rabbi Benjamin), 94–95, 102, 191
Reichman, Shalom, 154, 158, 160
Reilly, James, 37
Revisionists, 215, 216–217
Rhodesia, 9, 13
Rishon Letzion, 51, 52, 55, 63, 67, 93, 102, 105, 107, 108, 109, 118, 138, 140, 142, 169, 187
Rodinson, Maxime, 211–213
Ro'i Yaakov, 88, 141, 202, 208
Romny, 173, 174
Rosh Pina, 139, 200
Rothschild, Baron Edmund de, 190
  capital imports to Palestine, 132
  and First *Aliya's* plantations, 50–52, 148, 154, 187–188
  and French colonization model, 10–11, 79, 97, 160
  and labor forces in Palestine, 52–53, 61
  and land purchase in Palestine, 137, 187
  his tutelary administration in Palestine, 46, 53–54, 97, 127, 187
Rubin, David, 139
Ruppin, Arthur, 100, 149, 158, 196, 197
  and founding of Degania, 171, 172, 176–178, 182
  influence of Prussian internal colonization model on, 11, 154, 159–160, 176, 182
  and Jewish settlement pattern, 43, 44, 205, 214
  and Jewish–Palestinian conflict, 203, 206
  and *ashkenazi* Jewish agricultural workers, 71, 129, 133–134, 159–160
  and Yemenite Jewish agricultural workers, 92, 94–95, 101–102, 105, 112, 118, 134
  see also WZO
Rutenberg, Pinchas, 216

Safed, 92
Said, Edward, 202, 212–213
Samaria, 24
Santayana, George, xi
Sapir, Eliyahu, 95
satellite villages, 37, 39, 40
Sateria, 201
Schama, Simon, 51
Schapira, Hermann, 155–156
Schölch, Alexander, 28, 30, 38
Schulze-Delitzsch, Hermann, 151
Second *Aliya*, 1–5, 7, 17, 19, 42, 46, 49, 55–58, 59, 127, 129, 160–165
  and anti-philanthropy, 58–59
  and census of agricultural workers, 63–65, 75
  its demographic interest, 89, 125, 160, 165, 183, 193, 195, 215
  and guarding, 136–144
  and ideology, 124–125, 173, 188

Index

Tabenkin, Itzhak, 1, 131, 142
Tabib, Avraham, 118
Tanfilov, Tanchum, 173
Tanzimat, 23, 24, 27, 28, 31, 32, 34–36,
    41, 202; *see also* Ottoman Empire
Tayan, Anton Bishara, 200
Techiya, 173, 174, 175, 181
Tel Adash, 139
Templars, 29, 39
territorial maximalism, xi–xii, 219
Third *Aliya*, 1, 75, 132, 183, 184, 185,
    193, 194
Thompson, Leonard, 199
Thon, Yaakov, 203
Tiberias (and Lake Tiberias), 43, 92, 114,
    157, 169
Timar system, 31, 33, 35
training farms, 86, 88, 113–114, 121, 129
Transjordan, 24
Treitsch, Davis, 71
Trumpeldor, Joseph, 168
Tschlenov, Yehiel, 158
Tsemach, Shlomo, 124–125
Tunisia, 11
    colonization in, 10, 27, 75–78
    labor force in, 66–68, 75–76
Turner, Frederick Jackson, 13

Uganda proposal, 147
Ulster plantation, 9
Um Djunni see Degania
Umlabess, 200
United States, 213
    availability of land in, 13, 45
    exceptionalism of, 13
    land allocation in, 12
    land appropriation in, 23
    settlement in, 12
    state in, 13
    Zionists in, 143, 195–196, 197
Ussishkin, Menachem, 42, 43, 59, 99,
    101, 102, 124, 137, 159, 166

Vilkansky, Itzhak (A. Tsiyoni), 158, 164,
    167, 180, 191, 192
viniculture
    in Algeria, 75–77
    in France, 51, 66–68
    in Palestine, 51–53, 67–69, 96–97
    in Tunisia, 75–77
Virginia, 11, 12
Vitkin, Joseph, 56–57, 74, 124–125, 128,
    161–162, 166

Wadi-Ara, 38

wages, 61, 63–65, 69, 71, 99, 104, 107,
    109, 116–117, 120, 139–140, 165,
    169, 181
Wakefield, Edward Gibbon, 9, 80
Wallerstein, Immanuel, 35
War of Independence, 43, 219
Warburg, Otto, 149, 155, 157, 158, 175,
    177, 178–179
    influence of Prussian internal
    colonization model on, 11, 154, 159
Warriner, Doreen, 33
Weber, Max, xii, 32, 152
Weizmann, Dr Chaim, 143, 196
West Bank, 24
white labor, 9, 14, 82–84
white settlers, 12, 199, 213
Willard, Myra, 84
Wine Producers' Cooperative Association,
    54
wineries, 55, 102–103, 107–108
World Zionist Organization (WZO), 18,
    46, 127
    its alliance with Second *Aliya*, 19–20,
    90, 133, 146–147, 189, 193, 196, 197,
    198
    and capital imports, 132
    its congresses, 155, 156, 157, 178, 179,
    196–197
    and "conquest of labor," 62–63
    and cooperatives, 175, 178–179, 182,
    190
    dominated by labor movement, 123
    its executive, 102
    and First *Aliya*, 62–63, 195–196
    its guidance of Second *Aliya*, 7, 130,
    131, 176–179, 182, 190, 197
    and Hashomer, 139
    and influence of Prussian internal
    colonization model on, 151, 154,
    158–159, 169, 182, 190
    and Jewish demographic interest,
    62–63, 160
    leaders, 99, 149, 151
    and settlement, 112, 121, 130, 131, 139,
    179, 182
    and pure settlement method, 154–160,
    190, 196
    and pure settlement theory, 148, 154,
    182, 190, 196
    its training farms, 86, 88, 113–114,
    121, 129, 168–169
    and Yemenite Jews, 105–106, 111–116

Yaffe, Eliezer, 174
Yahud (Yahudia), 39, 200–201

286